Contents

Study Guide

for use with

Cost Management
Strategies for Business Decisions

Fourth Edition

Ronald W. Hilton
Cornell University

Michael W. Maher
University of California -- Davis

Frank H. Selto
University of Colorado -- Boulder

Prepared by
Janice Mereba

Boston Burr Ridge, IL Dubuque, IA Madison, WI New York San Francisco St. Louis Bangkok Bogotá Caracas Kuala Lumpur Lisbon London Madrid Mexico City Milan Montreal New Delhi Santiago Seoul Singapore Sydney Taipei Toronto

Study Guide for use with
COST MANAGEMENT: STRATEGIES FOR BUSINESS DECISIONS
Ronald W. Hilton, Michael W. Maher, Frank H. Selto

Published by McGraw-Hill/Irwin, an imprint of The McGraw-Hill Companies, Inc., 1221 Avenue of the Americas, New York, NY 10020.

1 2 3 4 5 6 7 8 9 0 BKM/BKM 0 9 8 7

ISBN 978-0-07-322111-3
MHID 0-07-322111-2

www.mhhe.com

The McGraw-Hill Companies

Chapter 1
Cost Management and Strategic Decision Making

Chapter Study Suggestions

This chapter introduces the entire concept of cost management as a new approach to managing a company. Cost management is an important element of modern management. In today's business environment, businesses must focus on cost management in order to maintain a competitive edge. In addition, Chapter 1 explains the importance of strategic decision making, and discusses how these two concepts work together to help organizations to reach their goals. It introduces key terms used in a management setting that apply specifically to cost management activities. It discusses the importance of ethical behavior, and introduces the use of benefit-cost analysis, to evaluate strategic plans.

This chapter introduces many terms and concepts that underlie materials presented in later chapters. Mastering them will greatly enhance understanding of materials that follow in the text.

Chapter Highlights

A. Cost Management Challenges. There are 3 questions addressed in this chapter.

1. What should cost-management analysts do when confronted with ethical dilemmas on the job?

2. How do cost-management analysts contribute to strategic decision making?

3. How should cost-management analysts prepare the information used to make strategic decisions?

B. Learning Objectives—this chapter has 4 learning objectives.

1. The chapter explains how cost management supports strategic planning and decision-making.

2. It presents a discussion of the importance of ethical behavior when decision-making takes place.

3. Chapter 1 describes the steps used in strategic decision-making.

4. The chapter introduces benefit-cost and variance analysis as ways to evaluate an organization's strategic plans.

C. Cost managers are members of the management team who have responsibility for managing the financial resources and financial personnel. The **chief financial officer (CFO)** is the top cost manager. This person usually has an educational background in accounting or finance, and may be certified as a certified public accountant (CPA), certified financial manager (CFM), or certified management accountant (CMA).

1. The CFO oversees the activities of all financial managers, and interacts with many other managers who are responsible for the use of an organization's resources.

2. Financial managers reporting to the CFO may have training as accountants, finance, engineering, or non-business disciplines. Since a financial manager has a role that extends far beyond that of the traditional cost accountant, the skill set possessed by a financial manager includes knowledge of customer profitability, process improvement, performance evaluation, and strategic planning.

3. Financial managers should possess a cost management attitude. They should be vigilant in their pursuit of cost control, but not at the expense of product quality or customer needs. They must know their organization, and the organization's goals. They need to possess high ethical standards.

D. Cost management is a crucial part of the strategy of a business. Good cost management arises when managers view it as a philosophy. Cost managers must have a proactive attitude, and must possess or acquire a set of reliable techniques to help them to implement and manage change in their organization.

E. Cost-management analysts must have high standards of ethical behavior. Since they have access to and control over information used to make strategic decisions, they cannot use that information unethically. Many organizations have developed and implemented a code of ethics, to describe approved and unacceptable practices. There are several reasons why cost-management analysts might stray from ethical behavior. A few are listed below.

1. Personal commitment to a wrong decision may make it hard for an analyst to take corrective steps.

2. Individuals may fear loss of prestige, position or compensation if a strategy fails. This makes it tempting to hide failures.

3. Greed and intentional behavior may contribute to fraud or other unethical behavior.

4. Unethical behavior by top executives during the late 1900's and through 2002 led to passage of the Sarbanes-Oxley Act of 2002. Though cost managers continue to be key players in maintaining the ethical behavior of businesses, the CEO and CFO are now held accountable for assuring that unethical behavior does not occur.

5. The Sarbanes-Oxley Act made internal controls much more important in organizations. Internal controls are processes, procedures, policies and mechanisms put in place to ascertain that organizations will comply with company policies and the law, perform efficiently, protect assets and provide reliable financial accounting information and

F. An organization's strategy is its overall plan to achieve its goals. When developing a strategy, two questions must be addressed.

1. Where do we want to go? The organization must define its mission, or strategic destination. There are four common types of strategic missions.

   a. The build strategy requires that the organization achieve high rates of growth. Organizations adopting this strategy seek new markets and customers with high growth potential.

   b. The hold strategy is used by organizations that want to maintain existing growth rates. This means an organization has to grow at the same rate as the surrounding population or community in order to retain market share. This strategy is less risky than the build strategy.

c. The harvest strategy is sometimes called the cash cow strategy. It means an organization sells products that are in mature markets, and growth has stabled off, or is even declining. Organizations may use this strategy for some units, and then use cash flows from the units being harvested to fund units in the build state. This strategy is generally viewed as low risk, but also may be less rewarding financially.

d. The divest strategy is used when a product or organization has reached the end of its useful life, or when an organization decides that certain products or units are not a good strategic fit. The divest strategy is risky primarily when a company uses it too long, and gets stuck with a product or unit that it cannot divest itself of.

2. How do we want to get there? The second question deals with the actual steps an organization must take to accomplish its organizational goals. In order to answer this question, managers must understand sources and threats to competitive advantages, and use effective decision making techniques.

   a. Some examples of competitive advantages include exclusive access to a process, employee talent, control over natural resources, or a cost or quality advantage.

   b. The value chain is a way to think about the entire process for a good or service, from its inception to the point at which the consumer receives the product. Effective use of an organization's value chain can be a competitive advantage by itself.

      i. The value chain begins with research and development, proceeds to product design, supply of inputs, production, marketing, distribution, and customer service. Linked to all of these stages of the value chain is support.

      ii. Evaluating the best strategy to getting there, using the value chain approach also helps managers to decide whether it is more advantageous to outsource certain functions or activities. While it may seem that cost savings is a good reason to outsource, having a competitive advantage due to exclusive access or control over some resource may lead organizations away from the outsourcing decision at times.

3. Organizations that identify their competitive advantages must always be conscious of the threats to their competitive advantage. There are five forces that threaten one's competitive advantage.

   a. Existing competition may be fighting for the same customers and market share. The size of this threat is based on the breadth, intensity, competence and basis of these competitors.

b. New competitors are also a threat. The more attractive a market is, the more likely it is that new entrants will emerge. Protection of relationships with customers and exclusive processes, employee talents or resources is a key to protecting against this threat.

c. Demand and stability of customers is a third threat to competitive advantage.

d. Reliability, quality and breadth of suppliers is also a threat to competitive advantage. Losing a key supplier can result in loss of customers if the quality of product is affected.

e. Availability or likelihood of substitutes is a fifth threat to competitive advantage. This threat emerges anytime a competitor finds a way to provide similar customer satisfaction, whether it is because substitute products cost less but are of comparable quality, are higher quality but cost the same, or provide a comparable level of customer satisfaction.

G. There is an eight-step process that organizations can use to implement strategic plans.

1. First, identify a need for change (why are you doing all of this anyway?)

2. Create a team to lead and manage the change. These teams need to be cross-functional and diverse. This team needs access to all of the information to implement the change, and access to all of the people needed to complete the analysis of the change.

3. Create a vision of and a strategy for the change. This requires input from people who are knowledgeable about the area being changed.

4. Communicate the vision and strategy for change to fellow employees. Solicit additional input from employees. Help co-workers, especially those most affected by the changes, to feel a part of the coming changes. The change team should be role models and advocates for the proposed changes.

5. Encourage innovation and remove obstacles to change. Top management should give the implementation team the leeway needed to successfully implement the changes proposed.

6. Ensure that short-term achievements are frequent and obvious. Given a major project that results in many changes, the project should be broken down into smaller pieces. This simplifies the work of the implementation teams, makes the setting of deadlines (and meeting them) more realistic, and helps management to see which parts of the plan work, and which parts do not.

7. Successes can be promoted as a way to create opportunities for improvement in the entire organization. When a large project is split into pieces, each piece when successfully implemented can be used to encourage and motivate employees to make even more suggestions to improve the operations of the organization.

8. Reinforce a culture of more improvement, better leadership, and more effective management. If employees believe that management appreciates and will use their suggestions then the operation of the organization can be continuously improved.

H. Strategic plans must be evaluated, to see if they are working. One way to evaluate a plan is to use operational performance analysis. This type of evaluation focuses on measurement of current operations, to see if ongoing organizational objectives are being met. A second evaluation tool is strategic performance analysis, which measures whether a strategic decision has met expectations. Operational performance analysis is short-term, while strategic performance analysis is long-term.

1. Benefit-cost analysis is one way to measure performance. This type of analysis compares expected costs and benefits to actual outcomes. There are both quantitative and qualitative aspects to benefit-cost analysis.

    a. The difference between expected outcomes and actual outcomes is called a variance. While managers expect variances to occur, it is the magnitude of variances that managers look at, to see what parts of a plan work or do not, and then to determine why.

REVIEW AND SELF TEST QUESTIONS AND EXERCISES

True or False

For each of the following statements enter a T or an F in the blank to indicate whether the statement is true or false.

_____ 1. Cost management means the same thing as cost accounting.

_____ 2. Financial managers are trained in accounting, finance, engineering, and other disciplines.

_____ 3. According to the Sarbanes-Oxley of 2002, the chief financial officer (CFO) and chief executive officer (CEO) are now the only ones responsible for ethical behavior in a business.

_____ 4. Cost management is an important consideration in decision-making in an organization.

_____ 5. When making a management decision, both quantitative and qualitative information must be considered.

_____ 6. The appropriate philosophy for good cost management always aims at managing costs regardless of customer needs.

_____ 7. Cost management represents an attitude that costs just happen, so it is hard to manage them.

_____ 8. One question that should be answered when developing organizational strategy is "Where do we want to go?"

_____ 9. One example of a competitive advantage is that an organization has talented employees.

_____10. It is always more expensive for a company to outsource an activity than it is to complete the activity internally.

_____11. It is acceptable for a manager to violate her company's code of ethics, as long as it improves her company's profits.

_____12. Benefit-cost analysis can be used to compare expectations to outcomes.

_____13. A variance is the difference between the expected results of two alternative decisions.

_____14. One important qualitative factor in decision-making is the effect of a decision on employee morale.

_____15. Cost-management analysts should **not** make suggestions to top management about the long-term strategy of the organization.

Multiple Choice

Choose the best answer by writing the letter corresponding to your choice in the space provided.

_____16. Which of the following is correct?

a) The sole responsibility of cost-management analysts is to record financial data.
b) Cost-management analysts are important members of the management team.
c) A cost-management analyst must be a trained accountant.
d) Only cost management analysts can make decisions about managing costs.

_____17. The chief financial officer (CFO) oversees all of the following **except**

a) the hiring activities of an organization.
b) the accounting activities of an organization.
c) the financing activities of an organization.
d) the investment activities of an organization.

_____18. Which of the following describe characteristics that a cost-management analyst should have?

a) High ethical standards
b) Ability to work well with others
c) A good understanding of the organization's objectives and goals
d) All of the Above

_____19. Which of the following correctly defines functional roles in an organization?

a) Functional roles are broadly defined jobs that require managers to have many diverse responsibilities.
b) Functional roles are narrowly defined jobs that focus on specific types of activities.
c) Managers performing functional roles traditionally have interacted heavily with other managers.
d) Modern management teams normally consist of people with the same functional roles.

_____20. Which of the following is **not** likely to be present in a cross-functional team?

a) People who work well with others.
b) People with a variety of backgrounds.
c) People who can lead, but cannot be easily led.
d) People with different functions.

_____21. Which of the following scenarios might lead a company to adopt a "hold" strategy?

a) New technologies have caused most of a company's products to become obsolete.
b) A U.S. company has recently opened a branch Toronto, Canada.
c) Acquisition of another company's division is being considered by a company.
d) A company has been the number one seller of a product, and expects to be number one for a long time even though demand has stabilized.

_____22. The term "cash cow" is most closely associated with which strategic mission?

a) Harvesting
b) Divesting
c) Holding
d) Building

_____23. Which of the following is the best way to respond to new competitors to a market by a company?

a) Sue all new competitors.
b) Safeguard any patents or processes that give the company an advantage over new competitors.
c) Reduce prices below that offered by new competitors.
d) Buy the competing company.

_____24. A performance measure allows

a) organizations to compare expected outcomes to actual outcomes.
b) organizations to compare their products to their competitors' products.
c) organizations to compare one job applicant to another job applicant.
d) organizations to compare existing results to planned future results.

_____25. Organizations that want to formulate a strategic action plan often create a team to lead and manage change. Which of the following is **not** a characteristic of a team responsible for developing the strategic plan?

a) The team should have members with diverse work backgrounds.
b) The team should consist of top management.
c) The team should act as role models, to encourage others to accept the strategic plan.
d) The team should have enough authority to develop the plan without the intervention of top management.

_____26. Bellsman Technologies has discovered its market niche is to sell computer software to small businesses. This means that

a) Bellsman cannot expand into related markets.
b) Bellsman should turn down contracts with larger businesses desiring their services.
c) Bellsman cannot compete against similar, but larger firms.
d) Bellsman should focus on becoming the best in this market.

_____27. Which of the following is **not** an example of operational performance analysis?

a) Net income was 4% lower than expected for 2003.
b) Employees were able to respond to 150 customer inquiries per day during the month of June. The standard is 160.
c) A new product failed to meet ISO standards.
d) Cost of materials for a product were $20 less per unit than budgeted.

_____28. The value chain is defined as

a) the way in which costs are contained, to maximize profits.
b) the processes beginning with an idea and ending with the product being received by customers.
c) a management decision-making process.
d) the sequence of events leading to proper cost management.

_____29. Research and Development (R & D) is

a) the first step in the value chain.
b) the most important part of the value chain.
c) not a necessary part of the value chain.
d) the part of the value chain where products are designed.

_____30. Which of the following is **not** a part of the value chain?

a) Design
b) Production
c) Cost analysis
d) Marketing

_____31. One key to making large projects more likely to succeed is to

a) make sure that top management is directly involved with the project.
b) only let people who will benefit directly from a project's success be on the project team.
c) keep all projects small enough in scope that they can be completed in short periods of time.
d) break the project into smaller, short-term pieces, to motivate people based on early successes.

_____32. Benefit-cost analysis is

a) a way to quantify a business problem.
b) a way to quantify the qualitative aspects of a problem.
c) the only way to solve a problem properly.
d) the team approach to problem-solving.

_____33. Outsourcing is an alternative to performing some activity internally. All of the following are valid reasons for outsourcing **except**

a) there is no expertise inside of the organization.
b) the cost is lower if the activity is outsourced.
c) there is less control over the activity if it is outsourced.
d) production capacity can be used for other production activities if outsourcing occurs.

_____34. Which of the following is a quantitative factors used in benefit-cost analysis?

a) Employee morale.
b) Product quality.
c) Customer satisfaction.
d) Production-related wages.

_____35. A variance can be due to all **except** which of the following?

a) Unexpected costs
b) Poor estimation
c) No budgeting or planning
d) Changes in demand

Exercises

Use the following information about Maxwell Entertainment, Inc. to answer the next 4 questions.

Maxwell Entertainment Inc. is in the business of videotaping events such as weddings, birthday parties, training sessions for businesses, and almost any event that a customer might want to have videotaped. In the past two years, business has nearly tripled, in part because one client has implemented a major training program that needs to be videotaped. This customer has been so pleased with the quality of the training tapes that word has spread to other potential customers who are interested in developing similar training tapes. Maxwell's management team must decide whether to stop videotaping weddings and parties in order to accept the increased jobs with the videotaping of training sessions. They feel that there would be some savings on travel costs to the weddings and parties (some are out of town). Also, corporate customers usually pay directly for the tapes, to assure that they get tapes that are compatible with their company's video systems. At the same time, training tapes require that documentation be produced to accompany the tapes. Additional technicians are needed for the training tapes, and more sophisticated equipment would be needed if training tapes are to be the main product.

Jenny Maxwell, founder and owner, decided to do training tapes for twelve months, and to compare that to her team's budgeted projections for training tapes alone, to see which direction she should take the company in.

The projected results for a year are shown below, along with actual results for the twelve-month trial period. Use this information to answer the following five questions.

Benefits of Shift to Training Tapes	Expected Amount	Actual Amount	Variance
Sales	$1,200,000	$1,000,000	($200,000)
Savings on travel	$25,000	$40,000	$15,000
Savings on videotapes	$3,000	$2,200	($800)
Revenue growth (monthly)	.6% (6/10 of 1 percent)	.5% (5/10 of 1%)	(.1%)
Costs of the Shift to Training Tapes	**Expected Amount**	**Actual Amount**	**Variance**
Additional staff	$80,000	$60,000	$20,000
Training documentation	$10,000	$12,000	($2,000)
Equipment	$15,000	$16,000	($1,000)

36. **Based on the variances shown between actual and expected results, what would your recommendation be to Ms. Maxwell?**

37. **What reasons can you give for making a recommendation that is not consistent with the variances?**

38. **What competitive advantages do you think Maxwell Entertainment might have that would make entry to the videotaping of training for businesses easier?**

39. **What competitive advantages do you think Maxwell Entertainment's competitors might have that would make entry to the videotaping of training for businesses harder?**

40. **Benefit-cost analysis should provide both quantitative and qualitative support for making a decision and for evaluating performance. Give at least three qualitative reasons for eliminating weddings and parties from the product offerings. Give at least three qualitative reasons for keeping weddings and parties in the product offerings.**

Answers to Questions and Exercises

True or False

1. F. Cost accounting is restricted to the collection, assimilation, and dissemination of financial and management accounting information. Cost management has a much broader scope, and encompasses the decision-making and strategic planning activities of managers of an organization.
2. T. Financial managers come from a variety of disciplines.
3. F. The CEO and CFO are accountable for assuring that unethical behavior does not occur. However, cost managers continue to be key employees in terms of preventing unethical behavior.
4. T. Cost management has become increasingly important, as companies realize that being competitive also means being cost-conscious.
5. T. Quantitative measures of costs and benefits for a given decision must be balanced with evaluation of the qualitative impact of that same decision.
6. F. Modern management philosophies recognize the importance of customer satisfaction, as well as managing costs.
7. F. Costs don't "just happen". Managers must be vigilant in identifying costs, and making sure that they are necessary and add value.
8. T. Organizational strategy is a plan to achieve long-term goals. Thus, an important question to ask is "where do we want to go?"
9. T. Employees with special skills or talents can give organizations a significant competitive edge.
10. F. Sometimes, for instance, if a company has no expertise, it is less costly to have an outside company perform some task.
11. F. A manager should behave ethically, regardless of its impact on company profits. That is one of the reasons organizations develop and implement codes of ethics.
12. T. Cost-benefit analysis is normally a useful tool to compare the costs to the benefits, based on expected results and actual results.
13. F. A variance is the difference between expected results and actual results.
14. T. The effect of a decision on employee morale can have long-term detrimental effects on an organization's productivity.
15. F. Cost management analysts are key participants in strategic planning since they can provide actual and estimated financial information needed to make decisions.

Multiple Choice

16. b. Cost management analysts do much more than record financial information, may be trained in other disciplines besides accounting, and seek input from other managers to manage costs.
17. a. The CFO oversees all accounting, investment and financing activities. The vice-president or director of Human Resources oversees hiring activities.
18. d. All of the described qualities are desirable in a cost management analyst.
19. b. A functional role is a narrowly defined job. Modern management teams bring together managers skilled in different functional areas, who work together to make management decisions.

20. c. Although team members should not be easily swayed from a correct position, they must be flexible enough to defer to others' suggestions. This is especially true when one manager has more expertise for making a particular decision than others on the team.

21. d. Introduction of technologies that make products obsolete should lead to a "divest" strategy. Expanding into new territory should lead to a "build" strategy. Acquiring another company could be done for different reasons, but would not necessarily lead to a "hold" strategy. D is correct because the market leader usually wants to sustain growth at the same rate as that occurring in the economy or the geographic location of the market.

22. a. Harvesting is a strategy adopted for mature products that have probably reached the peak of demand, but which generate cash that can be used to develop and introduce new products.

23. b. Since patents or processes are keys to maintaining a competitive edge, this is the best way to maintain that advantage. Suing or buying out competitors are both unrealistic solutions. It is not always possible or practical to reduce prices below that of competitors.

24. a. Performance measures should tell you what happened compared to what you expected to happen.

25. b. A team responsible for developing a strategic plan must feel that it can develop the plan freely, without the constraints imposed by top management and their immediate goals, which might not necessarily be consistent with the overall long-term goals of the organization.

26. d. The company should develop its competitive edge in the market where it is most competitive, and in future periods expand to related markets.

27. c. This is an example of a component of a strategic performance analysis.

28. b. The value chain describes an organization as a set of linked processes that begins with a good idea and ends with a customer receiving something they value.

29. a. R&D is the starting point. A good idea emerges, and then people explore the ways in which this idea can be made into a reality.

30. c. Cost analysis is not an explicit part of the value chain.

31. d. Breaking a major project up into smaller pieces gives organizations two benefits. One is that it allows employees to achieve goals on an ongoing basis. The other is that it allows employees to identify problems, mistakes and flaws in the project so that corrections can be made as necessary.

32. a. Benefit-cost analysis is a management tool that allows managers to identify all of the costs caused by a particular decision, and to compare these costs to the benefits that would be obtained by that decision.

33. c. This would be a compelling reason **not** to outsource an activity.

34. d. Employee morale, product quality, and customer satisfaction are all purely qualitative, or "soft" quantitative results of a particular decision. The impact on wages is easier to quantify.

35. c. Since a variance compares expected outcomes to actual outcomes, a variance can't be measured if there is no budgeting or planning to begin with.

Exercises

36. Based purely on the quantitative results, the company should not move in the direction of offering only training tapes. Sales revenues are lower than anticipated, and additional costs outweigh additional cost savings.

37. Even though the benefit-cost analysis would appear to indicate the training tapes are not the right choice, there are several reasons that could be given for moving forward, or at least considering the new strategy further.
    - Poor estimation of sales and growth could make the actual results look worse than they really are. Maxwell should consider how confident she is in the projections.
    - Since the idea to move to training tapes was based on the results from one existing client, it is hard to predict with certainty what the impact of getting a major client would be. This has to do with management using its judgment and business instincts to make decisions.
    - The analysis does not capture qualitative benefits or costs of choosing the strategy. They should be incorporated into the decision.
    - One of the costs, obtaining new equipment could be incorrect for two reasons. First, it might be a one-time (start-up) cost, which should not be incorporated into the annual costs presented. Second, they might be costs that the company would incur anyway, as video equipment currently used becomes obsolete.
38. One competitive advantage Maxwell Entertainment might have is the word-of-mouth recommendations of the client described in the exercise. Being recommended to a few key clients might be enough to launch the company in this new market successfully. Another is the company's talent and expertise. If the videographers have a reputation for the quality of work, this could contribute to new business. The business might also have some flexibility in terms of ability to move quickly out of one market and into another one without a large amount of additional cost.
39. Maxwell Entertainment would encounter competition on two fronts. Its main competition would be in-house HR training programs of businesses that choose not to outsource this function. Maxwell would then have to sell companies on the advantages of outsourcing. Maxwell Entertainment might also have competition from companies that already exist. In that case, Maxwell might have to identify a niche market, or identify some other competitive advantages (cost, quality, availability, creativity, etc.) that would attract customers.
40. Qualitative reasons for eliminating weddings and parties from the product offerings:
    a. Keeping these services might detract from the image of a corporate training videographer.
    b. Continuing to offer these services might tie up resources needed for the new venture.
    c. Employees might prefer concentrating on one area of expertise.
    d. Weddings and parties might be viewed as minor or unimportant compared with HR training tapes.

    Qualitative reasons for keeping weddings and parties as part of product offerings:
    a. Company might want to have an image of being able to offer diverse services.
    b. Employees might prefer the kinds of interaction with different types of customers instead of business employees.
    c. Employees might feel that taping weddings and parties is more creative and enjoyable than training tapes.
    d. Eliminating the weddings and parties might not be the mission of the business, even if it might be less profitable.

Chapter 2
Product Costing Systems: Concepts and Design Issues

Chapter Study Suggestions

This chapter presents some of the basics of assigning costs to units of product. It explains what costs should be assigned to products, and defines the difference between product costs and those costs that are not (period costs). The income statement is defined, discussed and demonstrated for service firms, retailers and manufacturing companies. Many concepts of cost or expense are introduced. Among these cost concepts are product and period costs; cost of goods sold; unit level, fixed and variable costs; direct materials, direct labor and manufacturing overhead; sunk costs, committed costs and opportunity costs; and direct and indirect costs.

Three ways to prepare an income statement are introduced based on different product costing methods. These are absorption costing, variable costing, and throughput costing. The three methods are presented for service, retail and manufacturing companies, so that the differences among the three types of companies can be illustrated. Cost of goods sold, usually the single largest expense for retailers and manufacturers is defined, and the ways to derive it are presented.

Chapter Highlights

A. Cost Management Challenges. There are 3 questions addressed in this chapter.

1. What inputs are needed during the production process? How are costs tracked as they flow through the production process?
2. How can alternative methods for calculating product costs create different incentives?
3. How should cost managers measure costs for internal decision making?

B. Learning Objectives—this chapter has 8 learning objectives.

1. The chapter compares product costs to period costs, and describes expenses in the income statement.
2. Chapter 2 shows how to prepare an income statement and, for manufacturing companies a schedule of cost of goods manufactured and sold.
3. It describes the components of manufacturing costs and shows how these costs flow through the production process.
4. Unit-level, variable and fixed costs are described and compared.
5. Explain the concepts of opportunity, sunk, committed, direct, indirect, controllable and uncontrollable costs.
6. Preparation of income statements using the absorption, variable and throughput costing methods is shown.
7. Reconciliation of absorption, variable, and throughput costing methods is presented.
8. The advantages and disadvantages of the three costing methods (absorption, variable and throughput costing) are discussed.
9. Discusses ethical issues especially related to inventory production and reporting.

C. In order to manage costs, cost management analysts must be able to identify the activities and processes that occur in their organization. They also need to assess the benefit of having some of these activities performed outside of their own organization. Cost analysts must be able to categorize costs so that they can be properly assigned to production or non-production areas, for financial reporting purposes.

The term "cost" has a basic meaning. It represents a sacrifice made – some resource being given up for achieving a specific purpose. The cost manager must, however, go far beyond identifying costs in this general sense. As a starting point, here are some types of costs to consider.

1. All costs occurring in a business can be categorized as product costs or period costs. Product costs are those costs incurred to make products or services available to customers. Product costs are also called inventoriable costs. Inventory is also an asset. When inventory is sold, it is treated as an expense called "cost of goods sold".

2. Period costs are costs that are incurred to support production activities or service-provision activities. They are necessary for the operation of a business, but are not directly related to production activities. Period costs are called that because they are recorded as expenses and reported on the income statement in the period when they are incurred.

D. Companies must report their financial results in financial reports. One of these reports is the income statement. An income statement always shows sales revenues first, and always shows net income last. The format and presentation of an income statement varies, depending on the type of business that is reporting.

1. Service firms offer products that are services. They do not have inventory or cost of goods sold. Expenses are usually listed in order of importance.

2. Retail companies buy products and sell them at a markup. Sales minus cost of goods sold equals a subtotal called gross margin. This subtotal is an important measure of profitability for a retailer.

    a. Cost of goods sold for retail firms consists primarily of costs to purchase inventory. A Schedule of Cost of Goods Sold gives details of cost of goods sold.

3. Manufacturing firms' income statements are complicated by the fact that such firms buy raw materials, which are converted to products for sale. Product costs for manufacturers are split into three broad categories.

    a. Direct materials are the raw materials, parts and components that go into the making of products.

    b. Direct labor is the cost of employees who are directly involved in the making of products. This includes their hourly wages as well as employee benefits.

    c. Manufacturing overhead consists of all costs incurred in making product besides direct materials and direct labor. Manufacturing overhead includes indirect materials and labor, depreciation of manufacturing facilities and equipment, utilities expense and any other expenses occurring in the manufacturing facility. Costs of departments that provide support services to the manufacturing facility are also treated as manufacturing overhead.

d. Another way to categorize production costs is to view them as prime costs and conversion costs. Prime costs are the direct material and direct labor costs. Conversion costs are manufacturing overhead costs and direct labor costs.

e. Non-manufacturing costs are period costs. They do not become part of product costs, and are not assigned to inventory accounts. Marketing and advertising, administrative, and salaries of top management are examples of non-manufacturing costs.

E. The flow of production costs and stages of production for manufacturing are described below. There are three inventory accounts for manufacturers. Production costs flow into these inventory accounts in sequence. They are Raw Materials Inventory, Work in Process Inventory, and Finished Goods Inventory. Production costs are recorded next as cost of goods sold, when finished goods inventory items are sold.

1. **Raw Materials Inventory** represents goods purchased from suppliers and vendors for use in making product. Raw materials are placed into production, and combined with direct labor and other production activities with the goal of manufacturing product. **Work in Process** is an inventory account that arises because production begins without regard to the timing of financial reporting. At the end of the accounting period, the value of the partially finished products are determined and recorded as an inventory account. **Finished Goods Inventory** is the value of units of product that are completed but not yet sold.

2. For a manufacturing firm, the income statement cannot be completed before another report, the Schedule of Cost of Goods Manufactured and Sold is completed. The Schedule of Cost of Goods Manufactured and Sold shows how production costs – direct materials, direct labor and manufacturing overhead (MOH) become the expense called cost of goods sold.

a. Direct materials are materials taken from the raw materials inventory (RMI) and placed into production. A formula can be used to determine the cost of direct materials for an accounting period:

Beginning RMI + Purchases – Ending RMI = **Cost of direct materials put into production.**

b. In order to complete the Schedule of Cost of Goods Manufactured and Sold, both the beginning and ending balances in the work in process (WIP) Inventory account must be known. The beginning and ending balances of finished goods inventory (FGI) must also be known.

c. The Schedule of Cost of Goods Manufactured and Sold can be summarized as follows:

Beginning WIP Inventory
\+ Direct materials put into production
\+ Direct labor for the accounting period
\+ Manufacturing OH for the accounting period
(here, two subtotals, total manufacturing costs incurred, and total cost of WIP are reported)
– Ending WIP Inventory
(here, another subtotal is reported – it is Cost of Goods Manufactured)
\+ Beginning FGI
(report a subtotal here, FGI available for sale)
– Ending FGI
= Cost of Goods Sold

3. To summarize, for manufacturing firms, costs flow through the accounting system as follows.

   a. Materials, labor and other manufacturing overhead costs are added to work in process inventory.

   b. When goods are finished, the costs are transferred to finished goods inventory.

   c. When finished units of product are sold, the expense account, cost of goods sold is increased, and finished goods inventory is reduced.

4. Service industries may also have production costs, but reporting for service firms is different because there are no inventory accounts to record the flow of costs through the system.

F. An alternative way to think about costs is to recognize that different costs occur in an organization for different purposes. In order to manage costs, managers should think about the activity that causes the cost, and determine whether the cost is necessary.

1. Cost drivers describe those activities that cause costs to occur. A simple example of a cost driver is the number of units of product made. The more one makes, the higher total costs will be.

2. Managers should also consider how costs behave. This means identifying costs based on whether they are fixed costs or variable costs.

   a. Fixed costs do not change with production activity. For instance, rent or depreciation expenses do not change just because production activity increases or decreases.

   b. Variable costs increase in total whenever activity increases. For instance, total variable costs will increase if more units of product are made because more direct materials and direct labor will be needed.

c. Closely related to fixed and variable cost distinctions are direct and indirect distinctions. Direct costs can be traced to specific activity, while indirect costs cannot.

3. The traditional meaning of variable costs has been modified in recent years to take into account that cost behavior needs more than two classifications of fixed and variable costs. What formerly was classified as variable cost in a manufacturing setting is more properly split into more different categories. The costs are divided into five cost hierarchies, described below.

   a. Unit-level costs occur any time a unit of product is produced.

   b. Batch-level costs are incurred when units of product are completed in batches.

   c. Product-level costs occur when one particular product is produced.

   d. Customer-level costs are incurred to meet needs of specific customers.

   e. Facility-level costs are overall operating costs that cannot be traced to lower level hierarchies.

4. Some other definitions of cost are **committed costs, opportunity costs,** and **sunk costs.**

   a. Committed costs are those costs that occur regardless of production activity. Committed costs cannot be reduced or eliminated easily in the short term.

   b. Opportunity costs are those that arise when an economic sacrifice is made. When one thing of value is obtained, it is typically the case that some other economic benefit had to be given up.

   c. Sunk costs are past costs, incurred because of past decisions. Sunk costs cannot be retrieved.

   d. Cost systems should be useful for making good business decisions. Decisions should be made after considering which costs are relevant to the decision. For decision-making purposes, sunk costs are generally not relevant. Relevant costs are future costs that differ among alternative decisions.

5. Another concern cost managers have with respect to cost is the traceability of resources. Costs caused by the using up of resources should be traceable to activities, so these costs can be assigned appropriately. Also, traceability of costs allows managers to be held accountable for the occurrence of costs traceable to their operations.

G. Cost accounting systems are needed to produce reports to managers for decision-making purposes. The system is also used to prepare and report financial results. Financial accounting mandates that product costs include materials, labor and overhead costs. While some costs are direct, and can be assigned directly to units, batches, customers or products, many overhead costs cannot. These costs must be allocated to units of product to determine inventory values and the cost of goods sold. This assignment approach is called **absorption costing, or full costing.**

1. While absorption costing is required for financial accounting purposes, managers find variable costing to be more useful for making management decisions. When a variable cost approach to assigning product cost is used, it is easier to see how costs change with production or other activity. The difference between absorption costing and variable costing is the treatment of fixed MOH costs.

2. The two costing approaches – absorption costing and variable costing can both be used to prepare income statements. The absorption-cost form is used for financial reporting, while the variable cost form is used internally, by managers.

    a. Profitability under the absorption is called **gross margin**, and equals sales revenues minus cost of goods sold.

    b. Profitability under the variable cost method is called **contribution margin**, and equals sales revenues minus variable expenses.

    c. The financial results obtained when these income statements are compared to each other differ based on differences in how much fixed overhead cost is inventoried and how much is included in the cost of goods sold. Since fixed MOH is an inventoriable cost under the absorption method, but is a period cost for the variable cost method, the difference arises when all units produced in a period are not sold in that same period.

       In a JIT manufacturing environment, where virtually all units produced are sold in the same period, there is virtually no difference in financial results between the two methods.

3. Comparison of the absorption cost method and the variable cost method highlights two different views of these methods.

    a. Advocates of full-cost reporting argue that in the long run, full costs reflect the true cost of products. Because full costing assigns fixed manufacturing costs, it takes into account the fact that such costs, in the long run, vary with production activity.

    b. Advocates of variable cost methods argue that reporting product costs purely based on activity gives a clearer picture of costs that can be managed when making product or selling services. Management decisions about managing production costs should not be based on product costing using the absorption method.

3\. A modification of the variable cost approach is throughput costing. With this costing method, only unit-level costs are included as product cost. Often throughput costing assigns only direct materials costs to units of product.

4. **Regardless of the arguments for or against absorption, variable or throughput costing, all three methods can be (and are) used in a single organization. As the cost of developing different reports became easier and less costly due to advancement in information technologies, many companies produce cost analyses using all three costing methods.**

5. **One criticism of full costing is that it may lead managers to intentionally over-produce inventory, merely for the purpose of shifting overhead costs to inventory, thereby reducing expenses and increasing profit. Doing so is viewed as an unethical practice by most managers and accountants.**

REVIEW AND SELF TEST QUESTIONS AND EXERCISES

Matching key terms

Match the following terms to the correct definition by writing the correct letter next to the correct definition.

a. manufacturing overhead
b. cost of goods sold
c. work in process
d. prime costs
e. absorption costing
f. fixed costs
g. period costs
h. product costs
i. direct labor
j. contribution margin

______ 1. Costs that are not related to production activity for a manufacturing firm.

______ 2. Production costs that cannot be traced directly to units of product.

______ 3. The difference between sales revenue and variable costs.

______ 4. The sum of direct labor and direct materials.

______ 5. The expense account charged when inventory items are sold.

______ 6. Labor costs that can be assigned to units of product.

______ 7. A costing approach where the full costs of production are assigned to units of product.

______ 8. The sum of direct materials, direct labor and manufacturing overhead costs.

______ 9. Costs of production associated with units of product that are incomplete at the end of an accounting period

______10. Costs that do not change with production activity.

True or False

For each of the following statements enter a T or an F in the blank to indicate whether the statement is true or false.

_____11. The word “cost” usually signifies spending cash to buy something.

_____12. In a manufacturing environment, all costs that occur in a business are either product costs or period costs.

_____13. Raw Materials Inventory is the name of an expense account.

_____14. There are five different hierarchies of resources used in business and production processes.

_____15. Businesses that offer services to their customers generally have an asset account called inventory.

_____16. In a manufacturing company, there is only one production cost. It is manufacturing overhead expense.

_____17. Work in process is an inventory account that represents the value of unfinished units of product.

_____18. Direct materials cost is an example of a traceable cost.

_____19. Gross margin is a profit measure used in the variable cost form of the income statement.

_____20. A cost driver is best described as a type of period cost.

_____21. A customer-level resource is one that can be traced to the serving of a particular group of customers.

_____22. The last item reported on an income statement is net income for a service firm, but it is cost of goods manufactured for a manufacturer

_____23. Cost of goods sold for a manufacturer is based on the value of finished goods sold to customers.

_____24. Period costs are expensed during the time period they are incurred.

_____25. A sunk cost is the same as an opportunity cost.

Multiple Choice

Choose the best answer by writing the letter corresponding to your choice in the space provided.

_____26. Which of the following is **incorrect**?

a) The three inventory accounts for a manufacturer are raw materials inventory, work in process inventory and finished goods inventory.
b) Service sector firms generally do not have any inventory
c) A retailer does not usually have production costs.
d) When raw materials are placed into production, the value of raw materials is added to the raw materials inventory account.

_____27. Which of the following lists the hierarchy of resources in the correct order (from lowest level to highest level)?

a) Batch-level, product-level, customer-level, facility-level, and unit-level resources
b) Product-level, batch-level, customer-level, facility-level, and unit-level resources
c) Unit-level, batch-level, product-level, customer-level, and facility-level resources
d) Facility-level, unit-level, batch-level, product-level, and customer-level resources

_____28. Which of the following is correct regarding committed costs?

a) Committed costs are never included as product costs, regardless of the costing method
b) Only production activities can cause committed costs – support activities cannot
c) A committed cost is very likely to change each time production activity changes
d) Usually, committed costs can be changed in the future, but cannot be changed immediately

_____29. One way to categorize costs is based is based on one's ability to trace the cost to some activity. Which of the following is true regarding costs that are traceable?

a) Traceable costs must be assigned to units of product using some type of allocation process.
b) Traceable costs are restricted to support activities.
c) Untraceable costs are not assigned to products when variable costing is used.
d) When absorption costing is used, traceable costs are treated as period costs.

_____30. Conversion costs in production equal the sum of

a) direct materials and direct labor
b) direct labor and manufacturing overhead
c) direct materials and manufacturing overhead
d) direct materials, direct labor and manufacturing overhead

_____31. Based on the variable costing approach, cost of goods sold consists of

a) all variable production costs, excluding unit-level production costs for products sold.
b) all variable costs, both production and non-production, for products sold.
c) all variable production costs and committed production costs for products sold.
d) All unit-level production costs and variable production costs for products sold.

_____32. What is a correct description of the flow of costs through a manufacturing company's inventory system?

a) Materials go to finished goods inventory from materials inventory, and conversion costs go from work in process to finished goods inventory.
b) Unused materials go to work in process, and unsold finished goods go back to work in process.
c) Materials go to work in process from materials inventory, and work in process is completed and goes to finished goods inventory.
d) The three types of inventory are not related to each other in any way.

_____33. If there is a large amount of unsold product in inventory at year-end, then which of the following correctly describes expenses and operating income reported on the income statement, based on the costing method?

a) Absorption costing results in lower total expenses and lower operating income than throughput costing.
b) Absorption costing results in higher total expenses and higher operating income than throughput costing.
c) Absorption costing results in higher total expenses and lower operating income than throughput costing.
d) Absorption costing results in lower total expenses and higher operating income than throughput costing.

_____34. Which of the following is an example of a resource that would be treated as a traceable product cost for a candy manufacturer?

a) Sugar to make salt water taffy for a candy company.
b) Energy costs to run machines to mix the candy ingredients.
c) Salary of the factory supervisor in the candy manufacturing facility.
d) All of the above are traceable product costs.

_____35. Which of the following is **incorrect** regarding completion of the schedule of cost of goods manufactured?

a) In order to complete the schedule, you would have to first know the cost of goods sold.
b) In order to complete the schedule, you need to know the beginning and ending balances of work in process inventory
c) In order to complete the schedule, you need to know the beginning and ending balances of finished goods inventory.
d) Total cost of direct labor is one of the costs listed on the schedule.

______36. If a large amount of units of product are unsold and they remain in finished goods inventory at year-end, what can be said about inventory balances given that absorption costing is used?

a) Production costs for the year just ended will all be expensed in that year.
b) A lot of production cost will not be expensed because it is included in the finished goods inventory balance.
c) Production expenses for the remaining unsold product will be treated as operating expenses for the year just ended.
d) Operating income for the year just ended must be increased by the amount of production cost included in finished goods inventory.

______37. Which of the following is most likely to be treated as a facility-level cost at a law firm?

a) Attorneys' time in court for specific cases.
b) Salaries of office staff.
c) Travel costs of attorneys who are going to meet with clients.
d) Costs of taking depositions for cases.

______38. Total production costs for May were as follows for a small manufacturer of hand-made leather bags. Unit-level production costs totaled $250,000. Variable production costs totaled $100,000. Variable non-production costs were $30,000. Indirect production costs were $400,000. Indirect non-production costs totaled $20,000. If 50,000 units of product were completed, then what would the average per-unit cost of inventory be? Assume absorption costing is used.

a) $7 per unit
b) $8 per unit
c) $15 per unit
d) $16 per unit

______39. A company has a rate of $12 per unit for electricity costs based on an estimated cost per kilowatt-hour, and an estimated amount of machine time for each unit of product. The rate was derived with the expectation that 1,500 units of this product would be made last month, and based on estimated electricity costs of $18,000. The amount of electricity costs applied to products was $19,200, and actual electricity costs were $21,000. Based on the three dollar amounts given, which of the following statements is true?

a) More units of product were made than originally estimated.
b) The rate of $12 per unit was too high.
c) The amount of electricity cost applied to products was based purely on the amount of electricity actually used.
d) Electricity costs are too unpredictable to use in an activity-based rate.

_____40. Production costs for one month for a food processing plant totaled $2 million for materials (unit-level costs). Variable production costs were $4,250,000, and indirect production costs totaled $3,750,000. If 100% of the product for the month was completed and sold, then how much of the cost described would be treated as non-production cost based on variable costing and absorption costing?

a) Variable costing = $5,750,000 and absorption costing = $3,750,000.
b) Variable costing = $4,250,000 and absorption costing = $3,750,000.
c) Variable costing = $4,250,000 and absorption costing = $0.
d) Variable costing = $3,750,000 and absorption costing = $0.

_____41. Which of the following is an example of a committed cost?

a) Cost of raw materials that will be ordered for production.
b) Salary of an NBA player with a 5-year contract.
c) Costs of paying seasonal workers for a lettuce farm.
d) Rental costs for a piece of equipment for which the 5-year lease is about to be signed.

_____42. If production activity is not completed by the end of a company's fiscal year, then which of the following is the most accurate statement?

a) There will be RMI, WIP and FGI at year-end as a result.
b) There will be RMI and WIP at year-end as a result.
c) There will be WIP at year-end as a result.
d) There will be FGI at year-end as a result.

_____43. The contribution margin (CM) is a profitability measure. Which of the following statements is **incorrect** regarding contribution margin?

a) CM is a subtotal that appears on the income statement for variable costing income statements.
b) CM is a concept that is associated with variable costing.
c) CM equals sales revenue minus variable production costs.
d) CM and gross margin mean the same thing.

_____44. Which of the following is **least likely** to be included as part of manufacturing overhead costs?

a) Costs for electricity is a production facility.
b) Factory supervisor's salary.
c) Costs of engines used in tractors being manufactured.
d) Cost of the paint used to paint the tractors being manufactured.

_____45. Which of the following is correct about the difference between absorption costing and variable costing for a manufacturer?

a) The only difference between these two methods is the treatment of fixed overhead costs.
b) The only difference between these two methods is the treatment of work in process inventory.
c) The only difference between these two methods is the treatment of unit-level costs.
d) The only difference between these two methods is the treatment of sunk costs.

Exercises

Brenda Goldman and Deb DiPietro recently graduated from the Food Sciences program at Wynn State University. After learning how to mass produce ice cream , the two women decided to start a manufacturing firm to make ice cream. After completing a thorough market analysis, and developing a business plan, operations began last year. Their company, BD Creamery Company had the following results.

		Production
Direct Material Used		$50,000
Direct Labor		$60,000
Variable MOH		$40,000
Fixed MOH		$90,000
Variable Selling and Administrative Costs		$10,000
Fixed Selling and Administrative Costs		$110,000
Total Costs		**$360,000**

300,000 cartons of ice cream were made. 250,000 cartons were sold for $1.50 per gallon to regional grocery store chains. The remaining 50,000 were completed by year-end, and were stored for sale the following year.

Complete the table below to answer questions 46–50.

	VARIABLE COSTING	ABSORPTION COSTING
46. Cost of goods sold		
47. Ending inventory		
48. Profit measure	Contribution margin =	Gross margin =
49. Operating expenses		
50. Operating income		

Answers to Questions and Exercises

Matching key terms

1. g 2. a 3. j 4. d 5. b 6. i 7. e 8. h 9. c 10. f

True or False

11. F. The term "cost" implies some expense has been incurred without regard to whether money has been paid for the expense.
12. T. Product costs are associated with production activities, while period costs are incurred in running the business.
13. F. Raw materials inventory is the name of an asset account on the balance sheet
14. T. These hierarchies are unit, batch, product, customer, and facility-level resources.
15. F Manufacturers and merchandisers have inventory accounts; service firms do not.
16. F. Manufacturing firms have three broad categories of manufacturing costs. They are direct materials, direct labor, and manufacturing overhead.
17. T. Work in process is an asset, and appears on the balance sheet as a type of inventory.
18. T. Direct materials can be traced to a unit of product. A traceable cost can be linked directly to a cost object like a unit of product.
19. F. Gross margin is associated with absorption-costed income statements. Contribution margin is associated with a variable-costed income statement.
20. F. A cost driver is an activity that causes costs.
21. T. Customer-level resources are costs that arise only because of the needs of specific groups of customers. They can be traced to one particular customer type.
22. F. Regardless of the type of business that is reporting financial information, the "bottom line" of the income statement is net income.
23. T. Cost of goods sold is based on the value of inventory items sold. For a manufacturer, the items sold come from finished goods inventory.
24. T. Period costs appear on the income statement in the period during which they occurred. Product costs are inventoried, and are not expensed until the inventory items are sold.
25. F. A sunk cost is one that has been incurred in the past, and which can't be retrieved. Opportunity costs represent a sacrifice – one thing is given up in order to obtain something else.

Multiple Choice

26. d. When raw materials are placed into production, they are added to the work in process inventory account.
27. c. Higher-level resources cannot be traced to lower-level activities, but lower-level resources can be traced to higher-level activities. There is a logical ordering of the hierarchies that reflects that fact.\
28. d. Committed costs are costs that may be fixed in the short run. That is, they cannot be easily changed. For instance, factory equipment that was acquired for production purposes can't be quickly replaced. It is expected to last for long periods of time.
29. c. Costs that are not traceable are considered to be period costs under the variable-cost approach, but are allocated to units of product under absorption costing.
30. Conversion costs consisting of direct labor and MOH are the costs incurred to change raw materials into finished product.

31. d. Cost of goods sold for variable-cost income statements consists only of variable production costs. All costs that do not vary with production activity are treated as fixed costs, and would be expensed as period costs.
32. c. When raw materials are placed into production, they become part of work in process (WIP). Direct labor and MOH are added to materials in WIP, and when production is complete, the completed units and their costs are transferred to finished goods inventory (FGI).
33. d. Absorption costing treats all production costs as inventory, so if a lot of inventory is unsold, then a lot of production cost remains in inventory accounts. This means the only production costs that become expense would be production costs for units sold (cost of goods sold). Throughput costing treats only unit-level and variable costs as product cost. Cost of goods sold would be only unit-level and variable production costs. However, all fixed costs would be treated as period costs instead of being inventoried. Thus, expenses would be higher under throughput costing, and operating income would be lower.
34. a. Energy costs and factory supervision are manufacturing overhead costs.
35. a. The Schedule of Cost of Goods Manufactured is used to determine cost of goods sold, so CGS cannot be used to complete it.
36. b. Since all production costs are inventoried under absorption costing, the FGI account will be large and CGS will be small.
37. b. Office staff salaries cannot be traced to one particular unit of product. Here, a "product" is legal service provided to clients. All of the other answers can be traced to particular cases or clients and would be treated as unit-level, batch (for instance preparing leases for a client renting office space to many tenants), product, or customer-level costs.
38. c. When absorption costing is used, the cost per unit is total production cost divided by total units. Then total production costs are ($250,000 + $100,000 + $400,000) = $750,000. $750,000/50,000 units = $15 per unit.
39. a. This question requires an understanding of how rates are applied. They are applied based on production activity. If 1,500 units were made, the amount applied would be 1,500 × $12, or $18,000. Since $19,200 was assigned to product cost, it must be the case that $19,200/$12, or 1,600 units were made.
40. d. Under variable costing, all indirect costs are treated as period costs, and under absorption costing all production costs are treated as product costs.
41. b. A five-year contract is a committed cost because it can't be easily eliminated. The other three costs in a, c, and d can be eliminated simply by opting not to incur them.
42. c. Work in process is an inventory account that measures the value of incomplete units of product at the end of an accounting period.
43. d. Contribution margin is a profitability measure for variable-costed income statements; gross margin is a profitability measure for absorption-costed income statements.
44. c. The cost of engines would probably be treated as a major direct material cost, so would not be an overhead cost, but would be a direct materials cost. The other three items are not traceable to individual units of product.
45. a. Under variable costing, fixed OH costs are period costs; under absorption costing, fixed OH costs are treated as period costs.

Exercises

46 and 47. For both methods, production costs are split between cost of goods sold and finished goods inventory. However, when absorption costing is used all production costs are included, while variable costing uses only unit-level and variable production costs. 250,000/300,000 is sold, and 50,000/300,000 remains as FGI.

- For variable costing, cost of goods sold is ($50,000 + 60,000 + 40,000)/300,000 units × 250,000 units sold = $125,000.
- For absorption costing, cost of goods sold is ($50,000 + 60,000 + 40,000 + 90,000)/300,000 units × 250,000 units sold = $200,000.
- Once CGS is computed, FGI can easily be determined. For variable costing it is $150,000 – 125,000 = $25,000.
- For absorption costing, FGI = $240,000 – $200,000 = $40,000

48. Even though each costing method has a different profit measure, all of the begin with revenues. Revenue was $1.50 × 250,000 gallons, or $375,000.

- For variable costing, contribution margin is $375,000 – 125,000 = $250,000
- For absorption costing, gross margin is $375,000 – 200,000 = $175,000

49. Operating expenses under variable costing are all non-production costs plus fixed MOH. For absorption costing, operating expenses are all non-production costs.

- For variable costing, operating expenses are $10,000 + 110,000 + 90,000 = $210,000
- For absorption costing, operating expenses are $10,000 + 110,000 = $120,000

50. Operating income is just profit margin from question 48 less operating expenses from question 49.

- For variable costing, operating income is $250,000 – 210,000 = $40,000
- For absorption costing, operating income is $175,000 – 120,000 = $55,000

The amounts are summarized below. Notice that the operating income differs under the two methods by the same amount as the difference between the ending inventory balances. This shows clearly that the only difference between these costing methods arises due to different treatment of the fixed overhead costs.

	VARIABLE COSTING	**ABSORPTION COSTING**
46. Cost of goods sold	$125,000	$200,000
47. Ending inventory	$25,000	$40,000
48. Profit measure	Contribution margin = $250,000	Gross margin = $175,000
49. Operating expenses	$210,000	$120,000
50. Operating income	$40,000	$55,000

Chapter 3
Cost Accumulation for Job-Shop and Batch Production Operations

Chapter Study Suggestions

Chapter 3 presents job costing. Job costing treats each individual job as a unit of product. Costs are assigned or allocated to each job as resources are used. The basic cost flow model provides a framework for recording costs of jobs. The assignment of costs occurs either by assigning actual costs for lower-level resources, or by applying costs using a predetermined cost-driver rate. If a cost-driver rate is used, then a variance usually results between actual costs and the amount of cost applied to jobs.

An overhead account is a general ledger account where higher-level resource costs are accumulated. Since at the end of an accounting period this account must be closed out, and there is almost always a balance, three methods for closing this account are discussed. Discussion of Work-in Process Inventory, Finished Goods Inventory, and Cost of Goods Sold is extended to the job-order costing environment.

Finally, this chapter discusses accounting for projects, which are similar to jobs, but are long-term in duration.

Chapter Highlights

A. Cost Management Challenges. There are 3 questions addressed in this chapter.

1. What factors should a cost management analyst consider when designing a product costing system?
2. What features should a job-cost system have, and how can they be developed?
3. How can cost managers use job-cost information to support planning and decision-making activities?

B. Learning Objectives—This chapter has 8 learning objectives.

1. This chapter explains the differences between job-order-, process- and operation-costing systems.
2. It explains how costs flow through manufacturing accounts.
3. The chapter shows how to assign costs to jobs or products in a job-cost accounting system.
4. Journal entries are explained, and use of journal entries to record job costs is presented.
5. Calculation and use of a predetermined overhead rate to assign indirect costs is presented.
6. Actual, normal and standard costing systems are introduced.
7. Use of job-order costing in service organizations is discussed.
8. It illustrates the use of job-costing information for planning and managing long-term projects.

C. Choosing the right product costing system should be based on the types of products a company sells. The three most common types of costing systems are job-order costing, process costing and operation costing. Other costing systems are variations of these three.

1. Job costing (or job-order costing) treats each job as a unit of product. Costs are allocated based on resource use in each job. A "unit" might also be a batch of units that are all identical. This variation of job-order costing is operation costing.
    a. Job costing helps managers to identify jobs that will be profitable, so organizations can more clearly define the scope and scale of its operations.
    b. Job costing provides data that is useful for predicting costs of future jobs.

c. Job costing allows costs of current jobs to be better managed and controlled.

d. It facilitates re-negotiation of job contracts if changes in jobs occur.

e. Job costing provides information that allows comparison between actual and expected outcomes.

2. Process costing, discussed in Chapter 8, treats all units of product the same. Process costing is useful when all units of product use virtually the same resources in the same way. A producer of sunflower seeds is not likely to keep track of each pound of seeds as a separate job.

3. Operation costing is a hybrid of the two extremes. Job order costing assumes each job is a unique, distinct unit of product. Process costing assumes each unit of product is virtually the same. Hybrid costing is most commonly used when batches of similar products are made that are virtually the same within the batch but each batch is a unique, distinct job. Large auto manufacturers use hybrid costing. Ford makes thousands of Ford Focus, a subcompact car, in batches. They also make Ford Freestar, a minivan whose production uses Ford Motor Company's resources differently.

D. The basic cost-flow model in accounting for WIP inventory can be used for job costing. The model is as follows.

1. Beginning balance + resources transferred in – resources transferred out = ending balance.

a. Costs in the beginning balance are from prior periods, and represent costs of resources used so far. They may be unit, batch, product, customer and facility-level costs assigned using cost-driver rates.

b. Resources used or transferred-in, in a subsequent period are assigned in the same way.

c. Resources transferred out reflect costs of goods or services that are either completed and ready for sale, or are partially completed goods being transferred to another department for additional production activities. Transferred-out may also represent defective or scrapped products.

d. The ending balance is the amount of cost that remains on a job. In job costing, an ending balance is an indication that the job has not been completed.

2. Because reporting of business activity occurs periodically, but completion of jobs generally does not occur at the end of a reporting period, job cost reporting must reflect the value of jobs at interim points before they are completed. There are two inventory accounts in which costs of jobs are accumulated. They are Work-in Process (WIP) inventory and Finished-goods inventory (FGI).

a. Work-in-Process inventory accumulates all costs of resources used on jobs that have not been completed. Each job has its own subsidiary account, where costs specific to the job are recorded.

b. Finished-goods inventory is an account where costs of all completed jobs are recorded. These costs are transferred from WIP inventory when a job is completed. The costs remain in FGI until the job is sold. Once sold, the costs of a job are transferred to the expense account, Cost of Goods Sold.

E. Companies using job costing usually have many jobs being worked on at the same time. An accounting system must allow the organization to keep track of all jobs separately, and must maintain records of all jobs in progress, completed, and sold. It must also record activity for WIP inventory, FGI, and cost of goods sold.

1. A job cost accounting system records information in a journal, usually maintained on a computer system. This information is summarized, and the totals are recorded in general ledger accounts. The general ledger accounts contain balances of all accumulated effects of transactions. Three general ledger accounts important in a job costing system are Work-in-Process inventory, Finished-goods inventory, and cost of goods sold.

a. Journal entries are used to record transactions. In a job-order shop, journal entries record the transactions in control accounts as well as assigning product costs to jobs.

b. The general ledger account, Work-in-Process inventory is a control account containing total costs for all incomplete jobs. There is also a subsidiary ledger account that contains details for each job.

c. General ledger accounts are depicted in textbooks as "T" accounts. The left-hand side of a T-account for inventory like WIP or FGI, or for an expense account like cost of goods sold (CGS) is called the "debit" side. The right-hand side of an inventory or expense account is called the "credit" side. Increasing an inventory or expense account is accomplished by "debiting" the account. Decreasing an account like WIP, FGI, or CGS occurs by "crediting" the account. Inventory accounts cannot have a credit balance. That is like saying that you have a negative amount of materials on hand.

A T-account for WIP inventory, for one job is shown below.

JOB 598

BB $5,000	
TI $ 500	
	$5,500 TO
EB $ 0	

BB is the beginning balance, TI is for costs transferred in during the period, TO is for costs transferred out of Job 598. In this example, the job is completed, and costs are transferred to FGI, so the ending balance (EB) is zero.

d. The simplest job costing system used to assign higher-level resource costs to jobs is one that uses one predetermined rate, called the overhead rate.

F. Journal entries are used to record costs. Entries are made to the control accounts and to the subsidiary ledgers. There are four journal entries that record production activity in a simple manufacturing system.

1. Purchase raw materials:
   DR Raw Materials Inventory
   CR Accounts Payable

2. Place raw materials into production:
   DR WIP
   MOH
   CR RMI

   WIP is charged for direct materials placed into production, and MOH is charged for indirect materials placed into production.

3. Record labor costs:
   DR WIP
   MOH
   CR Wages Payable

   WIP is charged for direct labor, and MOH is charged for indirect labor.

4. Record other manufacturing costs:
   DR MOH
   CR Accounts Payable
   Prepaid Expenses
   Cash
   Accumulated Depreciation

G. Job costs are summarized for three reasons. (1) A job is completed, and costs must be summarized to determine the total cost of the job. (2) A job is sold. (3) The end of an accounting period makes it necessary to report the status of all jobs.

1. When jobs are completed, amounts are transferred from WIP inventory to FGI. The journal entry to record this transfer is to debit FGI and to credit WIP.

2. When jobs are sold, balances are transferred from FGI to CGS. Price minus CGS = Gross Profit. The journal entry for this is to debit CGS and credit FGI.

3. At month-end or year-end, a company's books are closed, and financial statements are prepared. Since it is not likely that every job will be complete at the end of an accounting period, and every completed job will not have been sold, it is necessary to update the balances in the inventory accounts. Cost of goods sold must be closed at the end of each accounting period.

4. Adjustments must be made to the overhead account at the end of a period. Overheads are expenses, and expense accounts must be closed at the end of an accounting period. The overhead control account is a summary total of all indirect manufacturing costs. Subsidiary ledger accounts contain detail of the overhead control account. The detail is based on the type of cost.

   Actual costs are accumulated in the control and subsidiary ledgers by debiting these expense accounts. These costs are assigned to jobs using the predetermined overhead rate. Since the rate is derived using estimated costs and activity, but costs are assigned to jobs based on the rate and actual activity, there is usually a mismatch between the amount assigned and the amount that actually occurs.

   a. The difference between the amount applied to jobs and the amount of actual overhead expense incurred is called an overhead variance. There are two reasons an overhead variance occurs. Either actual spending differed from budgeted spending, or actual activity was different from budgeted activity. The first difference results in an overhead spending or budget variance. The second difference results in an overhead activity or volume variance.

   b. Overhead costs can be over-applied to jobs, meaning that more overhead costs were assigned than actually occurred. Overhead costs may also be under-applied, meaning that less cost was assigned to jobs than occurred.

   c. Since the overhead control account is an expense account, the amount of overhead over-applied or under-applied needs to be disposed of. There are two ways to dispose of overhead variances. One way is to assign them to cost of goods sold. The other way is to prorate them among WIP, FGI, and CGS. The latter method is necessary only if the amount of variance is considered to be material.

   d. The flow of overhead costs through the accounting system is as described below.

      Actual overhead costs are accumulated in the overhead control (and subsidiary) accounts. At the end of an accounting period, overhead costs are assigned to jobs in WIP inventory, based on predetermined overhead (or cost-driver) rates and actual activity for the jobs receiving the overhead costs. If more costs are assigned to jobs than actually occurred, then the overhead control account and corresponding subsidiary accounts must be closed by debiting them by amounts equal to the credit balance. If fewer costs are assigned than actually occurred then the overhead accounts must be credited by amounts equal to the debit balances.

      Some organizations set up separate accounts to reflect spending and activity variances, to separate them from the overhead account. In that case, it is the variance accounts that must be closed.

e. If the amounts of the variance are written off to cost of goods sold, then whatever amount is taken from the overhead (or variance) account is assigned to cost of goods sold. If the amounts are prorated among WIP inventory, FGI, and CGS then they are usually prorated based on the existing balances in each of the three accounts.

H. Job order costing is used by service-oriented companies. The cost driver is often different than the one used in a manufacturing environment, but the concepts are the same.

I. Assigning costs that are not traceable to jobs requires an allocation procedure. Assignment of manufacturing overhead costs usually requires use of a predetermined overhead rate, which is used to assign costs to jobs. Tracing and assigning costs to jobs requires (1) choosing methods for tracing costs to jobs, (2) setting predetermined cost-driver rates and (3) using the predetermined cost-driver rates.

1. Predetermined OH rates are developed for MOH costs, and these rates are used to apply costs to jobs.

2. Developing predetermined OH rates requires a lot of estimation, described below.

    a. For estimating OH rates, all OH costs to be included as indirect should be identified.

    b. Then all of these costs must be estimated. These cost estimates are usually based on past experience, current conditions, and expected changes.

    c. Next, cost-drivers must be chosen. The cost driver should be highly correlated with the costs that are to be assigned. Sometimes a cost-driver is obvious for a facility-level resource. At other times, a valid cost-driver cannot be identified. Traditionally, direct labor hours or machine hours have been used as cost drivers.

    d. Next, the quantity of the cost driver activity must be estimated.

    e. Finally, the predetermined cost-driver rate can be calculated by dividing the estimated cost of a resource by the estimated quantity of the chosen cost-driver base. These rates are then used to apply costs to jobs based on the actual amount of use of the cost driver.

3. Predetermined cost-driver rates are used to assign higher-level resource costs. Actual unit or batch-level costs can be assigned without a predetermined cost-driver rate. Some higher-level resources in a job-costing environment may be grouped together as general and administrative costs.

4. Use of a predetermined OH rate is the approach used when one cost assignment approach is used. That approach is called normal costing. There are two other methods that can be used.

    a. Actual costing assigns actual costs as they occur. Although accurate, only direct materials and direct labor (and batch-level when a unit is one batch) costs can be assigned immediately. Manufacturing overhead costs must be assigned later. In addition to the inability to assign MOH costs immediately, they also cannot be traced directly to a particular job.

    b. Standard costing is a widely used approach, where standard costs and rates are used to assign costs to products. For this method, direct material and direct labor rates are applied to jobs, similar to the way OH costs are applied to jobs under normal costing.

J. Complex jobs that take a long time (months or even years) to complete are called projects.

1. Unlike some jobs, which may be completed before a customer is identified, projects normally are not initiated unless a customer has requested that the work be performed. In most cases, organizations must submit bids for projects. Bids are based on estimated costs and estimated uses of resources and time. Profits are also estimated and factored into the bid. If an organization submits a low bid with unrealistically low cost estimates, any cost overruns come directly out of profits.

2. There are two control issues for the manager of a project. They are related to control and management of project cost, and proper budgeting and use of project time.

    a. Project cost is estimated before the project begins, and usually is developed from the estimates used in the bidding process. The project manager spreads the cost budget over the expected time to complete the project. As the project progresses, the manager periodically evaluates the budgeted cost of work completed versus the actual cost of work completed. Also evaluated is the budgeted percentage of work completed versus the actual percentage of work completed.

       If actual costs are greater than budgeted costs for the percentage of work done, then the project has "cost overruns".

    b. The manager must also see whether a project is on schedule, so periodically checks to see what percentage of the project is actually complete compared to what percentage should have been completed by pre-specified points in time.

    c. Project scheduling can be depicted using a Gantt chart, which shows the timing and sequencing of major project activities. All activities of a project are displayed on the chart month by month (or week by week). Both planned and actual times are shown. A Gantt chart allows a project manager to anticipate delays and bottlenecks, so that scheduling of subsequent activities can be revised accordingly.

3. Job and project costs can, at times far exceed estimates, or may be incorrectly reported or charged. The most common improprieties are (1) misstating the stage of completion, (2) charging costs to the wrong job intentionally, to reduce cost overruns on a job, and (3) misrepresenting costs on jobs in order to receive a larger payment for a job.

K. Job costing systems are indispensable for reporting and controlling the costs of jobs. Profitability can be easily assessed job by job if job costing is used.

REVIEW AND SELF TEST QUESTIONS AND EXERCISES

Matching key terms

Match the following terms to the correct definition by writing the correct letter next to the correct definition.

a.	actual costing	b.	process costing	c.	operation costing
d.	job-order costing	e.	predetermined OH rate	f.	subsidiary ledger
g.	applied overhead	h.	projects	i.	standard costing
j.	Gantt chart				

_____ 1. A costing system used when companies produce large batches of similar products.

_____ 2. Jobs that take a long time to complete.

_____ 3. A detailed set of records that supports a control account.

_____ 4. A way to show the timing, sequencing and overlap of project activities.

_____ 5. A way to assign MOH costs to jobs.

_____ 6. A method for assigning costs when a unit of product is a job.

_____ 7. A cost assignment approach where actual costs are assigned to jobs.

_____ 8. A costing approach where direct materials, direct labor and MOH all have a rate.

_____ 9. A costing system that is useful when all units of product are exactly the same.

_____10. The amount of OH cost allocated to jobs using a predetermined OH rate.

True or False

For each of the following statements enter a T or an F in the blank to indicate whether the statement is true or false.

______11. Job-order costing can only be used if all units of product are very similar to each other.

______12. Job-order costing cannot be used for service organizations.

______13. Job-order costing makes it necessary to maintain separate records for each job.

______14. Standard costing allows direct assignment of direct costs to jobs, and average cost assignment for indirect costs.

______15. Actual costing does not allow costs to be assigned to jobs on a timely basis.

______16. In a job-order costing environment, the work in process subsidiary ledger contains information by inventory account.

______17. When normal costing is used, the actual overhead costs are assigned to jobs.

______18. If jobs are completed and sold, FGI and CGS are two accounts that will be affected.

______19. Overhead control is a general ledger account where direct manufacturing costs are summarized.

______20. A predetermined OH rate is used to assign OH costs to jobs when normal costing is used.

______21. Once a job is completed, WIP inventory is credited, and FGI is debited.

______22. The amount of cost assigned to jobs using an overhead rate always equals the actual amount of cost that occurs.

______23. When the end of an accounting period occurs, the overhead account must be closed.

______24. If overhead variance is prorated, it is split among WIP inventory, FGI, and Raw Materials Inventory.

______25. A project is similar to a job, only it takes longer to complete.

Multiple Choice

Choose the best answer by writing the letter corresponding to your choice in the space provided.

_____26. Which of the following is the correct name for the following: "This costing method assigns actual unit-level costs to a job, and uses average past spending for higher-level resource costs."

a) Actual costing
b) Budgeted costing
c) Normal costing
d) Standard costing

_____27. One criticism of actual costing is that it

a) does not allow timely reporting or assignment of costs for specific jobs.
b) does not allow the use of actual costs for unit-level costs.
c) does not allow the use of job-order costing.
d) is not an accurate reporting method

_____28. Job-order costing is most appropriate when

a) all units of product are the same.
b) all units of product are different.
c) all units of product are very expensive to produce.
d) all units of product are very inexpensive to produce.

_____29. Jennings Brothers, DDS offers orthodontic services. Every patient has very specific needs, and is billed accordingly. Which of the following costing systems would be the most appropriate to use for this dental practice?

a) Operation costing
b) Process costing
c) Job costing
d) Any of the three costing systems would work

_____30. If the basic cost flow model is used to show job costing for inventory, what does the ending balance for the WIP control account show?

a) The balance of costs for completed jobs
b) The balance of costs for incomplete jobs
c) The amount of cost added to all jobs for the month
d) The amount of cost to be transferred to cost of goods sold

_____31. Two of the three inventory accounts used by most manufacturing companies that have inventory are Work-in-Process (WIP) inventory, and Finished-goods inventory (FGI). Which of the following correctly describes the relationship between these two inventory accounts?

a) These two accounts are not related in any way.
b) WIP balances get transferred to FGI.
c) FGI balances get transferred to WIP.
d) WIP is a subsidiary account to the FGI control account.

_____32. FGI contains costs of completed jobs. What happens to the amounts in this account?

a) When jobs are sold, costs are transferred from WIP to FGI.
b) When jobs are completed, CGS is closed to FGI.
c) When jobs are sold, FGI is transferred to CGS.
d) When jobs are completed, FGI is closed to an income summary account.

_____33. Which of the following shows the correct flow of costs of inventory through the accounting system?

a) Overhead costs go to WIP, and WIP goes to CGS.
b) WIP goes to FGI, and FGI goes to overhead.
c) WIP goes to overhead, and overhead goes to FGI.
d) WIP goes to FGI, and FGI goes to CGS.

_____34. The predetermined overhead rate for assigning OH costs to each job was based on an estimated OH cost of $720,000 and 36,000 machine hours. Job #168 used 250 hours of machine time. How much cost will be assigned to Job #168 for overhead costs?

a) $144
b) $2,880
c) $5,000
d) $720,000

_____35. A trucking company is trying to develop a way to assign costs of maintaining trucks to jobs. Which cost-driver base is the most appropriate to use?

a) Estimated number of miles driven to jobs in a year
b) Estimated number of trucking jobs per year
c) Estimated number of drivers employed per year
d) Estimated total weight transported per year

_____36. Which of the following costs is the **least** likely to have an obvious cost-driver?

a) Costs of the Human Resources Department.
b) Costs of billing customers.
c) Costs of using a travel agency to arrange travel to jobs.
d) Costs of salaries paid to the CFO and CEO.

_____37. Work-in-Process inventory had a beginning balance of $820,000. Direct material and direct labor costs for the month were $215,000, and overhead costs applied were $300,000. $570,000 for jobs completed was transferred to Finished-goods inventory. What is the ending balance of WIP inventory?

a) $265,000
b) $765,000
c) $875,000
d) $1,905,000

_____38. Which of the following statements is **false** regarding the T-account for Finished-goods inventory?

a) FGI is increased by receiving charges from WIP inventory.
b) FGI cannot have an ending balance on the right-hand side (credit balance).
c) FGI's ending balance represents jobs completed but not yet sold.
d) FGI is assigned costs from overhead control via the predetermined overhead rates and actual activity.

_____39. Cost of goods sold is an expense account. It represents costs of

a) jobs completed but not yet sold.
b) jobs not yet completed.
c) jobs completed and sold.
d) jobs sold in advance of completion.

_____40. The overhead control account is increased by all **except**

a) direct materials costs.
b) electricity costs.
c) the production manager's salary.
d) machinery repair expenses.

_____41. The amount of overhead cost assigned to jobs rarely equals the actual cost of overhead activities. Which of the following is **not** a reason for this mismatching of applied and actual costs?

a) Direct materials costs were unexpectedly high.
b) Actual spending for overhead activities is not equal to estimated spending for overhead activities.
c) Actual overhead activity is not equal to estimated overhead activity.
d) Budget estimates of overhead costs were unrealistically low.

_____42. If the overhead applied is greater than the amount of overhead cost incurred, then overhead costs are over-applied, resulting in an overhead variance. In this case, the variance implies that

a) actual costs were greater than applied costs.
b) actual costs were less than applied costs.
c) actual costs were greater than budgeted costs.
d) budgeted costs were equal to applied costs.

_____43. If over- or under-applied overhead costs are prorated, they are prorated among

a) WIP, FGI and overhead control
b) Overhead control, FGI, and CGS.
c) WIP, overhead control, and CGS.
d) WIP, FGI, and CGS.

_____44. The balance in WIP Control is $50,000. The ending balance in FGI is $110,000, and cost of goods sold was $240,000. The amount of overhead variance was an $18,000 debit, meaning more overhead needed to be applied. After prorating the variance, what are the new balances for WIP, FGI, and CGS?

a) WIP is $50,000, FGI is $110,000, and CGS is $240,000. OH variance does not effect the other accounts.
b) WIP is $50,000, FGI is $110,000, and CGS is $258,000. Assign all of the variance to CGS.
c) WIP is $56,000, FGI is $116,000, and CGS is $246,000. Prorate the amount evenly among the three accounts.
d) WIP is $52,250, FGI is $114,950, and CGS is $250,800. Prorate based on relative balances of the three accounts.

_____45. Which of the following is **not** correct about a project?

a) If actual project costs exceed budgeted costs, the customer must pay more.
b) A project is more complex, and takes longer than a job.
c) A project manager must manage a cost budget and a time budget.
d) If actual costs exceed budget costs, then the project has a cost overrun.

Exercises

Use the following information about Real Thrills, Inc. to answer the next 5 questions.

Real Thrills, Inc. is a corporation that builds rides for amusement parks such as Six Flags, Busch Gardens, and Disney Theme Parks. Each ride constructed is different from every other ride, so the firm uses a job order costing system to assign costs to each customer's order. During the month of January 2005, Real Thrills worked on four different jobs. One job was the construction of "The Fright Master". A second was a children's ride called "Parachute Alley". The third job was "Thunder Coaster", while the fourth job was "Virtual Reality in Space". Costs for direct materials and direct labor are accumulated on job cost sheets. Because there are many indirect materials added to each job, there is a separate pre-determined overhead rate that is used to apply costs for indirect materials. All other overhead costs are applied based on the number of hours a ride is **tested**. Testing is a critical and expensive part of the production process for amusement park rides because of the need for absolute safety of the rides. Thus, the **allocation base for all overhead costs, except for indirect materials is testing hours**. The WIP subsidiary t-accounts for each of the four jobs are shown below, at the beginning of January 2005.

The overhead rates for indirect materials and all other overhead costs are based on the following: Indirect materials costs are applied based on amount of direct materials costs used on a job. The rate is based on estimated direct materials costs of $7,500,000 in 2005. Estimated indirect materials costs are $1,800,000. The rate for all other overhead expenses is based on an estimated cost of $20,500,000 for overheads (excluding indirect materials), and estimated testing hours totaling 400,000.

The following activities were recorded for production on the four jobs in January:

Costs of direct materials assigned to jobs were $18,976 to Job 345, $278,488 to Job 347, $69,560 to Job 349, and $17,680 to Job 351.

Costs of direct labor assigned to jobs totaled $45,367 for Job 345, $136,200 for Job 347, $398,450 for Job 349, and $325,760 for Job 351.

Most of the testing occurs at critical stages during construction on the rides, but is especially important upon completion of the ride on-site. Testing times for the jobs were 654 hours for Job 345 (The Fright Master), 1,266 hours for Job 347 (Parachute Alley), 958 hours for Job 349 (Thunder Coaster), and 155 hours for Job 351 (Virtual Reality in Space). **Job 345 was completed and the WIP balance for this job was closed at the end of January. The other three jobs were not completed, and remained in WIP at the end of January.**

46. Determine the OH rate for applying indirect materials costs to jobs.

47. Determine the OH rate for applying all other overheads (besides indirect materials) to jobs.

Post entries to the t-accounts for each of the four jobs. Show the ending WIP balance (at 1/31/05) for each of the four jobs. Please label your entries to the t-accounts. Use DM for direct materials, DL for direct labor, OHIM for Indirect Materials Applied, and OH for other overheads applied. Do not forget to add in the beginning balances, which are given.

The Fright Master – Job 345			**Parachute Alley – Job 347**	
Bal., 12/31/04 $12,695			Bal., 12/31/04 $139,400	
Bal., 1/31/05			Bal., 1/31/05	

Thunder Coaster – Job 349			**Virtual Reality in Space – Job 351**	
Bal., 12/31/04 $212,750			Bal., 12/31/04 $0	
Bal., 1/31/05			Bal., 1/31/05	

48. Job 345 was completed. What was the total cost of Job 345? The WIP balance for Job 345 was closed. What is the journal entry to record the completion of this job?

49. Jobs 345, 347, and 349 had beginning balances, but Job 351 did not. What is the reason for this difference?

Answers to Questions and Exercises

Matching key terms

1. c 2. h 3. f 4. j 5. e 6. d 7. a 8. I 9. b 10. g

True or False

11. F. This describes process costing. Job costing should be used when all units of product are different.
12. F. Job costing can be used in any business that offers unique products to individual customers.
13. T. Costs of each job are accumulated separately, as supporting detail for cost control, management, and profitability analysis.
14. F. Normal costing assigns unit-level costs directly to jobs, and applies higher-level costs using predetermined rates that are based on average estimated cost. Standard costing uses predetermined rates for direct materials, direct labor, and MOH.
15. T. One of the criticisms of actual costing is that higher-level costs cannot be assigned on a timely basis.
16. F. Work-in-Process is an inventory account for jobs that are incomplete. Since each job is a unique unit of product, subsidiary ledgers must be maintained for each job.
17. F. When normal costing is used, a predetermined OH rate is used to assign OH costs to each job, based on actual amounts of cost-driver activity for each job.
18. T. When jobs are sold, the corresponding amounts in FGI are transferred to CGS.
19. F. The MOH control account is a summary account that contains total costs for all of the individual OH costs that occurred, not direct costs.
20. T. When a company uses normal costing, higher-level production costs cannot be assigned directly to jobs. Predetermined cost-driver rates are used to assign these costs to jobs, based on the actual activity that occurs in each job.
21. T. Costs of jobs are accumulated in WIP inventory accounts. Once the work is completed, the entire amount assigned to a particular job is transferred to FGI. Crediting WIP reduces its balance, and debiting FGI increases it.
22. F. The amount assigned to jobs using the cost-driver rates is based on actual activity, but the OH rate is developed based on estimates. It is virtually impossible to estimate what the exact amount of cost will occur in the future.
23. T. The overhead account is an expense account, and all expense accounts must be closed at the end of an accounting period.
24. F. When overhead variances are prorated, they are split among WIP, FGI, and CGS – nothing gets allocated to the Raw Materials Inventory account.
25. T. The length of a project is one characteristic that distinguishes it from a job.

Multiple Choice

26. c. Actual costing assigns costs based on actual costs – not average costs. Budgeted costing uses expected future average costs of higher-level resources instead of past average costs. Standard costing uses expected costs of unit-level resources as well as expected costs of higher-level resources.
27. a. Since actual costs may not be known at the time a job is completed, it is impossible to assign total actual costs to jobs on a timely basis. The other three answers are simply not true.
28. b. If all units of product are the same, process costing should be used. The product's status as expensive or inexpensive is not a basis for choosing a costing method. Gold mining produces very expensive products, but process costing is the best method. Having one's hair styled is a very inexpensive product offering, but would be better accounted for using job costing.
29. c. Any product that uses resources differently for each unit of product should be costed using job costing unless it is prohibitively expensive to do so.
30. b. The ending balance in WIP shows the amount of resource cost assigned to jobs that are incomplete at the end of an accounting period. Answer a describes the ending balance of FGI. Answer c describes transferred-in costs. Answer d describes the amount transferred from FGI to CGS when completed jobs are sold.
31. b. When jobs are completed, the total cost assigned to the job has been accumulated in WIP. This entire cost is then transferred to FGI. Answer c is wrong because the reverse happens. Answer d is wrong because both WIP and FGI have their own control accounts and subsidiary ledger accounts.
32. c. The amount in the finished-goods inventory account shows the value of the completed job. Once the job is sold, that value becomes an expense, called cost of goods sold. Answer a is incorrect because WIP costs are transferred when work is complete – not when jobs are sold. Answer b is wrong because FGI is transferred to CGS – not the opposite. Answer d is incorrect because it is CGS that is closed to an income summary account – not FGI.
33. d. Costs related to jobs that are incomplete are included in WIP. Once complete, these costs are transferred to FGI. When completed jobs are sold, the costs for the sold jobs are transferred to CGS. The costs accumulated in the overhead account are added to WIP, using predetermined overhead (or cost-driver) rates. FGI and CGS are not directly impacted by the overhead account unless there is an overhead variance and the variance is prorated.
34. c. The OH rate is $720,000/36,000 machine hours = $20 per machine hour. 250 hours * $20 = $5,000
35. a. Mileage is the most appropriate cost-driver to use. If a truck is never driven, it will likely have little or no maintenance cost. If it is driven a lot, it will likely have higher maintenance costs. Number of jobs is not as good a measure, since it does not factor in the distance trucks are being driven. Number of drivers has no impact on maintenance costs. Weight transported may have some impact, but not as much as mileage.
36. d. A cost-driver for HR costs would be some measure related to number of employees or number of hires. Billing costs could be based on something as simple as the number of bills sent to customers, or number of pages of billing. Travel agency costs could be based on the estimated number of job-related trips. The salaries of the CEO or CFO would be hard to allocate using a cost driver other than, perhaps, number of jobs, or relative value of each job. These are facility-level costs that do not have an obvious cost-driver.

37. b. Use the cost flow model, BB + TI – TO = EB. Unit-level costs and overhead costs applied are both transferred-in costs. $820,000 + $215,000 + $300,000 - $570,000 = $765,000 EB.
38. d. The predetermined OH rate is used to apply overhead costs to WIP. Then, those overhead costs are transferred to FGI as part of the amount in WIP.
39. c. Cost of goods sold is charged with amounts in FGI for those jobs that are sold. Jobs completed but not yet sold remain in FGI (answer a). Jobs not completed are in WIP (answer b). Jobs sold in advance of completion actually create a liability, and the cost of goods sold for such jobs would not be recorded until the job is completed and delivered.
40. a. Direct materials costs are unit-level costs that can be assigned directly. The other three costs are all higher-level, overhead costs.
41. a. Unit-level costs are applied directly, and would not affect the amount of overhead estimated or applied. All of the other answers would cause mismatching of actual and applied OH costs.
42. b. If overhead costs are over-applied, this means too much overhead cost was applied relative to the actual amount of OH cost.
43. d. The proration of overhead costs attempts to place the remaining overhead costs where they belong. Recall that overhead costs are applied to WIP. WIP is transferred to FGI as jobs are completed, and as jobs are sold FGI is transferred to CGS. The overhead costs are in all three of these accounts, so it makes sense to prorate the remainder of overhead costs (too much or too little having been applied) to these three accounts. The other three answers all have proration to the overhead account, which would defeat the purpose of prorating. The objective of prorating the overhead account is to bring the balance of the OH account to zero.
44. d. Prorate as follows: The total in the three accounts is $50,000 + $110,000 + $240,000 = $400,000. WIP represents $50,000/$400,000, or 12.5%. FGI is $110,000/$400,000 = 27.5%. CGS is $240,000/$400,000 = 60%. 12.5% of the $18,000 variance is $2,250. 27.5% of $18,000 is $4,950. 60% of $18,000 is $10,800. Add these amounts to the three accounts to get $52,250 (WIP), $114,950 (FGI), and $250,800 (CGS).
45. b. Once a customer agrees to pay a certain amount for a project, any cost overruns that occur affect profits – not the amount the customer must pay. The only exception to this is when the customer causes the cost overruns, and agrees to pay for them.

Exercises

46. The cost-driver (overhead) rate for indirect materials is $1,800,000/$7,500,000 = .24, or 24% of direct materials costs. Here is another way to think about this rate. For every dollar of direct materials cost, add another 24 cents for indirect materials cost.
47. The cost-driver (overhead) rate for other overhead costs is $20,500,000/400,000 testing hours = $51.25 per testing hour.
48. The completed t-accounts are shown below.

The Fright Master – Job 345		**Parachute Alley – Job 347**	
Bal., 12/31/04 $12,695.00		Bal., 12/31/04 $139,400.00	
DM $18,976.00 DL $45,367.00		DM $278,488.00 DL $136,200.00	
OHIM $4,554.24		OHIM $66,837.12	
OH $33,517.50		OH $64,882.50	
	$115,109.74 to FGI		
Bal., 1/31/05 $0		Bal., 1/31/05 $685,807.62	

Thunder Coaster – Job 349			Virtual Reality in Space – Job 351	
Bal., 12/31/04 $212,750.00			Bal., 12/31/04 $0	
DM $69,560.00 DL $398,450.00			DM $17,680.00 DL $325,760.00	
OHIM $16,694.40			OHIM $4,243.20	
OH $49,097.50			OH $7,943.75	
Bal., 1/31/05 $746,551.90			Bal., 1/31/05 $355,626.95	

The amounts for OHIM and OH were calculated as follows:

Job 345: OHIM = $18,976 × .24 = $4,554.24. OH = $51.25 × 654 testing hours = $33,517.50
Job 347: OHIM = $278,488 × .24 = $66,837.12. OH = $51.25 × 1,266 testing hours = $64,882.50
Job 349: OHIM = $69,560 × .24 = $16,694.40. OH = $51.25 × 958 testing hours = $49,057.50
Job 351: OHIM = $17,680 × .24 = $4,243.20. OH = $51.25 × 155 testing hours = $7,943.75

49. As the t-account for Job 345 shows, the total cost for the job was $115,109.74. The $115,109.74 in Job 345 was transferred from WIP and was added to finished-goods inventory. The journal entry is:

DR	FGI	$115,109.74	
	CR	WIP	$115,109.74

50. Jobs 345, 347, and 349 had beginning balances, meaning these jobs were begun in prior periods. Job 351 had a zero beginning balance, meaning this job was started in January 2005.

Chapter 4
Activity-Based Costing Systems

Chapter Study Suggestions

This chapter introduces activity-based costing, which is a valuable method to know when managing costs is important. By identifying the causes of costs that occur in an organization, costs can be better managed, controlled, and even eliminated. Chapter 4 discusses how to identify different levels of activities and costs. It describes the estimation process for activities that generate costs. The chapter introduces the use of cost-drivers, calculation of rates based on activities, and profitability analysis based on activity-based costing.

A concept used throughout the book is the classification of resources into hierarchies. These 5 hierarchies are unit-level, batch-level, product-level, customer-level, and facility-level resources. Understanding how costs occur at these different levels improves one's ability to manage costs.

Chapter Highlights

A. Cost Management Challenges. There are 3 questions addressed in this chapter.

1. Why is activity-based information useful for making business decisions?
2. What data and knowledge are necessary to support the development of activity-based information?
3. Is activity-based information always better than average-cost information?

B. Learning Objectives—This chapter has 7 learning objectives.

1. The chapter discusses the ways in which traditional costing could lead to overcosting or undercosting of products.
2. Chapter 4 describes the four steps used in an activity-based costing system.
3. It identifies five different levels of resources and activities used in production processes.
4. Estimation of the cost of activities, and calculation of a cost-driver rate are demonstrated.
5. The chapter explains how activity costs are assigned to goods and services.
6. The chapter describes how to analyze the profitability of products and customers.
7. Activity-based costing is applied to service and merchandising companies.

C. A traditional costing system does not trace indirect costs when assigning them to units of product. Instead, these costs are allocated, using an allocation base like direct labor hours. While this method is simple, it sometimes results in overcosting or undercosting of products. Activity-based costing (ABC) is a costing system that assigns costs based on how work is done in an organization, and based on the need to continuously provide incentives for improvements.

D. When using an ABC system, there are four steps to take in determining the costs of goods and services.

1. Step 1 is to identify and classify the activities related to the company's products.
2. In step 2, one should estimate the cost of activities identified in step 1.
3. Step 3 entails calculation of a cost-driver rate for each activity.
4. In step 4, activity costs are assigned to products.

These four steps are described further below.

E. **Step 1. Identify and classify activities**. The organization should try to identify as many activities as possible, because this information can be used both for process improvement and to develop product costs. It may not be cost-beneficial, however, to develop a cost-driver rate for each and every activity. One very useful way to assess the need for resources, and evaluate the use of resources and activities is to categorize them based on hierarchies. There are five resource and activity hierarchies.

1. Unit-level resources or activities are acquired and used for specific individual units of product or services. For instance, the raw materials used to make a table can be traced directly to that table.

2. Batch-level resources or activities are acquired and used to make a group (or batch) of similar products. For instance the use of outsourced supervision to complete a batch of products to meet a deadline is a cost directly traceable to that batch. The costs are indirect to each individual unit of product, but are directly related to the batch.

3. Product-level resources or activities are acquired and used to make a specific product. For instance, equipment useful only for the production of a certain product fits this category. These resources may be indirectly related to batches or units.

4. Customer-level resources or activities are acquired to meet the needs of specific customers or customer-types. For example, if a customer orders custom designed furniture, and a designer is hired to design it, the cost can be directly traced to one customer. The costs of this resource may be indirectly related to product, batch, or unit-level decisions.

5. Facility-level resources or activities are acquired and used to produce any products and services the organization may decide to offer for sale. Examples of the types of resources are buildings, land, employees and production equipment. These resource acquisition decisions are directly related to decisions about scale and scope of operations.

The purpose of dividing resources or activities into hierarchical levels is to accurately describe how an organization performs its work, and to allow costs to be traced to goods and services.

F. A necessary step in assigning costs is to identify, in as much detail as is practical, the activities. There are two approaches that may be used to generate these activity lists.

1. A "top-down" approach relies solely on an analysis team to develop the list of activities. A disadvantage of this approach is that the team may not have a thorough understanding of the processes and activities they are assigned to describe.

2. The "interview or participative" approach includes input from employees actually performing the activities under study. The analysis team might still develop the list, but incorporates information obtained from the employees who are most knowledgeable regarding the activities. Although this approach may result in a more accurate depiction of the activities performed, there is a risk that employees may be unwilling to divulge correct information, for fear of negative repercussions. Furthermore, employees' recollection of how activities are performed may be inaccurate. Finally, the interview approach is time-consuming.

G. **Step 2. Estimate the cost of activities.** This simply requires that costs be identified according to the activities that caused them. At the same time, they should be classified as to the level as outlined in step 1, above. Consumption of resources generates costs. A cost-driver is an activity that causes costs to rise as the activity rises. The simplest example is the direct relationship between unit costs and increased production of units of product. The more units that are made, the higher the total cost of materials will be. A cost-driver base is a measurable cause of performing an activity, and is what causes a cost to be incurred.

H. **Step 3. Calculate a cost-driver rate for each activity.** The cost driver rate is calculated based on the estimated cost divided by the estimated quantity of the activity. The rate is a dollar amount per unit of activity. Rates are calculated based on the five hierarchical levels. For instance, a cost-driver rate could be a cost per batch. Assignment of unit-level costs is the simplest cost-assignment problem. The cost-driver base can be the unit of product itself. The higher the hierarchy, the more difficult the cost assignment problem becomes.

I. **Step 4. Assign activity costs.** Cost assignment occurs in levels. That is, costs are assigned to units, batches, products, customers and facilities.

J. Product and customer profitability analyses are important because they allow managers to decide which products and which customers are profitable. These types of analyses address the questions regarding which products should be dropped (or added), and which customers create the most cost. Are some customers worth the extra costs they cause?

1. Product profitability requires analysis of only those costs that are related to a specific product – unit-level costs and product-level costs. If a product is produced solely for a particular customer then those costs are also customer costs. Managers assess profitability by identifying costs associated with a particular product and can also assess the need to revise pricing based on the better information obtained by use of product-specific costs.

   Looking at the product costs individually also allows managers to focus on the other, higher-level costs as a separate cost management issue.

2. Comparing customer costing with revenues generated by an individual customer or customer type is called customer profitability analysis. Customer costing occurs when cost information traceable to specific customers or customer type is collected and analyzed. Use of profit information at the customer level allows managers to see which customers it should focus on to maintain or build the relationship with. Other customers may be targeted by the company as customers to work with, to bring costs down.

3. ABC is a useful tool for estimating the costs of new products. If processes and activities for the new product are similar to existing activities and processes, then the costs of making the new product can be easily estimated using the ABC system.

K. Activity-based costing was first introduced in manufacturing. However, ABC has applications in service and merchandising industries as well. The process for developing and then applying ABC is the same. You must apply the four steps in activity-based costing. You also must identify the activities and classify them according to the hierarchical level.

REVIEW AND SELF TEST QUESTIONS AND EXERCISES

Matching key terms

Match the following terms to the correct definition by writing the correct letter next to the correct definition.

a.	cost driver	b.	batch-level resources
c.	activity-based costing	d.	unit-level resources
e.	full-cost ABC	f.	Customer profitability analysis
g.	allocation rate	h.	facility-level resources
i.	activity list	j.	product pricing

_____ 1. A cost assignment method based on the use of resources to make product.

_____ 2. The combined use of traditional product costing methods with ABC costing.

_____ 3. The process of assigning costs to units of product.

_____ 4. Resources that can be traced directly to an individual unit of product.

_____ 5. A summary of different production activities for which costs can be estimated, and for which ABC rates can be derived.

_____ 6. A way to assess what the costs are for servicing specific customers.

_____ 7. Something that causes costs to increase.

_____ 8. Expenses that occur at the highest level of activity.

_____ 9. Estimated cost divided by estimated activity.

_____10. Expenses that can be assigned to batches of similar products.

True or False

For each of the following statements enter a T or an F in the blank to indicate whether the statement is true or false.

_____11. Activities-based costing gives managers a more accurate way to assign costs to products than traditional costing methods.

_____12. Only manufacturing companics can use ABC.

_____13. The most important benefit of ABC is that it allows organizations to report product costs differently in the financial statements.

_____14. When using ABC, cost-driver rates should be consistent with the five levels of hierarchical costs.

_____15. ABC costing assigns production costs uniformly to all products, regardless of the level of the resource used to make them.

_____16. When first developing activities-based costing systems, many organizations begin by eliminating the existing costing system.

_____17. An important reason for using activities-based costing is that different products use different amounts of resources.

_____18. One question that must be answered in developing an ABC system is, how do processes use resources.

_____19. Product-level resources include all of the resources in a production facility.

_____20. A cost driver is an activity implemented to reduce costs.

_____21. A facility-level resource is usually the most difficult to trace to one unit of product.

_____22. Estimates of the cost of a resource can only be based on budget information.

_____23. When trying to classify costs according to different levels, one useful source of information comes from interviewing employees.

_____24. A cost driver rate is computed by dividing the quantity of cost driver activity by dollar amount of the resource supplied.

_____25. For a manufacturer, the most likely resource to be included as a unit-level resource is materials.

Multiple Choice

Choose the best answer by writing the letter corresponding to your choice in the space provided.

______26. Which of the following is **incorrect?**

a) The purpose of ABC is to make the costing of products and services more accurate than traditional costing systems.
b) ABC helps managers to make decisions about which products to make or discontinue.
c) A company using ABC still needs to prepare full-cost information.
d) Only cost managers can provide information to be used in developing an ABC system.

______27. Which of the following is **not** one of the four steps used in an ABC system?

a) Identify and classify activities related to the company's products.
b) Determine actual costs of the activity for the year.
c) Calculate a cost-driver rate for each activity.
d) Assign activity costs to products.

______28. Which of the following is correct?

a) Activities-based costing can be used for job-costing or batch costing, except for service sector companies.
b) Activities-based costing can be used for job-costing but not batch costing.
c) Activities-based costing can be used for job-costing or batch costing.
d) Activities-based costing can be used for batch costing, but not for job-costing.

______29. A company has recently purchased expensive robots to assemble some of its products, but continues to use a traditional costing system. One of the pitfalls of using a traditional costing system is that products may be over-costed or under-costed. Product X requires no robotics, while Product Z requires extensive robotics. Which of the following correctly expresses how over- or under-costing occurs in this scenario?

a) Too much cost will be assigned to Product X, and too little will be assigned to Product Z.
b) Neither Product (X or Z) will have enough cost assigned to it.
c) Too little cost will be assigned to Product X, and too much will be assigned to Product Z.
d) Both Products (X and Z) will have too much cost assigned to them.

_____30. One of the unit-level costs for making desks at Beckman Furniture Company is the wood. It takes 15 board feet of wood per desk to make the body of the desk and the drawer fronts. The wood costs $.75 per board foot. Each desk also has particleboard for the drawer bottoms and sides. Particleboard costs $.20 per board foot, and each desk uses 4 board feet. Handles and other hardware costs are $3.50 per desk. What is the unit-level cost for wood for each desk?

a) $4.45 per desk
b) $15.55 per desk
c) $12.05 (handles and hardware are not unit-level costs)
d) Not enough information is given to determine unit-level costs

_____31. When considering the traditional costing approach and ABC, one might argue that

a) the traditional costing approach is more costly than ABC.
b) ABC is not useful for service organizations.
c) ABC assigns costs more accurately than traditional costing does.
d) Traditional costing uses more realistic cost assignment methods than ABC does.

_____32. If cost assignment is to be done at the customer level, then which of the following costs is **least** likely to be included?

a) Costs of delivering product to customers
b) Costs of factory supervision
c) Costs of expediting customer orders
d) Costs of specialized design for a customer

_____33. Which of the following would be the best base to use for assigning costs of janitorial services in a 5-department office building?

a) Number of departments (assign costs equally to each department)
b) Number of employees in each department
c) Number of janitorial employees
d) Square feet in each department

_____34. If comparing unit-level ABC to full-cost ABC, which of the following is true?

a) The cost per unit will be higher based on full cost ABC than it will be based on unit-level ABC.
b) The cost per unit will be higher based on unit-level ABC than it will be based on full cost ABC.
c) The cost per unit will be the same regardless of which of these two methods is used.
d) For unit-level ABC, product cost cannot be determined, but with full cost they can be determined.

_____35. A small college has decided that as part of its conversion to activity-based costing, it will assign library costs based on the number of students in each department or school. The college has monthly costs of $64,000 for running the library. It projects enrollment of 4,000 in the fall. The rate calculated will be

a) $.625 per student.
b) $16 per school or department.
c) $16 per student.
d) $1 for every 16 students.

_____36. Which of the following is **incorrect** with respect to ABC?

a) It uses activities to assign product costs to units of product.
b) It can be used for non-manufacturing organizations.
c) It can be used in a job-costing system.
d) It is best used when an organization has a few, similar products.

_____37. Which of the following is **least** likely to be treated as a batch-level cost for a 100-dress batch at a dress manufacturer? Only 100 dresses of this type will be made.

a) Cost of fabric for the dresses
b) Depreciation expenses for the sewing machines
c) Cost of direct labor for the dresses
d) Costs of design of the dresses

_____38. Which of the following questions can be answered if an ABC framework is being used to assign costs?

a) Is production capacity meeting quality standards?
b) Should an organization outsource some part of production activity?
c) Is capacity adequate to complete activities being planned?
d) Is total profit higher or lower than last year?

_____39. A nail (manicure) shop has a rate of $8 per customer for the nail techs' time. The rate was based on an estimated number of customers per month and estimated wages and benefits paid to nail techs of $4,800. The rate was derived with the expectation that 600 customers would be served per month. The amount of nail techs' costs applied to products was $4,920, and actual wages and benefits paid were $5,100. Based on the three dollar amounts given, which of the following statements is true?

a) More customers were served than originally estimated.
b) The rate of $8 per customer was too high.
c) The amount of nail tech time applied to products was based purely on the amount actually paid to nail techs.
d) Wages and benefits fluctuate too much to be used as a cost-driver.

_____40. The salary of Linda McPhee is $60,000. Ms. McPhee is the supervisor of the Commercial Bottling Division of a spring water bottling company. Two other production divisions are the Residential Sales Division, and the Wholesale Sales Division. Due to a re-organization, the Commercial Division was combined with the Residential Sales Division, and renamed the Retail Sales Division. The supervisor of the Residential Division was named supervisor of the Retail Sales Division. Ms. McPhee did not lose her job with the company though. The company named Ms. McPhee the Director of Safety of the entire production facility. Which of the following is true regarding Ms. McPhee's salary?

a) Her salary was a facility-level cost before, and is still a facility-level cost now.
b) Her salary was a product-level cost before, and is a facility-level cost now.
c) Her salary was a batch-level cost before, and is a product-level cost now.
d) Her salary was a product-level cost before, and is still a product-level cost now.

_____41. One important purpose of customer profitability analysis is to allow organizations to

a) get rid of unprofitable customers.
b) increase customer service for all customers.
c) eliminate all costs associated with customer service.
d) identify costs caused by specific customers.

_____42. Batch-level costs are

a) costs that can be traced to one particular production facility.
b) costs that can be traced to one particular production department.
c) costs that can be traced to one type of resource.
d) costs that can be traced to one group of products being made.

_____43. Activity based costing requires that rates be developed based on estimates. Suppose a rate is developed for a facility-level resource that is based on production activity, and then production is unexpectedly halted due to a strike. Only half of the expected production is actually completed. Which of the following results is likely to occur?

a) Actual costs for this facility-level resource will be reduced by half.
c) The amount of cost assigned to products for this facility-level resource will be double what it should have been.
c) Only half of the estimated cost of this facility-level resource will be assigned to units of product.
d) The organization will need to take immediate steps to eliminate up to half of the costs for this facility-level resource.

_____44. If one particular product line at a company is discontinued, then which of the following costs might be eliminated immediately as a result?

a) Unit-level, batch-level, product-level, customer-level, and facility-level costs
b) Unit-level, batch-level, product-level, and customer-level costs, but not facility-level costs
c) Unit-level, and batch-level costs, but not product-level, customer-level, or facility-level costs
d) Unit-level and product-level costs, but not batch-level, customer-level, or facility-level costs

_____45. Which of the following is correct about a cost driver?

a) A cost driver is an activity that causes costs to increase when the activity increases.
b) A cost driver should allow any cost to be traceable to some activity.
c) Cost drivers for facility-level resources allow costs to be traced to unit-level activity.
d) A cost driver chosen for unit-level activity is very likely to also be chosen for customer-level activity.

Exercises

Use the following information about Chambers Bikes, LTD. to answer the next 5 questions.

Chambers Bikes, LTD. is a bicycle manufacturing firm that produces mountain bikes that range from very highly specialized bikes used by professional racers, to the more conventional bikes purchased by the more traditional customer (college and high school students, and non-professional biking enthusiasts). Some bikes are sold by Chambers for as much as $6,000, while bikes at the bottom of their product line are sold for about $175. The expensive bikes are produced on a made-to-order basis, and each bike is treated as one job. The less expensive bikes are manufactured in batches, and a batch of 100 bikes is treated as one job. The less expensive bikes are partially pre-assembled and tested by a supplier.

Currently, the firm uses two unit-level cost categories - materials and direct labor. There is just one indirect cost category - manufacturing overhead, which is allocated based on direct labor hours. The indirect allocation rate is currently $92.50 per direct labor hour. Because the types of bikes produced are very different (some very expensive and specialized, and some not), Corey Chambers, the vice-president of Operations, is concerned about the correct assignment of costs to each bike. Mariah Chambers, the vice president of Marketing and Customer Relations, is also concerned, because their customers (bike stores and professional racers) want the high prices to be justified. The accounting system does not provide her with any useful information about costs.

The CFO of Chambers Bikes, Sidney Chambers has asked the controller to revise the accounting system. The controller has, in turn, asked you, the new staff accountant to develop an activities-based costing system. After some investigation, you have compiled accounting and production data that should be helpful in developing the new system.

Develop the ABC system using the following information.

You are certain that some of the indirect costs can be assigned to individual jobs using the following five activity areas:

ACTIVITY AREA	**Cost Driver**	**Cost Allocation Rate**
Materials Handling	Number of parts	$6.00 per part
Lathe work (metal shaping)	Number of hours of lathe time	$50 per machine hour
Assembly (using robotics)	Number of robot hours	$38 per robot hour
Computerized Setting of Controls (Bike Calipers)	Number of speeds	$4 per speed
Testing	Number of components tested	$5 per component

Under ABC, remaining facility-level costs will be allocated to the jobs at a rate of $2.00 per direct labor hour.

To test the ABC system, you are to use the following two jobs recently completed by Chambers Bikes The ABC totals will be computed manually (by you), and will be compared to the cost assignments that would have occurred under the old costing system. The information to be used is below.

	Mountain Bike Supreme (Custom made Racing Bike)	**Mountain Bike II (one batch of 100 bikes)**
Materials cost	$1,400	$3600
Direct labor costs	$650 (26 hours)	$1,375 (55 hours)
Number of parts handled	60 parts	400 parts
Lathe work	10 machine hours	0 machine hours
Assembly	20 robot-hours	23 robot-hours
Computerized Setting of Controls	45 speeds	12 speeds per bike, 100 bikes, 1,200 speeds
Testing	28 components tested	300 components tested

46. Compute the costs for each job, using the old costing system.

	Mountain Bike Supreme (Custom made Racing Bike)	**Mountain Bike II (one batch of 100 bikes)**
Materials Costs		
Direct Labor Costs		
Allocated Costs		
Total Cost per Job		

47. Compute the costs per job using the ABC system being implemented.

	Mountain Bike Supreme (Custom made Racing Bike)	**Mountain Bike II (one batch of 100 bikes)**
Materials cost		
Direct labor costs		
Materials Handling		
Lathe work		
Assembly		
Computerized Setting of Controls		
Testing		
Indirect Costs Allocated		
Total Cost per Job		

48. Suppose these products were sold for $6,250 and $15,000. Compare and discuss the results you obtained in questions 46 and 47, comparing the costs and profitability, and discuss the advantages of using the ABC system.

49. For all of the cost categories identified, classify each cost as unit, batch, product, customer, or facility-level cost.

50. Describe at least 3 customer-level costs that might occur. Describe at least 3 facility level costs that might occur.

Answers to Questions and Exercises

Matching key terms

1. c 2. 3. j 4. d 5. I 6. f 7. a 8. h 9. g 10. b

True or False

11. T. Traditional costing allocates indirect costs without regard to activities causing the costs to occur.
12. F. Any organization with diverse products or services can utilize ABC.
13. F. Financial statement reporting of product costs is based on full costing, regardless of whether ABC is used or not.
14. T. Rates developed using ABC should take into account the presence of levels of cost. These are called hierarchies, and are unit, batch, product, customer, and facility-level resources.
15. F. ABC assigns costs to products based on how resources are used.
16. F. ABC does not replace the existing system – it changes the existing system.
17. T. In an organization with diverse product offerings, the use of resources (and therefore the underlying cost of products) is also likely to be diverse.
18. T. Understanding how different processes use resources allows managers to more accurately assign costs of the various activities.
19. F. Product-level resources include unit-level and batch-level resources, but do not include customer or facility-level resources.
20. F. A cost driver is an activity that causes costs.
21. T. Since facility-level costs benefit all production activities in that facility, they typically cannot be traced to a single unit of product.
22. F. Estimates are based on historical information, budgets, input from employees, and known changes.
23. T Employees using the resources are a valuable source of information regarding how resources are used.
24. F. The calculation is the opposite. The dollar amount is divided by the quantity of cost driver activity.
25. T. In many cases, materials are the only resource treated as a unit-level resource.

Multiple Choice

26. d. In addition to cost managers, employees using the resources may provide input. In addition, teams may be formed to direct the development of a new ABC system, and the team consists of people with diverse backgrounds.
27. b. The actual costs are not known in advance. Estimated costs are used to develop the cost-driver rate.
28. c. Activities-based costing can be used in any type of business, and can replace any type of costing system.
29. a. Easy-to-make products like Product X do not use as many resources as complex products, but with a traditional costing system, costs are assigned uniformly to products, whether they were easy (and inexpensive) to make or hard (and more expensive) to make. Some of the costs that should be assigned to Product Z will be allocated to Product X, so Product X will be over-costed and Product Z will be under-costed.
30. b. All of the costs described are unit-level costs because each desk requires these resources, and they can be readily identified. $.75 * 15 board feet = $11.25. $.20 * 4 board feet = $.80. Add to these amounts $3.50 for the hardware, to get $15.55.
31. c. Since ABC results in costs being assigned based on the activities that cause them, product costing is more accurate than product costing using traditional costing methods.
32. b. Costs of factory supervision are facility-level costs that cannot be traced to a particular customer.
33. d. Since the amount of physical space is what janitors are responsible for, this is the most appropriate cost driver. The other 3 answers are not good cost drivers. Unless each department is exactly the same, dividing the cost equally would not be an equitable solution (answer a). Number of employees in each department is not a good cost driver for this cost (answer b). Number of janitorial employees does not give good information on how to assign the costs (answer c).
34. a. Full-cost ABC assigns all production costs to units of product, while unit-level ABC only assigns unit-level costs to units of product.
35. c. A rate is calculated as the dollar amount divided by the quantity of the cost driver, or $64,000/4,000 = $16 per student.
36. d. ABC is best used when an organization has a wide variety of dissimilar products.
37. b. The other three costs – material, labor and design costs could all conceivably be traced to the batch. The depreciation expense of the sewing machines could not since they would also be used to make other dresses.
38. c. Since ABC rates are determined based on expected production needs, it is at this point that capacity needs would be identified. Quality, outsourcing decisions, and profitability assessment are not part of the ABC framework.
39. a. This question requires an understanding of how ABC rates are applied. They are applied based on actual cost-driver activity. If 600 customers were served, the amount applied would be 600 * $8, or $4,800. Since $4,920 was assigned, it must be the case that $4,920/$8, or 615 customers were served.
40. b. Ms. McPhee's salary was a product-level cost before, because it could be traced to Commercial Bottling, which was one of 3 product lines. After the re-organization, Ms. McPhee's job became a facility-level cost. Her responsibilities as Director of Safety cannot be traced to one particular product (Retail Sales or Wholesale Sales).

41. d. Once costs of a particular customer are identified, managers can determine whether the customer is generating enough profit to justify the costs. If costs are too high, the organization may try to work with the customer to bring down costs, or may pass the costs on to the customer in the form of higher prices.
42. d. For one particular product, production may occur in batches (e.g., 100 units of product at a time is a batch).
43. c. Since costs are assigned using production activity, if only half of the production activity occurs then only half of the facility-level cost will be assigned. Answer a is not true. Facility costs do not change when production activity changes. Answer b is not true. The rate should not be changed when an unexpected, temporary event causes activity to change. Answer d is not true. If the costs are eliminated, then when things go back to normal the organization would not be able to function normally.
44. b. Every type of cost except facility-level costs could potentially be eliminated if an entire product line is eliminated. Facility-level costs are not dedicated to one particular product, so would not be eliminated. Customer-level costs might be eliminated if customers had special needs (costs) associated with the discontinued service offering.
45. a. By definition, a cost driver is some activity that is directly related to costs.

Exercises

46.

	Mountain Bike Supreme (Custom made Racing Bike)	**Mountain Bike II (one batch of 100 bikes)**
Materials Costs	$1,400 (given)	$3,600 (given)
Direct Labor Costs	$650 (given)	$1,375 (given)
Allocated Costs	$2,405 ($92.50 * 26 hours)	$5,087.50 ($92.50 * 55 hours)
Total Cost per Job	**$4,455**	**$10,062.50**

47.

	Mountain Bike Supreme (Custom made Racing Bike)	**Mountain Bike II (one batch of 100 bikes)**
Materials cost	$1,400 (given)	$3,600 (given)
Direct labor costs	$650 (given)	$1,375 (given)
Materials Handling	$360 ($6 * 60)	$2,400 ($6 * 400)
Lathe work	$500 ($50 * 10)	$0
Assembly	$760 ($38 * 20)	$874 ($38 * 23)
Computerized Setting of Controls	$180 ($4 * 45)	$4,800 ($4 * 1,200)
Testing	$140 ($5 * 28)	$1,500 ($5 *300)
Indirect Costs Allocated	$52 ($2 * 26)	$110 ($2 * 55)
Total Cost per Job	**$4,042**	**$14,659**

48. Under the old costing system, both products have a markup on costs of about 40%, and appear to be quite profitable. If price is based on a markup of costs, then it is especially important to understand what costs are, and what activity causes costs to occur. Under the ABC system, the Mountain Bike Supreme is much more profitable than the Mountain Bike II. The Mountain Bike II is close to making no profit at all.

    The old method of allocating costs to manufacturing jobs led to misallocation of manufacturing costs among different jobs, because the old costing system ignored different uses of the manufacturing resources. As a result, the custom made racing bikes were over-costed, and the Mountain Bike IIs were under-costed. This would make it appear that the custom made bikes were less profitable than they really were, and the MB IIs appeared to be more profitable than they really were. To the extent that pricing is tied to costs of products, the prices were probably distorted by the inaccurate allocation of costs. Some of the advantages of converting to the ABC system include: (1) improved ability to identify cost-causing product lines; (2) improved pricing and profit planning; (3) better scheduling of the resources being used (for instance, custom made bikes used lathe time, but MB IIs did not - thus, work in this department could be better scheduled to meet production needs of the custom made bikes; (4) reduction of the cross-subsidization of costs among products.

49. For the Mountain Bike Supreme, materials and labor are unit-level costs. Materials handling, assembly, computerized setting of controls, testing, and indirect costs are facility level. If the lathe is used exclusively for Mountain Bike Supreme models, this resource is a product-level resource. Since these bikes are made one at a time, there are no batch-level costs.

    For the Mountain Bike II models, the materials and labor are unit-level costs, or could be viewed as batch-level costs as presented in this problem (100 bikes at a time). The other costs are facilities-level costs. One way to think about facility-level costs is to consider where these resources might be used. If they could be used for anything produced, they are likely to be facility-level costs because they will not be eliminated just by the elimination of a single product.

50. In this problem, no customer-level costs were given, to simplify the analysis. Some production costs that could be customer-level costs are 1) special features, 2) special labeling and/or packaging, and 3) expedited production costs (rush jobs).

    Some facility-level costs are 1) supervisors' salaries, 2) maintenance and repair costs, 3) janitorial services, 4) supplies, 5) utilities and 6) plant administration.

Chapter 5
Activity-Based Management

Chapter Study Suggestions

Chapter 5 extends the discussion of Chapter 4 on activities-based costing (ABC), by presenting activity-based management (ABM). Activity-based costing is merely a system for assigning costs. It provides important information about uses of resources, given existing processes. However, it does not identify opportunities for decreasing costs and increasing value. Activities-based management (ABM) uses ABC and perceived customer values to improve processes so that they create more value at lower cost.

ABM, combined with ABC and value-added analysis allows managers of organizations to improve processes that benefit the efficiency of the organization. Chapter 5 presents the actions and procedures necessary to develop and successfully implement an ABC/ABM system. First, the chapter shows how ABC is used. The use of ABC information in conjunction with value-added analysis is discussed next. Value-added analysis also includes the identification of non-value-added activities and costs, which must be eliminated in order for organizations to be competitive. Third, the purposes of ABM are discussed. Activity analysis is explained as a key tool used in ABM. Then, the steps needed to successfully develop and implement ABC and ABM are presented.

Chapter Highlights

A. Cost Management Challenges. There are 3 questions addressed in this chapter.

1. Is implementing ABC enough to improve efficiency? Does doing so mean that the organization will meet its efficiency goals?
2. Does the cost management analyst need to make recommendations for improvements based on ABC numbers?
3. How can ABM methods be evaluated for their value?

B. Learning Objectives—This chapter has 6 learning objectives.

1. This chapter provides understanding of an ABM system.
2. The chapter demonstrates how to use ABC for target costing.
3. It shows how to identify costs of activities that add value or do not add value in organizations.
4. Chapter 5 explains how to use the elements of an activity-based management system to identify opportunities for process management.
5. Capacity utilization can be evaluated by determining which resources are supplied and which ones are used.
6. The chapter presents methods and discusses problems associated with ABC and ABM.

C. Activities-based Management (ABM) allows managers to evaluate costs and values of process activities to identify opportunities for improved efficiency.

1. Activities based costing (ABC) focuses on (1) understanding how resources are used in current processes and (2) measuring accurate product and service costs, given those processes.
2. ABC provides input to, but is not a cost management system.
3. ABM combines ABC analysis and value-added analysis.
4. ABC determines major activities within the value chain, and identifies the organization's cost drivers and cost-driver rates appropriate for each activity. ABM adds customer-perceived value of each activity, identifies value-added and non-value-added activities, and gives managers opportunities to enhance value-added activities and to reduce non-value-added activities.

D. ABC is the foundation for process improvements. Once ABC is adopted and implemented in an organization, the next logical step toward achieving ABM is to combine ABC and target costing. Target costing is based on determining target revenues and subtracting target profits. If costs derived from the ABC system (called the currently feasible cost) exceed the target cost, then costs must be reduced. In a competitive environment, organizations must conclude that if their currently feasible costs exceed what target costs are, there may be inefficiency in their operations or there may be non-value-added activities and costs that need to be eliminated.

E. Value-added activities enhance the value of products and services in the eyes of the customer while meeting the goals of the organization. Non-value-added activities do not contribute to customer-perceived value.

1. Both internal and external customers determine what value-added activities are. However, the true measures of value-added qualities exhibit themselves when external customers agree to pay for them.

   Non-value-added activities do not contribute to customer-perceived value, and so eliminating such activities will not reduce customer value. Their elimination will, however, eliminate their cost.

2. Eliminating non-value-added activities is a competitive necessity. In a competitive environment, an organization should eliminate as much waste as possible, because competitors are constantly working to create more value for customers at lower cost. Failure to eliminate non-value-added activities and costs results in a price that is too high to be competitive. This results in lost sales. Alternatively, costs that are too high may result in profits that are too low to allow a company to remain in business.

   a. Even in environments where competition is non-existent, organizations cannot afford to become complacent. For instance, American automobile manufacturers were unprepared for the onslaught of less expensive, more reliable Japanese automobiles during the late 1970's and early 1980's. It took many years for American auto companies to restructure production activities so that non-value-added activities could be eliminated. Because of unionized workforces in the US auto industry, there are some non-value-added activities that cannot be eliminated because of contractual agreements between workers and the companies. Another noncompetitive setting that was redefined occurred with the deregulation of industries like telecommunications, trucking, and the airlines.

   b. It is critical to identify non-value-added activities so that they can be reduced or eliminated. In manufacturing firms, non-value-added activities include unnecessary inventory, bottlenecks that slow productivity, time and effort to move processing forward, and inefficient processing.

3. Value-added activities can be identified by answering two questions. First, one should ask whether an external customer would encourage the organization to do more of the activity. Second, one should ask whether an organization would be more likely to reach its goal by performing that activity.

a. Organizations must not only determine whether activities are value-added or not, they must somehow quantify the value of activities. Some activities, while clearly not viewed as value-added from a customer's perspective, may be necessary because of laws, organizational policy, or even societal norms.

Even if a dollar amount cannot be assigned to an activity, it needs to at least be ranked, or rated in some way. For instance, one could say that, on a scale of 1 to 5, some activities are rated as 1 (clearly non-value-added) to 5 (clearly value-added).

a. Measurement and evaluation of activities should be performed by someone who is objective and knowledgeable about what customers value. The evaluator must also know what the organization must do to meet its goals. There are two obvious barriers to finding such an evaluator.

i. Everyone's knowledge is limited to his or her own experiences and knowledge base.

ii. Everyone is potentially biased in his or her responses.

4. If organizations use a team approach to evaluating value-added activities, they must seek input not only from team members, but also from internal and external customers.

a. The process of identifying and ranking activities can be an overwhelming task. Moreover, since reducing or eliminating non-value-added activities may affect the livelihood of employees, it can become a politically sensitive endeavor.

b. Because functional areas and various departments and processes are linked, and depend on each other, activities cannot be evaluated in isolation. For instance, suppose materials inventory is evaluated, and it is judged to be too large. Some organizations view any inventory on hand to be non-value-added. Evaluation of inventory levels without considering production needs or lead times necessary to obtain adequate materials would be a pointless exercise that might lead to bottlenecks, another non-value-added event.

F. ABM requires that various tasks be performed. ABM has two objectives. First, ABM aims to identify non-value-added activities to reduce or eliminate. It also aims to identify value-added activities to enhance or build upon. Second, ABM aims to redesign processes so that productive activity can be completed without unneeded non-value-added activities.

1. Non-value-added activities cannot be eliminated without redesigning processes. A starting point for eliminating NVA activities is to perform detailed activity analysis.

   a. Activities must be listed, item by item, ranked according to perceived customer value, and a cost must be assigned to the activity.

   b. Once activities are split into broad categories, they should be broken down again into sub-categories. These sub-categories are ranked, costs assigned, and assessed for the contributions each makes to the total cost and its contribution to value.

   c. It is during this activity analysis that ideas for the redesign of the process begin to emerge. Activities with low ratings on the value-added scale should be reduced or eliminated.

G. A major objective of the activity analysis is to identify opportunities for process improvement.

   1. Part of the analysis process should involve a persistent asking of the question "why", in order to determine the real reason an activity is performed.

   2. After identifying NVA activities and taking steps to eliminate them, a next logical question to ask is what to do with the savings. If currently feasible costs exceed target costs, the first response must be to reduce costs to the level of the target. Any savings beyond that can be used to decrease prices, increasing the perceived value in the eyes of the customers, or to shift the saved resources to value-added activities.

H. In order to properly assess whether resources are being used efficiently or not, one must consider how capacity is utilized. There should be as close a match as possible between resources supplied and resources used. The ability to use resources varies based on the level of resources being evaluated. While it is relatively easy to match unit-level resource use to unit-level resources supplied, the matching of facility-level resources provided with facility-level resources used is only possible if the organization is operating at full capacity.

I. Activity-based costing and management offer feasible ways to evaluate and improve efficiency of processes. Their benefits may well exceed their costs. While ABC provides improved product or service cost information, ABM identifies opportunities for improving processes. Most organizations can benefit from process improvements.

Critics of ABC have cited its failure to generate product costs that are significantly different from traditional, functional costs, and argue that the costs of developing, implementing, and maintaining ABC far outweigh the benefits. However, advocates of ABM respond by arguing that ABC product costs should be viewed merely as a by-product of ABM and process improvement efforts. This is much more important than having accurate product cost information.

Activity-based costing and management, while conceptually appealing, are nontrivial to implement. There are several factors that appear to influence the likelihood of success or failure in implementing ABC or ABM. They are presented below.

1. Are ABC and ABM for every organization? ABC and ABM seem to be practical tools in complex organizations that produce many complex products. Organizations that have been confronted by intense competition have been at the forefront of the ABC/ABM movement. These organizations have chosen ABM as a way to improve processes and profitability. Organizations using ABM include manufacturing and service firms, as well as organizations facing competition because of deregulation of their industry.
2. Can the success of ABC and ABM be guaranteed? The obvious answer to this question is no. However, for those organizations that have found success in implementing ABC and ABM, a key to their success is planning properly. The six P's of planning that should be followed are *Prior Planning Prevents Particularly Poor Performance.* For ABC and ABM, there are 5 planning issues that should be considered.

    a. The intended scope of the ABC or ABM project needs to be decided upon. An ABC and/or ABM system can be implemented and used by cost managers or it can be expanded to encompass all activities of an organization. Regardless of the planned scope of the use of ABC and ABM, it is most wise to begin small. A pilot project is the best way to introduce ABC or ABM to an organization.

       Translating the technical requirements of ABC and ABM into a feasible pilot project gives people in an organization time to learn, provides experience in identifying links across departments, groups, processes and the data gathering and reporting requirements of the full-scale implementation.

    b. There are several factors that increase the likelihood of success in implementing an ABC and/or ABM system. The following resources need to be in place.

        i. Management commitment is critical to the success of planned development and implementation of ABC or ABM. Unless top management is willing to act on recommendations of the people who are planning and developing ABC/ABM, it is unlikely that the new system will have much impact on the organization. It is the responsibility of cost managers to clearly and accurately educate top management about the costs and benefits of the new system.

ii. Adequate personnel and time must be dedicated to the development and implementation of ABC and ABM. A 3 or 4-person team that is composed of cross-functional members must be freed of their other duties for as long as six months (sometimes longer). Failure to adequately man the project will result in a poorly planned endeavor that will, of necessity, include shortcuts and mistakes, and increase the likelihood of failure.

iii. Proper software and consultants to assist in the development and implementation of the system are also critical to the success of planned development and implementation of ABC/ABM. Most organizations must seek outside consultants to develop an ABC system. There is commercial software that can be purchased and adapted to the particular needs of an organization. Development of an ABC/ABM system in-house makes it necessary for employees to maintain and update the system on an ongoing basis. This is not always possible. Using outside consultants who specialize in the development, implementation and maintenance of computer systems will bring the needed technical expertise to the project.

c. A factor that spells doom for ABC and ABM, if not addressed from the very beginning of planned development of ABC and ABM is resistance to change. Employees may feel threatened by the changes that ABC or ABM will undoubtedly bring. For some employees, these fears are well-founded. One of the objectives of ABM is to identify and eliminate non-value-added activities. This may result in the elimination of employees. Preventing resistance to change can be minimized by educating and training employees, by encouraging widespread sponsorship and participation, and by rewarding change. The team responsible for planning may need to identify ways to shift employees doing non-value-added work to areas of value-added work. This is not always possible.

International companies need to be especially aware of cultural differences in deciding what roles should be played by employees. In some cultures, employees think it is unacceptable to challenge managers who are their superiors. In this case, a "bottom up", participative approach to implementing the new system may not work. A "top down" approach may be necessary.

d. Information that must be gathered by the team before the ABC/ABM system can be developed is not easy to obtain. First of all, the information is usually not available from the organization's information system. Observation, interview or survey of employees must be used to generate information needed. The information obtained must be as accurate as is possible and practical in order to develop a sound, workable system.

e. The analysis team must make recommendations to top management after the study phase is complete. The team is the only group with intimate knowledge of the proposed system, including its strengths and weaknesses. The team needs to convey its recommendations clearly and honestly if the system is to succeed.

REVIEW AND SELF TEST QUESTIONS AND EXERCISES

Matching key terms

Match the following terms to the correct definition by writing the correct letter next to the correct definition.

a. Activity-based management	b. currently feasible cost	c. target cost
d. value-added analysis	e. unused capacity	f. pilot project
g. resources supplied	h. process improvement	i. activity analysis
j. non-value-added activity		

_____ 1. Some activity that causes costs to occur, but does not increase product value

_____ 2. The highest cost of a good or service that meets the needs of customers, while allowing a company to meet its profit goals.

_____ 3. The process of listing activities, ranked according to customer-perceived value, and assigning cost to each activity.

_____ 4. A procedure where costs and values of process activities are evaluated; a combination of ABC and value-added analysis.

_____ 5. The process of determining each activity that occurs in order to complete some process, deciding what the cost is, and deciding whether it adds value.

_____ 6. The total capacity provided by an organization for use in operations.

_____ 7. The cost of all current operations being undertaken to produce a product.

_____ 8. The difference between resources supplied and resources used.

_____ 9. A way to test a new system, using a smaller number of activities than the actual system would have.

____10. A change in production caused by elimination or reduction in non-value-added costs.

True or False

For each of the following statements enter a T or an F in the blank to indicate whether the statement is true or false.

_____11. Activities-based costing (ABC) can be developed and used without activities-based management (ABM).

_____12. Activities-based management has been widely adopted and is in use in most organizations in the US.

_____13. ABC provides input to ABM.

_____14. Value-added activities enhance the value of products and services in the eyes of an organization's management.

_____15. Non-value-added production activities cause product costs to be higher than necessary.

_____16. If non-value-added activities exist, it will make achieving target costs difficult.

_____17. In a manufacturing company, having large amounts of inventory on hand is viewed as value-added.

_____18. Fierce competition may cause organizations to change non-value-added activities into value-added activities.

_____19. One way to identify a value-added activity is to ask whether an external customer would encourage the organization to do more of the activity.

_____20. If a production activity is to be evaluated to determine whether it is value-added or not, the evaluator must be a production manager.

_____21. Production activities can be ranked, for instance, on a scale of 1 to 5 as to their value.

_____22. Performing evaluation of activities to determine whether they are value-added requires that activities be evaluated in isolation from other activities.

_____23. A major objective of activity analysis is to identify opportunities for process improvement.

_____24. Advocates of ABM argue that ABC is the main benefit of having ABM.

_____25. A serious obstacle to the success of activities-based management is resistance to change among employees.

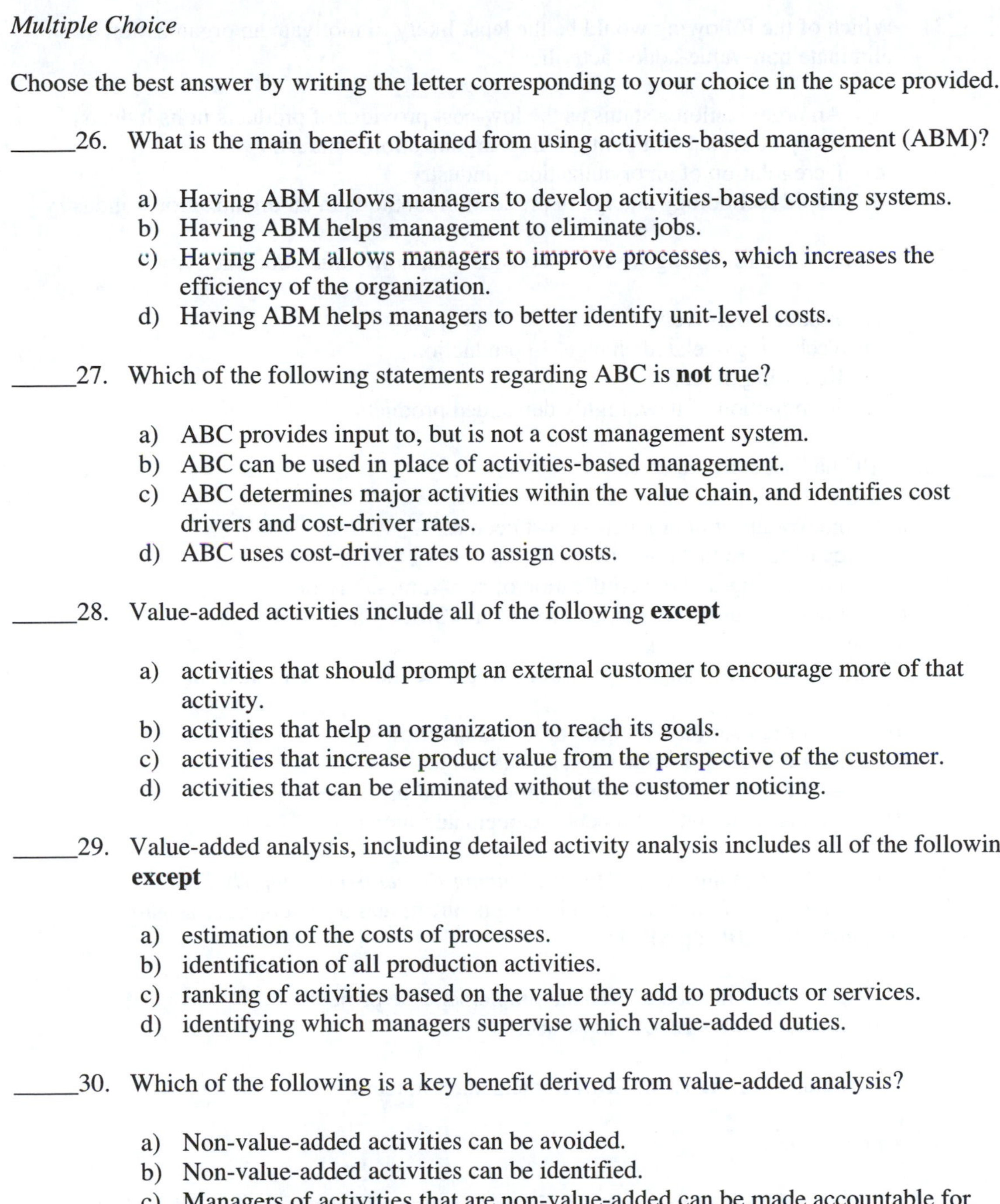

Chapter 5

Multiple Choice

Choose the best answer by writing the letter corresponding to your choice in the space provided.

_____26. What is the main benefit obtained from using activities-based management (ABM)?

a) Having ABM allows managers to develop activities-based costing systems.
b) Having ABM helps management to eliminate jobs.
c) Having ABM allows managers to improve processes, which increases the efficiency of the organization.
d) Having ABM helps managers to better identify unit-level costs.

_____27. Which of the following statements regarding ABC is **not** true?

a) ABC provides input to, but is not a cost management system.
b) ABC can be used in place of activities-based management.
c) ABC determines major activities within the value chain, and identifies cost drivers and cost-driver rates.
d) ABC uses cost-driver rates to assign costs.

_____28. Value-added activities include all of the following **except**

a) activities that should prompt an external customer to encourage more of that activity.
b) activities that help an organization to reach its goals.
c) activities that increase product value from the perspective of the customer.
d) activities that can be eliminated without the customer noticing.

_____29. Value-added analysis, including detailed activity analysis includes all of the following **except**

a) estimation of the costs of processes.
b) identification of all production activities.
c) ranking of activities based on the value they add to products or services.
d) identifying which managers supervise which value-added duties.

_____30. Which of the following is a key benefit derived from value-added analysis?

a) Non-value-added activities can be avoided.
b) Non-value-added activities can be identified.
c) Managers of activities that are non-value-added can be made accountable for performing them.
d) Non-value-added activities can be converted to value-added activities.

_____31. Which of the following would be the **least** likely to motivate an organization to eliminate non-value-added activities?

a) An organization's status as the low-cost provider of products in its industry.
b) Entry of global competition in an organization's industry.
c) Deregulation of an organization's industry.
d) Rapid technology change in production methods in an organization's industry.

_____32. Which of the following would be considered a non-value-added activity?

a) Product improvements
b) Technology-related changes in production
c) Repairing defects
d) Introduction of new, highly demanded products

_____33. ABC has been criticized for

a) not resulting in production cost decreases.
b) causing product costs to rise.
c) not helping in the identification of non-value-activities.
d) not being useful in conjunction with ABM.

_____34. Which of the following organizations would be the best candidate for ABC and ABM?

a) An organization with little or no competition
b) An organization with a loyal local market
c) An organization with simple products and processes
d) An organization in a recently deregulated industry

_____35. The 6 "Ps" of planning are "*Prior Planning Prevents Particularly Poor Performance*". Which of the following is **not** necessary to consider as part of planning for ABC or ABM?

a) Resources needed to plan and implement the project
b) Scope of the ABC/ABM project
c) Resistance to change
d) Salaries of the ABC/ABM implementation team

_____36. A pilot project

a) should be used to test the likelihood of success or failure of ABM projects.
b) should be used after implementation of ABM to find any flaws in the new system.
c) should not be used in ABM projects because they can't capture the complexity of ABM systems.
d) does not help managers to understand ABM projects.

_____37. Which of the following resources would **not** be helpful to ensure that ABM/ABC is successful?

a) Management commitment
b) Adequate personnel and time allotted to the development and implementation
c) Software and consultants
d) Employee resistance to ABC/ABM-related changes

_____38. Employee resistance to change may be an obstacle to the successful implementation of ABC/ABM. Which of the following is **not** a reason that employees are resistant to changes brought on by implementing ABC or ABM?

a) Fear of job loss
b) Value-added activities they perform may be changed to non-value-added activities
c) Lack of understanding of the new ABC/ABM system
d) More education and training is required

_____39. Which of the following is true regarding the use of software to develop an ABC/ABM system?

a) Most companies are better off developing their own (in-house) ABC/ABM software.
b) Outside consultants have too little expertise about various organizations to help in the development of an organization's ABC/ABM software or system.
c) The need to consistently update an ABC/ABM makes the purchase of software and consulting services appealing.
d) No one except the managers of various production departments can develop the software and ABC/ABM system for their departments.

_____40. Which of the following would be the most helpful in accomplishing the task of obtaining information to use in developing an ABC/ABM system?

a) Interview employees performing the various activities.
b) Obtain all of the information needed from the accounting information system.
c) Use activities as they are currently described in company documents.
d) Create information based on the views of the ABC/ABM development team.

_____41. A company has developed a ranking system for all of its production activities, in preparation for planned implementation of ABC and ABM. The 5-point scale ranges from 1, which is the ranking for an activity that is clearly non-value-added, to 5, which is clearly a value-added activity. One particular activity is ranked as a 4. This activity

a) would probably be treated as a non-value-added activity.
b) would probably be a noticeable omission (by customers), if removed from the production process.
c) could not possibly be improperly ranked.
d) would likely cause debate among the ABC/ABM members as to its value in the production process.

_____42. Which of the following statements is **not** true regarding non-value-added activities?

a) They may be difficult to eliminate from a production process if they use unionized workers.
b) Employees performing these activities will be resistant to their elimination.
c) Managers should eliminate these activities at any cost.
d) Sometimes employees performing these activities can be reassigned to performing value-added activities.

_____43. Which of the following customer-related activities would be viewed as adding the most value from an existing customer's perspective?

a) Customer support services—to answer questions about new purchases.
b) The customer complaint department—to return products for replacement and for customers to report dissatisfaction about products they have purchased.
c) Customer telemarketing—employees make calls to solicit new business.
d) Product delivery scheduling—employees schedule delivery of product, and are currently scheduling deliveries four weeks after the sale (there is a backlog).

_____44. What would be the best way to eliminate non-value-activities?

a) Establish across-the-board cost cuts of 10%.
b) Identify all activities, rank them, and then eliminate the activities with low rankings.
c) Give production managers the responsibility for eliminating non-value-added activities, and hold them accountable for reducing the costs associated with them.
d) Allow top management to determine which activities are non-value-added, and based on their instructions eliminate non-value-added activities and costs.

_____45. The US Postal Service delivers mail to and from its customers. Which of the following would rank the **lowest** in terms of the value added to mail delivery services?

a) Sorting mail before delivery.
b) Assigning zip codes to new subdivisions in the suburbs.
c) Delivering mail during a tornado.
d) Providing door-to-door mail delivery.

Exercises

Use the following information about HomeWare Home Delivery Company to answer the next 5 questions.

HomeWare Home Delivery Company is a large catalog company that sells its products to consumers exclusively through phone-orders. HomeWare buys products at wholesale prices and sells them to consumers at retail. In order to gain a better understanding of its costs and to control and eliminate unnecessary costs, HomeWare's management has committed to development and implementation of an activities-based costing and activities-based management system. One of their first steps was to rank activities in their distribution center on the East Coast, and estimate the costs of doing each one. Ten of these activities are listed below.

Activity	Cost Driver Base	Cost Driver Rate	Rank (1 to 5)
1. Taking phone orders	Number of orders placed	$20 per order	
2. Pulling ordered goods from inventory	Lines of orders	$3.00 per line	
3. Visually inspecting goods for defects, damages	Number of items per order	$.50 per item	
4. Packaging orders	Total weight	$1.25 per pound	
5. Addressing and labeling orders	Number of total orders being shipped	$.75 per order shipped	
6. Replace damaged items with good items	Quantity of damaged items	$5.00 per item	
7. Loading orders onto trucks	Cubic meters of truck space	$10.00 per cubic meter	
8. Changing orders (customer request)	Number of changes	$15.00 per change	
9. Customer service—order verification	Number of customers	$2.00 per customer	
10. Accepting customer returns	Number of items returned	$12.00 per return	

46. The first step for the company to take is to rank the above activities from 1 to 5. 1 is the rank given to an activity that is clearly non-value-added. A rank of 5 is for an activity that is clearly value-added. Rank the above 10 items from 1 to 5. Classify four items that have a rank of 1 or 2, and classify six items as activities with a rank of 3, 4, or 5. Write your answers in the above table.

47. Last week, the company had the following activities:

Activity	Cost Driver Base	Cost Driver Rate	Quantity
1. Taking orders	Number of orders placed	$20 per order	5,000 orders
2. Pulling ordered goods from inventory	Lines of orders	$3.00 per line	18,000 lines
3. Visually inspecting goods for defects, damages	Number of items per order	$.50 per item	25,600 items
4. Packaging orders	Total weight	$1.25 per pound	32,300 pounds
5. Addressing and labeling orders	Number of total orders being shipped	$.75 per order shipped	4,200 orders shipped
6. Replace damaged items with good items	Quantity of damaged items	$5.00 per damaged item	1,600 damaged items
7. Loading orders onto trucks	Cubic meters of truck space	$10.00 per cubic meter	3,000 cubic meters
8. Changing orders (customer request)	Number of changes	$15.00 per change	250 changes
9. Customer service—order verification	Number of customers	$2.00 per customer	3,800 customers
10. Accepting customer returns	Number of items returned	$12.00 per return	350 items returned

Based on this activity, how much cost will be assigned to the ordering and delivery department?

48. Suppose the managers decided that activities 3, 6, and 10 are non-value-added activities, but also recognize that they cannot be completely eliminated. Suppose 40% of activity 3 could be eliminated, 60% of activity 6 could be eliminated, and 80% of activity 10 could be eliminated. By how much would assigned costs be reduced?

49. Explain why the elimination of some of these activities would not necessarily eliminate the corresponding amount of cost (think about how costs are allocated, and what kinds of costs these are likely to be).

50. HomeWare's management thinks that any costs associated with damages are non-value-added. Discuss whether this is true, and discuss what the costs of eliminating damages might be.

Answers to Questions and Exercises

Matching key terms

1. j 2. c 3. i 4. a 5. d 6. g 7. b 8. e 9. f 10. h

True or False

11. T. Although it is more beneficial to do both, ABC can be implemented without implementing ABM.
12. F. ABM has not been adopted widely, and although a number of US companies have adopted it, it is far from the majority.
13. T. ABC is just a costing system, but it provides input to ABM which is a broader management tool.
14. F. Value-added activities are evaluated from the perspective of the customer—not the management of an organization.
15. T. Since non-value-added production costs are included in product cost along with value-added cost, they increase total product cost.
16. T. In a competitive environment, organizations cannot afford to include non-value-added costs because their presence either forces prices up or forces profits down.
17. F. Having excess inventory is viewed as **non**-value-added.
18. F. Non-value-added activities cannot be transformed into value-added activities. They must be reduced or eliminated.
19. T. Since value-added activities are determined by external customers, they are the real measure of an activity's worth.
20. F. The production manager's opinion may be biased. The opinions of several people should be solicited to rank activities.
21. T. Ranking activities is one of the steps taken in order to determine which activities are value-added, and which ones are not.
22. F. When evaluating activities, one must consider the impact one activity has on other activities. What appears, by itself, to be a non-value-added activity may in fact be a necessary link to performance of a value-added activity.
23. T. Activity analysis focuses attention on those activities that are essential, and those that are not. A product of this analysis should be an improved process.
24. F. Advocates of ABM argue that ABC should simply be a by-product of ABM.
25. T. Employees may feel threatened by the implementation of ABM.

Multiple Choice

26. c. This is the main benefit. Although jobs may be eliminated (answer b), and unit-level costs may be better identified via activity analysis (answer d), these are not the main benefits of ABM. Answer a is incorrect because ABC is usually developed and implemented before or in conjunction with ABM.
27. b. ABM is a cost management system, while ABC is a costing system, but is not a management system (ABM is more far-reaching than ABC).
28. d. Value-added activities result in product qualities that customers value, and therefore customers would miss them if they were eliminated.
29. d. Answers a, b and c are steps taken during detailed activity analysis. Answer d is incorrect because identification of managers is not a part of the detailed analysis.
30. b. Answer a is not true. Non-value-activities can't be avoided simply by doing value-added analysis. Answer c is not true. Rather than holding managers accountable, the whole idea is to minimize non-value-added activities. Answer d is wrong because non-value-added activities can't be converted to value-added activities.
31. a. An organization that is the low-cost provider is one that has most likely already eliminated non-value-added activities. The other three answers represent situations that will force organizations to evaluate their production processes.
32. c. Repairing defects would be a non-value-added activity, because any work that has to be re-done is non-value-added.
33. a. ABC has been criticized as simply leading to a rearrangement of costs, without changing them. However, ABC has the potential for reducing costs if it helps managers to identify and eliminate non-value-added activities and costs.
34. d. It is not true that every organization should adopt ABC and ABM. In some cases the costs far exceed the benefits. Organizations in recently deregulated industries are good candidates for ABC and ABM because they often allow non-value-added activities to exist. This occurs because regulated industries are usually allowed to recover whatever costs they have, even if they are non-value-added.
35. d. The team normally consists of employees with the expertise to successfully implement activities-based costing and management. Their salaries are not relevant to the planning activities of the team.
36. a. A pilot of a major change like ABM helps managers to identify problems and bugs in the system before the entire (costly) system is implemented. Answer b is incorrect because a pilot project after the implementation of ABM is too late. Answer c is incorrect. Even though a pilot project can't capture every bit of the complexity, it often can highlight unanticipated problems. Pilot projects help managers to understand ABM projects by taking them "live" on a small scale (answer d).
37. d. Employee resistance to change is one of the obstacles to successful implementation of ABM.
38. b. Value-added activities can't be changed to non-value-added activities.
39. c. Many organizations do not have the technical expertise to develop and implement a sophisticated ABM system. In that case, it is more cost-effective to hire software and computer consultants to develop and help in the implementation of a new information system.
40. a. Interviewing employees is helpful because the employees can provide the best description of production processes in sufficient detail to develop the detailed activity analysis used in developing the ABM system.

41. b. The ranking of 4 means that external customers place a high value on this activity. Therefore, it would probably be a noticeable omission. It would not be treated as a non-value-added activity (answer a). It could be improperly ranked (answer c). It is not likely, given a rank of 4, that team members would dispute its value.

42. c. Although theoretically, non-value-added costs should be eliminated, there are times when the costs of doing so exceed the benefits.

43. a. If these four activities were ranked, having customer service after the sale would probably be the activity that customers saw as the most beneficial. Answer b would probably be viewed as non-value-added activity. Answer c would probably not be viewed as value-added by existing customers, but would be an activity that is necessary for the company to achieve its goals. Answer d is an activity that would probably receive a low ranking because of the backlog.

44. b. Identification, ranking, and systematic elimination of non-value-added activities would be the best approach to eliminating non-value-added activities.

45. c. Despite the motto of the Postal Service to deliver the mail regardless of inclement weather, the other three services would likely be more valuable to postal service customers than getting mail during a tornado.

Exercises

46. Ranking of the activities requires some judgement on the part of the reader. However, if all value-added activities were given rankings of 4 or 5, items 1, 2, 4, 5 and 7 would probably be viewed by anyone as the most valued processes occurring. Activity 9 is of value, but may be viewed by some as having questionable value since it should not be necessary to verify orders (they should be right in the first place). Items 3, 6, 8, and 10 are all activities having to do with some unacceptable event, and would probably be viewed as non-value-added. Items 8 and 10, accepting customer changes and returns might be viewed as value-added to the customers making the changes, but to other customers who are not causing the associated costs, these activities would not necessarily be viewed as value-added.

    For purposes of this exercise, items 3, 6, 8, and 10 are given ranks of 1 or 2 (non-value-added).

47. The ordering and delivery department would have the following costs.

    1. Taking orders: $100,000. 2. Pulling inventory: $54,000. 3. Inspect for defects: $12,800. 4. Packaging orders: $40,375. 5. Addressing and labeling orders: $3,150. 6. Replacing damaged goods with good items: $8,000. 7. Loading orders onto trucks: $30,000. 8. Changing orders: $3,750. 9. Customer service—order verification: $7,600. 10. Accepting customer returns: $4,200.

    Total cost for the week is $263,875.

48. If items 3, 6, and 10 could be completely eliminated, then \$25,000, or 9.47% of the costs assigned could be eliminated. A more realistic assumption, that some, but not all of these activities could be eliminated, would give the following results.

Item 3. Inspect for defects: \$12,800×40% = \$5,120.
Item 6. Replacing damaged goods: \$8,000×60% = \$4,800.
Item 10. Accepting customer returns. \$4,200×80% = \$3,360.

Reduction in assigned costs = \$13,280, or a little more than 5%.

49. The costs would not automatically go away. The reduction in activity does not immediately eliminate the costs unless the costs are proportionate to the activity. For instance, if part of the cost of accepting returns is for shipping costs, then these costs would go away. If, on the other hand, part of the cost is for employees accepting the returned items, then these costs would not go away unless employees were terminated. In the short run, employee costs for this activity would simply make the allocation rate higher for each item returned.

50. It is correct in theory to view any damages as non-value-added. Customers obviously do not want damaged goods. However, it is more realistic to recognize that damages are inevitable in a high-volume warehouse such as the one described for HomeWare. Instead of eliminating damages completely, HomeWare should try to minimize the amount of damages. Trying to completely eliminate damages would likely slow down the productivity rates of warehouse employees, and this might be more expensive than the cost savings from undamaged merchandise.

Chapter 6
Managing Customer Profitability

Chapter Study Suggestions

Chapter 6 presents the topic of customer profitability analysis. The chapter discusses the importance of recognizing that different customers cause different costs. It then shows how to identify customer costs, and explains how managers should respond when customer costs lead to lower profits.

The chapter applies ABC analysis to this specific area of operations. The sales revenues, by customer and product or service are identified. Next, costs of servicing individual customers must also be identified. Then cost management analysts can assess which costs can be reduced or eliminated as necessary. Analysts can also identify weaknesses or gaps in customer service that will enhance customer satisfaction.

Chapter Highlights

A. Cost Management Challenges. Chapter 6 addresses five cost management challenges.

1. How can you determine in advance whether it is worth the time, effort and information systems to perform profitability analysis?

2. How can customer profitability analysis be more relevant for service and governmental organizations than for others?

3. What are the tradeoffs among relevant, accurate and timely information and the time and cost of getting and using the information?

4. How can cost management analysts help an organization plan and execute changes that result in more customer value at lower cost?

5. How can one determine whether operational changes in customer service levels have been harmful or beneficial?

B. Learning Objectives—This chapter has 3 learning objectives.

1. Chapter 6 explains the value of analyzing customer profitability by major customer types.

2. The chapter explains the use of an activity-based approach to customer profitability analysis.

3. It shows how to identify alternative actions, and explains how to present recommended improvements for customer profitability.

C. Customer profitability is a management approach that considers the costs and benefits of serving specific customers. This is one way to improve overall organizational profitability. If a company decides to perform this type of analysis, it must be able to measure profitability by customer, identify effective and ineffective customer-related activities, and move away from traditional methods of assessing profitability.

1. Some organizations spend significant amounts of money to satisfy customers, but often do not know whether these costs do anything to increase revenues (or profits). Customer profitability analysis is a cost-benefit approach that attempts to identify profitable and unprofitable customers. This is the first objective of customer profitability analysis.

2. Although customer profitability analysis is mainly quantitative, there often are qualitative issues to consider as well. Even if a customer is identified as unprofitable, there may be other factors that justify keeping that customer. For instance, a customer may be a source of referrals to other customers. Unprofitable customers might also prove to be profitable if they are served more efficiently.

3. An important early first step in doing customer profitability analysis is to identify effective and ineffective customer-related activities. Clearly, the information technology to perform analysis at this level of detail requires far more than a traditional cost accounting system.

4. Customer profitability analysis begins with the estimation of costs, customer by customer, to see which customers cause how much cost. Revenue information is combined with variable costs, to get contribution margin by customer.

    a. Customer satisfaction and customer profitability should go hand-in-hand. If they don't, companies need to figure out what to do differently so that there is a closer match between these two things.

    b. Some companies use customer profitability analysis to decide what the quality of service should be.

D. Before considering costs of providing goods and services, as well as customer service, organizations should consider the nature of sales revenues. Using an ABC approach, sales data can be segmented in a variety of ways, from customer to product type to distribution method.

1. A customer profile categorizes individual customers or types of customers according to the major activities or factors that drive revenues and costs.

2. Customer sales patterns are also useful for the analysis of customers. A matrix of sales activity should show at a minimum, sales by product line and by customer (or customer type).

E. To the extent possible, organizations should trace operating costs, or sales and administrative costs to customers. There are five categories of sales and administrative costs for which cost-causing customers can be evaluated.

1. Customer selling costs include all of the costs of personnel, databases, equipment and facilities used to support sales activities. The easiest selling costs to identify are those related to direct sales. For instance, a sales rep who travels to customers on a route can link his or her costs directly to those customers. Not so easy to trace are costs of sales administrative staff. These are comparable to overhead costs in manufacturing.

2. Customer marketing costs are another type of cost that can be analyzed. Customer marketing costs include costs of market research, marketing strategy, and marketing plans. Although it is not always possible to trace marketing costs to specific customers, it may be possible to at least trace them to product lines or regions.

3. Customer distribution costs include the costs of getting the product to the customer. If different customers can choose their delivery method, it is likely that distribution costs can be traced to them. For instance, if a customer requires expedited delivery, then these costs are higher than regular delivery, and that customer should be charged differently.

4. General and administrative costs, including research and development costs may be the most general type of operating expense, and may not be traceable to individual customers. However, some of these costs could probably be traced to types or classes of customers based on the products they buy.

F. Development of the information in the form described above allows a company to perform customer profitability analysis. Information captured in a traditional accounting system does not provide the necessary detail to do this type of analysis.

G. Customer profitability analysis should result in improved decision-making with respect to servicing customers more efficiently and more profitably. In the case where customers or segments of a business appear to be a drain on profits, management can make one of several choices. One way to quickly assess poor performers by customer class is to prepare common-size profit statements, which show which customer classes generate what percentage of profits.

1. Managers can choose to continue to serve a class of customers in the same way. To do so is basically recognition that these customers demand service at costs that differ from other customers.

2. Management can choose to drop customers that seem unprofitable. This is an alternative that is difficult and may be avoidable if costs attributable to these customers can be reduced, eliminated, or charged to the customers.

3. Management can use the information obtained from the profitability analysis to increase efficiency and/or reduce costs of serving the unprofitable customers.

REVIEW AND SELF TEST QUESTIONS AND EXERCISES

Matching key terms

Match the following terms to the correct definition by writing the correct letter next to the correct definition.

a. distribution costs b. common-size profit statements c. customer profile
d. customer profitability analysis e. customer sales analysis

_____ 1. Income statements divided into customer class.

_____ 2. A way to use financial information traceable to specific customers for use in improving profits and quality of service.

_____ 3. Information showing how much revenue is generated by a particular customer or customer class.

_____ 4. The costs associated with getting goods or services to the customer.

_____ 5. A description of individual customers or types of customers that categorizes them based on activities or factors that drive revenues or costs.

True or False

For each of the following statements enter a T or an F in the blank to indicate whether the statement is true or false.

_____ 6. The main reason for using customer profitability analysis is to get rid of cost-causing customers.

_____ 7. Customer profitability analysis is possible without some form of ABC analysis.

_____ 8. If customers who are unprofitable are identified via customer profitability analysis, the next logical step is to see whether any of the costs they cause can be reduced or eliminated.

_____ 9. The primary purpose of a customer profile is to identify customers who constantly pay their bills late.

_____10. Marketing research is one part of marketing costs that might be traceable to customer types.

_____11. Distribution costs that result from expedited delivery are good targets for cost reductions by customer.

_____12. The traditional accounting system can usually provide information needed to perform customer profitability analysis.

_____13. A common-size profit statement makes different customer types comparable, when considering their contribution to profitability.

_____14. If a customer type appears to be unprofitable, it is always because there is some non-value-added activity associated with that customer.

_____15. Any reduction in costs to serve customers will result in lower quality customer service.

_____16. Customer profitability analysis requires an information system that can provide very detailed data by customer class.

_____17. Customers who generate the least cost generate the most profit.

_____18. A qualitative reason for keeping a customer who appears unprofitable is that they enhance the (selling) company's reputation.

_____19. Businesses that have customers with very different delivery costs would probably not benefit from using customer profitability analysis.

_____20. General and administrative expenses are often difficult to trace to different customer types.

Multiple Choice

Choose the best answer by writing the letter corresponding to your choice in the space provided.

_____21. Which of the following is **not** a reason to perform customer profitability analysis?

a) Companies want to find out which customers cause a lot of cost, and which ones generate high profits.
b) Once costly customers are identified using profitability analysis, a company should work with these customers to help them to reduce the costs they are causing.
c) Once costly customers are identified using profitability analysis, companies should use price discrimination to eliminate unprofitable customers.
d) Customer profitability analysis helps companies to identify unnecessary customer costs.

_____22. All of the following are examples of customer-related activities that should be evaluated during customer profitability analysis **except**

a) requiring expedited production and delivery of product.
b) requiring frequent delivery of small orders.
c) placing very large orders without allowing for adequate lead time.
d) returning defective product to the manufacturer.

_____23. Customer profitability analysis **cannot** be successfully implemented without

a) use of a standard costing system.
b) use of an activity-based costing system.
c) a customer service department being in place.
d) an existing mechanism for reducing customer-related costs.

_____24. What is the purpose of a customer profitability profile?

a) It allows a company to rank customers based on their relative profitability.
b) It helps companies to see why particular customers are profitable or not.
c) It gives customers important feedback on the amount of cost they cause.
d) It helps companies to see which customers to drop.

_____25. Which of the following businesses is **least** likely to benefit from using customer profitability analysis?

a) A furniture manufacturer whose customers include home improvement stores, furniture stores, and hotels.
b) A retail grocery store selling thousands of different products.
c) A computer software store selling anything from educational software to schools, to information systems to medium companies.
d) A tax consulting company providing services for international companies, large partnerships, and professional athletes.

_____26. Which of the following is a distribution cost?

a) Costs of outsourced delivery services.
b) Costs of returning defective product.
c) Production costs for a manufacturer.
d) Customer service costs.

_____27. Vail's Furs requests delivery of coats from Zeff's Mfg. Company on an expedited basis every time an order is placed. Vail's Furs is one of Zeff's largest customers. This results in higher delivery costs and higher production costs since Zeff employees must speed up production to get the furs to Vail's in time. Which of the following is a true statement regarding this business/customer relationship?

a) Zeff's should automatically add the additional charges to Vail's bill.
b) Zeff's should drop Vail's Furs as a customer to cut costs.
c) Zeff's should treat these extra costs as normal, and recover them by raising prices for all of its customers.
d) Zeff's should request a meeting with Vail's management to discuss ways to reduce or eliminate these costs.

_____28. Which of the following is **not** a valid response to reducing customer costs that have been identified by profitability analysis?

a) Seek ways to make operations more efficient.
b) Try to reduce or eliminate costs.
c) Try to get the customer causing the costs to modify their operations if possible, to reduce or eliminate costs.
d) Drop the cost-causing customers immediately.

_____29. Which of the following statements is correct regarding allocating costs to different customer classes?

a) Allocated costs are readily traceable to customer types.
b) Allocation of costs is necessary when costs can't be traced.
c) Allocation is the best way to assign customer-level costs.
d) If one customer type is dropped, allocated costs will decrease.

_____30. The Smallins Group provides financial services to customers locally. Two service offerings are Retirement Planning and Tax Services. Retirement Planning generated \$600,000 in revenue last year. Tax Services generated \$400,000 in revenues. Both customer types have about the same number of customers. Given this, which of the following statements is correct?

a) Customer-level costs for Retirement Planning will be greater than customer-level costs for Tax Services.
b) Retirement Services will be more profitable than Tax Services.
c) These two customer-types may be different enough to warrant customer-level profitability analysis.
d) This business is required to use customer-level profitability analysis.

_____31. The Matey Company completed a customer profitability analysis and discovered that their top 100 customers generated 140% of the total profit. This result means that

a) All of Matey's customers generated more than 100% in profit.
b) Some of Matey's customers are generating losses.
c) The top 100 customers must also be generating 140% of the revenue.
d) Matey must have earned a profit.

_____32. What is the financial basis for deciding to drop a particular customer type?

a) The customer type is causing too many costs.
b) The customer type is not generating enough revenues.
c) The customer type has too much allocated cost.
d) The customer type is generating more customer-level cost than revenue.

_____33. Which of the following is **incorrect** with respect to general and administrative (G&A) costs?

a) G&A costs should always be treated as customer-level costs.
b) G&A costs exist whether customer profitability analysis is used or not.
c) G&A costs are often allocated costs.
d) G&A costs are not the same as marketing costs.

_____34. Herd Communications is an outsourcing telecommunications company that services medium-sized businesses. The company has 10 customers. Sales-related expenses are easily traceable because each of these major customers is assigned a half-time consultant. One of the customers is demanding the attention equivalent to a three-fourth time consultant instead, while another customer requires only one-fourth time. Which of the following is true based on this information?

a) The customer using three-fourth time should be charged the same as the other customers.
b) The customer using three-fourth time should be charged more than the other customers.
c) All of the customers should be charged equally. The customer using one-fourth time should be charged for half-time as long as he does not find out.
d) The customer using three-fourth time should be dropped.

_____35. What is the benefit of using a common-size profit statement?

a) It allows one to make all customer-types comparable
b) It helps managers to reduce costs
c) It shows how much overall profit a company has earned.
d) It is guaranteed to increase profits.

_____36. Suppose the company wanted to eliminate any customers that did not generate profit, but also did not want to lay off employees or downsize its sales or customer support staff. Which of the following correctly describes the result of eliminating an unprofitable customer type with respect to customer support staff costs?

a) Customer support costs would increase and revenues would decrease.
b) Customer support costs would decrease and revenues would decrease.
c) Customer support costs would stay the same and revenues would decrease.
d) Customer support costs would decrease and revenues would stay the same.

_____37. Which of the following is **not** a marketing cost?

a) Delivery costs
b) Marketing research
c) Advertising
d) Promotion

_____38. Which of the following is a disadvantage of choosing to do customer profitability analysis?

a) It usually results in lost customers.
b) It usually causes revenues to decline.
c) It usually requires a very detailed information system
d) It usually results in employees losing their jobs.

_____39. Which of the following is a qualitative consideration when deciding whether customers should be dropped?

a) Legal requirements
b) Reputation of the customer causing the costs
c) Financial accounting requirements
d) Whether the costs can be reduced.

_____40. Which of the following is **least** likely to be treated as a customer-level cost?

a) The salary of a sales consultant.
b) The technician installing equipment after the sale.
c) The salary of a delivery truck driver with a set route.
d) The salary of the chief executive officer (CEO).

Exercises

Please use the following information to answer the next five questions.

Melange Inc. sells and installs security equipment, and offers monitoring services after the sale. The company has three customer types—residential, churches, and small businesses, and is planning to begin performing customer profitability analysis. Sales were $312,000 for residential customers, $394,200 for churches, and $493,800 for small businesses. The company has identified two expenses that it wants to include in the analysis right away. They are sales employees' salaries and customer support costs. Sales salaries totaled $240,000, and customer support was $150,000. Based on time reporting for salespeople and customer support staff, residential customers use 25% of salespersons' time and 60% of customer support. Churches use 45% of salespersons' time and 18% of customer support. Small businesses use 30% of salespersons' time and 22% of customer support.

41. What percentage of revenue is generated by each customer type?

42. What percentage of profit is generated, by customer type after subtracting sales salaries and customer support costs?

Use the table below to answer questions 41 and 42.

	TOTAL	**Residential**	**Churches**	**Small Businesses**
Revenues	$1,200,000	$312,000	$394,200	$493,800
41. Revenues as a percentage	100%			
Dollar amount of Sales Salaries	$240,000			
Dollar amount of Customer Support	$150,000			
Total Sales Salaries and Customer Support	$390,000			
Dollar amount of profit remaining after subtracting customer costs	$810,000			
42. Profit remaining as a percentage, by customer type	100%			

43. A third set of costs that will likely be incorporated into the customer profitability analysis is distribution costs. These include costs of delivery and installation of the security systems. The company will need to modify its reporting requirements for delivery and installation activities in order to better track the costs by customer type. Preliminary estimates of these costs by customer type are as follows. Total distribution costs are $280,000. $172,600 is estimated to be due to residential customers, $68,400 is the result of churches, and the remaining $39,000 is due to small businesses. After accounting for the estimated distribution costs by customer type, what is the dollar amount of profit remaining?

44. After accounting for the estimated distribution costs by customer type, what is the percentage of profit remaining by customer type?

Use the table below to answer questions 43 and 44.

	TOTAL	Residential	Churches	Small Businesses
Dollar amount of profit remaining after subtracting customer costs (from table above)	$810,000			
Distribution costs	$280,000			
43. Profit remaining after subtracting distribution costs.	$530,000			
44. Profit remaining after subtracting distribution costs as a percentage.	100%			

45. Compare your answers in questions 42 and 44. What do the results show for each customer? What actions should Melange Inc. management take based on this preliminary analysis?

Chapter 6

Answers to Questions and Exercises

Matching key terms

1\. b 2. d 3. e 4. a 5. c

True or False

6\. F. The objective of customer profitability analysis is to identify the profits and costs of individual customers. Those customers who generate a lot of costs should not be eliminated. Instead, the company should work on reducing unnecessary costs.

7\. F. Activity that can be traced to specific customers or customer types is the whole basis for customer profitability analysis. Customer profitability analysis is just a special type of ABC analysis.

8\. T. Some costs can be eliminated or reduced internally. Other customer-related costs must be eliminated or reduced by getting the customer involved, and letting them know that they need to either help to reduce unnecessary costs, or accept being charged extra for those costs.

9\. F. A customer profile is intended to identify characteristics of specific customers or customer types, based on qualities that impact revenues and/or costs.

10\. T. Marketing research is a type of marketing cost. Some can be traced to specific products, customer types or customers.

11\. T. Expedited delivery costs often are the result of sales to customers who demand immediate delivery. These customers may need to be advised as to the additional costs they are causing. Then they could be given the option of paying higher delivery costs or requiring regular delivery.

12\. F. A traditional accounting system does not allow activity-based analysis. Customer profitability analysis is an activity-based analytical method.

13\. T. Since profits are expressed as percentages instead of absolute dollar amounts, different customer types are comparable regardless of their relative sizes.

14\. F. Since customers are the ones who determine whether a cost is value-added or not, it may be the case that they cause costs that make them less profitable, but which are value-added.

15\. F. If non-value-added costs are identified and eliminated, that would not have a detrimental effect on quality of customer service.

16\. T. A very detailed information system that allows costs to be traced to specific customers or customer types is needed to successfully complete customer profitability analysis.

17\. F. One of the reasons customer profitability analysis is useful is that it helps managers to see what customers generate what costs. There is not always a correlation between costs and profits for each customer type.

18\. T. The selling company's reputation as the supplier to high-profile customers may attract additional customers.

19\. F. Businesses whose customers cause costs to occur in differing amounts are always good candidates for customer profitability analysis.

20\. T. Since general and administrative costs often occur at a higher level than the customer level, they cannot always be traced to individual customers or customer types.

Multiple Choice

21. c. Price discrimination is illegal. Aside from that, customer profitability analysis should be used to help eliminate unnecessary costs—not to eliminate customers.
22. d. Returning defective product is not a customer cost, so is not part of customer profitability analysis.
23. b. Without detailed cost information traceable to specific customers, customer profitability analysis cannot be performed.
24. a. Customers can be ranked along important dimensions, and then further analysis of customers or customer types can be done with those dimensions in mind.
25. b. A retail grocer's customers are likely to be fairly homogenous in terms of the costs they cause. The other three answers are all for companies whose customers are very diverse.
26. a. Costs of getting product to customers are distribution costs whether they are accomplished internally or via outsourcing. (b) is not a customer cost; (c) is product cost, and (d) is a separate category of customer costs.
27. d. Once a customer is identified as one who causes unnecessary costs, an important next step is to try to reduce or eliminate those costs. The costs of expedited delivery are likely viewed by the customer as value-added (delivery on demand often is). However, the added costs would probably not be viewed in the same way once the customer was informed of them.
28. d. Dropping cost-causing customers without first trying to reduce, eliminate, or charge the customer would be an inappropriate first step.
29. b. The word "allocation" implies that there must be a somewhat arbitrary way to assign costs. Traceable costs are not arbitrarily assigned to cost objects. Answer (c) is incorrect because customer-level costs should be traceable. Answer (d) is incorrect because allocated costs are usually unaffected by dropping a customer type. The allocated costs remain, and must then be allocated to the remaining customers.
30. c. The fact that two customer types generate different revenues per customer is an indicator that costs might also be generated differently. At a minimum, Smallins should look at the potential for doing customer profitability analysis.
31. b. In order for one customer type to generate more than 100% of total profit, it is mathematically impossible for there **not** to be at least one customer type that is generating losses.
32. d. From a purely quantitative standpoint, revenue minus customer-level cost is the basis for considering whether a customer type should be dropped. One cannot look at costs alone or revenues alone, and allocated costs are not a factor in this decision.
33. a. G&A costs are often difficult to trace to customer types, so they can't always be treated as customer costs.
34. b. The cost-causing customer should be properly charged after informing that customer of the billing policies. If the customer has a contract specifying what the charges are but is demanding more consultant time than the contract specifies, the company should meet with the customer's management to resolve the differences.
35. a. A common-size profit statement shows profits by customer type, expressed as a percentage. This makes different sized customers comparable.
36. c. If no customer support level costs were eliminated, those costs would remain the same. Revenues would decrease because sales to the dropped customers would not generate revenues anymore. The customer support staff costs would remain the same, and would be assigned to the remaining customers.

37. a. Delivery costs are distribution costs. The other three answers are all marketing costs.
38. c. Customer profitability analysis requires a great deal of detail. The other three answers might occur, but do not necessarily need to.
39. b. Dropping a customer may have negative repercussions that are not quantifiable. If the customer is high profile, or has influence on what other customers do it could indirectly affect profits in the long run. Legal or accounting requirements do not factor into the decision to drop a customer (answers (a) and (c)). Answer (d) is a quantitative reason.
40. d. Salary of the CEO cannot be traced to any one group of customers.

Exercises

41. Revenues for residential customers are $312,000/$1,200,000, or 26%. Revenues for church customers are $394,200/$1,200,000, or 32.85%. Small business customers generated $493,800/$1,200,000, or 41.15% of revenues.

42. **Profit remaining after subtracting sales salaries and customer support costs are as follows:** Residential customers caused 25% of the sales salaries, or $60,000. They caused 60% of customer support, or $90,000. Profit attributed to residential customers is $312,000–($60,000 + $90,000), or $162,000 of profit. As a percentage, it is $162,000/$810,000, or 20%.

    Church customers caused 45% of the sales salaries, or $108,000. They caused 18% of customer support, or $27,000. Profit attributed to church customers is $394,200–($108,000 + $27,000), or **$259,200 of profit.** As a percentage, it is $259,200/$810,000, or **32%.**

    Small business customers caused 30% of the sales salaries, or $72,000. They caused 22% of customer support, or $33,000. Profit attributed to small business customers is $493,800–($72,000 + $33,000), or **$388,800 of profit.** As a percentage, it is $388,800/$810,000, or **48%.**

43. **Residential customers** caused $172,600 of distribution costs, leaving a loss instead of profit of $162,000–$172,600 =**–$10,600**.

    Church customers caused $68,400 of distribution costs, leaving a profit of $259,200–$68,400 = **$190,800.**

    Small business customers caused $39,000 of distribution costs, leaving a profit of $388,800–$39,000 = **$349,800.**

44. As a percentage, **residential customers** generated–$10,600/530,000, or **–2%. Churches generated** $190,800/$530,000, or **36%,** and **small business customers generated** $349,800/$530,000, or **66%** of profits.

45. This brief analysis illustrates the benefits of using customer profitability analysis. A customer type that generates 26% of the revenues actually contributes nothing to profits. Instead, residential customers appear to cause a drain on profits of –2%. Small business customers generate almost 42% of revenues but because their customer costs are relatively low, they generate a sizable 66% of profits. Profits for church customers appear to be somewhat consistent with the revenues they generate. This does not mean the company should not investigate, to see whether costs could be reduced or quality of service could be increased for church customers. The company could look at all three customer types to determine how to reduce costs and improve customer service.

Before the company decides to drop residential customers, remember the following. These costs can all be looked at, to determine whether they include avoidable and/or NVA costs. The distribution costs are preliminary estimates, so the assignment of these costs could actually be different. The price structure of different customer types might need revision. Dropping customers should be a last resort after taking action to make a customer type profitable. Qualitative aspects of dropping a customer type should also be taken into consideration. For instance, if residential customers were the ones recommending Melange to their churches, would they recommend to their church administrators that Melange be dropped as the provider of security services?

Chapter 7
Managing Quality and Time to Create Value

Chapter Study Suggestions

Chapter 7 presents the topic of quality, and describes methods adopted by organizations to stay ahead of competition by properly managing quality and time. The chapter describes a number of important quality management tools: histograms, control charts, run charts, cause and effect diagrams, scatter diagrams, flowcharts, Pareto charts, and cost-of-quality reports. These tools are all presented as effective ways to monitor quality and process time. Use of such tools should prevent the occurrence of mistakes in meeting customer needs. Two views of quality management—total quality management (TQM) and return on quality (ROQ) are described and contrasted with each other. The dimensions of quality are presented. They are product or service attributes, and customer service before and after the sale.

Another important feature of quality issues focuses on identifying, evaluating and categorizing costs of quality. The cost of quality is the cost of activities to control quality. Costs of quality can be categorized as prevention, appraisal, internal failure, or external failure costs.

The importance of managing time is presented in the context of product development time, customer response time, and cycle time. The importance of measuring and managing productivity and capacity is introduced and related to time and quality management. The chapter also discusses how Just-in-Time methods combine concerns for managing quality and time.

Chapter Highlights

A. Cost Management Challenges. Chapter 7 presents three challenges.

1. What can cost managers provide to better manage quality?

2. Is there a conflict between meeting quality and time goals, or do these goals reinforce each other?

3. How should cost managers choose among all the available quality and time management tools?

B. Learning Objectives—This chapter has 5 learning objectives.

1. It teaches how to evaluate similarities and differences of total quality management and return on quality approaches to managing quality.

2. The chapter demonstrates how to measure and analyze dimensions of quality with commonly used diagrams, charts and reports.

3. Chapter 7 aids in one's understanding of the importance of managing process time.

4. The chapter shows how to manage productivity and capacity.

5. It demonstrates how just-in-time methods create benefits by combining management of quality and time.

C. Quality is important for organizations to offer to its customers. Poor quality results in lost customers, and high quality attracts new customers and assures that existing customers will remain loyal. Improving quality translates into improved customer satisfaction. In a globally competitive market, improving quality is a high priority for organizations.

D. Should organizations strive for quality at any cost, or quality up to a cost-defining limit? There are two views on what the ideal level of quality is.

1. Total Quality Management (TQM) promotes the view that perfect quality is never achieved, and that organizations must constantly seek improved quality. TQM advocates argue that customers will seek the highest quality, and are willing to pay a premium for the highest quality.

   a. TQM is a concept attributed to W. Edwards Deming.

   b. TQM advocates believe that improving quality pays for itself by creating higher profits.

2. Return on quality (ROQ) is a more pragmatic view of quality. This view of quality assumes that there is a tradeoff between the costs and benefits of improving quality. The optimum quality level of products and services maximizes profits rather than maximizing quality.

3. TQM has a goal of "total delight" for customers. This means that the customer's expectations are exceeded. With total delight there are zero defects. ROQ seeks an optimum quality level. This level of quality is almost always lower than total delight.

   TQM assumes that the amount of profit is highest when quality is at its peak. ROQ assumes that the amount of profit is highest when quality is at some optimal level, usually lower than maximum quality. Beyond that optimal level, the cost of improving quality exceeds the amount of additional profit that can be earned from increasing prices.

4. The ROQ view has been the traditional view of quality, but the TQM view emerged in the 1980s when quality became a competitive advantage for companies in global markets.

5. The theoretical definitions of TQM and ROQ conflict with each other. In practice, organizations try to use ideas generated from both philosophies.

E. There are two dimensions of quality that organizations need to be concerned about. They are product or service attributes and customer service before and after the sale.

1. Product and service attributes are described as the tangible and intangible features. Tangible features include performance, adherence to specifications, and functionality. Intangible features include reputation, taste, appearance, style and appeal.

2. Customer service before and after the sale influences whether purchasers of products will become new customers and remain as repeat customers. Customer service features include provision of pre-sale information, proper treatment of customers by salespeople, on-time delivery, follow up with customers, timeliness and accuracy of resolution of questions and complaints, and warranty and repair services.

F. How do organizations measure quality? This question can be answered in many ways. To ensure that an organization is meeting expectations on the two dimensions of quality (product attributes and customer service), the organization should use measures that are lead indicators of customers' expectations for product quality. The organization should then measure customers' satisfaction with the products or services they have purchased.

1. Lead indicators of quality can be used to evaluate tangible features of products, such as physical dimensions and functional performance before they reach customers. It is more difficult to measure tangible features of services because the service is not complete until the customer receives it. Service organizations must focus their attention on evaluating the capabilities of personnel and technology that will provide the service. Measurement of the intangible features of products and services are even harder to measure since the value of intangible features differs from customer to customer. Measures of intangible features may be obtained by customer surveys or other methods. Evaluating some features, like quality of service received from salespeople, customer service staff, or on-time delivery must be obtained after the customer has had contact with the organization.

2. A primary source of poor quality is variation in process outcomes. Variability provides a greater chance for product and service attributes to disappoint customers. A bakery, for instance, does not want to undercook a pie (the crust will not be brown). It would also not want to overcook a pie (it will be burnt). Three tools to use for measuring lead indicators are histograms, run charts, and control charts.

   a. A histogram is a chart that displays the frequency distribution of an attribute's measures, showing its range and the degree of concentration around an average attribute value. The wider the range, the greater the variation, and the higher the chances that a customer will receive poor quality products or services.

   b. A run chart shows trends in variation in product or service attributes over time. It reflects measures of quality features taken at defined points in time. Run charts are especially useful after some process change has been made, because it shows whether the change has improved product or service quality.

   c. A control chart shows variation in product or service attributes over time, just as a run chart does. However, it goes further by including maximum and minimum desired levels. In this way, variations outside the acceptable range can be quickly and easily identified.

3. Although lead indicator information identifies potential quality problems, it usually does not diagnose the cause of the problem. The next step, then, is to diagnose the problem. This can be accomplished by using cause-and-effect diagrams, scatter diagrams, flow charts, and Pareto diagrams.

   a. Cause-and-effect diagrams take the information related to potential causes of product or service defects, and then identifies the causes that may contribute to the problem. The cause-and-effect diagram splits probable causes into five distinct sources.

      i. Human resources (human error)

      ii. Physical resources (insufficient capacity)

      iii. Procedures (inadequate, improper procedures)

      iv. Information technology (information not available, incorrect)

      v. Communication (failure to communicate)

   Using the simple example of baking times for pies, if a large bakery finds that too many pies are overcooked, it should ask "why" questions that can be answered in the context of these five different potential causes of the effect (the effect being poor quality).

b. Scatter diagrams consist of a plot of two measures that may be related. These diagrams are used to diagnose cause and effect between outcomes and activities that may drive them. Scatter diagrams are useful for determining whether a suspected cause of a quality problem is really the true cause. The frequency of the suspected cause of the problem is paired with the quality attribute being evaluated. If the suspected cause is truly the reason for a quality problem, the scatter diagram will show a pattern that looks like an upward or downward line. If the suspected cause is not the true reason for a quality problem, the scatter diagram will not reflect any discernible pattern.

   One problem with using a scatter diagram is that it requires that the organization have reliable data on both the quality measures and the suspected causes.

c. A flowchart can sometimes be used to show the cause-and-effect linkages among process activities. This can help to pinpoint where quality problems arise. Flowcharting the ideal process, and then flowcharting the actual process may also pinpoint where the quality problems emerge in the process.

d. A Pareto chart (named after an Italian economist) prioritizes the causes of problems or defects as bars of varying heights, in order of frequency or size. Pareto charts help analysis teams to focus on the causes that may offer the greatest potential for improvement.

4. Customer satisfaction is the degree to which expectations of attributes, customer service, and price have been or are expected to be met. In addition to measuring lead indicators of tangible and intangible product and service features, as described above, organizations should also try to measure customer satisfaction. Measures of customer satisfaction may be used as both lead indicators of future sales and as diagnostic tools to discover causes of unexpectedly low or high sales.

   The most common method of measuring customer satisfaction is customer surveys. Focus groups may also be used. Some organizations use phantom shoppers, who are actually employees sent out as customers, to see how regular customers are treated.

G. Customers seeking high quality products understand that they must pay a higher price for higher quality. Customers may be willing to pay a higher price for a product or service if it clearly has higher quality than comparable products offered at the same price. Managers of organizations also understand the need to offer high quality products, but realize that increased quality comes at a cost. Managers must, therefore, balance the desire for high quality against the cost of that quality. This results in a quality/price tradeoff. An important part of keeping the balance at the correct level is based on the ability to identify the costs of quality.

1. Cost of quality (COQ) is the cost of activities to control quality. It is also the cost of activities to correct failure to control quality. Costs of controlling quality are associated with lead indicators of imminent quality problems. Costs of correcting failures may be lead indicators of future decreased sales.

   Organizations usually prefer to devote most of their costs of quality on activities intended to control quality rather than correcting quality failures.

2. Controlling quality requires that two activities take place. One is prevention. The other is appraisal, or detection.

   a. Prevention activities seek to prevent defects in products or services being produced. Prevention activities may include certifying suppliers, designing products to be manufactured defect-free, quality training, quality evaluations, and process improvement. TQM advocates argue that prevention activities are the most efficient use of resource use in the area of quality. ROQ advocates argue that preventing defects is effective, but suggest that preventing **all** defects may be prohibitively expensive. The ROQ philosophy does not prevent all quality problems before they occur. It attempts to detect them in ways that TQM advocates view as non-value-added activities. ROQ advocates also recognize that costs of quality beyond prevention costs are non-value-added costs. However, their view is that prevention costs may be too high to justify, and they opt instead to incur non-value-added costs.

   b. Appraisal activities, also called detection or inspection activities, require that inputs be inspected or that outputs (units of product) be inspected in order to detect whether they conform to specifications or customer expectations. Appraisal activities include inspecting materials, inspecting machines, inspecting processes, automated inspection, statistical process control, testing at the end of a process, and field testing (at a customer site).

3. Failing to control quality leads to two types of failure. One type is internal failure, while the other type is external failure.

   a. Internal failure activities are required to correct defective processes or products and services, which are detected before being delivered to customers. Internal failure activities include disposing of scrap caused by defective products, rework to correct defects, re-inspecting or re-testing, and delays in processes. Internal failure can be very expensive. It is obviously a non-value-added activity, particularly when bottlenecks are affected (worsened) by defects.

b. External failure activities are required when defective products or services are detected after customers have received them. These activities include warranty repairs, settling product liability claims, resolving customer complaints, restoring reputations, and lost sales. External failure activities are the most costly of all failure costs because they may permanently damage the reputation of an organization. This type of failure affects future sales, but this effect is difficult to quantify.

4. Organizations must effectively measure costs of quality in order to manage them. Organizations using ABC and ABM have the activity-based information needed to compile cost of quality information. With ABC information, cost managers can take the additional step of classifying activities based on cost of quality category.

   Those organizations without ABC in place may find it expensive or time-consuming to develop the kinds of cost information to properly identify costs of quality.

5. Reporting costs of quality may occur in a variety of forms. A cost of quality report always, however, will split the costs into the four categories—prevention, appraisal, internal failure, and external failure. Typically, the reports then provide more detail on the actual type of activity (inspection of materials, rework of defective product), the cost of the activity, and the cost as a percentage of sales. Reporting costs of quality as a percentage of sales places emphasis on the fact that profits are consumed by costs of quality just like any other type of cost consumes profits.

   Organizations may set benchmarks for costs of quality, for instance setting a ceiling on COQ of 5% of sales revenue.

H. Quality has become so important to success that there are now international awards given to companies for the quality of their product, services, or processes. The Malcolm Baldrige award, created by the US Congress in 1987, recognizes US firms with outstanding records of quality improvement and quality management. The Deming Prize is a Japanese award for companies around the world that excel in quality improvement.

   The International Organization for Standardization is a European organization best known for its development of international standards for quality management called ISO 9000. ISO 9000 is a set of global guidelines for the design, development, production, final inspection and testing, installation, and servicing of products, processes and services. To be certified, a company must document its quality systems and pass a rigorous third-party audit of its manufacturing and customer service processes.

I. When activity-based costing (ABC) systems are used, it becomes important to incorporate time management into the ABC system. When time-based ABC is used, the basic cost-driver rate is Total cost of supplying capacity to complete activities/Total time available to complete activities. This measure places emphasis on the need to reduce time needed for an activity, which in turn reduces costs.

J. In addition to having to address the need to manage quality and control costs of quality, cost managers must be conscious of the need to manage time. There are three specific areas of concern with respect to time. They are new product and service development time, customer response time, and production cycle time.

1. New product and service development time is the period between the first consideration of a product and its initial sale to the customer. Businesses that respond quickly to demand for new products and services may develop a competitive advantage over competitors. The shorter the product development time is, the more likely it is that an organization will be the first to offer the new product.
2. Customer response time is another important time dimension that organizations need to properly manage. Customer response time is the amount of time between a customer's placing an order or requesting service and the delivery of the product or service to the customer. The shorter the response time, the more competitive the company is on this dimension. Organizations work to reduce customer response time by automating ordering activities, scheduling bottleneck resources carefully, and by keeping reserve capacity for unexpected but valuable orders. When necessary, companies may use expedited services. If orders are placed before products are produced, the customer response time may be reduced by eliminating non-value-added activities in production processes. This reduces the cycle time.
3. Production cycle time is the time between starting and finishing a production process, including any time needed to correct mistakes. Identifying and eliminating non-value-added activities can shorten cycle time.

4. Since timeliness is so important in a competitive environment, organizations have come to recognize that longer process times mean more than higher production costs. They may also cause lost sales or opportunities. To motivate efficiency in cycle times, some organizations reward employees based on their ability to meet or exceed targeted cycle times.

K. Another key component in successfully managing quality and time is measurement of process efficiency. Process efficiency is the ability to transform inputs into outputs at lowest cost. There are two types of processes to consider.

1. **Production processes** result in the production of products or services. **Business processes** support production processes. These support activities are essential to the smooth running and operation of any organization. Measures of the efficiency of both production and business processes are lead indicators of financial performance. Three measures of efficiency are discussed below.

2. One measure of efficiency is measure of productivity.

    a. The simplest measure of productivity is total factor productivity. It is calculated as Total Revenue/Total Cost. Factor productivity can be benchmarked against competitors. The higher the total factor productivity is, the more efficient an operation is.

    b. Other measures of productivity include sales revenue per employee, trends over time and cost savings from new processes.

3. A second measure of efficiency is average cycle time. Average cycle time is the total processing time/number of good units produced. This represents the time from a unit of product being ordered to the time the unit is shipped to the customer. Ideally, the shorter the average cycle time, the better.

4. A third measure of efficiency is called throughput efficiency. It is measured using the throughput time ratio, which is value-added time/total processing time. The lower the ratio is, the more inefficient the process is. This ratio gives managers information about non-value-added activities, which should be eliminated or minimized.

L. Managing process capacity is another key to successful production management. There are three different measures of capacity one might encounter.

1. Theoretical capacity is the maximum possible amount of capacity. For instance, the maximum theoretical capacity of an employee who works 8-hour days is 480 minutes per day (60 minutes times 8 hours). Although theoretically an employee can work every minute of his or her workday, it is not likely to happen. Similarly, a machine can theoretically operate for 24 hours per day, but is not likely to be operated non-stop no matter how well the machine was constructed.

2. Practical capacity is a more realistic measure of capacity. Practical capacity takes into consideration the time needed for breaks, training, and other interruptions in an employee's workday. A machine needs to have downtime for maintenance, repairs and improvements.

3. Excess capacity is the difference between practical capacity and capacity demanded. If capacity demand is greater than practical capacity then a bottleneck exists.

M. The successful use of time and quality management processes, as well as managing productivity and capacity effectively leads to a JIT process. Just-in-Time (JIT) is a process that requires that products be made and delivered just when they are needed. Organizations that use JIT expect to reduce or eliminate inventory carrying costs, which are costs of receiving, handling, storing, and insuring inventory. Obsolescence of inventory is another cost of having inventory on hand.

Since JIT precludes stocking inventory in anticipation of sales, and materials are not ordered and stockpiled, a JIT operation requires high-quality processes. Defective products are incompatible with JIT since there is no product on hand in reserve just in case defective products are made, and have to be replaced for pending customer orders. Defects in a JIT organization trigger an investigation of processes to eliminate their causes.

1. JIT manufacturing makes it necessary to minimize inventory, shorten cycle times, and eliminate defects. To a customer, inventory on hand represents a non-value-added cost. Costs of rework, or other cost-causing, non-value-added activities are also undesirable in the eyes of the customer. JIT manufacturing is a radical departure from traditional manufacturing. Both approaches are described below.

   a. Traditional manufacturing is referred to as "push" manufacturing because production is "pushed" through the production and sales processes based on forecasted sales orders. The sequence of events for a traditional manufacturing shop would be to forecast sales in advance of production; order all parts and other necessary inputs; prepare a production schedule in anticipation of production needs, and finally, when a customer order is received, sell it from finished goods inventory, or place the order on backorder to be filled as soon as the production schedule allows it.

      i. This traditional manufacturing approach has some drawbacks. First, it is driven by sales forecasts, which may be inaccurate. If the forecast is too optimistic, the company will overproduce, which results in unsold inventories and could result in obsolete product. If sales are higher than anticipated, there will not be enough product, resulting in the need to backorder sales, which increases the customer response time. Sales could be lost if customers can buy products from competitors. An alternative to backordering is to expedite production, which usually leads to overtime costs for employees and increases the costs of obtaining resources because their delivery must be rushed (at higher cost). A second drawback to traditional manufacturing is that it does not allow the organization to arrange production activities around the bottleneck production activities. This can result in a wasteful and costly buildup of incomplete inventories.

   b. JIT manufacturing is referred to as "pull" manufacturing. JIT production is pulled through the production and sales process by actual customer orders instead of forecasted orders. The sequence of events for a JIT manufacturer is as follows. First, a customer places an order. The sales order triggers a production order. Then, the production order triggers the acquisition of materials and other resources needed to fill the order. Finally, the customer receives the product on the promised delivery date.

      i. JIT has some drawbacks too. The main drawback is that any defect or obstacle in the production process may cause the entire production process to shut down, and there is no inventory in reserve to replace the item being manufactured "just in case" something goes wrong. JIT manufacturers try to avoid this problem by being certain that the production process does not have any flaws in it. Some companies that are JIT maintain minimal levels of inventory on hand just in case something goes wrong.

c. Cost managers can play a key role by measuring the costs of excess inventories and costs of quality that are encouraged by traditional push production methods. Revealing the cost inefficiencies caused by traditional manufacturing may induce companies to consider adopting a JIT approach.

2. There are several advantages offered by the use of JIT manufacturing. Six success factors are linked in such a way that failure to include any one threatens the likelihood of the success of JIT at an organization.

   a. JIT mandates that the organization maintain a strong commitment to quality. Defects cause delays, and require buffer inventories. If defects occur, the sooner an employee can detect and correct the problem, the less time is lost.

   b. Capacity must be flexible, and setup times must be short. As much as possible, JIT manufacturers of mass-produced products should seek long-term purchase agreements.

   c. Suppliers must be reliable. In order for JIT manufacturers to complete production on time, they must be sure that suppliers can provide needed inputs on time. JIT manufacturers typically require that suppliers meet a stringent set of tests, and the number of suppliers may be reduced so that the quality and scheduling of inputs can be better managed.

   d. Production flow must be smooth. Unbalanced production leads to delays at bottlenecks, and makes it necessary to have buffer inventories.

   e. A well-trained, motivated, flexible workforce is critical. Workers need to be cross-trained so that they can work on production areas as needed.

   f. Cycle and customer response times must be minimized.

3. Even if JIT is not adopted, organizations can benefit from adopting some of these success factors because they make any production environment more efficient.

Chapter 7

REVIEW AND SELF TEST QUESTIONS AND EXERCISES

Matching key terms

Match the following terms to the correct definition by writing the correct letter next to the corresponding definition.

a. histogram	b. ISO 9000	c. total quality management
d. Pareto chart	e. internal failure	f. total factor productivity
g. practical capacity	h. run chart	i. return on quality
j. flowchart		

______1. A defective product is detected before it reaches customers

______2. A chart that shows the frequency distribution of an attribute's measures, compared against some benchmark.

______3. A diagram that shows cause-and-effect as well as sequential links among process activities.

______4. A management philosophy that weighs the costs of improved quality against the benefits gained by that improved quality.

______5. International standards for quality management.

______6. The total quantity of output possible for a process after taking into consideration downtime and idle time.

______7. A management philosophy that argues that any quality improvement will improve overall organizational performance.

______8. A way to show variation in product or service attributes; a way to identify persistent trends.

______9. The value of goods and services (total sales revenue) divided by total cost to provide them.

______10. A chart that shows problems or defects, prioritized by frequency of occurrence or magnitude.

True or False

For each of the following statements enter a T or an F in the blank to indicate whether the statement is true or false.

_____11. Business efficiency is the same as process efficiency.

_____12. Most organizations have external customers but do **not** have internal customers.

_____13. Cycle time covers the time from customers placing orders to product being received by customers.

_____14. Throughput efficiency measures how quickly product is delivered to customers.

_____15. Total quality management (TQM) advocates argue that there should be no limit on costs incurred to improve quality.

_____16. The return on quality view says that a business should expect to meet every aspect of customers' expectations with respect to a product.

_____17. On-time delivery is considered to be a part of customer service.

_____18. The less variability there is in a production process, the more likely it is that poor quality will result.

_____19. A control chart shows variation in product or service attributes over time, and also allows comparison between actual outcomes and maximum and minimum levels of acceptance.

_____20. If a scatter diagram shows an upward or downward pattern, there is probably a relation between some cause and some effect.

_____21. One type of quality cost is prevention cost. This is the cost to prevent customers from filing product liability suits against an organization.

_____22. Internal failure is an undesirable cost of poor quality. Internal failure happens once the customer obtains a poor quality product.

_____23. If customers buy poor quality merchandise, then one of the costs of (poor) quality is lost future sales.

_____24. The main reason new product development time is important to managers is they want to be sure that plenty of time is taken to make the product just right.

_____25. Just-in-time manufacturing requires little or no buildup of inventory.

Multiple Choice

Choose the best answer by writing the letter corresponding to your choice in the space provided.

_____26. Process efficiency is

a) the ability to transform inputs into outputs in the shortest feasible time.
b) the ability to transform inputs into outputs at the lowest feasible cost.
c) the ability to transform inputs into outputs with the smallest feasible number of workers.
d) the ability to transform inputs into outputs with the smallest feasible number of parts.

_____27. Business processes are best described as

a) any activity that results in products being made or services being provided to customers.
b) any activity that improves operations.
c) any activity that supports production processes.
d) any activity that generates profits for a business.

_____28. Which of the following is correct?

a) Business processes support production processes, and production processes support business processes.
b) Business processes support production processes, but production processes do **not** support business processes.
c) Business processes do **not** support production processes, but production processes support business processes.
d) Business processes do **not** support production processes, and production processes do **not** support business processes.

_____29. An internal customer is someone who is

a) a repeat customer.
b) a customer who comes into a store or warehouse to buy product.
c) an employee who receives partially completed product.
d) a production worker who gets paid based on the authorization of management of the corporation.

_____30. Average cycle time is calculated as

a) total units/total processing time.
b) total processing time/total good units produced.
c) total processing time/total units produced.
d) total good units produced/total processing time.

_____31. Osage Computer Manufacturers requires 37.5 hours' total processing time to produce 100 good keyboards, resulting in average cycle time of .375 hour per good unit. Unfortunately, in order to produce 100 good keyboards the company also produces 50 keyboards that are defective, and require rework. If the number of defects could be reduced by 50%, then what would the new average cycle time be?

a) 1.50 per good keyboard
b) .375 per good keyboard
c) .30 per good keyboard
d) .25 per good keyboard

_____32. Osage Computer Manufacturers has determined that it takes 7.5 hours of value-added time to make a particular model of PC. Total processing time is 18.75 hours per computer. The throughput time ratio for this computer is

a) 562.50%
b) 52.50%
c) 2.50%
d) 40%

_____33. Which of the following statements about TQM is **not** true?

a) TQM is a concept attributed to Malcolm Baldrige.
b) TQM is a concept that embraces the belief that improving quality pays for itself by creating profit.
c) Adopting TQM is not a guarantee that a company will become more profitable than it was before.
d) TQM advocates argue that perfect product quality can never be attained.

_____34. Which of the following is **not** a valid reason to place more emphasis on quality issues?

a) In service organizations, customer satisfaction drives repeat business.
b) Organizations need to charge higher prices to cover non-value-added costs.
c) Some organizations are in highly competitive global markets.
d) Organizations want to be the market leader in their industry.

_____35. When trying to decide how much to spend on quality-related issues, a TQM advocate would

a) use most cost of quality resources on appraisal activities.
b) use most cost of quality resources on correcting internal failure problems.
c) use most cost of quality resources on correcting external failure problems.
d) use most cost of quality resources on prevention activities.

_____36. A cause-and-effect diagram can do all of the following **except**

a) identify a particular product defect.
b) identify possible human error that causes a particular defect.
c) categorize probable causes of a particular defect into one of five categories.
d) give managers information that may be useful in reducing or eliminating a particular defect.

_____37. What should a Pareto chart be used for?

a) To show the linkages among process activities so that the point at which a defect occurs in the production process can be identified.
b) To plot a suspected cause of a problem with a quality problem so that it can be determined whether the suspected cause is the true cause of the defect.
c) To show the frequency of causes of defects, so that the cause with the highest frequency can be easily identified.
d) To show variation in product or service attributes over time so that the amount of variability can be assessed.

_____38. The cost of quality is a measure of all of the following **except**

a) the costs to prevent defects.
b) the costs to inspect products.
c) the costs to repair defective product.
d) the costs of disposing of normal scrap.

_____39. Which of the following is an example of an internal failure?

a) Costs of settling a customer product liability suit.
b) Costs of inspecting a product just before it is shipped.
c) Costs of replacing components broken during production.
d) Costs of certifying suppliers.

_____40. Which of the following external failure activities is the most difficult to quantify?

a) The amount of profit lost on future sales.
b) Costs of customer service in the complaints department.
c) The amount of profit lost on current sales.
d) The cost to replace defective products.

_____41. A cost of quality report will provide information about all of the following **except**

a) the total cost of quality.
b) ways to correct problems with defects.
c) the costs of prevention.
d) how much of revenue is consumed by quality costs.

_____42. Time management is a concern for cost managers, particularly for which of the following areas?

a) New product and service development time.
b) Time it takes to replace defective equipment.
c) Time it takes to inspect completed product.
d) Time it takes to identify production problems.

_____43. Customer response time is defined as

a) the time between a customer's returning defective product and the product being replaced.
b) the time between a customer's placing an order and the delivery of the product to the customer.
c) the time between a customer's placing an order and the time taken to produce the product.
d) the time between the customer's filing of a product liability claim and the point at which the claim is settled.

_____44. Which of the following statements is **not** true regarding Just-in-time manufacturing?

a) JIT manufacturing makes it unnecessary to build up large amounts of inventory.
b) JIT is based on producing only to fill orders already placed by customers.
c) JIT production activities rely heavily on sales forecasts.
d) JIT manufacturing requires that defects be minimized or eliminated altogether.

_____45. To the customer of a JIT manufacturer, the presence of inventory represents

a) the capacity of the organization to acquire resources.
b) the financial stability of the organization.
c) the ability to provide product on demand.
d) a non-value-added cost.

Exercises

Use the following information about Wood Goods, Inc. to answer the next 5 questions.

Wood Goods, Inc. is a rapidly growing furniture manufacturer, specializing in high-quality kitchen and dining room furniture. Recently, the management at Wood Goods decided that it would be to their competitive advantage to convert their manufacturing activities to a JIT shop. This management decision was hastened by a warehouse fire that destroyed over $2 million in inventory two years ago. The insurance company only paid $.60 on the dollar for the estimated value of the inventory because the company's information system did not adequately measure the true value of the furniture that was destroyed.

The plant accountant has compiled some preliminary information for use in evaluating the cost savings and additional costs that will occur because of the change to JIT.

- Average inventory can be reduced from $2.5 million to $180,000 as a result of JIT manufacturing. The company will continue to keep minimal inventory.
- Carrying costs from having inventory have been consistently around 14% of the average inventory balance. Of this percentage, $150,000 is for salaries and other committed costs. The remaining portion is variable cost that is directly proportional to average inventory values. $100,000 of the committed cost is for salaries of three employees, who will be reassigned to other open positions in the company. $50,000 of the committed cost is for expenses of having the warehouse that burned down. This cost will become variable because the company will warehouse its inventory in the warehouse of another business for a fee, based on the value of inventory. The rest of the carrying costs totaled $200,000 for $2.5 million in inventory. This part of the inventory cost is truly variable with the average inventory value.
- The company has decided to outsource its warehouse activities, and will pay a fee of 10% of inventory value to the warehouse company. The fee covers all carrying costs previously paid by Wood Goods.
- The costs of quality will change because the company will shift its emphasis away from failure costs to prevention and appraisal costs. Prevention costs will increase annually by $100,000. Appraisal costs will increase by $60,000 per year. Internal failure costs will decline by an estimated $180,000, while external failure costs will decrease about $210,000.

46. What is the true percentage of variable inventory-related cost that will be eliminated by implementing JIT and reducing inventory? What is the new amount of inventory-related cost that will be incurred?

47. What is the total amount of cost savings that will result from reducing inventory and their associated costs? Assume the new inventory balance of $180,000 is the expected average balance under JIT.

48. Ignoring the information related to inventory, what is the total change in the costs of quality under JIT?

49. Name the six factors that Wood Goods, Inc. must have in place in order for JIT to work.

50. Name at least three qualitative factors that might justify the company's shift to JIT?

Chapter 7

Answers to Questions and Exercises

Matching key terms

1. e 2. a 3. j 4. i 5. b 6. g 7. c 8. h 9. f 10. d

True or False

11. F. Process efficiency is related to production activities, or activities related to providing services to customers; business efficiency relates to support activities
12. F. The majority of organizations have both internal and external customers.
13. T. Cycle time is the time that elapses from the customer order being placed to the time at which product is shipped to customers.
14. F. Throughput efficiency measures how much total production time adds value to a product.
15. T. TQM advocates believe that improving quality pays for itself, and that improvements to quality never end.
16. F. ROQ advocates recognize the tradeoffs between quality improvements and profits. When the benefits of improving quality are exceeded by the costs of improving quality, quality improvements should stop.
17. T. Customer service begins before the sale, and continues after the sale. On-time delivery is part of good quality customer service.
18. F. The more variability there is in a production process, the more likely it is that poor quality will result.
19. T. By showing the maximum and minimum tolerance levels for some process, the manager can see whether the process is in control or out of control.
20. T. If plotting a problem and its suspected cause, a pattern indicates that the cause and effect are related to each other.
21. F. Prevention costs are expenditures made to ensure that quality meets or exceeds standards. If prevention activities work, there will be no product liability suits.
22. F. Internal failure occurs before the product is sold to customers.
23. T. Lost future sales is the hardest external failure cost to quantify, because the number of repeat and referred sales lost due to poor quality can only be estimated.
24. F. New product development time is important to manage so that an organization can be first to introduce a new product. The first entrant in a new market has the competitive advantage.
25. T. JIT manufacturing mandates little or no inventory.

Multiple Choice

26. a. Although answers b, c, and d are desirable attributes to have in the production process, they are not measures of process efficiency.
27. c. Answer a describes the production process. A business process is activity that helps organizations to accomplish the production processes smoothly.
28. b. The second half of answer a is incorrect; all of answer c is incorrect; and the first half of answer d is incorrect.
29. c. An internal customer is not the final consumer of a product or service. Internal customers receive the product before it is complete, and perform some process or activity to move it closer to completion.

30. b. Inclusion of the word "good" is important. It places emphasis on the fact that production of "bad" units makes cycle time higher, and customers only want "good" product.
31. c. If defects are reduced by 50% then 100 + 25, or 125 good units would be produced. The new average cycle time would be 37.50/125 = .30.
32. d. The throughput ratio is calculated by dividing value-added time by total processing time. This is 7.5 hours/18.75 total hours = .40, or 40%.
33. a. TQM is attributed to W. Edwards Deming.
34. b. Costs of completing non-value-added activities should be eliminated—not recovered through higher prices.
35. d. TQM advocates believe that appraisal, internal failure and external failure costs are non-value-added.
36. a. In order to prepare a cause-and-effect diagram, the defect must already have been identified.
37. c. Answer a describes a flowchart. Answer b describes a scatter diagram. Answer d describes a run chart.
38. d. The occurrence of normal scrap is a natural part of the production process. However, scrap from production of defects is an internal failure cost.
39. c. Detection of a defect during production is considered to be internal failure. Answer a is an example of external failure cost. Answer b is an example of appraisal cost. Answer d is an example of prevention cost.
40. a. When customers are unhappy about the quality of products they buy, it is difficult to track their response to poor quality unless they complain. Those customers who do not complain may, in many instances, simply never buy any more products from the company. It is these lost sales that are hard to quantify. In addition, reputation effects may result in loss of additional sales once other potential customers become aware of quality problems.
41. b. A cost of quality report provides information about costs and types of quality costs, but does not provide ways to correct quality problems.
42. a. New development time is critical to managers. It should be minimized so that an organization is the first to introduce a new product or innovation. The first entrant to a market gains a competitive advantage.
43. b. Customer response time is a quality attribute, because a customer would rather have product sooner rather than later. Answer b is the correct definition of customer response time.
44. c. Traditional manufacturing firms rely on sales forecasts. JIT manufacturers only make product for actual customer orders. The other three answers are all characteristics of JIT manufacturing.
45. d. Having inventory on hand costs money. There are warehousing costs, insurance, handling, breakage, obsolescence, and other costs. The less inventory there is on hand, the lower inventory costs will be. In a JIT setting, there is no need for inventory because product is made only when it is ordered by customers, and after its production is complete it can be delivered immediately to the customer.

Exercises

46. The truly variable portion of inventory-related costs under the old system were \$200,000/\$2,500,000 = 8%. The total costs were \$350,000, but \$150,000 of this cost was committed. The new inventory-related cost is 10% of \$180,000, or \$18,000.

47. The old costs were \$350,000. \$100,000 of this cost, for salaries, will not be eliminated. Instead, the employees will be transferred. The other \$250,000 will be eliminated. The new arrangement will cost 10% of average inventory. If inventory is \$180,000, then the new cost will be \$18,000. \$100,000 + \$18,000 = \$118,000, the new cost. This is compared to the old cost of having inventory of \$350,000.

48. Costs of quality would decrease by \$230,000. Prevention costs would increase by \$100,000. Appraisal costs would increase by \$60,000. Internal failure costs would decrease by \$180,000, and external failure costs would decrease by \$210,000. Total change is \$230,000 less cost.

49. There are six success factors that must be present to ensure the success of JIT manufacturing. They are:

    1. JIT mandates that the organization maintain a strong commitment to quality. Defects cause delays, and require buffer inventories. If defects occur, the sooner an employee can detect and correct the problem, the less time is lost.

    2. Capacity must be flexible, and setup times must be short. As much as possible, JIT manufacturers of mass-produced products should seek long-term purchase agreements.

    3. Suppliers must be reliable. In order for JIT manufacturers to complete production on time, they must be sure that suppliers can provide needed inputs on time. JIT manufacturers typically require that suppliers meet a stringent set of tests, and the number of suppliers may be reduced so that the quality and scheduling of inputs can be better managed.

    4. Production flow must be smooth. Unbalanced production leads to delays at bottlenecks, and makes it necessary to have buffer inventories.

    5. A well-trained, motivated, flexible workforce is critical. Workers need to be cross-trained so that they can work on production areas as needed.

    6. Cycle and customer response times must be minimized.

50. There are several qualitative factors that might justify a shift to JIT operations. Company reputation is an important consideration. An organization that has a reputation for on-time delivery, top-quality product, and competitive prices will earn a position at the top of its industry. Customer satisfaction is another benefit. Elimination of external failure will result in elimination of complaints and dissatisfaction with products. Shortened customer response time may be another benefit gained by operating under a more efficient production schedule afforded by JIT. Other qualitative benefits may include improved product quality, improved employee morale, better relations with customers at one end of the value chain and suppliers at the other end, and smoother operations in general.

Chapter 8
Process Costing Systems

Chapter Study Suggestions

Chapter 8 presents process costing. Process costing is a system that assigns costs equally to homogeneous units of product within a particular time period. All production costs are averaged over the number of units produced. Products for which process costing are appropriately used also have short cycle times, making it more efficient to focus on the costs of a period instead of focusing on the cost of an individual unit of output.

If all production began and ended in one accounting period (one month or one year), process costing would be a simple averaging of all costs over all units of product. Process costing is made complicated by four factors. First, production is not all completed in one accounting period. This results in partially completed units of product at the end of each month and the beginning of another month. Product costs for these partially completed units must be assigned. The second factor is that resources used to make product are used at different points, and in different quantities during production. This makes it necessary to assign costs to units of product based on what portion is complete for each different resource used. The third factor that complicates the process costing method occurs when more than one production department exists. In that case, production may be completed in one department, and then instead of being transferred to a warehouse as finished goods inventory, it is transferred to another production department, where additional production processes take place. Finally, some units of product may be spoiled, and they must be accounted for. The chapter presents discussion of these four complicating factors using the weighted average method.

Chapter Highlights

A. Cost Management Challenges. There are two questions addressed in this chapter.

1. How should a company's costing system measure costs of products, services, and operations when outputs are numerous and indistinguishable?

2. How should organizations recognize and measure the costs of spoilage and waste?

B. Learning Objectives—This chapter has 6 learning objectives.

1. The chapter explains how to decide whether a company should use process costing or job costing.

2. It explains why process-costing information is useful for decision-making.

3. The chapter presents a five-step procedure for assigning process costs to units of product.

4. The most commonly used method of process costing is described. It is the weighted-average method.

5. Chapter 8 explains how to use process costing when costs must be transferred between processes.

6. The chapter shows how to analyze and manage normal and abnormal spoilage.

C. Process costing is a method for assigning product costs to units of product when all units of product are virtually the same. Products are completed in a short time, and costs for a single period can be averaged over the number of units produced.

1. With process costing, costs are not traced to units of product. Instead, all production costs (unit-level and otherwise) are assigned, or allocated based on total production costs and total units produced.

2. Job costing and process costing differ in the way costs are assigned, and they differ because of differences in product characteristics. With job costing, many costs are traceable to jobs, or can be assigned to specific jobs using cost-driver rates. For products in a process costing environment, all costs must be assigned using a cost-driver approach. The key difference is that the only cost-driver is the actual number of units produced.

D. A very basic model of process costing assumes there are only two cost categories—materials and conversion costs. Materials costs (also called direct materials) are unit-level costs, but they are assigned to units of product based on the cost of materials and the actual number of units produced. Conversion costs include all other costs for resources used besides materials. These other costs may be batch, product, or facility-level costs. Resources are recorded as processes rather than activities. Simplifying assumptions in the basic process costing model presented in Chapter 8 preclude the use of ABC. The chapter presents five examples of costing when process costing is appropriate.

E. **Example 1.** The simplest case for assigning costs using a process costing approach assumes all production is started and completed within a single accounting period. This simplifying assumption makes it easier to see how materials and conversion costs are used and applied to units of product. If all units of product are completed in one month, there is no work-in-process inventory. It is the presence of WIP inventory that makes process costing complex.

1. There are only two cost categories to consider in a simple process costing model. They are direct material and conversion costs. Each of these resources is assigned to units of product separately. That is because, except in the simplest case, these two resources are added and used in production in differing amounts and points in time.

2. There is only one cost-driver. The cost-driver in process costing is the actual number of units produced. Calculation of a rate for direct materials is calculated as total direct materials cost divided by total number of (equivalent) units = direct materials cost per unit of product. The rate for conversion costs is total conversion cost divided by total (equivalent) units = conversion cost per unit of product. The process costing system described is an actual costing system which measures actual resources used.

3. Calculation of the cost per unit for conversion costs includes higher-level resources. For decision-making purposes, the cost per unit information can be misleading. Managers should separate higher-level costs from unit-level costs when making cost decisions, or when trying to assess profitability.

F. **Example 2.** A slightly more complex case for process costing occurs when there is production that is not completed at the end of an accounting period. In other words, there is no beginning work-in-process inventory, but there is ending WIP inventory. This case better illustrates the need to segregate the costs and activities of different resources like materials and conversion activities. It is useful at this point to explain the five steps used to assign costs to units of product.

1. First, summarize the flow of physical units. What is the total number of units being made when all production is complete?

   a. The basic cost flow model can be used to depict the flow of physical units through WIP inventory. Beginning WIP + units transferred in (or units started)—units transferred out (or completed) = ending WIP.

   b. In the simplest case, beginning WIP and ending WIP are zero. Then, the number of units transferred in (started) equals the number of units transferred out (completed). That was the case in Example 1, above.

c. In the case where there is no beginning WIP but there is ending WIP, the number of units transferred in (started) does not equal the number of units transferred out (completed). Transferred in units are greater than units transferred out because some units are not completed at the end of an accounting period.

d. This first step expresses the number of units to account for, and then accounts for them. It shows where units of product came from (beginning WIP and units started), and where they went (transferred out and ending WIP).

2. The second step requires that the number of equivalent units (EUs) be computed. Equivalent units equal the number of whole units that could have been completed given the amount of resources actually used. For instance, if 5,000 toys had 90% of the direct materials needed for the toys to be complete, this would be the equivalent of having 5,000×90%, or 4,500 toys being fully completed. Suppose 2,000 physical units were started and 1,500 were fully complete as far as conversion activity goes, and the remaining 500 were 60% complete as far as conversion activity goes. This is the equivalent of 1,500 + (60%×500) = 1,500 + 300 = 1,800 equivalent units.

   a. The number of equivalent units must be computed separately for each different resource. In the simplest case there are just two resources—direct materials and conversion costs.

   b. The equivalent units calculations could be expanded to include as many different categories as the accounting system needed to improve information, but the calculations for each resource would be accomplished the same way.

3. The third step requires that costs to account for be identified, and classified as direct materials cost or conversion cost. This information comes from the beginning WIP balance and costs transferred in for the period. In the case where there is no beginning WIP, just the costs transferred in are the costs to account for. This cost information can be obtained from the accounting system.

4. Step 4 requires that cost per equivalent unit be calculated. It is simply the cost obtained in step 3 divided by the number of equivalent units calculated in step 2. Separate costs per equivalent unit must be calculated for direct materials costs and for conversion costs.

   a. The total cost per equivalent unit is the sum of direct materials cost per equivalent unit plus conversion cost per equivalent unit. This represents the cost of producing one whole unit.

   b. Managers should compare monthly calculations over time, to see whether costs are stable. Costs per equivalent unit should not fluctuate erratically from month to month, because the corresponding price cannot usually fluctuate the same way. This would result in erratic profits.

5. The last step shows the assignment of costs to the ending WIP inventory balances and to units transferred out (to FGI, or the next production department).

   a. This step shows how costs to account for in step 3 are accounted for.

   b. The number of equivalent units transferred out times the cost per EU = total dollar amount transferred out. Since the number of equivalent units transferred out is the same for both materials and conversion costs, it is not necessary to calculate costs transferred out separately for materials and conversion costs. This is true when the weighted average method is used, but is not true when the FIFO method (discussed in the Chapter Appendix) is used. The number of equivalent units in ending WIP times the cost per EU = total dollar value of ending WIP. For ending WIP, calculations must be made separately for materials and conversion costs because the number of equivalent units will probably not be the same for these two resources.

6. Steps 1 and 2 divide the cost flow model into two pieces for quantities. Beginning WIP and units transferred in (started) are used in step 1 to identify the number of physical units. These amounts show where the units came from. Units transferred out and units remaining in ending WIP are converted to equivalent units, and in step 2 these units are identified as either completed and transferred out or as incomplete units in ending WIP.

7. Steps 3 and 5 divide the cost flow model into two pieces also, but instead of quantities identified in steps 1 and 2, steps 3 and 5 divide costs into two pieces. Step 3 uses the beginning WIP balance and costs transferred in, indicating the costs to account for. Step 5 uses costs transferred out and ending WIP, indicating how the costs were accounted for. The basic cost flow model, Beginning WIP + units transferred in (or units started)–units transferred out (or completed) = ending WIP can be restated as Beginning WIP + units transferred in (or units started) = Units transferred out (or completed) + ending WIP. This restatement is what is accomplished in steps 3 and 5.

G. **Example 3.** The next layer of complexity in process costing arises when there are units from the prior period included in the assignment of production costs. There are two methods that can be used in process costing. These methods are the weighted average (WA) method, and the first-in, first-out (FIFO) method. The only difference between these two methods is the way in which beginning WIP units and costs are treated. The FIFO method is presented in the appendix, and is not discussed further here.

1. The weighted average method treats the units in beginning WIP as if they are part of the current month's production activity. The amount of work completed on these units in prior months is assumed to be zero. The costs in beginning WIP are added to the current month's costs, and this total cost is used to compute cost per EU. Steps 1 through 5 of the five-step costing approach are reviewed based on the WA method.

   a. Step 1 is exactly the same as before, except now there are some physical units that came from beginning WIP

b. Step 2 is different. The beginning WIP units are treated as units that were started and completed in the current period. The calculation of equivalent units is based on the assumption that 100% of the work for the beginning WIP units was completed in the current month. Thus, for units completed and transferred out, the number of EUs is 100% of the physical number of units transferred out. Calculation of EUs for ending WIP is the same as described before.

c. Step 3 is the same as before, except that now there is a dollar amount for beginning WIP.

d. Step 4 is the same as before also, except that the number of equivalent units now includes some from beginning inventory. The calculation is the same though.

e. Step 5 is also the same. Costs assigned go to units completed and transferred out, and units in ending WIP.

e. A disadvantage of the WA method is that it combines current period costs with prior period costs. This makes it difficult to isolate fluctuations in current period costs.

H. **Example 4.** Many companies that use process costing have more than one production process. Instead of completing production and transferring finished goods to finished-goods inventory, some portion of production may be completed, and then partially completed goods are passed on to the next production department. In this case, there are three types of costs to be assigned to units of product in a subsequent production department. These costs are direct materials and conversion cost, as well as transferred-in costs. All units transferred in are 100% complete in terms of the prior department's process costs, so cost computations are simple since the number of EUs equals the number of physical units for this resource called transferred-in costs.

I. **Example 5.** The fifth example of process costing and cost assignment adds another layer of complexity to the process costing approach by including spoilage. Spoilage is the cost of wasted resources and defective products that cannot be recovered by rework or recycling

1. Spoilage is a normal part of production costs. One way to handle spoilage costs is to view them as a normal part of production. Spoilage, if material in amount, should be identified and reported, at least internally, so that managers can assess spoilage and waste as a cost to be managed and minimized. Calculations for spoiled units are made the same way as for good units, using the five-step approach described earlier. However, the number of physical units must be split between good units and spoiled units. Equivalent units are also split so that costs can be assigned to the spoiled units. The percentage of completion for spoiled units depends on when the spoilage is detected, and what portion of the work has been completed for those units.

a. Step 1 of the five-step process is the same as described before—determine the total number of physical units.

b. Step 2 is different. Now, units must be split three ways instead of two. Before, units were split between those that were completed and transferred out and those remaining in ending WIP. With spoiled units included, there is a third group of units—those that are spoiled. The number of equivalent units for each of these three groups must be calculated separately.

c. Step 3 is the same as before—it consists of determining what costs are to be accounted for.

d. Step 4 is the same, except now the number of equivalent units will be calculated and shown for spoiled units, and therefore the cost per EU will be different.

e. Step 5 is different. Now, costs must be assigned to units completed and transferred out, ending WIP inventory, and spoiled units.

2. Spoilage costs can be reported as a period cost, and expensed right away (as part of cost of goods sold), or they can be treated as part of production costs, and flow through the inventory system until product is sold.

a. Normal spoilage is waste that is considered to be part of the production process. It is generally counted as a normal cost of good units produced.

b. Abnormal spoilage is waste in excess of normal spoilage. Abnormal spoilage is usually treated as a period cost, regardless of how normal spoilage is treated.

c. Spoilage is usually not listed as a separate expense on financial statements. Regardless of how spoilage is reported on financial statements though, the amount and associated cost of spoilage is important information for managers to have.

REVIEW AND SELF TEST QUESTIONS AND EXERCISES

Matching key terms

Match the following terms to the correct definition by writing the correct letter next to the correct definition.

a. weighted-average method
b. process costing
c. normal spoilage
d. production cost report
e. equivalent units
f. abnormal spoilage
g. physical units
h. transferred-in costs
i. FIFO method
j. conversion costs

_____ 1. Costs of production that came from earlier production activities.

_____ 2. Costs of resources used to convert raw materials into finished products.

_____ 3. A costing method used when all units of product are the same.

_____ 4. The actual quantity of units resulting from production activity.

_____ 5. A way to calculate equivalent units, based on the assumption that all units in beginning inventory were started and completed in the current period.

_____ 6. That portion of production output that cannot be sold.

_____ 7. A way to calculate equivalent units that assumes beginning inventory units are completed first.

_____ 8. The estimated number of whole units that could have been completed based on the resources used so far.

_____ 9. A report showing the status of production activity.

_____10. Damaged units of product that are beyond the norm.

Chapter 8

True or False

For each of the following statements enter a T or an F in the blank to indicate whether the statement is true or false.

______11. Process costing is most useful when all units of product are alike.

______12. Process costing uses many different cost-drivers.

______13. Calculation of equivalent units of production provides a measure of how many fully completed units could have been produced with the resources used.

______14. If all production is started and finished in one month, the cost per equivalent unit is total cost divided by total number of units.

______15. Equivalent units cannot be calculated separately for direct materials and conversion costs.

______16. All production costs must be assigned to either beginning WIP or ending WIP.

______17. If all direct materials are added at the beginning of the production process, the number of equivalent units will equal the number of physical units.

______18. If a company never ends a month with all production being completed, there is no need to calculate equivalent units.

______19. If the number of spoiled units is material, costs should be assigned to them.

______20. Process costing and job costing are very similar costing systems.

______21. When process costing is used, it is harder to trace product costs to individual units of product than it is with job costing.

______22. With process costing, one must keep track of both production costs and the number of units of production.

______23. If there are two or more production departments, costs from the first department are never combined with costs of the next department.

______24. If there is abnormal spoilage, the associated costs should be charged to a special account.

______25. If there is normal spoilage, this will not affect the number of completed good units.

Multiple Choice

Choose the best answer by writing the letter corresponding to your choice in the space provided.

_____26. Which of the following best explains how process costing works?

a) Only materials costs are assigned to units of product.
b) Only conversion costs are allocated to units of product, while materials costs are traced directly to each unit of product.
c) Both production and period costs are averaged and assigned to units of product.
d) Materials and conversion costs are averaged and assigned to units of product.

_____27. If a company uses process costing, then it is likely that

a) all units of product are uniform (all units are alike).
b) all units of product are distinct (each unit is different).
c) products change from month to month.
d) production costs are insignificant.

_____28. When process costing is used, when is it necessary to calculate equivalent units of production?

a) When all units of product are completed in one month.
b) When there is no ending WIP and no beginning WIP.
c) Only when there are transferred-in costs.
d) When there is WIP.

_____29. For process costing, which of the following is true about cost drivers?

a) There is just one cost driver—the number of units produced.
b) There is one cost driver for conversion costs and a different one for direct materials.
c) There are at least three cost drivers (sometimes more).
d) There are as many cost drivers as there are units of product.

_____30. When comparing job costing and process costing, which of the following statements is correct?

a) Job costing uses direct cost assignment of all resource costs used in production, while process costing allocates all resource costs used in production to units of product.
b) Job costing directly assigns all traceable resource costs used in production, and allocates all indirect resource costs of production, while process costing allocates all resource costs used in production to units of product.
c) Both job costing and process costing directly assign all traceable resource costs used in production and allocate all indirect production costs to units of product.
d) Both job costing and process costing allocate all resource costs of production to units of product.

______31. A manager of a facility where process costing is used must keep track of

a) the number of units produced only (does not need to keep track of costs).
b) the number of units produced and production costs.
c) the production costs only (does not need to keep track of number of units).
d) non-production costs only (does not need to keep track of production costs).

______32. Equivalent units equal

a) the number of whole units of product that are actually completed in a month, excluding any units from beginning WIP.
b) the number of whole units of product that are completed from beginning WIP.
c) the number of whole units of product that could have been completed given the amount of resources actually used.
d) the number of units of product in beginning WIP and ending WIP.

______33. Which of the following statements is true regarding the calculation of equivalent units?

a) The number of equivalent units is usually the same for direct materials and conversion costs.
b) The number of equivalent units is usually different for direct materials and conversion costs.
c) Equivalent units are not calculated for direct materials and conversion costs. They are only calculated for non-production costs.
d) Equivalent units are calculated for direct materials and conversion costs, and then the quantities are added together.

______34. If a company using the weighted-average method has ending WIP for direct materials and conversion costs, then

a) the number of equivalent units will be greater than the number of physical units.
b) the number of physical units will be equal to the number of physical units.
c) the number of equivalent units is always greater than the number of physical units.
d) the number of equivalent units will be less than the number of physical units.

______35. 2,000 physical units are 60% complete with respect to materials. This means that

a) there are 1,200 equivalent units with respect to materials.
b) there are 800 equivalent units with respect to direct materials.
c) there are 2,000 equivalent units with respect to direct materials.
d) equivalent units cannot be determined based on the information given.

______36. For 600 physical units, 50 units were found to be spoiled after 80% of the direct materials costs were added. 90% of the direct materials cost was completed on the remaining 550 units. Actual costs for materials totaled $6,420. How much cost should be assigned to normal spoilage?

a) $0 (costs are not assigned to spoiled units)
b) $428
c) $480
d) $535

______37. There are five steps used to assign costs to units of product. Step 3 requires that costs to account for be identified. These costs consist of

a) ending WIP and beginning WIP.
b) costs transferred out and ending WIP.
c) beginning WIP and costs transferred in.
d) costs transferred in and costs transferred out.

______38. The main difference between the weighted average and FIFO methods for process costing is that

a) treatment of beginning WIP costs and units differs between the two methods.
b) treatment of ending WIP costs and units differs between the two methods.
c) costs to account for are different.
d) treatment of conversion costs is different.

______39. If there are spoiled units in a production run, which of the following is correct?

a) They must be reported in the financial statements.
b) They should be ignored.
c) They should be reported in management reports.
d) Presence of spoiled units will reduce the unit cost of good units.

______40. If a company has abnormal spoilage,

a) The number of good units will be higher than expected.
b) The number of good units will be smaller than expected.
c) The number of good units will be unchanged.
d) There will be no normal spoiled units.

______41. If the weighted average method for assigning costs is used, the beginning WIP units

a) are ignored in the calculation of equivalent units.
b) are treated as if only the prior months' work was done in the current month for calculation of equivalent units.
c) are treated as if only current month's work was done in the calculation of equivalent units.
d) are treated as if 100% of the work on them was done in the current month for calculation of equivalent units.

_____42. If an organization has more than one production department then units transferred in to a subsequent department will have

a) transferred-in costs associated with the prior production department.
b) conversion costs only (no materials costs) associated with the prior production department.
c) materials costs only (no conversion costs) associated with the prior production department.
d) no costs associated with the prior production department.

_____43. 5,000 physical units had 75% of the work for direct materials completed on 3,600 of the units. 100% of the work was completed on the remaining 1,400 units. How many equivalent units were there from this production activity with respect to direct materials? Assume these units were all started in the current month.

a) 5,150 equivalent units
b) 5,000 equivalent units
c) 4,100 equivalent units
d) 2,300 equivalent units

_____44. Which of the following production activities is **least** likely to use process costing?

a) A coal mining company
b) A pineapple producer
c) A landscaper
d) A textile mill (manufactures fabric)

_____45. When the weighted-average method is used, which of the following is correct about the costs in beginning WIP inventory?

a) Beginning inventory costs are not used to calculate cost per equivalent unit for current month's production activity.
b) Beginning inventory costs must be included in the calculation of cost per equivalent unit for current month's production activity.
c) Beginning inventory costs are added exclusively to spoiled units.
d) Beginning inventory costs are only added to ending inventory costs to arrive at the ending inventory balance.

Exercises

Use the following information about Bottle-Up, Inc. to answer the next 5 questions.

Bottle-Up, Inc. is an independent sports drink manufacturer. The company uses process costing to apply production costs to its WIP and FGI inventory accounts. The company only accounts for direct materials as a direct cost category. All other costs are treated as indirect costs, using a conversion costs account for all other manufacturing costs (i.e., labor and overhead costs are combined). A "unit" of product is 20,000 2-liter bottles of soft drink.[1] The plant accountant has compiled the following information for the month of February 2005:

Physical Units for February, 2005:	
WIP, beginning inventory (February 1)	500 units
Started during February	2,500 units
Completed and transferred out during February	2,700 units
WIP, ending inventory (February 28)	300 units
Direct materials, 90% complete	
Conversion costs, 60% complete	
Costs for February, 2005:	
WIP, Beginning Inventory:	
Direct Materials	$ 3,451,065
Conversion Costs	899,850
Direct Materials added during February	15,028,275
Conversion costs added during February	5,436,150

46. Using the weighted average method, compute equivalent units of production for direct materials and conversion activities, for February 2005.

	Direct Materials	**Conversion Costs**
Number of Equivalent Units of Production:		

47. Compute **costs** per equivalent unit of production for direct materials and conversion costs (**HINT**: Your costs per EU should be even dollar and cents amounts).

Direct Materials	**Conversion Costs**

[1] The number of bottles per unit is given to you only to help you in evaluating whether your answers make sense. Think about how much one bottle of sports drink is being inventoried at. Then think about how much a bottle of sports drink sells for at retail. Does your answer make sense?

48. Based on the information used to answer questions 46 and 47, what are the balances in ending WIP, and how much was transferred to finished goods inventory in February?

Ending WIP

Transferred to FGI

49. Assume the company discovered spoilage. Instead of the 300 units in ending WIP, assume that 120 units are in ending WIP and 180 units were spoiled. The spoiled units were 24% complete for direct materials, and 24.44% for conversion costs.

a. Compute the equivalent units of production for direct materials and conversion costs.

	Direct Materials	**Conversion Costs**
Number of Equivalent Units of production:		

b. Based on the 180 spoiled units described above, compute **costs** per EU for direct materials, conversion costs, and total costs. (**HINT:** your costs per EU should be even dollar and cents amounts).

Direct Materials	**Conversion Costs**

50. Based on the information used to answer question 49, what are the balances in ending WIP, and how much was transferred to finished goods inventory in February?

Ending WIP

Transferred to FGI

Answers to Questions and Exercises

Matching key terms

1. h 2. j 3. b 4. g 5. a 6. c 7. i 8. e 9. d 10. f

True or False

11. T. Process costing basically averages production costs over units of product, which is practical only if units of product are homogeneous.
12. F. The only cost-driver is the number of units of product.
13. T. Calculation of equivalent units tells how many units could have been made given the resources used.
14. T. This is the simplest case for process costing.
15. F Equivalent units must be calculated separately for each type of resource used, because the resources are used in differing quantities at different points in time.
16. F. Units are not assigned to beginning WIP. They are assigned to units completed and transferred out, ending WIP, or spoiled units.
17. T. The number of equivalent units is based on the amount of resources used to make a complete unit. If all direct materials are added at the beginning of production, equivalent units equal physical units.
18. F. It is because accounting information is reported at the end of an accounting period (a month, quarter or year), but production of units is not complete at the end of the period that calculation of equivalent units is necessary.
19. T. Even if the cost of spoiled units is not reported in the financial statements, it should be reported to managers so that they can see what costs of spoilage are.
20. F. Job order costing should be used when each unit of product is distinctly different from each other unit of product. Process costing should be used when each unit of product is indistinguishable from each other unit of product.
21. T. Production costs are averaged over units of product. In fact, it is not informative to be able to trace costs to individual units of product.
22. T. The costs are kept track of in process costing as they are for job costing. The number of units must be kept track of because number of units is the cost-driver used to assign costs.
23. F. The costs of the first department are "transferred in costs" to the next department.
24. T. Abnormal spoilage should be charged to a separate account. Abnormal spoilage is an expense that should not occur on a regular basis. It should not merely be lumped into normal spoilage, because that would distort the costs of normal production activity.
25. F. If there are spoiled units, the total number of physical units to be completed will be smaller. Thus, the number of units completed and transferred out will also be smaller.

Multiple Choice

26. d. For process costing, there is no direct cost assignment of any resource, even for unit-level costs like materials. Only product costs are assigned to product, but all production costs are averaged over the number of units produced.
27. a. The homogeneity of units of product is the reason costs can be averaged. Answer b describes products for which job costing would be more practical. If products change from month to month there is no homogeneity, so process costing would not work. Answer d is not correct. If production costs are insignificant, an entire costing system may not be necessary.
28. d. When all units are completed, the number of physical units equals the number of "equivalent units" (answer a). If there is no beginning or ending WIP, this means the same thing as answer a. Answer c is not correct because presence of transferred-in costs does not affect the need to calculate equivalent units.
29. a. Process costing recognizes that all costs are driven by one activity, and that is the production of units of product. Since each product uses up resources in the same way, it is not necessary to search for other cost drivers.
30. b. Answer a is incorrect because job costing allocates indirect costs. Answer c is incorrect because process costing does not directly assign any costs. Answer d is incorrect because job costing directly assigns traceable costs.
31. b. In order to assign costs to inventory accounts, the manager needs to know what production costs are as well as the number of units in each inventory account, since the cost per EU and the number of EUs is the basis of cost assignment. The number of physical units must be known in order to compute the number of equivalent units.
32. c. Calculation of equivalent units provides an estimate of the number of whole units could have been made for the resources used.
33. b. Since resources are added and used in production differently, it is usually the case that units of product have different percentages of completion for direct materials and conversion. This is why equivalent units must be calculated for each separate category of resource used in production.
34. d. At the most, the number of equivalent units equals the number of physical units. That only happens if the units started in a month are also completed in the same month. The number of equivalent units in ending WIP is always less than the number of physical units. Otherwise, those units would be complete.
35. a. 60% of 2,000 is 1,200.
36. c. There are 535 equivalent units. 80% of 50 spoiled units equals 40 equivalent units. 90% of 550 good units equals 495 EUs. Total EUs equal 40 + 495 = 535. $6,420/535 = $12 per EU. $12 × 40 EUs equals $480, assigned to normal spoilage.
37. c. Using the cost flow model, BB + TI – TO = EB. Step 3 accounts for BB and TI.
38. a. The WA method treats beginning WIP units as if 100% of the work on them was completed in the current month. The beginning WIP costs are included in the calculation of cost per EU under the WA method. The FIFO method only considers the amount of work needed to complete beginning WIP units in the current month. Beginning WIP costs are transferred out with completed units, but these costs are not used to calculate the cost per EU.
39. c. Spoiled units do not have to be reported in financial statements, but they should be reported to managers so that spoilage can be better managed. They should not be ignored since they cause costs that managers should be aware of. Answer d is incorrect because spoilage raises the cost of good units instead of lowering the per unit cost.

40. b. Since the number of good units is based on the total number of physical units, the occurrence of abnormal spoilage will result in lower production of good units.
41. d. The procedure for assigning costs to units completed and transferred out is simplified under the WA method because the beginning WIP units and costs are just combined with those units started and completed in the current month. Thus, the beginning WIP units are treated as if all of the work was completed on those units in the current month.
42. a. The direct materials and conversion costs from the prior department are 100% complete, and are called "transferred-in costs" when those units get passed on to the next production department. The costs move with the units.
43. c. 75% of 3,600 is 2,700 equivalent units. 100% of 1,400 is 1,400 equivalent units. Total equivalent units is 2,700 + 1,400 = 4,100 equivalent units.
44. c. A landscaper's units of product would be clients' property (land). Each job would be different, so process costing would not be a feasible cost assignment method. The other three production activities all produce homogeneous units of product, so process costing would be a practical cost assignment approach.
45. b. Beginning inventory units are assumed to be 100% completed during the current month. The costs in beginning WIP should be included when calculating the cost per EU.

Exercises

Questions 46, 47 and 48 can be answered by using the five-step procedure for assigning product costs to inventory accounts. The five steps are shown below, for the weighted average method.

The Weighted Average Method:
Step 1: Determine the number of physical units (Where did units come from, and where did they go?)

Where did the units come from?
Beginning WIP = 500 units, and units started were 2,500 units, for a total of 3,000 physical units.

Where did the units go?
Ending inventory = 300, and units completed and transferred out = 2,700, or 3,000 physical units.

Step 2: Calculate the number of equivalent units. Calculate EUs for direct materials and conversion costs.

The weighted average method assumes that 100% of the work was completed on all units transferred out. Thus, 2,700 physical units transferred out = 2,700×100% = 2,700 equivalent units for both direct materials and conversion costs.

Ending inventory has 300 physical units. For materials, these units are 90% complete, so there are 270 EUs for direct materials. The 300 units are 60% complete for conversion costs, so there are 180 EUs for conversion costs.

Physical Units	**Direct Materials**	**Conversion Costs**
Transferred out = 2,700	2,700 × 100% = 2,700 EUs	2,700 × 100% = 2,700 EUs
Ending WIP = 300	300 × 90% = 270 EUs	300 × 60% = 180 EUs
TOTALS	**2,970 EUs**	**2,880 EUs**

Step 3: Identify costs to account for (from beginning WIP and costs added). Costs are split into materials and conversion costs.

Costs	Direct Materials	Conversion Costs
Beginning Inventory	$ 3,451,065	$ 899,850
Costs added	$15,028,275	$5,436,150
TOTALS	**$18,479,340**	**$6,336,000**

Total cost to account for is $18,479,340 + $6,336,000 = $24,815,340.

Step 4: Calculate cost per equivalent unit. Divide the results from step 3 by the results from step 2.

Direct Materials	Conversion Costs
$18,479,340/2,970 EUs = **$6,222 per EU**	$6,336,000/2,880 EUs = **$2,200 per EU**

Step 5: Assign costs to transferred out (to FGI) and ending WIP. Use cost per EU from step 4, and EU information from step 2.

	Direct Materials	Conversion Costs	Total
Transferred out (to FGI)	2,700 × $6,222 = **$16,799,400**	2,700 × $2,200 = **$5,940,000**	**$22,739,400**
Ending WIP	270 × $6,222 = **$1,679,940**	180 × $2,200 = **$396,000**	**$2,075,940**
TOTALS	**$18,479,340**	**$6,336,000**	**$24,815,340**

46. The number of equivalent units using the WA method is shown in step 2. It is 2,970 for direct materials and 2,880 for conversion costs.
47. The cost per equivalent unit under the weighted average method is $6,222 per EU for direct materials and $2,200 per EU for conversion costs.
48. Ending WIP is $2,075,940, and costs transferred to FGI are $22,739,400.
49. a. If 180 units are spoiled, the equivalent units are 2,700 + 43.2 (24% of 180) + 108 (90% of 120), or 2,851.20 for direct materials. These are the EUs for direct materials for transferred out units, spoiled units, and ending WIP, respectively. For conversion costs, equivalent units are 2,700 + 44 (24.44% of 180) + 72 (60% of 120), or 2816 for conversion costs. These are the EUs for conversion costs for transferred out units, spoiled units, and ending WIP, respectively.

    b. If 180 units are spoiled, the cost per EU is $18,479,340/2,851.20 = $6,481.25 per EU for direct materials, and 6,336,000/2816 = $2,250 per EU for conversion costs.

50. The costs transferred out when there are spoiled units equals 2,700 EUs × ($6,481.25 + $2,250) = 2,700 × $8,731.25 = **$23,574,375**. Spoiled units are assigned a cost of 43.2 × $6,481.25 = $279,990 for direct materials. Spoiled units are assigned a cost of 44×$2,250 = $99,000 for conversion costs. Total assigned to spoiled units is **$378,990**. Ending inventory is $6,481.25 × 108 = $699,975 for direct materials. For conversion costs, ending inventory gets $2,250 × 72 = $162,000. Total cost assigned to ending WIP is **$861,975.** The results for questions 49 and 50 are summarized in the table below.

	Direct Materials	**Conversion Costs**	**Total**
Transferred out (to FGI)	2,700 × $6,481.25 = **$17,499,375**	2,700 × $2,250 = **$6,075,000**	**$23,574,375**
Spoiled units	43.2 × $6,481.25 = **$279,990**	44 × $2,250 = **$99,000**	**$378,990**
Ending WIP	108 × $6,481.25 = **$699,975**	72 × $2,250 = **$162,000**	**$861,975**
TOTALS	**$18,479,340**	**$6,336,000**	**$24,815,340**

Chapter 9
Joint-Process Costing

Chapter Study Suggestions

This chapter explains the problems that arise when two or more products (joint products) result from a single input or process. Production of joint products results in a need to assign costs associated with the single input. Selling or processing these products further depends on the net realizable value of the products. There are two ways that can be used to assign these costs. One is based on physical measures of the products. The other is based on the relative net realizable values of the joint products. Proper treatment of by-products is also addressed in this chapter, and by-products are contrasted with main products of a joint process. Scrap, an undesirable outcome of joint processes is also discussed.

Chapter 9

Chapter Highlights

A. Cost Management Challenges. There are two questions asked in this chapter.

1. How do cost managers anticipate and resolve potential conflicts between joint-product and process decision making and external reporting?

2. If joint-cost allocations are arbitrary, does that mean they are meaningless?

B. Learning Objectives—This chapter has 5 learning objectives.

1. It teaches how to use cost management information to increase profits from using scarce resources of joint production processes.

2. It demonstrates how to use cost-management data in the sell-or-process further decision.

3. Chapter 9 presents explanations of the net-realizable-value and physical-measures joint cost allocation methods.

4. The chapter explains the differences between the joint-cost methods and why one way or the other may be preferred.

5. It shows how to account for by-products.

C. In order to understand joint processes and joint products, there are five terms to understand.

1. A joint process is some common set of inputs or activities that result in two or more products. The cost of the inputs/activities must be allocated to the separate products because they represent part of inventory costs for different inventory items. In Chapter 3, where job costing was explained, there were many costs that could be traced directly to one unit of product because each job represented a unit of product. Costs that were not directly related to a particular job had to be allocated.

   In Chapter 8, process costing was described as an appropriate costing method when every unit of product is homogeneous. The types of products that occur in a joint process environment are dissimilar from each other, yet a significant portion of the cost cannot be directly traced to any one of the two or more products being produced.

   Joint processes create a different type of cost assignment problem. One input or process is used to create two or more types of output. The costs that result from the joint process must be allocated to the joint products because the costs are production costs, which must be inventoried, and eventually included as part of cost of goods sold.

2. Joint products are the result of a joint process. That is, two or more outputs result from the common set of inputs. Since the joint process cannot be split into the portions that each product causes separately, allocation of joint costs is used to assign these costs.

3. Joint costs (or joint-process costs) are costs that arise from the common set of inputs. These are the costs that must be allocated among the joint products. Joint costs occur before the joint products emerge as separate, distinguishable products. Joint costs use batch and facility-level resources.

4. The split-off point is the point at which individual products from the joint process emerge, and can be identified as unique products. This is the point after which costs can be traced to a particular joint product. Costs occurring after the split-off point do not have to be allocated.

   It is also at the split-off point that a management decision must be made regarding what should be done with the joint products. Products can be sold at the split-off point, or they can be processed further. Some products are "final products" at the split-off point, and do not require further processing. Other products are "intermediate products" at the split-off point. Such products can be sold to others, who complete the production process, making it into the "final product". These products could also be processed further, to the point at which they are "final products". For instance, a chemical company that produces coatings for cookware could make the final product, treated cookware. Alternatively, it could make the intermediate product, the coating for the cookware, and sell this intermediate product to a company that makes the cookware.

5. Further processing costs (also called separate or separable costs) are costs that can be traced directly to one of the joint products. These costs occur after the split-off point. If products are not processed further, either they are already in their final form at this stage, or they are sold as intermediate products that are finalized by other organizations. If the products are processed further, there are costs associated with these additional processing activities.

D. Evaluating profitability when there are joint products should be based on the fact that joint costs do not change the degree of profitability of individual profits. Managers should look at maximizing overall profitability by choosing the best set of joint products possible. Correct decisions must be made with respect to process further decisions.

   Part of the analysis of profitability is the decision to sell intermediate products or process them further. The correct choice is based on measuring a product's net realizable value. This is the product's sales revenue less any further processing costs. When a product is processed further it becomes more valuable than a product that is not processed further. Thus, the price of such products should increase. The decision to process further is based on a comparison of the additional revenue generated by selling the product at a higher price, to the additional cost of processing the product further. If the incremental revenues are greater than the incremental costs, the product should be processed further.

E. Joint costs are part of product costs, which is the main reason for assigning them to products. Joint cost allocation is necessary for several other reasons.

1. Joint costs are inventory costs, and subsequently become part of the cost of goods sold. A portion of the joint costs must flow through the accounting system to reflect the recovery of the expense through sales.

2. Joint costs are allocated in response to regulatory requirements that mandate assignment of such costs as a basis for price-setting.

3. Estimation of casualty losses makes joint cost allocation necessary.

4. Performance evaluation may include some joint costs (although caution should be used whenever allocated costs are included in an evaluation).

5. Joint costs should **not** be used to make profitability decisions for individual joint products.

F. There are two ways commonly used to allocate joint costs.

1. The Net Realizable Method assigns joint costs to joint products based on the relative values of the products. For each product, estimated sales revenue minus estimated separate costs for that product equals estimated net realizable value (NRV). Total estimated NRV of all joint products is the allocation base. Product NRV divided by total NRV is multiplied by total joint cost to get the joint cost allocation for each product.

   a. The income statement for companies with joint products is detailed for managers' use so that it is obvious which products generate profit, and how much profit they generate. The income statement shows each product separately. Cost of goods sold is split into two dollar amounts. One is the further processing costs, which are traceable to individual joint products. The other is the amount of joint cost allocated to each product.

   b. The presentation of the income statement in this segmented form illustrates an important feature of the NRV method. If a product is profitable before allocation of joint costs, it is at this point that the profitability of the individual joint product should be evaluated.

2. The Physical Measures Method assigns joint costs based on physical characteristics of the products, like weight, size or other quantities. The final weight (or length, volume, content, etc.) of each product is determined. Then the total weight of production is determined. The total weight is the allocation base. The weight of one product divided by the total weight is multiplied by the joint cost to get the joint cost allocation for each product.

   a. As with the NRV method, the income statement details joint products separately, and splits cost of goods sold into the further processing costs and joint costs.

b. A major benefit of using a physical measures method is its simplicity. If products are relatively comparable in their weights, this is a practical approach. If the joint products have very different weights relative to each other, this method is likely to distort product gross margins.

c. A major drawback to using the physical measures method is that it bears no relation to the relative profitability of each joint product. Thus, using this method may distort the relative contributions of each joint product to overall profit.

3. The flow of costs through the accounting system is based on the use of control accounts for WIP and FGI, similar to job costing. Subsidiary ledgers are maintained for each of the joint products. There are two types of costs added to the subsidiary accounts for particular joint costs. They are the further processing (or separate) costs, and the joint cost allocation.

4. When deciding which of the two joint cost allocation methods is best to use, managers should consider the following 3 points.

   a. Product decisions should not be based on gross margins, which include the joint cost allocation, unless the product must comply with a regulatory requirement.

   b. When possible, joint costs should be allocated in such a way that regulated profits of cost reimbursements are maximized. This is usually only an issue for government contracts or regulated industries.

   c. The joint cost allocation procedure should be clearly specified in contractual agreements between the customer and product provider.

G. By-products are outputs from a joint production process that are minor in quantity or NRV in comparison to main products. A joint process may result in by-products, but joint costs are allocated only to the main products that result from a joint process. By-products do not receive any joint cost allocation. Accounting for revenues and costs of by-products (i.e., NRV) is described below.

Accounting for by-products differs from accounting for main products. There are **two ways** to account for by-products.

1. Treat by-product net realizable value as other revenue. This is a simple method, which allows NRV of by-products to be reported as a single line-item in the income statement. Many companies use this reporting approach because by-product revenues and costs are so small relative to revenues and costs from the main products.

2. Deduct by-product net realizable value from joint costs of main products. This approach, while more accurately reflecting the link between main products and by-products, is more complicated to use. This is especially true if all main products are not sold. Then, NRV of by-products must be split between cost of goods sold and ending inventory of the main products.

H. What to do with scrap and waste is another concern to deal with in a joint cost environment. Production activities often result in waste, or scrap. Waste and scrap can either be disposed of at a cost, or management can look for ways to dispose of them for a profit. Disposal costs for scraps or revenues from sale of scraps are included as part of the joint-processing costs. Revenues generated from waste or scrap are subtracted from joint costs. Costs of disposing of scrap or waste are added to joint costs.

REVIEW AND SELF TEST QUESTIONS AND EXERCISES

Matching key terms

Match the following terms to the correct definition by writing the correct letter next to the correct definition.

a. joint-process
b. by-product
c. scrap
d. split-off point
e. physical-measures method
f. main product
g. intermediate product
h. final product
i. joint products
j. net realizable value (NRV)

_____ 1. A joint output that generates a significant portion of the value of multiple outputs.

_____ 2. Output that is not worth anything, or has negative net realizable value.

_____ 3. The measure of a product's contribution to profit after the split-off point; sales revenue minus additional processing costs.

_____ 4. Two or more outputs resulting from a single input.

_____ 5. A way to allocate joint costs, based on relative weight or volume of joint products.

_____ 6. The point in production at which joint products become distinguishable from each other.

_____ 7. An output of a production process that is not the main purpose of the production activity.

_____ 8. A product that is incomplete.

_____ 9. Production activity that is used to produce two or more products

_____10. The output that results when production is complete.

True or False

For each of the following statements enter a T or an F in the blank to indicate whether the statement is true or false.

______11. Further processing costs must be allocated to joint products.

______12. Joint process costs should **not** be included in the cost of inventory.

______13. The split-off point is the point in a production process where the joint production process ends.

______14. By-products are usually viewed as an unexpected benefit of a joint process.

______15. As long as a company has the ability to process a product further, the product should be processed further.

______16. Revenues generated from the sale of by-products can be recorded as "other revenues".

______17. Costs of processing a joint product further are a type of cost that should be assigned to inventory for a joint product.

______18. Net Realizable Value is one method for determining how much of the separate costs to assign to one of the joint products.

______19. Scrap resulting from a joint process never has any value.

______20. Total profits resulting from joint products are determined in part by the method in which the joint costs are allocated.

______21. If waste can be sold for more than the costs to dispose of it, then NRV for the waste can be subtracted from joint costs.

______22. Given a joint process, the profits from a joint process can be maximized by producing only profitable joint products.

______23. Revenues generated from by-products can be added to revenues from the sale of one of the joint products.

______24. The decision to process a joint product further depends on the incremental costs and incremental revenues that would occur as a result.

______25. The incremental revenue obtained by processing a product further is $5,000. The additional cost of processing a product further is $3,500. From a quantitative standpoint, the product should be processed further.

Multiple Choice

Choose the best answer by writing the letter corresponding to your choice in the space provided.

______26. Midland Farms produces corn, soybeans, and wheat on its land. In the spring, the seeds for all three crops are purchased. Before planting the seed, farm employees prepare the land by plowing it and spreading an all-purpose fertilizer on the entire area where crops are grown. The costs of plowing and fertilizing are one cost to consider. The cost of the seeds is another cost to consider. Which of the following is correct about these two costs?

a) Both of these costs are joint costs.
b) Neither of these costs is a joint cost.
c) Costs of plowing and fertilizing are not joint costs, but cost of the seeds is a joint cost.
d) Costs of plowing and fertilizing are joint costs, but cost of the seeds is not a joint cost.

______27. Midland Farms could choose to have the wheat it grows ground on site, or it could choose to sell it as soon as it is harvested. The decision to process the wheat further should be based on

a) what is done with other joint products (all should be processed further or not processed further).
b) whether the additional revenue from processing the wheat further exceeds the additional cost of processing further.
c) whether the farm has the ability to process further—if it can grind the wheat, it should always choose to process further.
d) the farm should never process further—it is beyond the scope of a farm's operations.

______28. Depreciation expenses for the tractor and other farm equipment used to farm the land at Midland Farms are treated as joint costs. Which of the following is **not** an appropriate way to allocate depreciation expenses to the three crops grown there?

a) The net realizable value method
b) The physical measure method
c) Split depreciation expenses equally three ways
d) Neither a) or b) is appropriate

_____29. Bechtel Mines produces coal. In one of its mines, a large vein of diamonds was discovered. The estimated value of the coal is $8 million, while the value of the diamonds is $20 million. The coal weighs about 10 tons, and the diamonds weigh approximately 600 pounds (3/10 of a ton). Which of the following is correct about the handling of the coal and diamonds?

a) The diamonds should be assigned most of the joint costs because they are worth far more than the coal.
b) The diamonds should be treated as a by-product, and should not be assigned any joint costs.
c) The coal should be assigned most of the joint costs because there is more coal than there are diamonds.
d) The physical measure method is the only allocation method to use since both joint products can be measured by weight.

_____30. Which of the following is **not** a reason for joint cost allocation?

a) Joint products must be assigned joint costs as part of the value of inventory.
b) Costs of further processing joint products cannot be traced to one single product.
c) Joint products cannot be produced without some common costs.
d) Joint processes are a common input that result in two or more outputs.

_____31. If there are joint products then which of the following will always occur?

a) Joint costs and a split-off point
b) Further processing costs and joint costs
c) Further processing costs and a split-off point
d) All three (joint costs, split-off point, and further processing costs) must always be present

_____32. Which of the following approaches is acceptable to account for by-products?

a) Add NRV from by-products to NRV of the joint products.
b) Treat NRV from by-products as "other revenue".
c) Subtract NRV from by-products from costs of disposing of scrap.
d) Treat by-products the same as other joint products.

_____33. Recently, companies have been seeking ways to profit from the natural occurrence of scrap in production processes. The Rainbow Clothing Company has just agreed to sell its scraps of fabric to a toy manufacturer, who will use the scraps for the inside of its stuffed animals. This activity will cause

a) a reduction in joint costs to the Rainbow Clothing Company.
b) increased costs to process joint products further for the Rainbow Company.
c) reduction in materials used for joint products for the Rainbow Company.
d) increased joint costs for the Rainbow Company.

_____34. Casey Inc. produces chocolate candies. Two popular products are chocolate bunnies and chocolate Easter eggs. Both the bunnies and the eggs use milk chocolate. The candies are poured into molds, wrapped and packaged. Joint costs include the raw chocolate, sugar and other ingredients used to make milk chocolate. One month's production resulted in joint costs totaling $120,000. The joint process resulted in production of 400,000 pounds of bunnies and 240,000 pounds of eggs. Costs to finish production of the bunnies were $65,000, and costs to finish the eggs totaled $171,000. Bunnies sell for $3.60 per pound, and eggs sell for $5.40 per pound. Using the physical measure method, how much of the joint cost should be allocated to the bunnies, and how much should be assigned to the eggs?

a) $48,000 to the bunnies and $72,000 to the eggs
b) $63,158 to the bunnies and $56,842 to the eggs
c) $75,000 to the bunnies and $45,000 to the eggs
d) $66,000 to the bunnies and $54,000 to the eggs

_____35. Use the information from question 34. If the NRV method is used, how much joint cost would be allocated to the bunnies, and how much would be allocated to the eggs?

a) $48,000 to the bunnies and $72,000 to the eggs
b) $63,158 to the bunnies and $56,842 to the eggs
c) $75,000 to the bunnies and $45,000 to the eggs
d) $66,000 to the bunnies and $54,000 to the eggs

_____36. The split-off point is the point at which

a) joint products must be processed further.
b) joint products can be distinguished from each other.
c) joint products are combined.
d) joint production costs can be identified.

_____37. A company that has joint products

a) cannot use process costing systems.
b) cannot use job costing systems.
c) cannot use operations costing systems.
d) must choose a costing system to assign costs to units of product.

_____38. Which of the following statements is **not** true regarding joint costs?

a) Joint costs are part of production costs.
b) Joint costs are period costs for financial reporting purposes.
c) Joint costs can only be assigned by an allocation process.
d) Joint costs occur because there is one input that generates two or more products.

_____39. Which of the following statements about by-products is **incorrect**?

a) By-products are minor in quantity and/or net realizable value compared to main products.
b) By-products have less value than main products, but have more value than scrap.
c) By-products usually result from having to re-work main products.
d) By-products do not receive allocations of joint costs.

_____40. Organizations producing joint products categorize production costs into two types. They are

a) joint costs and allocated costs.
b) joint costs and indirect costs.
c) joint costs and period costs.
d) joint costs and further processing costs.

_____41. Which of the following is **not** a standard method for accounting for by-products?
a) Add by-product revenue to revenue of main products.
b) Deduct by-product NRV from costs of main products.
c) Any of these three methods would be acceptable.

_____42. Which of the following is true regarding scrap?

a) Scrap always has value to organizations.
b) Scrap is an unnecessary part of any production activity and can always be eliminated.
c) Scrap can only occur when joint products are being made.
d) Costs to dispose of scrap are normally included as part of joint costs.

_____43. Which of the following would be the best information to use in assessing profitability of a joint product?

a) Use estimated sales revenue minus allocated joint cost.
b) Use estimated sales revenue minus joint costs and separate costs.
c) Use estimate sales revenue minus separate costs.
d) Use estimated sales revenue.

_____44. All of the following are qualitative reasons for processing a joint product further **except**

a) excess capacity.
b) competition.
c) marketability of the further processed product.
d) synergism with existing products.

_____45. Which of the following is correct regarding the salary of the CFO in a company with joint products?

a) The salary should be allocated among joint products.
b) The salary is a joint cost.
c) The salary will eventually be included as cost of goods sold.
d) The salary is not a production cost—it is a period cost.

Exercises

Use the following information about the Warsaw Meat Co. to answer the next 5 questions.

The Warsaw Meat Company buys beef and pork from nearby slaughterhouses. Beef and pork are both used to make Warsaw Company's famous bologna and hot dog products. Last month, Warsaw Meat Co. bought 50,000 pounds of beef for $.45 per pound. The company bought 75,000 pounds of pork for $.50 per pound. All of the meat purchased was used in production of bologna and hot dogs last month.

After adding filler and spices, a total of 120,000 pounds of bologna and 40,000 pounds of hot dogs were produced. Cost of further processing the bologna was $12,800, while costs of processing the hot dogs further totaled $3,200.

Bologna is sold by Warsaw Meat Co. for $.90 per pound to grocery stores. Hot dogs are sold for $1.10 per pound.

46. If the physical measure method is used, what amount of joint cost would be allocated to the hot dogs, and what amount would be allocated to the bologna?

47. If the NRV method is used, what amount of joint cost would be allocated to the hot dogs, and what amounts would be allocated to the bologna?

48. If the NRV method is used, what is the value of the inventory for bologna? What is the inventory value for hot dogs?

49. Suppose the physical measure method was used. At the end of last month, 75% of the production for hot dogs had been sold, and 80% of the bologna had been sold. What is the cost of goods sold for the company for last month?

50. Warsaw Meats Company employees have suggested that the beef and pork scraps be used for a new product. Dubbed "PeopleFood for Dogs", the scraps could be made into dog food, and sold for $.50 per pound. The scraps would be molded into hamburger shapes, packaged in 4 quarter-pound plastic packages, and sold in one pound boxes. Costs to process and package the dog food would be approximately $.15 per one-pound box. Should Warsaw Meats market this product? Provide both a quantitative and a qualitative response.

Answers to Questions and Exercises

Matching key terms

1. f 2. c 3. j 4. i 5. e 6. d 7. b 8. g 9. a 10. h

True or False

11. F. Further processing costs can be traced to a single product
12. F. Joint costs and further processing costs are both inventoriable costs
13. T. The split-off point is the point in the production process where individual products emerge.
14. T. Main products are the reason a joint process is undertaken
15. F. Further processing should occur only if the additional benefits exceed the additional costs (both quantitative and qualitative)
16. T. This is one of two correct ways to treat revenues from sale of by-products. The other way to handle such revenues is to subtract them from joint costs.
17. T. Costs of processing further are a separate cost, to be assigned to the product for which the costs were incurred.
18. F. The NRV method is used to assign joint costs—not further processing (separate) costs.
19. F. Some scrap can be sold, in which case the proceeds should be subtracted from joint costs.
20. F. Joint costs are irrelevant to the evaluation of total profits.
21. T. Proceeds from the sale of waste can be offset against joint costs.
22. T. If NRV for a product is not positive, it is unprofitable and cannot contribute to recovery of joint costs, or even cover its own costs.
23. F. Revenues from by-products can either be treated as other revenue or netted against joint costs.
24. T. Only the incremental costs and incremental revenues are used in decision-making related to further processing a joint product
25. T. The incremental benefit ($5,000) exceeds the incremental cost ($3,500) by $1,500, so the product should be processed further.

Multiple Choice

26. d. Costs of the seeds are identifiable with the specific products, and are treated as further processing costs. Plowing and fertilizing costs cannot be traced to any single crop.
27. b. Answer a is incorrect because each product needs to be evaluated based on its own profitability. Answer c is incorrect because it is not true that a business should **always** process further. Answer d is incorrect because the farm may be interested in growth, and growth often requires expansion beyond the current scope of a company's operations.
28. c. Splitting joint costs evenly is not correct or justifiable.

29. a. This is an example of a joint cost problem where the physical measure method would lead to very distorted cost allocation. Because the diamonds are very lightweight, they would receive almost no cost. Yet, they are the more valuable of the two products. The NRV method should be used so that the larger portion of the joint cost of mining will be allocated to the most profitable product. Note, b is incorrect because the diamonds are not a by-product. Why is this true? Because even though the coal company did not anticipate that they would discover diamonds, once they did the economic value became more than that of their main product. Economic value helps companies to define the status of a product as main, by-product or scrap.
30. b. Costs for processing further can be traced directly to a product. Therefore, these costs do not need to be allocated.
31. a. By definition, joint costs arise as a result of some joint process, and costs are associated with that process. There must be some split-off point—otherwise, the individual products could not be identified. Costs to process further may or may not be present.
32. b. NRV of by-products can be treated as other revenue or can be subtracted from joint costs. No other way is used or acceptable in practice.
33. a. NRV of waste that is sold should be subtracted from joint costs.
34. c. 240,000 pounds of eggs were produced. 400,000 pounds of bunnies were produced. 640,000 pounds of product were produced. 240,000/640,000 × $120,000 = **$45,000** of the joint cost is allocated to the Easter eggs. 400,000/640,000 × $120,000 = **$75,000** of the joint cost allocated to the bunnies. Answer a allocated joint costs based on the prices. Answer b allocated based on revenues generated from the sale of the products. Answer d allocated based on the NRV of each product.
35. d. The NRV of the bunnies is $3.60 × 400,000 = $1,440,000 revenue. Subtract costs to process further, $65,000, giving a NRV of $1,375,000. The NRV of the Easter eggs is $5.40 × 240,000 = $1,296,000 revenue. Subtract further processing costs of $171,000 to get NRV of $1,125,000. Total NRV is $2,500,000. Allocate $120,000 × $1,375,000/$2,500,000 = **$66,000** to the bunnies. Allocate $120,000 × $1,125,000/$2,500,000 = **$54,000** to the eggs.
36. b. Answer a is incorrect because joint products might not need further processing. Answer c is not correct because joint products are not combined. Answer d is incorrect because joint costs can be identified when they are incurred—not only at the split-off point.
37. d. Joint products must be assigned costs using some type of costing system. The system chosen depends on the characteristics of the products.
38. b. Joint costs are not period costs because they need to be included in inventory, and subsequently are included in cost of goods sold.
39. c. By-products are not damaged or reworked main products.
40. d. Answers a and b are incorrect because joint costs are both allocated and indirect costs. Answer c is wrong because period costs are not production costs.
41. b. Revenue from by-products cannot be added to revenue of joint products.
42. d. Scrap may or may not have value (answer a). It usually cannot be completely eliminated (answer b). Scrap often occurs in production, whether there are joint products involved or not.
43. c. Only revenue and separate costs should be used to evaluate profitability of a single product.
44. a. Excess capacity is not a qualitative reason for processing further. It is a quantitative reason.
45. d. Executive salaries are not production costs, and therefore are treated as period costs.

Exercises

Information used to answer questions 46-50:

Total joint costs to be allocated:
Beef = \$.45 × 50,000 pounds = \$22,500
Pork = \$.50 × 75,000 pounds = \$37,500
Total joint costs to be allocated = \$60,000

120,000 pounds of bologna were produced. 40,000 pounds of hot dogs were produced. Total weight of production was 160,000 pounds.

Total NRV: Bologna is \$.90 × 120,000 pounds = \$108,000. Subtract \$12,800 separate costs to get NRV of \$95,200. The hot dogs generate revenue of \$1.10 × 40,000 = \$44,000. Subtract separate costs of \$3,200 to get NRV of \$40,800. Total NRV is \$136,000.

46. The physical measure method results in an allocation of \$60,000 × 120,000/160,000 = **\$45,000** to bologna

    The allocation to hot dogs is \$60,000 × 40,000/160,000 = **\$15,000** to hot dogs

47. The NRV method yields the following results: bologna is allocated \$95,200/\$136,000 × \$60,000=**\$42,000**. Hot dogs are allocated \$40,800/\$136,000 × \$60,000 = **\$18,000**.
48. Bologna has \$42,000 of joint costs plus \$12,800 separate costs from processing further. Total inventory cost for bologna is **\$54,800**. Hot dogs have \$18,000 joint costs plus \$3,200 = **\$21,200**.
49. If 75% of the hot dogs were sold then cost of goods sold would be 75% of (15,000 + \$3,200), or \$13,650. Ending inventory would be \$4,550 (\$18,200 – \$13,650). The cost of goods sold for bologna would be 80% of \$57,800, or **\$46,240**. Then, inventory would be \$57,800 – \$46,240 = **\$11,560**.
50. This is a "process further" problem for scraps. Should the company use the scraps to make dog food? The quantitative answer would say to proceed. The company stands to make \$.35 per pound of scraps processed. What qualitative considerations are there? How would the company's existing customers feel about having the producers of their luncheon meats producing dog food? Is there synergism among the existing products and the proposed one? Is there another way to benefit from processing scraps (sell to a dog food company)? A decision to market dog food might have a negative effect on existing products' sales.

Chapter 10
Managing and Allocating Support-Service Costs

Chapter Study Suggestions

Chapter 10 addresses the need to manage costs of support-service departments in an organization. Support-services are provided to facilitate completion of production activities, which are the purpose for an organization's existence. Although organizations are formed to accomplish certain objectives, they cannot function without performance of various ancillary activities that allow the organization to operate smoothly.

Support-service costs have historically received little attention in the cost management arena. However, as these costs have increased, managers of organizations have begun to place more emphasis on managing these costs along with the costs of production activities. Moreover, it has become clear that managers of production activities need to understand the link between activities they are responsible for, and the costs of support services. In order to help managers to better understand support department costs, they are assigned to production (or direct) departments. Chapter 10 presents different methods for allocating support-service costs to production departments. The direct method and the step method are two commonly used approaches for allocating support department costs. Activities-based methods are used by organizations wanting more accurate allocations. Another method, the reciprocal method is presented in the appendix to Chapter 10.

Chapter Highlights

A. Cost Management Challenges. There are 3 challenges offered in this chapter.

1. Since cost allocations are arbitrary, does it matter how costs are allocated in an organization?
2. How can a cost allocation approach be chosen that allows proper evaluation of tradeoffs that may result from the allocations made?
3. How can managers be educated to understand the complexities of the cost allocation process chosen?

B. Learning Objectives—This chapter has 5 learning objectives.

1. The chapter explains the importance of managing support service costs and tells why these costs are allocated.
2. It provides understanding of the need to choose cost pools.
3. Chapter 10 illustrates how to choose appropriate allocation bases.
4. The chapter presents two commonly used allocation methods—the direct method and the step method.
5. The repurcussions associated with alternative cost allocations are discussed.

C. Service cost challenges exist in virtually every type of organization. Organizations exist for a variety of purposes. For-profit organizations exist to provide goods and services that generate profit. Non-profit organizations and government units operate to provide goods and services that benefit members of a community or society at large.

Most of the focus on use of resources in organizations is properly placed on the resources used to meet the objectives of the organization. However, resources are also used to support productive processes. Employees provide services such as Human Resources, information systems, accounting, janitorial services, and top executives' expertise. Additional resources are expended to house and equip these services.

Historically, support services have been viewed as relatively minor costs compared to costs of productive activity. As these costs have increased though, organizations have shifted some of the cost management focus to controlling, reducing and minimizing costs of support services.

1. Support services may be outsourced. Some organizations have chosen to focus exclusively on their core business. These organizations have consciously chosen to eliminate in-house performance of support activities. When making a decision to outsource or not, there are several factors that should be considered.

a. The knowledge base needed by outsourcing service providers must be considered. If the skills or expertise needed to successfully perform services cannot be obtained outside of an organization, they must be completed internally. On the other hand, there are some activities that an organization may not have the skills or expertise to perform. For instance, an organization that is expanding into the global market may not have in-house expertise in dealing with complex customs and trade laws, or international tax issues. In these instances, it may be more practical to obtain such expertise from outside sources.

b. Some information or certain activities may be too sensitive to outsource. In this case, an organization must retain control of these support-service activities by providing them internally.

c. The costs of outsourcing compared to the cost of performing services internally must also be considered.

d. The reliability of outside service providers must also be considered. This is particularly important if outsourced activities are associated in some way with the reputation of the organization.

D. For those support services that continue to be performed internally, the costs of these services must be managed. There are several options for managing support-service costs. Two opposing views are to either provide the services to internal customers at no charge, or to charge internal customers for support services. Each is discussed below.

1. Internal customers who receive support services might be charged nothing for the services. In that case, support service costs are recovered from revenues generated from sale of product (or as illustrated in the text, by tax revenues for a government entity). Users of the support services do not have the financial information that helps them to recognize the costs of using support services. While this approach is simple, it does nothing to encourage efficient, cost-effective use of the services offered.

2. The costs of support services can be charged to using departments, and costs can be recovered from these internal customers. This is accomplished by use of a system of cost allocations. Since support services cannot be directly traced to users, allocation is the only way that support department costs can be assigned.

   Allocation of support department costs is somewhat arbitrary, and may not be accurate measures of resource use. Assigning costs may also create tension and dissension internally if managers do not agree with the charges to their department for the use of support department services.

E. Support services exist to facilitate direct, or production activities. Direct activities may also be referred to as line activities. Direct services or production activities exist to meet the objectives of an organization. Support services exist only to help the entire organization to function more smoothly.

1. Direct or production departments are those departments that generate revenue. Even in the case of nonprofit organizations, or government agencies, certain departments are the source of cash inflow, and can be viewed as direct departments. Support-service departments, on the other hand, only generate costs.

   a. Support-service costs are often facility-level resource costs that don't vary directly with production activity.

2. The use of support department costs is not easily observable. For instance, unit-level production costs are directly related to production activity, and changes in production costs can be traced to changes in unit-level activity. Support department costs cannot be traced this way, even though costs may be indirectly related to unit-level production activities.

   For instance, support services of the Payroll Department are necessary because of employees in direct and other departments. In other words, without the production activities, there would be no need for a Payroll Department. However, since Payroll Department employees are paid a salary that is not based purely on production activities, there is no direct way to trace Payroll Department activities to different production departments. Even if Payroll Department costs could justifiably be assigned based on number of employees in each production department, they would not be directly traceable to units of product unless labor costs themselves could be traced that way.

F. Allocation of support service costs is really a full cost problem, similar to the problems described in Chapter 2. Recall, in Chapter 2 the problem of assigning higher-level production costs to lower-level activities made cost allocation necessary. Allocation of support-services costs creates the same type of problem, because non-production facility-level costs are allocated to production departments.

1. The impact of cost allocation on managers' decision-making activities must be considered. Cost allocation from support departments should be excluded from consideration in making certain decisions. For instance, decisions about profitability of products or product lines should not include support department cost allocations.

   a. Cost allocations from support departments should be used to highlight the fact that direct departments are the **reason** for support department costs. The cost-causing direct department should pay for support department costs. In order for them to pay though, there must be a way to determine the amounts due.

   b. Allocation of costs to direct (production) departments makes the cost-causers conscious of the need to manage these costs. If there is no cost attached to support services then users may not be efficient in their use of such services.

c. Allocation of costs aids managers in planning and budgeting. To the extent that support department costs change with direct department activity, managers can better anticipate these changes in support department costs. For example, if a production department anticipates that a large number of new hires will be necessary in the coming year, it should also be conscious of the attendant costs that will occur in the Human Resources Department.

2. In addition to managing support-service needs of internal customers, there may be other reasons for allocating support department costs.

   a. Some organizations may be required to report allocations to government agencies.

   b. Cost-plus contracts, which are often used by government agencies, nonprofit organizations, and academic institutions make support department allocations critical to recovery of the entire cost of providing products and services to external customers.

   c. Allocation of facility-level support service costs like the salaries of top executives motivates managers at lower levels to increase profits needed to cover these higher-level costs.

3. Once the decision to allocate support-service costs is made, a system for allocating these costs must be chosen and implemented.

G. The choice of methods for cost allocation from support departments to internal customers should accomplish several objectives. A key objective is to allocate costs in a way that motivates using departments to use support services wisely. A second objective is to choose an allocation procedure that is fair, and does not cause internal disputes. A third objective is to help managers of an organization to know what amounts of support services are necessary. A fourth objective is to assure that the costs of the allocation system do not outweigh the benefits.

There are four steps to use that aid in the degree of success achieved in meeting these objectives. These steps are explained in detail below.

H. Step 1. Costs of support-services must be identified, and decisions must be made regarding how or if various support-service activities should be combined (pooled).

1. Support service spending must be identified. Identifying support department costs depends on how and at what level support departments acquire resources. The use of resources may also differ by level (i.e., facility- or lower-level). Some support department costs can be traced to direct departments. More often, however, support-service costs cannot be traced, and must be allocated.

   a. Support-service costs can be identified and pooled based on resource type. For instance, human resource costs could be separated from equipment and space costs for a given support department, or one type of support department may be separated from another type of support department.

2. Support service uses must be identified. Organizations may identify, and then pool costs based on uses of facility-level support-service resources. This is especially useful when a support department has both facility-level and lower-level components.

    a. Managers need to be cognizant of the costs associated with having many cost pools. At the same time, expanding the number of cost pools will increase the accuracy of cost allocations. There is a tradeoff between controlling the costs of having an accurate allocation system and limiting the degree of accuracy the system can provide.

    b. Often, organizations may have support-service department pools for each department, or for each function, or for broad categories of functions.

3. Costs to be allocated must be measured. Allocation of support department costs cannot be based on the actual costs, because they are not known early enough to allocate them. This makes it necessary to develop estimates of support-service costs.

I. Step 2. Choose the appropriate cost allocation bases and calculate rates. Once the costs and cost pools are identified, an allocation base must be chosen and allocation rates, or amounts to allocate must be calculated. The allocation base should mirror, as closely as is practical, a cost-driver base. This means that the base should be indicative of a causal link between the cost and the cost allocation. Such a link improves the planning and decision-making activities of managers. It may also influence behavior if managers see that their actions affect support-service costs.

1. An activities-based cost approach can be used to assign support department costs. This entails the following.

    a. Measure each support department's resource spending (costs) by level. This means that unit, batch, product, customer and facility-level costs must be identified.

    b. Identify and measure activities demanded by internal customers that require support-service spending. This allows cost-driver bases to be chosen.

    c. Derive cost-driver rates by dividing costs by the activity. Rates derived are percentages that can then be used to assign the support department costs to the departments.

2. A cost allocation approach that is more traditional than ABC is used by many organizations. Traditional cost allocations often use allocation bases such as number of employees, space occupied, hours of use, or other activities that are more general than those used in an ABC system.

a. If allocation bases are not cost drivers, they must at a minimum be justifiable for use as an allocation base.

J. Step 3. A cost allocation method must be selected and implemented. Two commonly used methods are the direct method and the step method. A third method, the reciprocal method, is not widely used, and is presented in the appendix to Chapter 10. The direct and step methods are described below.

1. The direct method of cost allocation charges support department costs only to internal customers in direct (production) departments. This allocation method ignores the use of support services between support service departments. The direct method places emphasis on the fact that, ultimately, all support-service costs are paid for by production departments.

   a. Suppose that an organization has two support departments, S1 and S2, and it has two production departments, P1 and P1. Costs of department S1 would be allocated to departments P1 and P2. Costs of department S2 would be allocated to departments P1 and P2. With the direct method, no costs of department S1 would be allocated to department S2, and no S2 costs would be allocated to department S1.

   b. The chief criticism of the direct method is that it ignores the use of support departments by other support departments. For instance, the Accounting Department hires new employees and therefore uses the services of the Human Resources Department. Human Resources uses the Accounting Department whenever it needs to have a bill paid. Neither of these support departments receives a cost allocation from the other support department. This is justifiable for two reasons. First, support department costs are fairly small relative to production department costs, so the degree of accuracy needed in assigning support department costs to other support departments need not be extensive. Second, since all support department costs are ultimately allocated to production departments anyway, an interim allocation between support departments is viewed by some as an unnecessary complication.

   c. The rates (percentages) are then used to allocate actual costs to production departments.

2. The step method partially addresses the criticisms leveled against the direct method. The step method allocates costs from the support department with the largest proportion of its total allocation base in other support departments to other support and production departments. This first support department is the most general support department. Then costs from the second most general support department are allocated to the remaining support departments and all of the production departments. The support department with the smallest proportion of its costs in other support departments has its costs allocated only to production departments.

   a. The procedure for calculating the allocation rates is the same, except with the step method some support departments are assigned costs of other support departments.

b. Once a support department's costs are allocated, nothing is ever allocated back to it, even though it may use the services of the remaining support departments. Thus, allocations from support departments are made in only one direction.

c. Using the example presented in the discussion of the direct method, suppose there are two support departments, S1 and S2, and two production departments, P1 and P2. If department S1 is the most general support department, then its costs will be allocated to departments S2, P1, and P2. Department S2 would then have its own costs plus the allocated amount it received from department S1. Then department S2's adjusted cost would be allocated to production departments P1 and P2.

d. The step method is viewed as an improvement over the direct method, because it partially recognizes the reciprocal relationships among support departments. Many companies opt for the direct method because it is easier to use and maintain.

3. Critics of the step method argue that if a more complex method is to be used, it should be the reciprocal method. The reciprocal method assigns costs of every support department to every other department that uses it. Thus, if department S1 uses department S2, and department S2 uses department S1, then each support department will receive an allocation from the other support department. The main criticism of the reciprocal method is that it unnecessarily complicates the cost allocation process, particularly since all of the support department costs end up being allocated to the production departments anyway.

K. Step 4. Evaluation of the choices among allocation methods should reveal whether the desired results will be achieved by the allocation method chosen. The desired results include accuracy, effects on departments, and linkage between costs and benefits.

1. The allocation process cannot be perfectly accurate. Since cost allocations are always arbitrary to some extent, managers must balance their degree of tolerance for the inaccuracy with their degree of tolerance for costs of having a more expensive and complex allocation method. It may not be cost-effective to modify allocation of support department costs to improve accuracy.

2. Another way to evaluate cost-allocation methods is to look at the effects of alternative methods on production departments. If costs are allocated to managers of production departments, managers will be resistant to any allocation method that increases support department costs to their department.

a. One factor that should influence the choice of methods—ABC, reciprocal, step, or direct, is the amount of support services used by other support departments. If the amount of use is high between support departments, use of the direct method will distort the true costs of support services used by the various production departments.

b. If support department costs are used to evaluate managers, then managers will prefer whichever cost allocation method assigns the least cost to them.

c. All support department allocation methods are assigning the same amount of total cost to production departments. However, the method chosen can change the amount of cost allocated to individual departments. An undesirable result of assigning support department costs to a production department is that the manager of the production department may cut back on the use of the support departments' services just to reduce his or her departments' costs. While this may have the desired effect in that production department, it simply means that the cost will be reassigned to another department in the short run. In the long run, costs and services would be reduced, and that manager would have access to lower levels of service.

   Suppose a trucking company revised its cost allocations in such a way that resulted in truck maintenance costs (a support service) being allocated differently. If the allocation base is mechanic hours, then the manager of a truck facility would be tempted to reduce mechanics' time to reduce maintenance costs. This is certainly not a desired effect of cost allocation.

d. The choice of allocation method could affect amounts allocated in cost-plus contracts. If an organization has a mix of external customers, some with cost-plus contracts, and others with market-based contracts, the tendency would be to allocate as much support department cost to the cost-plus contracts. Customers with such contracts need to recognize this tendency, and must insist on knowing how costs are determined and assigned. Many federal government contracts are cost-plus, and contractors are given very specific limits on allocation methods and amounts.

3. A third consideration in evaluating which cost allocation method to choose is the relation between costs and benefits of setting up, administering, and maintaining the system. Complex systems are much more difficult to maintain than simple systems. Each year, allocation bases and cost estimates change. New rates must be calculated for every cost base used. Organizational structure also changes, making it necessary to revise estimates of the use of support department services.

   a. At times it is necessary to fine-tune an allocation system, especially if it is causing undesirable results.

   b. Ethical considerations may lead to challenges in how cost allocations are made, especially in cost-plus contracts, or when government agencies charge taxes based on cost-plus estimates of taxes charged.

REVIEW AND SELF TEST QUESTIONS AND EXERCISES

Matching key terms

Match the following terms to the correct definition by writing the correct letter next to the correct definition.

a. cost allocation base	b. step method	c. support department
d. reciprocal services	e. internal support services	f. direct method
g. production department	h. internal customers	i. cost-based contracts
j. discretionary cost allocations		

_____ 1. Activity occurring in an organization that benefits production departments.

_____ 2. An allocation method that ignores the reciprocal relationship between support departments.

_____ 3. A way to assign costs that may be inaccurate in measuring use of resources.

_____ 4. A department that performs needed work in a business, but that does not make product.

_____ 5. Production departments and other support departments.

_____ 6. An allocation method that only partially recognizes the reciprocal relationship between support departments.

_____ 7. A way to assign costs to a job or project that allows inclusion of support department costs.

_____ 8. A basis for assigning indirect costs to cost objects.

_____ 9. Support departments provide services to each other in addition to servicing production departments in this instance.

_____10. A department that receives support department services but does not provide anything to support departments.

True or False

For each of the following statements enter a T or an F in the blank to indicate whether the statement is true or false.

______11. Support-service departments generate revenue for an organization.

______12. The objective of support departments is to facilitate direct (production) departments in meeting their objectives.

______13. A support department is the same as a direct department.

______14. Only service organizations (whose products are services) can have support departments.

______15. Support-service department costs typically must be allocated to production departments rather than being directly assigned to them.

______16. Support departments usually generate more costs in total than production departments do.

______17. Organizations can use an ABC approach to assign support department costs.

______18. Production department costs are usually assigned to support departments.

______19. The direct method for allocating support department costs is called that because it can be used when support department costs are traceable to production activities.

______20. The step method for allocating support department costs gives different results from the direct method if the amount of support department services provided to other support departments is high.

______21. Cost-plus contracts should include support department cost allocations.

______22. Support department costs are production costs, and that is why they must be allocated to production departments.

______23. If choosing between ABC, step, and direct methods for allocating support department costs, the ABC method will be the most accurate.

______24. If choosing between ABC, step, and direct methods for allocating support department costs, the ABC method will be the least expensive.

______25. After allocation of support department costs is completed, none of the support departments will have costs in them.

Multiple Choice

Choose the best answer by writing the letter corresponding to your choice in the space provided.

_____26. Which of the following correctly describes support departments?

a) Support departments always generate profit.
b) Support departments exist to facilitate activities of direct (production) departments.
c) Support departments do not have any costs—only revenues.
d) Support department costs are always traceable to other departments.

_____27. Why should support department costs be allocated?

a) Because they are part of the costs of products, and need to be included in cost of goods sold.
b) Because that is the only way to recover them.
c) Because it helps managers of production departments to see that these costs exist.
d) Because allocation is required by law.

_____28. Who benefits the most from support services?

a) Internal customers
b) Production managers
c) External customers
d) Support departments

_____29. When comparing support departments to production (direct) departments, which of the following statements is correct when the direct method is used?

a) Production department costs should be allocated only to support departments.
b) Support departments costs should be allocated only to other support departments.
c) Production department costs should be allocated only to other production departments.
d) Support department costs should be allocated only to production departments.

_____30. To calculate the allocation rate used to allocate support department costs to production departments, one should use

a) actual support department costs and the actual quantity of the allocation base.
b) actual support department costs and an estimated quantity of the allocation base.
c) estimated support department costs and an estimated quantity of the allocation base.
d) estimated support department costs and the actual quantity of the allocation base.

_____31. Regardless of the allocation method chosen, when allocation of support department costs is complete, which of the following is true?

a) Costs in all production departments will be zero.
b) Costs in all support departments will be zero.
c) Costs in all support departments will be greater than zero.
d) Costs in some of the support departments will be greater than zero.

_____32. The best choice of an allocation base for assigning support department costs is one that

a) will discourage production departments from using support services.
b) will increase the use of support services.
c) will increase costs of production departments evenly.
d) will motivate managers to use support services efficiently.

_____33. Cleaning and janitorial services are one support department. Which of the following would be the best allocation base to use for allocating these costs to production departments?

a) Number of janitorial employees
b) Amount of money spent on cleaning supplies
c) Square feet of production departments
d) Number of restrooms per floor

_____34. A cost-plus contract should

a) include as much support department cost allocation as a company can justify.
b) include as little support department cost allocation as a company can justify.
c) include no support department cost allocations.
d) include equal amounts of support department costs and production costs.

_____35. Which of the following is **false** regarding the step method for allocating support department costs?

a) The step method allocates some support department costs to other support departments as well as to production departments.
b) The step method is more complicated than the direct method.
c) After all allocations are complete, the total support department cost allocated to production departments will be less than total support department costs.
d) The step method partially recognizes the use of support departments by each other.

_____36. The step method differs from the direct method for allocating support department costs because

a) the total amount of support department cost allocated to production departments is different.
b) the direct method allocates only to production departments, while the step method allocates to support departments and to production departments.
c) the direct method only allocates costs to production departments and the step method only allocates costs to support departments.
d) the two methods are the same (just different names).

_____37. A company uses the direct method to allocate support-service costs. When costs of its Human Resources Department are allocated using this method, it means that

a) no support departments can use Human Resources services.
b) no Human Resources costs are allocated to production departments.
c) Human Resources costs are directly traceable to production departments.
d) no Human Resources costs are allocated to other support departments.

_____38. The Accounting Department uses Information Systems (IS) Services, and IS uses the Accounting Department's services, but Accounting uses IS more than IS uses Accounting. Which of the following correctly describes the cost allocation procedure for the direct and step methods.

a) The direct method will allocate no Accounting cost to IS, and no IS cost to Accounting. The step method will allocate some Accounting cost to IS, and no IS cost to Accounting.
b) The direct method will allocate some Accounting cost to IS, and some IS cost to Accounting. The step method will allocate no Accounting cost to IS, and no IS cost to Accounting.
c) The direct method will allocate no Accounting cost to IS, and no IS cost to Accounting. The step method will allocate no Accounting cost to IS, and some IS cost to Accounting.
d) The direct method will allocate no Accounting cost to IS, and no IS cost to Accounting. The step method will allocate some Accounting cost to IS, and some IS cost to Accounting.

_____39. Wonderland Daycare budgeted Administrative costs at $60,000, and allocations are based on direct department costs. Food Services costs were budgeted at $36,000, and allocations are based on the number of meals served. The two direct departments are Toddlers Classes, for children aged 2 and 3, and Pre-K Classes, for children aged 4 and 5. The Toddlers department had a budget totaling $103,680, while the Pre-K department had budgeted costs totaling $220,320. Toddlers were to be served an estimated 8,100 meals, and Pre-K children were expected to be served 9,900 meals. Administrative staff also receives meals, and were budgeted to be served 750 meals. If the direct method for allocating support department costs is used, which of the following shows the correct allocation of Food Services to the Toddlers Classes?

a) $12,960
b) $14,400
c) $15,552
d) $16,200

_____40. Use the information provided in question 39. Suppose the step method of allocating support department costs is used, and Administrative costs are allocated first. Which of the following shows the correct allocation of Food Services to the Toddlers Classes?

a) $18,900
b) $18,144
c) $16,200
d) $15,552

_____41. The main criticism of the step method is that it

a) does not assign any production department costs to any other production department.
b) only assigns costs to support departments in one direction.
c) does not assign any support department cost to any other support department.
d) does not assign any support department cost to production departments.

_____42. One negative repercussion of allocating support department costs to production departments is that

a) it may cause support department costs to rise.
b) it may cause managers to use more support department services.
c) it might result in lower levels of production activity.
d) it may cause managers to use less of needed services.

_____43. If, due to a revised allocation method a particular production department receives a smaller allocation of support department costs, then which of the following will occur?

a) Total support department costs will go down.
b) Other production departments' allocations will go up.
c) Use of support services in other production departments will increase.
d) The amount of support services available will increase.

_____44. Which of the following is **not** a valid reason for allocating support department costs?

a) Allocating support department costs helps production managers to see that these costs exist.
b) If support department costs are not allocated to production departments, production departments have no incentive to be efficient in use of these services.
c) Allocation of support services helps management to see what amounts of support services are necessary.
d) Allocation of support department costs helps production managers to evaluate the profitability of their products.

_____45. Which of the following is **not** a support department activity?

a) A staff attorney prepares leases for clients.
b) A staff attorney defends the company in an employment discrimination suit.
c) A staff attorney prepares documentation needed to patent a process developed in the company she works for.
d) A staff attorney files legal documents with a federal government agency in compliance with the law.

Exercises

Use the following information about Mallory and Tiffany Designs to answer the next 5 questions.

Mallory and Tiffany Designs are interior decorators. Mallory and Tiffany have noticed that even though their three direct divisions, Home Interiors, Multi-Unit Interiors, and Business Interiors are profitable, the costs of their support departments are increasing and apparently uncontrollable. Their most recent hire is an accountant, Leon Rogers. Leon thinks that one way to highlight support department costs is to assign the costs to the users of the support departments' services. The interior decorators' firm has divided all of its support costs into three departments also. One is General Administration, one is Human Resources, and the other is Procurement (Purchasing). Leon has compiled the costs and allocation base amounts for each of the departments for the year. He has decided that General Administration costs should be allocated to the other departments based on the **amount of budgeted expenses in the other departments.** Human Resources costs are to be allocated based on the **number of employees** of the other departments. Costs of Procurement will be allocated based on the **number of purchase orders** required by the other using departments.

	General Administration	Human Resources	Procurement	Home Interiors	Multi-Unit Interiors	Business Interiors
Number of Purchase Orders	100	50	–	750	330	420
Number of Employees	10	–	15	27	25	48
Budgeted Department Costs	$600,000	$300,000	$500,000	$3,000,000	$4,000,000	$5,000,000

46. If Leon uses the direct method for allocating support department costs, how much support department cost will be allocated to Home Interiors, Multi-Unit Interiors, and Business Interiors?

	Home Interiors	**Multi-Unit Interiors**	**Business Interiors**	**Total Allocated**
General Administration to:				
Human Resources to:				
Procurement to:				

47. If Leon uses the step method for allocating support department costs, and Human Resources is allocated first and Procurement is allocated second, how much support department cost will be allocated to Home Interiors, Multi-Unit Interiors, and Business Interiors?

	General Administration	**Procurement**	**Home Interiors**	**Multi-Unit Interiors**	**Business Interiors**
Human Resources to:					
Procurement to:		XXXXXX			
General Administration to:	XXXXXX	XXXXXX			

48. Based on your answer to question 47, what is the total support department cost assigned to each direct department?

Home Interiors:

Multi-Unit Interiors:

Business Interiors:

49. Explain why the ordering of allocations using the step method was chosen for question 47. Use numbers to support your answer.

50. For this company's allocation problem, which method would you choose—the direct method or the step method? Explain your response.

Chapter 10

Answers to Questions and Exercises

Matching key terms

1. e 2. f 3. j 4. c 5. h 6. b 7. i 8. a 9. d 10. g

True or False

11. F. Support-service departments generate costs but no revenues.
12. T. The only purpose for support departments is to facilitate meeting the organization's objectives.
13. F. Direct departments exist to meet an organization's objectives, while support departments exist to help direct departments meet those objectives.
14. F. Any type of organization can have support departments.
15. T Support department costs are generally not traceable to direct departments.
16. F. Support department costs are relatively minor compared to production costs.
17. T. ABC systems for allocating support department costs are more accurate, but also more expensive and complex.
18. F. Production department costs are **never** allocated to support departments.
19. F. The direct method is called that because it assigns support department costs directly to production departments without regard to use of support department services by other support departments.
20. T. If one support department uses another's services a lot, then the costs of that support department are really not accurate. They should be higher.
21. T. Failure to include an allocation for support department costs would cause the contract to be under-priced.
22. F. Support department costs are not production costs—they appear on the income statement below gross margin (after cost of goods sold).
23. T. The benefit of ABC is that it is more accurate than other allocation methods.
24. F. The drawback to use of an ABC allocation approach is that it is more complex and more expensive than simpler approaches.
25. T. The whole idea behind allocating support department costs is to assign support department costs to production departments. Regardless of the method used, after allocation is complete, all support department costs will have been assigned to production departments.

Multiple Choice

26. b. Facilitating activities of production (direct) departments is the sole purpose for the existence of support departments. Answer a is incorrect because support departments do not generate profits. Answer c is wrong because support departments generate costs instead of revenues. Answer d is incorrect because support department costs are generally not traceable to direct departments.
27. c. Support department costs are not production costs, they can be recovered from general revenues without assigning them to direct departments, and allocation is not required by law.

28. a. Internal customers are different parts of an organization who use the services of support departments. External customers are the purchasers of products and services of an organization. Production managers' departments are the beneficiaries of support services—not the managers themselves. Support departments only benefit as a by-product of support department activities.

29. d. Answers a and c are incorrect because they incorrectly state that costs of direct departments should be allocated someplace else. Answer b is incorrect because support department costs are only allocated to other support departments as an interim step (in the step and ABC methods) to assigning them to production departments.

30. c. No actual costs or quantities can be used because they are known too late to use for allocating the support department costs.

31. b. The purpose of allocating support department costs is to assign them all to production departments.

32. d. Answer a is not correct because the objective is not to discourage use of support departments. Instead, it is intended to help managers to make better decisions about efficient use of the services. Answer b is incorrect because the allocation base should not cause unwarranted increased use of services. Answer c is incorrect because assigning the costs evenly across departments would ignore the uneven demand and use of support services across production departments.

33. c. Only answer c would provide a quantitative link between the production department and the resources used.

34. a. Unless support department costs are included, cost-plus contracts will include too little cost.

35. c. After all allocation of support departments is complete, the total amount to allocate should be included in production departments.

36. b. Although the final outcome of the allocations is to have all support department costs allocated to production departments, the step method does this by first assigning some support department costs to other support departments.

37. d. The direct method does not assign any support department costs to other support departments. This method has no impact on which departments can use the services (answer a), and HR costs can't be traced to direct departments (answer c). Answer b is wrong because allocations are made precisely in order to allocate to production departments.

38. c. The direct method will allocate no support department costs to other support departments. The IS department is more general, so some of its costs will be allocated to the Accounting Department, but no Accounting Department costs will be allocated to IS.

39. d. Food Service is allocated as follows: $36,000 × 8100/18000 = **$16,200**. The allocation base is total estimated meals served to the direct departments. 8100 meals to the Toddlers classes plus 9900 meals to the Pre-K classes totals 18,000 meals, the allocation base.

40. a. First, Administrative costs must be allocated to Food Services and the two direct departments. The allocation base for Administrative Services is $36,000 + $113,400 + $210,600 = $360,000. Food Services gets $60,000 × $36,000/$360,000 = $6,000. Of course, Administrative costs are also allocated to the direct departments ($36,720 to Pre-K, and $17,280 to Toddlers). Now, Food Services has $36,000 + $6,000 = $42,000. Now, allocate $42,000 from Food Services to the two direct departments. Toddlers classes get $42,000 × 8,100/18,000 = **$18,900**.

41. b. The step method goes further than the direct method, but it only allocates support department costs in one direction. Answer a describes allocations that should not occur during the support department allocation process. Answer c describes the direct method. Answer d is simply untrue.

42. d. Although organizations want managers to be conscious of the costs associated with support services they use, allocation of support department costs is not intended to cause managers to eliminate services that are actually needed.

43. b. Revising the allocation method generally causes shifts in the amounts allocated to individual departments, but it does nothing to change the total amount of support department cost to allocate. Since this is true, revised allocation just results in individual departments getting different allocations.

44. d. Production managers should not include support department allocations in assessing profitability of the products coming out of their production area.

45. a. Answers b, c, and d are all support department activities, none of which generate revenues. Answer a is a direct department activity that generates revenue.

Exercises

46. General and Administrative has an allocation base totaling $12,000,000 ($3 million + $4 million and $5 million). Allocation of $600,000 results in $600,000 × 3/12 = $150,000 to Home Interiors; $600,000 × 4/12 = $200,000 to Multi-Unit Interiors, and $600,000×5/12 = $250,000 to Business Interiors.

Human Resources has an allocation base of 100 employees. Home Interiors gets 27% of the $300,000 in HR costs, or $81,000. Multi-Unit Interiors gets 25%, or $75,000. Business Interiors gets 48%, or $144,000.

Procurement's allocation base is 1,500 purchase orders. Home Interiors gets 750/1,500 × $500,000 = $250,000. Multi-Unit Interiors gets 330/1,500×$500,000 = $110,000. Business Interiors gets 420/1,500 × $500,000 = $140,000.

47. The step method requires that the order of allocating support department costs be decided before any allocations are made. Human Resources costs are allocated first. Now the allocation base is increased from 100 employees to 125 employees because the employees in the support departments must be included in the base. The allocations are as follows:

General Administration gets 10/125 × $300,000 = $24,000
Procurement gets 15/125 × $300,000 = $36,000
Home Interiors gets 27/125 × $300,000 = $64,800
Multi-Unit Interiors gets 25/125 × $300,000 = $60,000
Business Interiors gets 48/125 × $300,000 = $115,200

Next, allocate Procurement. Procurement now has its own cost of $500,000 plus the $36,000 of costs allocated from Human Resources. The allocation base is 1,600 purchase orders, because the purchase orders from General Administration are included in the base. Notice, the purchase orders from HR are not included because with the step method once a department's costs are allocated, you never return to it with allocations from other departments. Allocated costs are as follows.

General Administration gets 100/1,600 × $536,000 = $33,500
Home Interiors gets 750/1,600 × $536,000 = $251,250
Multi-Unit Interiors gets 330/1,600 × $536,000 = $110,550
Business Interiors gets 420/1,600 × $536,000 = $140,700

Last, allocate the least general support department, General Administrative. General Administrative has its own costs, $600,000, plus costs from HR and Procurement, $24,000 + $33,500. General Administrative now totals $657,500, and it is allocated only to the direct departments. The allocations are shown below.

Home Interiors gets 3/12 × $657,500 = $164,375
Multi-Unit Interiors gets 4/12 × $657,500 = $219,167
Business Interiors gets 5/12 × $657,500 = $273,958

48. Total costs assigned to each direct department based on the step method are shown in the table below.

	Home Interiors	**Multi-Unit Interiors**	**Business Interiors**	**TOTALS**
Human Resources to:	64,800	60,000	115,200	$240,000
Procurement to:	251,250	110,550	140,700	$502,500
General Administration to:	164,375	219,167	273,958	658,500
TOTALS	**$480,425**	**$389,717**	**$529,858**	**$1,400,000**

49. Human Resources has 25/125 employees in support departments. This means that 20% of its base is in the other two support departments. Procurement has 9.09% of its base in the other two support departments. Even though General Administrative has the most support department cost, it is the least general. Only 6.25% of its allocation base (department cost) is used in support departments. This is $800,000/$12,800,000 = 6.25%. The order of the allocations is based on the support departments that are the most general (Human Resources) to the least general (General Administration).

50. The results for the step method are shown in the answer to question 48. The direct method's results are shown below, to allow comparison.

The direct method:

	Home Interiors	Multi-Unit Interiors	Business Interiors	TOTALS
Human Resources to:	81,000	75,000	144,000	$300,000
Procurement to:	250,000	110,000	140,000	$500,000
General Administration to:	150,000	200,000	250,000	600,000
TOTALS	**$481,000**	**$385,000**	**$534,000**	**$1,400,000**

The direct method is easier to use. When a pencil-and-paper calculation is used, it is the preferred method. A real example could have hundreds of support depart allocations, and a computerized system of allocation would likely be used, making use of the step method (which is more accurate) a more likely candidate for use. However, even with the help of the computer, analysts would still have to revise the estimates used to arrive at the correct allocations each year. Unnecessary complexities could be avoided by adopting the direct method, as long as the allocations do not result in material differences in the amounts allocated to the individual production departments. In this particular example, there does not appear to be a significant difference between results obtained from using the direct method, when compared to the step method's results. Although individual amounts allocated to the direct departments are different when the two results are compared, the totals allocated to direct departments are very close.

Chapter 11
Cost Estimation

Chapter Study Suggestions

Chapter 11 presents the methods commonly used for estimating costs. Organizations need to estimate costs for three reasons. First, cost estimation is used to manage costs. Second, it is used to make decisions. Third, cost estimation helps managers to plan and set standards. In order to estimate costs, a manager must understand the characteristics of the costs in his or her organization. Cost patterns can be simple or complex. They can be linear or nonlinear. They can be a combination of cost types, and they will probably change over time.

Chapter 11 describes linear, step (semi-fixed), and mixed (semi-variable) cost patterns, and provides ways to estimate these different types of costs. Regression analysis is a way to separate mixed costs into their fixed and variable components. Account analysis and the engineering method are two methods for estimating costs that require a more detailed estimation approach than regression.

Chapter Highlights

A. Cost Management Challenges. Chapter 11 addresses six cost management challenges.

1. Why must an organization estimate costs?

2. What cost patterns exist in different organizations?

3. What is multiple regression analysis? What is account analysis? How are the two similar and different from each other?

4. What is the engineering method of cost estimation, and how is it used?

5. How can cost estimation be used to predict profitability in the future?

6. Based on cost estimation, how should managers respond to profits that appear to be non-optimal?

B. Learning Objectives—This chapter has 5 learning objectives.

1. Chapter 11 explains why companies need to estimate the relation between costs and cost drivers.

2. The chapter demonstrates how to recognize cost patterns when they are fixed, step (semi-variable), and variable.

3. Chapter 11 explains the uses of simple and multiple regression for cost estimation purposes.

4. It presents the uses and interpretation of account analysis for cost estimation.

5. The engineering method of cost analysis is presented, and it's use and interpretation of results is discussed.

C. Cost estimation is the process of estimating the relation between costs and the cost drivers that cause them. Some costs are directly related to an activity, and can be estimated based on the activity. Other costs are indirectly related to an activity, and are not as easy to predict because they are indirect. This is one of the challenges that cost managers must address in estimating costs. Another challenge exists because costs and expenditures do not always occur at the same time. The main purposes of cost estimation are to manage costs, make decisions, and to plan and set standards.

1. A cost is what occurs when resources are acquired for production or other activity in an organization. Expenditures are the payments for the activities in an organization. Expenditures do not always occur at the same time as the cost. When there are big time differences between the cost activity and the expenditure for cost activity, cost managers need to distinguish between them. In most cases, managers assume that costs and expenditures match reasonably well. This simplifies the cost estimation process.

2. The understanding that "costs do not just happen" is tied to an understanding between costs and activities. Managers must identify activities that cause costs in order to estimate costs. They must then manage the activities in order to manage costs.

D. There are three reasons why organizations find it necessary to estimate costs. Cost estimation is used to (1) manage costs, (2) make decisions, and (3) plan and set standards.

1. Cost management is best accomplished by determining which activities drive costs, and then managing these activities. This topic has been addressed in Chapter 4 (ABC) and Chapter 5 (ABM).

2. Decision-making in a business setting is based on cost and profit information. Since resources are limited, organizations are always confronted with choosing among alternatives. Given two cost-causing alternatives, managers must use estimated costs before deciding which alternative to choose. Cost estimation requires that managers understand the underlying behavior of costs being estimated. Cost behavior is described below.

a. A simple cost behavior pattern is one in which costs are some combination of fixed and variable. Total variable costs change in proportion with total activity. In the simplest case, there is only one activity driving variable costs. Fixed costs are those costs that do not vary with activity. This simple cost pattern can be expressed mathematically. It is,

$$TC = F + VX,$$

where

TC = Total costs

F = Fixed costs

V = The cost driver rate

X = The number of cost driver units.

This simple mathematical expression is just the equation for a line, suggesting that the cost pattern shows a linear relationship between costs and activity.

E. Real-world applications of cost estimation can be depicted as a simple linear expression. However, a more realistic expression considers multiple cost drivers and complex cost behaviors. As always, managers must weigh the costs and benefits of using a more complex estimation method.

1. Another cost pattern commonly encountered is one with step costs, also known as semi-fixed costs. Step costs change with activity of the cost driver, but not in direct proportion. These costs increase in chunks. For instance, rent on a store is a fixed cost. However, if the store is not large to accommodate rapidly increased sales activity, then a larger, more expensive store may be rented, increasing this seemingly fixed cost based on increased activity (units sold).

2. When trying to determine the pattern of costs, one must take into consideration the relevant range of activity. The relevant range is the range over which an organization expects to operate, and over which assumed cost patterns are reasonably accurate. As long as the relevant range falls below the point where the next higher level of a step cost will be expended, one can assume the simpler cost estimation (TC = F + VX) model is useful for cost estimation.

3. Another cost pattern that might be encountered is a mixed cost. Mixed costs have elements of fixed costs and variable costs. Utility costs are a simple example. If, in a given month an organization shut down, it would still have some amount of electricity costs. When that same organization is open and operating, electricity costs will rise because the use of electricity has risen. There are many semi-variable costs that occur in a business setting.

4. Some cost patterns are even more complex than the three just described. The simple cost line, semi-fixed, and mixed cost patterns are all linear in nature. Some cost patterns are curved, and trying to predict such costs is more difficult than costs that are linear. These are called non-linear costs.

F. Once a cost pattern has been established for a cost or set of costs, the next step is to try to estimate those costs. There are three methods that are commonly used in practice: (1) statistical methods, especially simple and multiple regression analysis, (2) account analysis, and (3) engineering estimates. Since estimates may differ based on the estimation methods used, managers may choose two or all three of these methods to aid them in making the right decision. Each of these methods is discussed below.

1. Statistical cost estimation using simple regression analysis is one way to mathematically express the relation between costs and cost drivers. Regression analysis uses terminology that must be explained before the mechanics of its use can be illustrated.

   a. A dependent variable (or left-hand-side variable, or the "Y" variable) represents total costs in a cost model.

   b. The independent variable (or the right-hand-side variable, or the X variable) represents cost driver activity. The purpose of a regression model is to estimate the total costs, particularly the total cost driver amounts, given some level of activity.

   c. The independent variable (cost driver activity) drives the dependent variable (total cost). The dependent variable and the independent variable are correlated, meaning they move together.

   d. The regression model is used to estimate the Y variable. It estimates the variable rate. The intercept in the regression model is an estimate of fixed costs. The estimate is based on historical cost observations of cost driver activity, paired with total costs. In order for a regression analysis to be informative, there must be a logical relationship between costs and the chosen cost driver. The regression model must be limited to analysis within the relevant range of activity.

e. A simple regression model is based on the simple, linear cost estimation equation described earlier:

TC = F + VX, where TC represents total costs, F represents fixed costs, V stands for variable costs per unit for the cost driver, and X is the cost driver quantity. In a simple regression model, there is only one independent variable.

2. There are five steps to follow when a simple regression model is used to estimate costs.

a. First, identify the cost driver. This is the independent, or X variable.

b. Second, gather relevant data. This is the total cost per period (dependent, or Y variable), and the activity for the cost driver.

c. Third, plot the data in a scattergraph. This allows one to identify patterns and to look for errors. The Y-axis shows total costs. The X-axis shows cost driver activity. The scattergraph can be used as a preliminary assessment of the validity of assumptions about the cost driver and total costs. If there is a linear relationship, the scattergraph will show a pattern that would allow a line to be drawn as a rough estimate of costs for any point in the graph.

d. Fourth, run a regression analysis. A short tutorial for use of MS excel to run simple regression analysis is given in the Exercises at the end of this chapter.

e. Fifth, interpret the regression results. If there is a linear relationship between the independent variable and total cost, then regression will show a fixed cost component and a variable rate. Interpretation of the regression model helps one to understand whether the results will be good predictors of future costs. The most important measure of the validity of the results is the "r-square (R^2), which measures the proportion of the variation in the dependent variable (total costs) explained by the independent variable (cost driver activity). R^2 can range in value from 0 to 1. An R^2 of zero implies there is absolutely no relationship between the dependent and independent variables. An R^2 of one implies the dependent and independent variable are perfectly correlated with each other. A statistical rule of thumb is that an R^2 that is greater than .30 implies there is some relationship between the dependent and independent variables.

f. Here is an example of a regression problem's results. Suppose one wanted to estimate monthly costs of electricity. The cost driver is kilowatt-hours.

TC = \$500 + .06X, where X is the number of kilowatt-hours. If 10,000 kilowatt-hours of electricity is used, then total cost would be an estimated \$500 + \$.06(10,000) = \$500 + \$600 = \$1,100 per month.

See exercises 46-50 for a brief tutorial of regression analysis using Microsoft Excel.

3. A method that is even simpler than the simple regression method is the high-low method. With the high-low method, the only information needed is the highest observation-pair of costs and activity, and the lowest observation of cost and activity. The high-low method estimates the slope of one's cost line. Mathematically, the high-low model is:

    Slope = (Highest cost – lowest cost)/(highest quantity of cost driver – lowest quantity of cost driver)

    The answer obtained by using the high-low method is the variable (cost driver) rate per unit. Armed with the cost driver rate, substitute this value into another equation that allows one to solve for the intercept. This equation is:

    Intercept = Total cost at lowest cost driver level minus (Variable cost per unit times lowest quantity of cost driver).

    The intercept represents fixed costs. Using the highest cost-quantity pair will give the same answer for the intercept.

    Estimates of fixed costs and the variable rate using regression are more accurate Than the high-low method because regression uses more observations.

4. A more complex and sophisticated type of regression analysis is useful when more than one cost driver affects total costs. This is called multiple regression. Multiple regression is a regression model that has more than one independent variable. Multiple regression is a better predictive model. However, it requires that more information be collected. A multiple regression model that is structured based on the hierarchies described in earlier chapters of the text would be an informative one to predict costs. A cost driver at the unit-level, batch-level, product-level, and customer level would be a very useful predictive tool. The intercept could represent facility-level costs and activities. The regression model for different organizations could use such cost drivers in different combinations.

    a. For each total cost observation, the corresponding activity quantity must also be known in a multiple regression model. Each piece of information is used as input in the regression model. Notice that the R-square discussed in a simple regression model is replaced with an adjusted R-square in multiple regression. The interpretation is essentially the same.

    b. The 5 steps described for simple regression should be followed for multiple regression, except there are multiple X-variables.

5. Account analysis is another estimation tool that can be used by itself or in addition to regression analysis. Account analysis is based on past costs associated with each cost driver. Total costs are separated into categories that tie to the cost drivers. Costs are categorized by hierarchy (unit, batch, product, customer, and facility-level). With an activities-based cost system, total costs must be categorized into each activity. A complex ABC system with 100 cost drivers would greatly complicate account analysis.

a. The account analysis method follows three steps.

   i. Identify the activity accounts (unit, batch, product, customer, facility).
   ii. Collect cost and cost-driver amounts for each activity.
   iii. Calculate a cost-driver rate for each activity account.

b. Account analysis gives results that are similar to multiple regression. It offers two benefits. First, it allows decision makers to have a comparison with regression results (to validate or invalidate them). Another benefit is that account analysis may help analysts to spot trends or errors that might be overlooked if a computerized regression analysis is used. Account analysis is more labor intensive and time consuming than regression analysis.

6. There are five data problems that might arise when using regression or account analysis.

   a. Missing data can lead to inaccuracies of results. The more detailed the analysis is, the more likely it is that this problem will arise.

   b. Outliers are extreme, unusual observations. Outliers should be taken out of the group of regular outliers. For instance, if an air conditioner manufacturer is trying to estimate production costs, the costs for a month of production during a record-breaking heat wave may be an outlier. The manufacturer may have a lot of overtime and expedited costs for such an unusual month.

   c. Allocated and discretionary costs should be included in regression and account analysis with caution. Allocated costs may appear to be variable if they are allocated based on some volume of a cost driver. Discretionary costs like advertising may also appear to be variable when assigned to segments of an organization.

   d. Since historical costs are not usually adjusted for inflation, use of historical costs may give misleading results in highly inflationary period.

   e. Activities may sometimes be mismatched with expenditures (for instance, billing for long distance costs may be a month later than recorded activity). Managers should recognize and correct such mismatches.

7. The engineering method is the third cost estimation method in use by organizations. Engineering estimates are cost estimates based on measurement and pricing of the work involved in the activities that go into a product. The engineering method differs from regression and account analysis in one important way. It uses cost and activity projections instead of historical costs. Cost analysts prepare detailed step-by-step analysis of each activity required to make a product, together with the costs involved.

   a. The engineering method has several advantages. The detailed cost information it provides allows managers to predict future costs with more accuracy than account analysis or regression. The detailed information provides a benchmark to be used to evaluate future activities. Since it does not rely on historical information, it can be used to estimate costs for totally new activities. The engineering method also helps managers to identify non-value-added activities.

Results can also be used for sensitivity analysis related to product and process variety, and revised cost estimation.

b. The engineering method has some drawbacks too. One obvious one is that it is expensive and time-consuming. Another is that it is based on estimates, and may not be properly adjusted for conditions that are non-optimal.

8. The three cost estimation methods all have benefits and drawbacks. If all three methods are used, they may give conflicting results.

9. Use of the cost estimation analyses requires an understanding of which information to use when, and how to use it. Suppose an organization is using cost estimates to decide if part of their operations should be outsourced? The cost estimation analysis should be modified to show which costs will go away, and which ones will be added.

G. Cost managers must resist any temptation to manipulate cost estimation results to their advantage. Statistics can be inappropriately used to support one's decision, when the decision should probably be a different one.

H. Managers must choose the estimation method or methods that are best for their organization. Regression is the least costly, and probably the easiest to collect data for. Managers who want more detailed, insightful information should consider account analysis or the engineering method. The practical reality is that the cost of estimation procedures, as well as the human resources needed to develop, implement and maintain the estimation models may be a driving factor in which method to choose.

Managers must also consider how well their own costs fit the different estimation methods, using logic, good sense and judgement to decide which models make the most sense for them to use.

1. Regression analyses are the easiest, but do not give a lot of insight into the underlying reasons for costs.

2. Account analyses allow one to look at patterns of cost, and help managers to see how and why resources are being used. Account analysis is more labor-intensive and time-consuming (and therefore more expensive) than regression analysis.

3. Engineering analyses force managers to think about every cost being incurred to achieve some objective, and help them to identify non-value-added costs. It is very expensive to do, and most of the information is estimated. Thus, cost estimates are based on numbers that are also estimates.

Chapter 11

REVIEW AND SELF TEST QUESTIONS AND EXERCISES

Matching key terms

Match the following terms to the correct definition by writing the correct letter next to the correct definition.

a. mixed cost	b. simple regression	c. multiple regression
d. dependent variable	e. goodness of fit	f. high-low method
g. account analysis	h. R-square	i. engineering estimates
j. outliers		

_____ 1. A measure of how closely variation in the independent variables matches variation in the dependent variable.

_____ 2. A cost estimation method that relies on measuring and pricing work involved in activities that go into a product.

_____ 3. A way to estimate fixed costs and a variable rate when there is only one cost driver.

_____ 4. The occurrence of some activity that is beyond the normal range of activity.

_____ 5. A cost estimation method that uses multiple cost drivers.

_____ 6. A simple cost estimation method that uses the highest and lowest cost-driver activity to estimate future costs.

_____ 7. A cost estimation method based on past costs associated with each cost driver.

_____ 8. In a cost model, total costs.

_____ 9. A statistical measure that shows the proportion of variation in the dependent variable explained by the independent variable.

_____10. A cost that has a fixed portion and a variable portion.

True or False

For each of the following statements enter a T or an F in the blank to indicate whether the statement is true or false.

_____11. Cost estimation is needed by managers in order to manage costs.

_____12. Cost estimation is required by users of financial statements.

_____13. When total cost is due to more than one activity, multiple regression is a good cost estimation method to consider

_____14. A semi-fixed cost is the same as a semi-variable cost.

_____15. Within a relevant range, a step cost may be treated as a fixed cost.

_____16. A variable cost increases in proportion with increases in a cost driver's activity.

_____17. A fixed cost stays the same regardless of activity, within a relevant range of activity.

_____18. The relevant range represents the range of activity that an organization is likely to operate at.

_____19. Simple regression analysis is the best cost estimation method to use when costs are nonlinear.

_____20. A dependent variable in a regression equation for cost estimation represents total fixed costs.

_____21. In regression, R-square is a measure of the correlation between total costs and a cost driver's activity.

_____22. Account analysis is a way to estimate costs that relies on estimated costs and activities.

_____23. The engineering method is the simplest, least expensive method, compared to regression and account analysis.

_____24. Cost managers can use cost estimation to plan and set standards.

_____25. The engineering method of cost estimation may reveal non-value-added activities.

Multiple Choice

Choose the best answer by writing the letter corresponding to your choice in the space provided.

______26. Which of the following is **not** a valid reason for estimating costs?

a) Cost estimation is useful for planning purposes.
b) Cost estimation is useful for making decisions.
c) Cost estimation is useful for eliminating non-value-added costs.
d) Cost estimation is useful for managing costs.

______27. A cost can be estimated by using the following equation: Total cost = Fixed costs + a cost driver rate × quantity of the cost driver. If a cost can be estimated this way, it is probably

a) a mixed cost.
b) a nonlinear cost.
c) a fixed cost.
d) a curvilinear cost.

______28. Which of the following correctly describes the relevant range?

a) The relevant range is the range over which an organization expects to operate, and over which cost patterns are presumed to be reasonably accurate.
b) The relevant range is the range over which an organization plans to operate in the future, after capacity is expanded.
c) An organization must operate above the relevant range to remain profitable.
d) An organization must operate below the relevant range in order to control costs.

______29. A manufacturing facility has reached its maximum production capacity, and in order to accommodate its increased production needs, it will have to invest in additional production equipment. What kind of cost pattern is being described by this situation?

a) This describes a fixed cost pattern.
b) This describes a semi-fixed cost pattern.
c) This describes a variable cost pattern.
d) This describes a mixed cost pattern.

______30. Which of the following best describes an instance where multiple regression is an appropriate cost estimation method to use?

a) Total costs are due almost completely to number of units produced.
b) Total costs are almost all fixed, and are unlikely to change much within a relevant range.
c) Total costs occur because of numerous different activities and some fixed costs.
d) Total costs are partly fixed, but some costs vary with number of employees.

_____31. The high-low method is a simplified cost estimation procedure. The purpose of the high-low method is to determine the slope of a cost line. The slope measures

a) the total amount of cost at a given level of activity.
b) the cost rate for one unit of the cost driver.
c) the total amount of fixed cost.
d) the quantity of activity.

_____32. The simple regression model can be used to estimate costs. The equation for the simple regression model is based on the simple, linear cost estimation equation. It is: TC = F + VX, where TC represents total costs, F represents fixed costs, V stands for variable costs per unit for the cost driver, and X is the cost driver quantity. Regression uses observations of total costs and corresponding quantities of activity. The regression solution gives you

a) the estimated fixed costs and estimated total variable costs.
b) the estimated total costs and estimated total fixed costs.
c) the estimated total fixed costs and estimated total quantity of the cost driver.
d) the estimated fixed costs and the cost rate per unit of a cost driver.

_____33. The R-square is a measure of the quality of results obtained from regression analysis. R-square expresses

a) how closely related fixed costs are to variable costs.
b) how closely related total costs are to cost driver activity.
c) how closely related fixed costs are to total costs.
d) how closely related variable costs are to cost driver activity.

_____34. A more complex cost estimation than simple regression is multiple regression. Multiple regression is more complex because it calculates

a) estimates of more than one type of cost.
b) estimates of rates for more than one cost driver.
c) estimates of fixed costs and a variable rate.
d) estimates of fixed costs and variable costs.

_____35. A simple regression was run to derive estimated monthly costs of pizza delivery for each delivery truck, for a major pizza chain. With miles driven as the cost driver activity, the regression provided the following results. TC = $1,500 + .12X. If, in a given month the pizza company expects a truck to be driven 1,960 miles, what is the estimated total cost of using this truck?

a) $1,500.12
b) $3,460
c) $1,735.20
d) Not enough information is given to determine total estimated cost for the truck.

______36. Suppose the regression analysis from question 35 had an r-square of .88. This means which of the following?

a) The dependent variable is closely related to the independent variable.
b) The dependent variable is not closely related to the independent variable.
c) The dependent variable is 88% of the independent variable.
d) The independent variable has a rate of $.88 per unit of the cost driver.

______37. A cost manager has decided to use multiple regression, using several cost drivers to estimate overhead costs in a production facility. Which of the following would **not** be a logical cost driver to use?

a) Number of hours of production workers (to estimate contribution of labor costs to total OH costs).
b) Number of batches completed per month (to estimate contribution of batch-level costs to total OH costs).
c) Number of square feet of space in the production facility (to estimate contribution of machinery costs to total OH costs).
d) Number of setups (to estimate the contribution of setup costs to total OH costs).

______38. Account analysis is another cost estimation method that can be used instead of simple regression analysis. Which of the following is an advantage of account analysis over simple regression analysis?

a) Account analysis is usually less expensive to implement and use than regression analysis is.
b) Account analysis may provide more detailed breakdowns of the cost-activity relationships than simple regression provides.
c) Account analysis does not use historical cost information like regression analysis does.
d) Account analysis does not require that any information for costs be categorized based on cost-driver activity.

______39. Which of the following is **not** a data problem that might be encountered when using regression?

a) Outliers may distort the results of the analyses.
b) Historical costs not adjusted for inflation may distort estimates of future costs if inflation is expected to be high in the future.
c) Missing or omitted data may lead to inaccuracies of results.
d) Use of future costs in the analyses may be subjective.

______40. The engineering method is a way to estimate future costs that is based on

a) historical cost estimates of activities.
b) future cost estimates of activities.
c) historical projections of new products that might be introduced.
d) calculating the costs of value-added activities (ignoring non-value-added activities).

_____41. The greatest advantage that the engineering method has over regression and account analysis is that

a) it forces managers to think about every cost incurred to meet some objective.
b) it is the least expensive cost estimation method to use.
c) it provides the most statistically sound estimation information.
d) it relies on historical cost information.

_____42. What is one thing that the engineering method allows that regression and account analysis do **not** allow?

a) It can help managers to develop cost estimates based on historical cost information, while regression and account analysis cannot.
b) It can be used to estimate costs of production activities, while account analysis and regression cannot.
c) It can be used to estimate costs for totally new activities, while regression and account analysis cannot.
d) It can be used to manage costs, while regression and account analysis cannot.

_____43. Even though simple regression and the high-low methods do the same thing, the results obtained for the same cost estimation may be different. Which of the following is **not** a reason for differences between the two methods?

a) The high-low method uses only two observations for its cost estimation, but regression uses more than two observations.
b) The observations in the high-low method might be outliers at the high end or the low end. Regression automatically ignores outliers.
c) The observations used in the high-low method may not be truly representative of the typical observations that occur for a particular cost/activity.
d) The high-low method is a less accurate estimation than the regression method.

_____44. A multiple regression analysis was run using four independent variables. They were number of deliveries (X_1), number of products (X_2), number of units of product (X_3), and number of labor hours (X_4). The regression analysis provided the following results.

Total Costs = \$35,000 + \$500X_1 + \$3,000X_2, + \$15X_3 + \$20X_4

If an organization projects that they will have 10 deliveries, 20 different products, 30,000 units of product, and 50,000 labor hours, how much will estimated total costs be for that month?

a) \$35,000
b) \$38,535
c) \$115,030
d) \$1,550,000

_____45. When comparing multiple regression to simple regression, which of the following is a key difference between the two methods?

a) Simple regression uses one cost driver, and multiple regression uses more than one cost driver.
b) Simple regression can be used to estimate total costs, and multiple regression can be used to estimate variable costs.
c) Simple regression uses historical cost information, and multiple regression uses future cost information.
d) Simple regression is not a statistical method, and multiple regression is a statistical method.

Exercises

The exercises that follow require that you use Excel to run a simple regression analysis. Before attempting to complete the exercises, a brief tutorial and a simple example are given for you to practice on.

A Tutorial for Running Simple Regression Using Microsoft Excel

1. Get into Microsoft Excel. You'll see an empty worksheet. First, look under tools in the menu. If one of your options is "data analysis", go to **step 4**. If data analysis is <u>NOT</u> one of the options, then go to step 2.
2. Go to tools. Under tools, choose "add-ins". You'll be given a menu of additional options that can be added to the tools menu.
3. Choose "Analysis Toolpak" (click on the box for it, and click on "OK". You might be prompted to install this function. Analysis Toolpak contains regression. Now you can proceed.
4. Enter the dependent variables (total cost information) in column A.
5. Enter independent variables (cost driver activity) in column B.
6. Under Tools, choose Data Analysis. A menu for data analysis will appear. Scroll down, and choose Regression.
7. A menu asking for ranges will appear. The Y range is for the **dependent** variables (total costs). The X range is for the **independent variables** (cost driver activity). Enter A1:A10 (if you have 10 observations), for the Y range, and B1:B10 for the X range. Go to the output range, and enter C1 for the output range. Otherwise, the regression analysis will appear on another worksheet.
8. Click on OK. The regression analysis will be done, and output will appear in cells C1 through K18. Since some of the columns for the output are not wide enough, widen columns C, D, E, and F so that you can print and read your results. To widen columns, place the arrow at the top of the column you want to widen, look for a black cross symbol at the top of a column (lower right-hand side), and click twice. This automatically widens the column to accommodate the largest entry in the column.
9. Print the input and your results.
10. Your results should make sense. Note that the output for EXCEL prints ANOVA results, which are not needed for simple regression. From the output, you need the R Square, number of observations (to check your data input), and the coefficient values for the intercept and the X variable. A common mistake is to enter the dependent variable (total cost) in place of the independent variable (cost driver activity), and vice versa. If you do this, you will get answers that are probably not logical for the problem you are trying to solve.

A SIMPLE EXAMPLE

A college student, Mildred, wants to finance her education by running a food wagon on campus, but she doesn't know how to estimate costs. Based on her father's costs in his wagon on campus, she has kept track of his expenses, and his hot dog sales (that is his main product). She has a friend at school who is learning regression in Accounting 102. Mildred's friend just bought a new computer, and she is eager to use the software loaded on it. She can help Mildred to estimate future costs, based on historical costs. The actual total costs and quantity of hot dog sales are given below, for ten weeks.

TOTAL COST	**HOT DOGS**
189	700
206	830
227	755
179	729
234	803
240	889
198	712
206	815
192	764
347	1500

RUN A SIMPLE REGRESSION USING EXCEL for this example.

Solution to the Sample Problem for Regression

TOTAL COST	HOT DOGS
189	700
206	830
227	755
179	729
234	803
240	889
198	712
206	815
192	764
347	1500

SUMMARY OUTPUT

Regression Statistics	
Multiple R	0.953367087
R Square	**0.908908802**
Adjusted R Square	0.897522403
Standard Error	15.47936822
Observations	10

ANOVA

	df	*SS*	*MS*	*F*
Regression	1	19126.71328	19126.71328	79.82407322
Residual	8	1916.886724	239.6108405	
Total	9	21043.6		

	Coefficients	*Standard Error*	*t Stat*	*P-value*
Intercept	**55.68797872**	19.22592776	2.896504107	0.01999863
X Variable 1	**0.195494906**	0.021881067	8.934431891	1.9554E-05

The information that is needed from the regression analysis is in bold. The intercept coefficient, 55.68797872 represents fixed costs. The weekly fixed cost of running the food wagon is $55.69. The X Variable 1 is the estimate of the cost driver rate. It is $.195 per hot dog sold. The r-square of .908908802 suggests a very high correlation between total costs and the number of hot dogs sold. If 1,000 hot dogs are sold, estimated costs would be $55.69 + $.195(1,000) = $250.69.

Exercises

Please use the following information about Just Taxes, Inc. to answer the following 5 questions.

Just Taxes, Inc. is a business operating in the northeastern US. The firm prepares income tax returns for individuals and small businesses. Recently, the firm's owner has been considering the acquisition of Burnette's Bookkeeping Services Company as a diversification strategy. Burnette's does the books for small to medium sized businesses. Before buying the firm, the controller of Just Taxes wants to estimate the monthly production costs of Burnette's Bookkeeping Services. Since some of the costs are fixed, and some are variable, and bookkeeping and associated costs will fluctuate from month to month the controller of the firm has assigned the newest accountant (you) to complete an analysis of estimated costs for completion of a bookkeeping job for a one month period for Burnette's Bookkeeping Services. Since the planned acquisition of Burnette's is a hostile takeover, Burnette's Bookkeeping Services does not want to release any cost information to Just Taxes, Inc. However, from monthly industry reports, Just Taxes has obtained the following information about Burnette's Bookkeeping Services for 2004.

MONTH	TOTAL MONTHLY COSTS	NUMBER OF BOOKKEEPING JOBS COMPLETED
January	$9,050,000	36,900
February	18,450,000	57,900
March	23,580,000	90,500
April	27,980,000	96,800
May	14,450,000	34,300
June	895,000	4,260
July	4,525,000	14,700
August	1,472,000	3,725
September	7,600,500	17,600
October	3,380,000	7,200
November	5,960,000	15,200
December	10,250,000	26,700

46. Using Microsoft Excel, run a simple regression analysis. Use your output to answer questions 47 to 50.

47. For Just Taxes, one big consideration in acquiring Burnette's Bookkeeping Services is that operating costs that are fixed could probably be reduced. At a minimum, some operating costs could be eliminated since some of Burnette's offices would be closed, and those offices would be merged with a Just Taxes office. Based on your regression results, what are monthly fixed costs for Burnette's estimated to be?

48. **What is the estimated variable cost associated with the completion of one bookkeeping job?**

49. **What is the r-square for the regression? What does r-square mean regarding the regression analysis? For Burnette's, what can be said about the firm's costs, based on r-square?**

50. **Using the results of your regression, estimate the total costs for the month for Burnette's if 30,000 bookkeeping jobs are completed.**

Answers to Questions and Exercises

Matching key terms

1. e 2. i 3. b 4. j 5. c 6. f 7. g 8. d 9. h 10. a

True or False

11. T. Cost management is one of three reasons managers estimate costs. They also use cost estimation to make decisions and to plan and set standards.
12. F. Cost estimation is used by cost managers, not by users of financial statements.
13. T. Multiple regression provides estimates of fixed cost plus multiple cost-driver rates.
14. F. Semi-fixed, or step costs are fixed costs that increase in chunks, when activity increases beyond some upper range. Semi-variable costs consist of both fixed costs and variable costs.
15. T. As long as activity falls below a certain range, it is not necessary to invest in more fixed resources to accommodate higher amounts of activity.
16. T. This is the definition of a variable cost.
17. T. This is the definition of a fixed cost.
18. T. When estimating costs, it is good to know what the relevant range is. Estimation outside of the relevant range may give managers inaccurate estimates.
19. F. Simple regression is most useful when costs and activities have a linear relationship.
20. F. The dependent variable in regression for cost estimation represents total costs—not fixed costs.
21. T. Total cost is the dependent variable, and the cost driver is the independent variable. R-square measures the correlation between the dependent variable and the independent variable.
22. F. Account analysis relies totally on historical costs.
23. F. The engineering method is the most complex and most expensive cost estimation method, compared to regression and account analysis.
24. T. Planning and setting standards is one of the main uses for cost estimation.
25. T. Since the engineering method requires that a process be evaluated step-by-step, it may reveal the presence of non-value-added activities.

Multiple Choice

26. c. Although one of the cost estimation methods, the engineering method may help managers to identify non-value-added costs, it does not provide a method for eliminating them.
27. a. The equation has a fixed component and a variable portion (the cost driver rate). That is what a mixed cost is—one that has a fixed component and a variable component. A nonlinear cost can't be estimated by using the equation described (answer b), because the equation is linear. The equation does not describe a pure fixed cost (answer c); nor does it describe a curvilinear cost (answer d).
28. a. Cost estimation is done under the assumption that activities will fall within a pre-specified range. This assumption is needed to avoid having step costs be estimated inaccurately.
29. b. This situation describes a semi-fixed, or step cost. Costs that increase in chunks, after some activity has exceeded a threshold are semi-fixed because they remain the same unless that threshold is exceeded.
30. c. Multiple regression is most appropriate when there are numerous activities that contribute to total costs of a business. If the appropriate cost drivers are identified, multiple regression is a good way to estimate total costs with some level of accuracy.

31. b. The slope represents the variable rate. Once you obtain the estimated variable rate, the high-low method can be used to obtain an estimate of the fixed costs, by using the cost equation at either the high observation or the low observation.
32. d. The input to the regression analysis consists of observations of total costs and cost driver activity. The output consists of an intercept term, which is an estimate of fixed costs, and an X variable, which is an estimate of the cost rate for one unit of the cost driver.
33. b. The r-square in regression measures the correlation between the dependent and independent variables. In a regression analysis used to estimate costs, total cost is the dependent variable and cost driver activity is the independent variable.
34. b. Multiple regression has two or more independent variables. The independent variable for cost estimation is the cost driver, and a rate is calculated for each one in a multiple regression model. Answer a is wrong because it still provides a way to estimate total costs, for chosen levels of activity. Answer c is the description of simple regression. Answer d is incorrect because regression (multiple or simple) does not provide estimates of fixed and variable costs.
35. c. Fixed cost is estimated at $1,500. Variable costs are $.12 × 1,960 miles = $235.20. $1,500 + $235.20 = $1735.20.
36. a. The closer r-square is to 1.00, the more closely related the dependent and independent variables are to each other. A statistical rule of thumb says that an r-square greater than .30 implies correlation between the dependent and independent variables.
37. c. The cost driver should have a meaningful relationship with the cost. Square feet of space would not have a meaningful relation with the cost of operating machinery. All of the other answers correctly relate to the costs that they would be used to estimate.
38. b. Simple regression only allows one cost driver to be used to estimate costs. Account analysis is more like multiple regression because it requires that costs be separated into many categories.
39. d. Future costs are not used in regression analysis.
40. b. The engineering method differs from regression and account analysis because those methods both use historical cost and activity information as a basis for estimating future costs. The engineering method uses estimates of future activities and their related costs.
41. a. Since the engineering method is based on a step-by-step analysis of the activities that are needed to complete a process, it helps managers to think about whether each step is necessary. It is not the least expensive—it is the most expensive of the three estimation methods described (answer b). Regression provides the most statistically sound information (answer c). It uses future and current cost and activity information (answer d).
42. c. Regression and account analysis cannot provide estimates for new products or processes because they rely wholly on historical costs and activities for existing processes.
43. b. The first statement in answer b is true—the high-low method may be using an outlier since it only uses the two most extreme observations to estimate the cost equation. The second statement is not true though. The outliers are not automatically eliminated from the regression analysis. The other three answers are true reasons for differences between the two methods.
44. d. The total cost is estimated at $35,000 + ($500 × 10) + ($3,000 × 20) + ($15 × 30,000) + $20 × $50,000) = $35,000 + $5,000 + $60,000 + $450,000 + $1,000,000 = $1,550,000.
45. a. Cost driver activity is an independent variable in regression. In multiple regression, two or more independent variables are identified and used.

Exercises

46. The output from Microsoft Excel is given below.

SUMMARY OUTPUT

Regression Statistics	
Multiple R	0.978416388
R Square	**0.957298628**
Adjusted R Square	0.953028491
Standard Error	1901307.454
Observations	12

ANOVA

	df
Regression	1
Residual	10
Total	11

	Coefficients
Intercept	**1569949.858**
X Variable 1	**268.0067073**

47. Fixed costs are the Intercept coefficient in the Excel output. They are estimated at $1,569,949.86.
48. The X Variable 1 coefficient is the estimated variable rate. For Burnette's Bookkeeping Services, the cost of one bookkeeping job is estimated at $268.01.
49. R-square is .95729. This means that the cost driver, bookkeeping jobs is nearly perfectly correlated with total costs. This would make cost estimation for the takeover candidate fairly reliable.
50. If 30,000 jobs were completed for Burnette's, estimated total cost would be $1,569,949.86 + (30,000 × $268.01), or $1,569,949.86 + $8,040,300 = **$9,610,249.86**

Chapter 12
Financial and Cost-Volume-Profit Models

Chapter Study Suggestions

Chapter 12 presents some techniques for analyzing profitability based on financial models. A financial model, which is a representation of reality, allows managers to make decisions without having to implement ideas first. Financial modeling gives managers insights into possible outcomes of decisions, so that they can identify bad decisions (or good ones) ahead of time. One model, the cost-volume-profit (CVP) model shows how managers can determine what it takes to break even on a project or business venture. The CVP model also shows what it takes to make pre-specified amounts of profit on such ventures. The basic CVP model is extended to one that allows two or more products to be treated as one bundle of goods, and then goes a step further by describing an activity-based CVP model. Sensitivity and scenario analyses are introduced.

A good financial model should be designed to meet three objectives. First, the model should be useful for making decisions, and the cost of having a model should not exceed the benefits gained by having them. Second, in order for the model to be useful, the model must be capable of accurately and reliably depicting the relevant factors and relations. Third, financial models should be flexible, so that different assumptions can be made regarding inputs, activities and results. Computerized financial models can provide this flexibility.

Chapter Highlights

A. Cost Management Challenges. Chapter 12 offers three cost management challenges.

1. What do cost managers need to know to build useful financial planning models?

2. Can financial models help to define risk so that managers know what uncertainties lie ahead?

3. Should managers always focus on maximizing revenues from the most profitable products without regard to resource constraints?

B. Learning Objectives—This chapter has 5 learning objectives.

1. Chapter 12 introduces financial modeling, and illustrates the design of models to match strategic and operational decisions.

2. The chapter shows how to build a basic cost-volume-profit (CVP) model.

3. It shows how a computerized model can be developed.

4. The basic one-product, one-cost driver CVP model can be extended to a multiple-product model with multiple cost drivers.

5. Use of sensitivity analysis to evaluate the risks associated with different scenarios is introduced.

C. Financial models are representations of reality in the business world. A model allows one to see how something is supposed to work. A financial model allows an organization to test the interaction of economic variables in a variety of settings. Financial models require that analysts develop a set of equations that represent a company's operating and financial relationships. These may include things like the relation of sales to variable costs, inventory turnover, and the relative proportions of various products sold. Once a financial model is developed, it can be used to explore different combinations of the variables that interact with each other, to see what outcomes to expect given different scenarios.

Financial models offer several benefits to users. Once the model is developed, users can concentrate on business analysis instead of number crunching. It gives managers insight into possible business outcomes without the risk of trying them first. It is, therefore, possible to identify bad business decisions ahead of time.

On a cautionary note, models are only as good as the information that goes into them. Faulty assumptions in building a model will lead to faulty predictions and bad business decisions.

D. One model that has proven to be especially useful is the cost-volume-profit (CVP) model. This model shows the effects of volume changes on an organization's costs, revenues, and income. This basic model combines four important variables—volume of sales, costs, revenue and profits. Although the model is called cost-volume-profit, it can be used by nonprofit organizations as well. Such organizations perform analyses to assure that they spend only the funds they have. An important calculation using the basic CVP model is the breakeven point. This is a special type of CVP analysis. The breakeven point is the volume of activity that generates just enough revenue to cover all costs for an organization. It is the level of sales volume where an organization is not making any profit, but they are not losing money either.

1. The breakeven point is best understood if costs and revenues are expressed in a manner that departs from the traditional presentation of costs and revenues. The format that aids in understanding how to achieve the breakeven point is called the contribution margin (CM) format. This type of profit-reporting approach splits costs into two categories—fixed costs and variable costs.

    a. The CM format of the income statement is shown in brief form as follows:

        Sales revenue
        Less Total Variable Cost
        = Total contribution margin
        Less total fixed costs
        = Operating income
        Less income taxes, other non-operating income
        = Net income

    b. This format is useful because variable costs change with sales activity. Since this is true, sales revenue, variable costs and total contribution can all be expressed in terms of volume times a dollar amount per unit sold. For instance, suppose a product can be sold for $40. Variable cost for each unit is $25. This leaves a contribution per unit of $15 ($40–$25). For every unit sold, $15 in contribution margin is generated. The contribution margin can be used first to cover fixed costs, and then what is left after covering fixed costs and income taxes is net income.

2. Calculation of the breakeven point can be accomplished using the contribution-margin approach. In order to use this approach, the CM per unit must be known, and estimated fixed costs must be known. Suppose in the example given above, the CM of $15 per unit must be used to cover $45,000 in fixed costs. Then, $45,000/$15 = 3,000 units. To check the accuracy of this, multiply 3,000 units times the $15 CM, to get $45,000 in contribution margin. This is the breakeven point.

3. Another way to calculate the breakeven point is to use the equation approach. To see how the equation approach is derived, look at the equation showing how operating income is obtained:

    1) Sales revenue – Total cost = Operating income. Total cost can be split into fixed and variable costs:
    2) Sales revenue – Variable cost – Fixed cost = Operating income. Sales revenue and variable costs can be expressed differently, based on number of units sold:
    3) (Selling price per unit × sales volume) – (Variable cost per unit × sales volume) – Fixed costs = Operating income. Since, at the breakeven point, Operating income is zero, the equation can be written as:
    4) (Selling price per unit × sales volume) – (Variable cost per unit × sales volume) – Fixed costs = $0. Next, rearrange the equation by adding Fixed costs to both sides of the equation, to get:
    5) (Selling price × sales volume) – (Variable cost per unit × sales volume) = Fixed costs. Rearrange the left-hand-side of the equation, combining the sales volume terms, to get:
    6) (Selling price – Variable cost per unit) × Sales volume = Fixed costs. Finally, to get Sales volume on one side of the equation by itself, divide both sides by (Selling price – Variable cost):
    7) Sales volume = Fixed costs/(Selling price – Variable cost). This gives you the sales volume at the breakeven point.

    Use the example given above to see if this approach works. Sales volume = $45,000/$40–$25) = $45,000/$15 = 3,000 units, which is the same result obtained before.

4. The CVP model can also be graphed. Graphing the model helps managers see what it will take to break even, and then they can see what it takes to make profit. It also shows how much sales would have to decline before an already profitable business begins to lose money.

E. Organizations in business to earn profits want to perform beyond the breakeven point. CVP analysis can be used to estimate the sales volume needed to attain target amounts of profit. If the target amount of operating income is known, then extending the CVP model beyond the breakeven point is fairly simple. All that is required is that target operating income be added to estimated fixed costs. In the example given above, suppose the organization wanted to earn operating income of $30,000. In order to determine the sales volume needed to achieve this income, use the equation form of the CM model:

    Sales volume = Fixed costs/(Selling price – Variable cost). This model needs to be expanded to include operating income of $30,000. Then, Sales volume = Fixed costs + Target operating income/(Selling price – Variable cost). Using the amounts given before, Sales volume = ($45,000 + $30,000)/$15 = 5,000 units.

F. Another useful result that can be derived from the CVP model is operating leverage. Operating leverage measures the risk of missing sales targets. Measured as contribution margin divided by operating income, it shows what amount of contribution margin is needed to cover operating (i.e., fixed or committed) costs.

G. Computer software such as MS Excel or Lotus can be used to set up a CVP model. This provides the ability to easily change the assumptions so that sensitivity analyses can be performed. There are also commercially sold financial management packages that allow CVP analyses to be completed. The variables can be revised, manipulated, and rearranged, to see what the profit outcomes would be if assumptions about price, volume, and costs were changed. These changes are best accomplished using computer software. This computer-based sensitivity analysis shows how the outcome of a decision process changes as assumptions change.

H. Organizations making profit must also pay income taxes. A business only gets to keep income after taxes (net income). Thus, the CVP analysis is more informative if it shows what it will take to generate a target amount of net income. In order to calculate the sales volume needed to achieve a specified amount of net income, a tax rate, as a percentage of operating income is assumed. Mathematically, the amount of net income can be expressed as a percentage of operating income. Look at the following equations to see why this is true. Let net income be represented by after-tax income, and before-tax income represent operating income. Let t equal the tax rate.

1) After-tax income = Before-tax income – income taxes. The amount of income tax is Before-tax income × t. Restated:
2) After-tax income = Before-tax income – (Before – tax income × t). Rearrange the right-hand-side of the equation, to get:
3) After-tax income = Before-tax income × (1 – t). Divide both sides of the equation by (1 – t) to get:
4) After-tax income/(1 – t) = Before-tax income.

1. Since organizations may establish target net income, now it is a straightforward step to calculate the amount of sales volume needed to achieve some target operating income as well. Extending the earlier example, suppose the tax rate is 20% and target operating income is, as before, $30,000. Then net income is 1–the tax rate of 20%, or 80% of $30,000 = $24,000. Suppose the net income of $24,000 is the stated target and target operating income is not known. It can be obtained by using the rearranged equation above: After – tax income/(1 – t) = Before – tax income – $24,000/(1 – .20) = Before-tax income = $24,000/.80 = $30,000. Then, the sales volume needed could be determined as before.

I. The basic model can be extended to assess the impact of price, cost and volume changes, along with changes in product mix and income taxes. CVP analysis as described so far is fine for a very simple business with only one product and a simple cost structure. Most organizations have many products, adding complexity to the CVP analysis. The CVP model can quickly become a modeling tool that can only be used via computer software. A simple example with two or three products can be used to illustrate how a multiple-product CVP model works. In this simple example, another simplifying assumption is made. It is assumed that the relative proportions of each type of product sold remains the same.

1. When two or more products are sold, and the sales mix is held constant, a weighted average unit contribution margin (WAUCM) can be computed. The best way to think about the WAUCM is to think of a "unit" as a bundle, consisting of the number of items in each bundle, for each product. For instance, if the sales mix for a beauty salon is five trims for every perm, then one "unit" will be five trims and one perm. The contribution margin will be the one that is generated by that bundle of products.

2. When calculating the breakeven point, or computing target income, the WAUCM must be revised any time the sales mix is revised.

3. CVP uses the idea of sales mix in calculating the breakeven point and beyond the breakeven point. The sales mix assumptions are also used for performance evaluation, and to assess profitability and for decision making related to which products to sell.

J. There are limitations in the usefulness of the CVP model. First, the sales mix must be held constant in order to calculate a breakeven point or to estimate sales volume needed to achieve some target income amount. This is usually not a realistic assumption. Other variables are assumed to remain constant—costs, efficiency of operations, technology in operations, and cost characteristics. This assumption is also not a realistic one. A third assumption is that there is a linear relationship between revenues and costs, thus ignoring quantity discounts and other effects that threaten the accuracy of the model's results. Perhaps the biggest criticism of the CVP model is the use of one activity—units sold—as the cost/activity driver. The CVP model ignores market conditions such as product demand, competitive pricing, sales resulting in pricing changes, quality issues, general economic conditions, inflation, among other variables. Some argue that CVP is too simplistic to be useful as a management tool. Others argue that the model needs to be extended to an activities-based model. Extension to activities-based modeling virtually precludes developing the CVP model any way other than via a computer-based analysis. Furthermore, ABC financial planning should incorporate multiple cost drivers at the unit, batch, customer, and facility-levels as necessary if the model is to provide relevant, accurate and reliable information.

1. CVP and ABC together can provide managers with a comprehensive estimation model. By using an ABC approach and taking into account that costs can be categorized as unit, batch, product, customer, or facility-level costs, the CVP model needs to be modified so that the costs are characterized differently than simply fixed or variable. Total costs should be categorized as: (Unit variable cost × number of units) + (Batch costs × number of batches) + (Product cost × number of products) + (Customer cost × number of customer orders) + (Facility costs × facility cost driver). This characterization of costs takes some costs that might have been treated as fixed before, and now treats them as variable, but the variability is based on activity other than number of units sold.

2. By using account analysis and multiple regression (see Chapter 11), a CVP model can be extended to incorporate multiple layers of cost drivers and activity. The extension of the simple CVP model provides many benefits. The main benefit is that it provides much better information regarding what must be done to ensure profitability. It also clarifies different costs that exist.

3. Although the CVP model is much more complex when adapted to allow inclusion of multiple cost drivers, it is easier to perform sensitivity analysis via computer software. Once the time and money are invested in an intricate system like the one described, it is to the advantage of the organization to use the model as much as possible, to evaluate performance and examine profitability options.

K. Financial planning models provide an important benefit for decision-makers. Since managers don't know the outcomes of future events, it is useful to try to anticipate numerous possible outcomes. Using CVP and other planning models to assess different scenarios is called sensitivity analysis. Sensitivity analysis allows managers to assess the benefits and costs of choosing different options before implementing one.

1. Sensitivity analysis allows analysts to use different assumptions about inputs like price, cost per unit, fixed costs and quantities. Assumptions about the sales mix can also be changed.

2. One measure that is useful when doing sensitivity analysis is model elasticity. This is measured as percentage change in profit divided by percentage change of input. Model elasticity shows how much the change in price of one product will affect overall profits.

3. Best and worst-case scenarios can be developed and used to enhance decision-making. Looking at the worst possible outcome gives managers information that helps them to focus on how to improve a plan for future operations.

L. When developing financial models for decision-making, managers must be cognizant of the fact that they do not have unlimited resources. The most fundamental resource, money, must be used in the manner that will provide the greatest benefit. Thus, different managers often compete for resources that are scarce. The characteristics of information used to make decisions on the use of scarce resources are described below.

Choosing which goods and services to produce and sell is a common managerial decision. Successful organizations are likely to be confronted with limited capacity, at least in the short run. These limitations are called capacity constraints. Examples of capacity constraints include shortage of skilled tax accountants during tax season, not enough computer programmers to write code for new video games needed for holiday sales, or too few cooks at a large restaurant. Ideally, managers faced with capacity constraints should direct resources needed to alleviate the constraint before expending resources on less constrained activities. Sometimes it is not possible to correct the capacity constraint problem soon enough to avoid choosing between profit-making alternatives.

1. When an organization is faced with choosing among alternative profitable activities, the contribution margins generated by each alternative should be compared. The opportunity that provides the highest contribution margin per unit of the scarce resource is the one that should be chosen.

2. Although managers might have to resolve capacity constraints related to one bottleneck resource, it is often the case that two or more capacity constraints must be dealt with at the same time. When this is the case, the analysis of which activity or group of activities is optimal can be completed using a mathematical model called "linear programming". Linear programming is a mathematical model used to maximize profits or minimize costs. It is presented in the appendix to Chapter 12.

REVIEW AND SELF TEST QUESTIONS AND EXERCISES

Matching key terms

Match the following terms to the correct definition by writing the correct letter next to the correct definition.

a. contribution margin	b. weighted-average unit CM	c. model elasticity
d. breakeven point	e. scarce resources	f. CVP model
g. operating leverage	h. sensitivity analysis	i. financial model
j. product mix		

_____ 1. Contribution margin based on a fixed group of products being sold.

_____ 2. The amount of profit left after subtracting total variable cost from total revenues.

_____ 3. The ratio of contribution margin and operating income.

_____ 4. The financial result that occurs when total revenues equal total costs.

_____ 5. A measure of the relationship between the price of one product and overall profitability.

_____ 6. Goods or services that are in short supply.

_____ 7. A financial planning model that is based on costs, profits, and units sold.

_____ 8. A modeling approach that allows analysts to assess different outcomes.

_____ 9. An accurate, reliable simulation of business activities, useful for making decisions.

_____10. The combination of different products sold.

True or False

For each of the following statements enter a T or an F in the blank to indicate whether the statement is true or false.

_____11. A financial model shows exactly how a future decision will work.

_____12. Financial models are as good as the information that goes into them.

_____13. The cost-volume-profit (CVP) model uses only cost information—not revenues.

_____14. The CVP model combines volume of sales, costs, revenues and profits.

_____15. The cost-volume-profit model can be used by nonprofit organizations.

_____16. Contribution margin is calculated by subtracting variable costs from sales revenue.

_____17. Contribution margin is used exclusively to cover fixed production costs and profits.

_____18. At the breakeven point, total revenues equal total costs.

_____19. If a company has a contribution margin of $50,000, and fixed costs of $35,000, it is breaking even.

_____20. The use of contribution margin to assess profits is useful because variable costs change with production and sales activity.

_____21. If a manager uses a CVP model to determine needed sales volume to earn target operating income, she should treat target operating income as a variable cost.

_____22. Operating leverage measures the risk of missing sales targets.

_____23. A CVP analysis that measures target profits should ignore taxes for purposes of the analysis

_____24. Sensitivity analysis allows managers to consider best and worst-case scenarios.

_____25. Companies with multiple products cannot use CVP analysis.

Multiple Choice

Choose the best answer by writing the letter corresponding to your choice in the space provided.

_____26. Which of the following correctly describes a characteristic of a financial model?

a) A financial model is a physical representation of planned production facilities.
b) A financial model cannot be used to plan for future business activities.
c) A financial model gives managers insight into possible business outcomes without the risk of trying them first.
d) A financial model can only be useful if a pilot has been completed for planned business opportunities.

_____27. One type of financial model used by businesses is called a cost-volume-profit (CVP) model. Which of the following can this model be used to do?

a) CVP can be used to estimate total fixed costs.
b) CVP can be used to determine the breakeven point for a new business venture.
c) CVP can be used to set product price
d) CVP can be used to establish an estimated variable cost per unit of product.

_____28. The breakeven point describes the point at which

a) total sales revenues equal total production costs.
b) total profits equal total costs.
c) total sales revenues equal total profits.
d) total sales revenues equal total costs.

_____29. The contribution margin (CM) is a measure of profitability. Which of the following is the correct way to compute the total CM?

a) Total sales revenue minus total costs = total CM.
b) Total fixed costs minus total variable costs = total CM.
c) Total sales revenue minus total variable costs = total CM.
d) Total costs minus total variable costs = total CM.

_____30. At the breakeven point,

a) profits equal zero and total sales revenues equal total costs.
b) profits are greater than zero, and sales revenues are greater than total costs.
c) profits are less than zero, and sales revenues are equal to total costs.
d) profits equal zero, and total sales revenues are less than total costs.

_____31. Walter's Bookbinders has estimated sales revenues must total $36,000 for a new process it will sell to book publishers, in order to break even. Variable costs at the breakeven point will be $12,000. What does this information imply about estimated fixed costs?

a) Estimated fixed costs must be $48,000.
b) Estimated fixed costs must be $24,000.
c) Estimated fixed costs must be $36,000.
d) Estimated fixed costs cannot be determined from the information given.

_____32. A new video game system will be sold at one location of a large toy store chain for $180 each. Variable costs per system are estimated at $60. Fixed costs are an estimated $360,000. What is the breakeven point for the new video game system?

a) 1,500 video game systems
b) 2,000 video game systems
c) 3,000 video game systems
d) 6,000 video game systems

_____33. The manager of the toy store described in question 32 thinks that demand will not allow the sale of more than 2,500 video game systems. The variable cost cannot be reduced because this is the cost specified by the manufacturer in a contract that has been agreed upon by the store. The price must be changed in order to keep from losing money on this product. Assuming variable costs remain at $60 per unit, and fixed costs remain at $360,000, what price must be charged in order to break even?

a) $204
b) $144
c) $84
d) The price cannot be determined from the information given.

_____34. Which of the following is a valid criticism of the CVP model?

a) It cannot be expanded to include analysis of more than one product.
b) It cannot be used to estimate profits beyond the breakeven point.
c) It only uses one cost and revenue driver (units sold).
d) It only measures profits, and completely ignores costs.

_____35. If calculating the sales volume needed to obtain a certain amount of operating income, you should

a) treat the operating income as part of sales revenues.
b) treat the operating income as an addition to fixed costs.
c) treat the operating income as an addition to variable costs.
d) treat the operating income as a part of total production costs.

_____36. A simplifying assumption applied when two or more products with different contribution margins are used in a CVP analysis is that the sales mix is constant. For instance, if 5 units of one product are sold for every 7 units of another product, this means that

a) actual sales that differ from this sales mix should be turned down.
b) actual sales that differ from this sales mix will change the breakeven point.
c) actual sales that differ from this sales mix will always result in profits that are higher than estimated by the CVP analysis.
d) actual sales that differ from this sales mix will always result in profits that are lower than estimated by the CVP analysis.

_____37. The breakeven point

a) can be expressed in units sold or as a dollar amount of revenue.
b) can be expressed as total revenue or total cost.
c) can be expressed as number of units or fixed cost per unit.
d) can be expressed as a variable cost per unit.

_____38. If a company wants to determine the necessary number of units sold in order to achieve a target net income, it should assume

a) income taxes are going to be zero.
b) income taxes are going to be some estimated percentage of net income.
c) income taxes are going to be at least as much as net income.
d) income taxes are going to be some estimated percentage of operating income.

_____39. Which of the following statements is **false**?

a) Target operating income is greater than target net income.
b) At the breakeven point, target operating income is zero.
c) Target operating income cannot be achieved unless the breakeven point is achieved first.
d) Target operating income is the same as target net income.

_____40. Operating leverage is a measure of risk associated with CVP analysis. If an organization has substantial committed (or facility) costs, which of the following results correctly describes the impact of decreased sales?

a) Lower sales will increase operating leverage.
b) Lower sales will have no impact on operating leverage.
c) Lower sales will sometimes increase operating leverage, and sometimes will decrease operating leverage.
d) Lower sales will decrease operating leverage.

_____41. Which of the following correctly describes how ABC is used in financial modeling?

a) If ABC analysis is used, all costs will be treated as fixed costs.
b) If ABC analysis is used, all costs will be treated as variable costs.
c) If ABC analysis is used, costs should be split among unit, batch, product, customer and facility levels, and then costs that vary with activity should be identified along those same dimensions.
d) If ABC analysis is used, breakeven point can be estimated for only one product at a time.

_____42. If breakeven point is calculated for a mix of products, which of the following is true?

a) Once the breakeven point for the bundle of products is determined, the number of units to be sold for each individual product can be determined.
b) Even after the breakeven point for the bundle of products is determined, the number of units to be sold for each individual product cannot be determined.
c) Once the breakeven point for one of the individual products is determined, the number of bundles in the mix of products can be determined.
d) Even after the breakeven point for the bundle of products is determined, the number of units to be sold for each individual product is variable.

_____43. Which of the following correctly describes model elasticity?

a) If the model elasticity is greater than 1, it means that given a price decrease of 1%, the percentage increase in profit will be higher than 1%.
b) If the model elasticity is greater than 1, it means that given a price increase of 1%, the percentage decrease in profit will be lower than 1%.
c) If the model elasticity is greater than 1, it means that given a price decrease of 1%, the percentage decrease in profit will be lower than 1%.
d) If the model elasticity is greater than 1, it means that given a price increase of 1%, the percentage increase in profit will be higher than 1%.

_____44. Sensitivity analysis allows analysts to prepare best-case and worst-case scenarios. A worst case scenario tells analysts

a) The minimum amount of loss an organization will incur in the coming year.
b) The lowest profit or largest loss likely to occur, compared to all other scenarios analyzed.
c) The maximum amount of loss an organization will incur in the coming year.
d) The minimum amount of profit an organization will earn in the coming year.

_____45. Which of the following is a correct statement?

a) Only organizations with manufacturing operations are likely to have scarce resources.
b) Most organizations have unlimited resources.
c) Most organizations have limited resources.
d) The only important scarce resource is cash.

Exercises

Please use the following to answer the next five questions.

Marilyn Blanding is considering starting a new business. A recent graduate of a prestigious art school, she plans to open an art gallery. She intends to sell each painting for an average price of $200. The artists of the paintings will be paid a commission of 25% of the price. Paintings will be framed, packed, and delivered to the customer. Marilyn estimates that framing, packing and delivery costs should be about $10 per picture. There will be additional expenses associated with running the gallery. Rent on the storefront Marilyn wants to use is $1,800 per month. Utilities, which will not vary much from month to month, will be approximately $330 per month. Insurance and other expenses will be $250 per month. She plans to pay herself and one sales associate salaries of $3,500 per month ($2,500 for herself, $1,000 for the associate). The tax rate is assumed by Marilyn to be 30%.

46. Based on the information, how many paintings per month would Marilyn need to sell in order to break even?

47. If Marilyn wanted to earn net income of $4,900 per month in 2002, assuming all of the same prices and costs given above, what amount of revenue would she need to make?

A friend of Marilyn's, Dan Bishop, is a business major at the local university. Dan is Marilyn's unpaid business consultant for her entrepreneurial plans. Dan suggested that Marilyn consider offering more variety in her gallery. He suggested that she sell paintings for a variety of prices, and that she sell artists' supplies, especially since some of her customers will be art students. To illustrate to her what her profits would look like given a mix of products, he showed her the following.

Large paintings, sold for $300 each. Commission, framing, packing and delivery, $150. Medium-sized paintings, sold for $200 each. Commission, framing, packing and delivery, $75. Small paintings, sold for $60 each. Commission and framing, $15 (customers could take small paintings with them). Art supply packs could be sold for $24 each. Variable costs are just the wholesale price of the art packs, $8. Finally, sculptures could be sold for $500 each. Commission, packing and delivery would be $100.

To make the analysis simpler, Dan assumed the sales mix is constant. He assumed Marilyn would sell an average of 1 sculpture for every 4 large paintings. For every 4 large paintings, she could sell 12 medium sized paintings. For every 4 large paintings, she could probably sell 20 small paintings. For every 4 large paintings, she could sell 40 art packs.

In order to sell this larger variety, Dan thinks Marilyn would need to rent a bigger store, and would probably have to hire one more sales associate. These additional fixed costs would total $6,240 per month (this is in addition to the fixed costs noted above).

48. How many of each product would Marilyn have to sell each month in order to break even?

49. To check your results obtained in question 48, prepare a segmented income statement in the contribution margin format. The format for the income statement is given.

	Art Packs	**Small Paintings**	**Medium Paintings**	**Large paintings**	**Sculptures**	**TOTALS**
Price						
Variable Cost per unit						
CM per Unit						
Units sold						
Sales Revenue						
Variable Cost						
Total CM						
Fixed Costs						
Operating Income						
Income Taxes						
Net Income						

50. Based on the sales mix proposed by Dan, in order to earn operating income of $16,160 per year how much of each product would Marilyn need to sell?

Chapter 12

Answers to Questions and Exercises

Matching key terms

1. b 2. a 3. g 4. d 5. c 6. e 7. f 8. h 9. i 10. j

True or False

11. F. Financial models are not perfect predictors of the future, and can only give managers some idea as to how a potential future action will turn out.
12. T. A financial model can only help managers to make the right decision if the information is relevant, accurate, and timely.
13. F. The CVP model uses sales volume, all costs, and revenues.
14. T. The CVP model combines these important performance variables to help managers see what it takes to achieve profitability.
15. T. Even though the model's name might suggest otherwise (the P stands for profit), nonprofit organizations can use the model to see what the breakeven point is. For a nonprofit organization, this the point at which charitable contributions or other cash inflows equal total expenses, or total cash outflow.
16. T. This is the definition of contribution margin.
17. F. Contribution margin is used to cover **all** fixed costs and to contribute to profits.
18. T. Total revenues generated by selling just enough units to break even will cover all fixed costs and all variable costs.
19. F. At the breakeven point, total contribution margin equals total fixed costs. This company has profit of $15,000, so is beyond the breakeven point.
20. T. CM is just total revenue minus total variable cost. If sales increase, variable costs increase, and if sales decrease, variable costs will decrease.
21. F. Target operating income should be treated like a fixed cost.
22. T. Operating leverage is contribution margin divided by operating income. Since committed (facility) costs do not decrease with lower sales, and lower sales result in a lower CM, this will mathematically increase operating leverage. This means it will become harder to cover committed costs.
23. F. Since for-profit organizations pay taxes, income taxes should be factored into the CVP analysis. Otherwise, the analysis will show results that are too low to meet the target.
24. T. One of the benefits of sensitivity analysis is that it allows managers to see what could happen, given different sets of circumstances.
25. F. CVP analysis can be expanded to include multiple products, especially if the analysis is computerized.

Multiple Choice

26. c. One of the benefits of a financial model is that it allows managers to see what outcomes to expect if they try different business ventures. A physical representation is not a financial model (answer a); the main purpose of a financial model is to plan for future activities (answer b); a pilot does not need to be completed in order to use a financial model (answer d).

27. b. The CVP model can be used to calculate the number of units of product that must be sold in order to cover total costs. The other three answers are incorrect because they must already be known in order to use the CVP model.
28. d. The breakeven point is the point at which there is no profit, but there are no losses either. Sales revenues are just enough to cover all costs.
29. c. Contribution margin is, by definition, sales revenue minus variable costs. Answer a describes calculation of operating income; answer b doesn't describe anything useful; answer d describes calculation of total fixed costs.
30. a. This is the definition of the breakeven point. There are no profits, making answers b and c incorrect. Revenues must equal costs, so answer d incorrect.
31. b. Sales revenue minus variable costs equals contribution margin. At the breakeven point, contribution margin equals fixed costs. $36,000 – $12,000 = $24,000, the CM. This means fixed costs must be $24,000.
32. c. Contribution margin per unit is $180 – $60 = $120 per unit. At the breakeven point, fixed costs equal total contribution margin, so TCM is $360,000. $360,000 divided by $120 = 3,000 units.
33. a. In this question, sales volume is known to be 2,500, variable cost per unit is known, and total fixed costs are known. Only the price is not known. First, determine the amount of CM per unit. Divide $360,000 by 2,500 units to get $144 CM per unit. Add the $60 variable cost per unit, to get a price of $204. To check this, see what contribution margin would be generated by selling 2,500 units for $204, and then subtract 2,500 times $60 (total variable cost).
34. c. The entire focus in the CVP model is on units sold. A modified version of the CVP model should incorporate other activities.
35. b. Treat operating income as another lump sum to be recouped from contribution margin.
36. b. The breakeven point is based on the assumption that the sales mix is held constant. One "unit" consists of 5 units of one product and 7 units of another. If the mix changes, the contribution margin of the "unit" will change. Answer a is wrong because sales should not be turned down to achieve some target set by a model. Answers c and d are incorrect because the profits could either be higher or lower than expected. It depends on whether the actual mix results in the sale of more or less of the product with the higher CM (or more or less of the one with the lower CM).
37. a. Breakeven point equals number of units times $CM per unit, expressed as a dollar amount. In order to calculate this dollar amount, the number of units must be known.
38. d. The income statement shows operating income less income taxes equals net income. CVP analysis assumes that income taxes are a percentage of operating income in order to estimate target net income.
39. d. If there is operating income, there will normally be income taxes. Therefore, target net income will be less than operating income.
40. a. Operating leverage is a measure of a company's ability to cover both variable and fixed (committed, or facility) costs. If sales decline, contribution margin declines. This makes it harder to cover fixed costs. Since operating leverage is contribution margin divided by operating income, lower sales make CM smaller, but the impact on operating income is more severe because fixed costs did not change.
41. c. CVP analysis can be extended by recognizing that costs vary based on more dimensions than number of units sold. By splitting estimated cost information into unit, batch, product, customer and facility categories, it is likely that the CVP analysis will be more accurate. Answers a and b are both wrong because costs cannot all be classified as fixed or all variable. Answer d is wrong because the analysis can still include multiple products, even if ABC analysis is used.

42. a. A simplifying assumption used in CVP analysis for multiple products is that the sales mix is constant. That is, for each "bundle" of products sold, the quantity of individual products stays the same. CVP analysis treats each bundle as one unit. Therefore, once the breakeven point is known for the number of "units" (i.e., bundles), the quantities of individual products can be easily determined.
43. d. Model elasticity is measured as percentage change in profit divided by percentage change in product price. If price (denominator) increases, but profit (numerator) increases even more, the result will be greater than 1.
44. b. One of the chief benefits of sensitivity analysis is that it allows cost managers to look at "what if" scenarios before putting a plan into place. Analysis of different outcomes allows analysts to rank different options, from best to worst. Answers a, c, and d are all wrong because they imply that the analysis is a perfect predictor of future outcomes.
45. c. Virtually every organization has some resource that is limited. This problem is not restricted to manufacturers (answer a), and the type of resource is not restricted to cash (answer d)

Exercises

46. 42 paintings. This is a simple CVP analysis problem. Price is $200. Variable costs per painting are 25% commission, or $50, plus the cost of framing, packing and delivery, $10. Total variable cost per painting is $60 per painting. CM per painting is $200 – $60 = $140. Fixed costs are ($1,800 + $330 + $250 + $3,500) = $5,880. The CVP problem is: $140X = $5,880, where X is the number of paintings to be sold. $5,880/$140 = 42 paintings.
47. 92 paintings. Net income of $4,900 is the same as operating income of $4,900/(1 – tax rate). The tax rate is 30%, so operating income is $4,900/.70 = $7,000. Add $7,000 to the fixed costs of $5,880 to get $12,880. Now, solve as before, except the amount to recover from total CM is $12,880. $12,880/$140 = 92 paintings.
48. This is a multiple-product CVP problem. First, determine the contribution margin generated from a "unit", consisting of one sculpture, four large paintings, twelve medium-sized paintings, 20 small paintings, and 40 art packs. CM for one sculpture is $500 – $100 = $400. CM for four large paintings is $1,200 – $600 = $600. CM for twelve medium-sized paintings is $2,400 – $900 = $1,500. CM for 20 small paintings is $1,200 – $300 = $900. CM for 40 art packs is $960 – $320 = $640. Total CM for one "unit" is $400 + $600 + $1,500 + $900 + $640 = $4,040. Total fixed costs are $5,880 plus an additional $6,240 = $12,120. Now, the CVP equation is $4,040X = $12,120. X represents one "unit" consisting of one sculpture, four large paintings, twelve medium-sized paintings, twenty small paintings, and 40 art packs. X = 3. This means that Marilyn must sell 3 sculptures, 12 large paintings, 36 medium-sized paintings, 60 small paintings, and 120 art packs to break even.

49. The income statement, in segmented CM format is shown below.

	Art Packs	Small Paintings	Medium Paintings	Large paintings	Sculptures	TOTALS
Price	$24	$60	$200	$300	$500	XXXXX
Variable Cost per unit	$8	$15	$75	$150	$100	XXXXX
CM per Unit	$16	$45	$125	$150	$400	XXXXX
Units sold	120	60	36	12	3	XXXXX
Sales Revenue	$2,880	$3,600	$7,200	$3,600	$1,500	$18,780
Variable Cost	$960	$900	$2,700	$1,800	$300	$6,660
Total CM	$1,920	$2,700	$4,500	$1,800	$1,200	$12,120
Fixed Costs	XXXXX	XXXXX	XXXXX	XXXXX	XXXXX	$12,120
Operating Income	XXXXX	XXXXX	XXXXX	XXXXX	XXXXX	$0
Income Taxes	XXXXX	XXXXX	XXXXX	XXXXX	XXXXX	$0
Net Income	XXXXX	XXXXX	XXXXX	XXXXX	XXXXX	$0

50. In order to earn operating income of $16,160, divide ($12,120 + $16,160) by $4,040, to get 7 bundles. This translates to 7 sculptures, 28 large paintings, 84 medium paintings, 140 small paintings, and 280 art packs.

Chapter 13
Cost Management and Decision Making

Chapter Study Suggestions

Chapter 13 presents a five-stage framework for decision-making. A necessary condition for good decision-making is that one must decide what goals and objectives are to be met. Based on this, decision-makers should gather the information needed to make the decision. One should next try to identify the alternative solutions from which to choose. Once the alternative solution is selected, the next stage involves implementing it. Finally, feedback should be obtained to allow one to assess whether the decision made was appropriate.

This five-stage framework applies to almost any business decision one might need to make. However, it is most applicable to strategic decisions that dictate how some future activities should be completed. Chapter 13 focuses on the first, second and third of these five stages. Specifically, Chapter 13 presents decision-making as it relates to choosing among alternatives. It also presents some common business decisions. They are the make-or-buy (outsourcing) decision; adding or dropping a product, product line or business unit; replacing equipment, and pricing decisions. The chapter also discusses the importance of deciding what information is relevant to making good decisions. Some important characteristics of information used for management decision-making are the relevance of information, the accuracy of information, and the timeliness of information. There are some tradeoffs between the degree of accuracy and the timeliness of it. However, it is always the case that managers must identify which pieces of cost and revenue information are relevant to making a decision.

Chapter Highlights

A. Cost Management Challenges. Chapter 13 offers two cost management challenges.

1. How can managers make correct choices, given alternative uses of their organization's resources and given an organization's mission?

2. Should prices be based on costs or should they be market-based?

B. Learning Objectives—This chapter has 4 learning objectives.

1. Chapter 13 divides decision-making problems into objectives, alternative actions, and expected outcomes.

2. It shows how cost managers can decide which information is relevant to a decision—both qualitative and quantitative.

3. Chapter 13 demonstrates how decision trees can be used to describe business decisions.

4. The chapter presents ways to use cost-benefit analysis for common strategic decisions.

C. Managers must make decisions every day. Since resources are not limitless, managers are constantly faced with choosing among alternative activities. When doing that, managers should choose the best alternative based on cost-benefit analyses that will provide the correct quantitative solution. They should also focus on qualitative issues in making right decisions.

Several common decisions made by managers are explored in Chapter 13. One of these decisions is the decision to make or buy products or product components. Outsourcing activity can be a useful alternative to in-house activity. There may be cost savings, less use of scarce resources, or improved quality as a result of making this choice. The decision to make products or components internally might be a better alternative when there are concerns about maintaining control over quality, processes or when a company wants information about its production activities to remain private.

A second common decision is related to adding or dropping a product, product line, or business unit. This can be something as straightforward as dropping a product that has become obsolete to something as complex as deciding whether to enter a market in a foreign country.

The third decision-making issue relates to the need to replace equipment. There are times when it is most cost efficient or there are higher returns from disposing of old equipment before it stops being useful.

The fourth decision-making problem presented in Chapter 13 deals with pricing issues. In addition to discussing use of target costing to determine price, the use of cost-plus pricing, pricing for special orders, and some legal aspects of pricing are factors in setting prices.

D. One framework for leading to correct decision-making divides the process into five stages. Three of these stages are discussed in Chapter 13. In the first stage setting goals and objectives takes place. In the second stage information is gathered that is needed to make the correct decision. In the third stage, alternatives are evaluated. These three stages are discussed in more detail below.

E. The first stage consists of setting goals and objectives. One tangible, specific goal is to determine a target profit, and then determine what target costs and target prices must be to achieve that.

1. Target profit per unit is calculated as market price times target profit percentage. In a competitive market, market price is the same as target price. Target cost is the most cost that can be incurred, if a target profit is to be achieved. This is because target price—target profit = target cost. Formally, target costing requires four steps.

   a. Determine the target price per unit. Target price is either the market price or what one would expect customers to be willing to pay.

   b. Set the target cost per unit and in total. Target cost per unit = Target price—target profit per unit. Total target cost is target cost per unit times total unit sales.

   c. Compare the total target cost to the currently feasible cost. Currently feasible total cost is the cost as it currently exists. If currently feasible total cost exceeds total target cost, then costs must be reduced.

   d. Redesign products and processes to achieve the cost-reduction target.

F. The second stage in the decision-making process consists of gathering information. The most important aspect of the information-gathering process is that it must produce relevant information. Relevant information must be accurate and timely. In addition, relevant information must differ among alternatives, and must be information related to future costs or revenues.

1. Three characteristics that are critical to making decisions are relevance, accuracy, and timeliness. Information is relevant only if it is pertinent to a particular decision. When making decisions about what should be done in the future, relevant information is defined as information that differs among alternatives in the future. Information must also be accurate in order to be useful. Inaccurate information could cause cost managers to approve unwise business decisions or to reject wise ones. Relevant, accurate information has absolutely no value if it arrives too late to be used in making a decision. The degree of accuracy of information may be reduced by the need for it to be made available on a more timely basis.

2. Other types of decision-making information are qualitative rather than quantitative in nature. Although most business decisions are related in some way to meeting profit objectives, qualitative concerns must also be factored in. Qualitative information includes things like effect on employee morale, loss of control by giving work to outsourcing providers and effects on a community or the environment. When faced with making a decision that includes hard to quantify factors such as these, managers must employ skill, experience, judgement and ethical standards.

3. Relevant costs and revenues are costs and revenues that occur in the future and differ among alternatives. When faced with a decision-making dilemma, managers should consider the following factors.

   a. The first question that should be answered is "Will the costs or benefits change as a result of selecting the alternative under study?" If the answer is "yes", then those costs and benefits must be considered in making the decision.

b. The second issue that must be considered is what time period will be affected by the decision to be made. The events of the past do not affect the decision. Only costs and benefits that will occur in the future are relevant to the decision. Costs that have already been incurred are called "sunk costs".

c. Although sunk costs are not factored into the assessment of costs and benefits to be gained in the future, past decisions should not be ignored completely. Information from past events should be looked at, at least to understand where mistakes and successes occurred. The past can be a good predictor of the future.

G. The third stage of the decision-making framework is evaluating alternatives. A number of tools and procedures are helpful in accomplishing the evaluation.

1. A helpful tool to use for this purpose is called a decision tree. A decision tree can be built by following 3 basic steps.

    a. Display the decision alternatives in the order in which the decisions must be made.

    b. Trace the path of each decision to its ultimate outcomes and identify the set of outcomes that result from each decision path.

    c. Measure the benefits and costs of each set of outcomes.

2. After identifying all of the alternative solutions to some problem, the manager should attempt to anticipate the future outcomes of each action. This includes considering past results as well as trying to predict future outcomes. Choosing the best alternative should be based on a quantitative cost-benefit analysis for each possible solution. Qualitative aspects of each alternative should also be considered.

3. Four common decisions for which the decision-making framework are appropriate are (1) the make-or-buy decision (outsourcing), (2) adding or dropping a product, (3) equipment replacement, and (4) various pricing decisions.

H. A make-or-buy decision is any decision by a company to acquire goods or services internally or externally. The decision to buy goods or services externally is also known as "outsourcing". Outsourcing is more commonly associated with decisions by organizations to shift their focus toward accomplishing core activities internally, and allowing outside organizations to accomplish peripheral activities. In recent years, many companies have chosen to outsource support service activities such as information systems technology, human resources, accounting, and payroll activities.

The make-or-buy decision is often part of a company's long-run strategy. Some organizations integrate vertically, meaning that they perform all activities from the beginning to the end of their value chain. Other organizations rely on outsiders for some inputs and specialize only on certain portions of the total process.

1. Outsourcing can sometimes result in the elimination of non-value-added activities. This is especially true when an organization does not have a lot of expertise in a particular area.

2. When making a decision to perform an activity internally or externally, the information used must be relevant, timely, and accurate. The best way to think about the decision is to consider which costs will differ based on the choice to make or to buy.

I. Managers must sometimes decide whether to add or drop a business unit. A business unit may be a product, market territory, department, facility, or any other type of segment that can be identified as a distinct unit. The decision to drop a business unit may occur for a variety of reasons, including decline in market demand, obsolescence of the product or inability to remain competitive. Companies may decide to add a business unit because of new product development, expansion to new markets, acquisition of other companies, or ability to meet demands of new customers. Making the decision to add or drop a business unit cannot be made based on segmented income statements. Financial statement information contains allocated costs that are not relevant to the decision. Cost managers deciding whether to add or drop a business unit must base their decision only on relevant costs and revenues. If a segment is dropped, what revenues will go away? What costs will go away? If the costs to be eliminated exceed the revenues, then it is probably wise to discontinue the segment.

1. One factor to consider in making the decision whether to drop or add a business is the opportunity cost associated with making one choice over another. This means that one should consider what can be done with resources that are freed up by dropping a unit, or what resources will be tied up by adding a unit? The value of the opportunities foregone by making the add or drop decision should be factored into the decision

2. Other factors to consider when deciding to close (drop) a business unit are qualitative ones. Discontinuing a business unit, while the correct financial choice is sometimes not viewed as the correct qualitative choice, especially when employees or communities are affected negatively by the decision. Completely eliminating a business unit almost always results in downsizing. Outsourcing also results in the elimination of jobs, since employees performing activities being outsourced are no longer needed.

   Discontinuing a segment is a difficult, sometimes emotional business decision that must, nevertheless be made by managers.

J. A third activity for which the decision-making framework is appropriate is deciding on whether to replace equipment. Organizations that make substantial investments in production equipment are sometimes faced with the decision of when it is better to replace equipment that is still operating.

1. There are several reasons that might lead to a decision to replace equipment. New equipment might produce higher quality product. Replacing old equipment might improve efficiency, or reduce maintenance and repair expenses. It might cost less to operate (lower electricity cost). It might be capable of doing more things that result in higher revenue.

2. As with all of the decisions discussed in the chapter, only relevant costs should be used to make the replacement decision. Irrelevant costs include things like remaining book value of the old equipment, gain or loss on disposal of the old machine, or depreciation expenses that could be taken on the old machine. Relevant costs and benefits include differences in revenues generated from the two options, differences in operating costs, cost to purchase the new equipment, and proceeds from the sale of the old equipment.

K. A fourth type of activity appropriate to the decision-making framework presented in Chapter 13 is the pricing decision. Trying to decide what the right price is for goods and services is not easy. Setting prices too high discourages customers from buying the product. Setting the price too low makes the profit margin smaller.

1. There are several factors that must be considered when the pricing decision is being made. Pricing must be considered from the perspective of the customer. The competitive environment may allow customers to find adequate substitutes for a product if an organization sets its prices too high. Competitors also react to prices charged. If one organization sets a high price, a competitor may offer a lower price. If an organization lowers its price, competitors may respond by lowering prices also. In an increasingly global competitive market, companies must also consider differential pricing in markets outside of their home base. Customers, markets and competitors are all market-based pricing considerations.

2. Costs must also be considered when setting price. In order to make profit, all costs of an organization must first be recovered through the sale of goods and services. Some industries' prices are very heavily market-driven. Prices are based on competitive pressures. In these industries, profit is made only if costs are managed properly. In other industries, prices are set, at least partially, based on the underlying production costs. In most industries, some components of market-driven and cost-driven pricing are present. Companies that use a cost-plus pricing approach benefit from use of a good costing system and from use of activities-based management that will have identified non-value-added costs. Companies cannot afford to use a pure cost-plus pricing strategy without first managing costs. Such a strategy coupled with out-of-control costs will result in too-high prices and lower sales volume as a result, or lower profit margins, and lower profits as a result.

3. In addition to customer, market, competitor and cost considerations, companies must be aware of legal, political, and reputation issues as they relate to pricing decisions. Companies should be aware of legal issues such as price discrimination, international laws related to dumping, and activities taken to monopolize a market (antitrust violations). There may be political repercussions if a company is perceived as one that is taking unfair advantage of its customers or society as a whole (for instance, the oil industry). Companies also base prices on the reputation they have for high quality, or low quality. High quality producers can demand higher prices than low quality producers.

a. Prices cannot, by law, be charged differentially to different customers for the same products (where there is intent to harm competitors). This is price discrimination. Companies in the United States must comply with antitrust laws. The Robinson-Patman Act prohibits price discrimination. Other laws—the Clayton Act, and the Sherman Act prevent pricing that results in monopolistic or anti-competitive behavior. Another illegal pricing tactic is predatory pricing. This occurs when organizations set prices below cost temporarily to increase demand for a product, and to damage competitors' sales of competing products.

4. Managers must consider short and long-run strategies in making pricing decisions. Decisions for price-setting should take into account the life cycle of products offered. Managers should also consider the effect of special, one-time orders that have no long-term implications. Product mix and volume adjustments must also be considered in a highly competitive market.

   a. When looking at short-run pricing decisions, there are some costs that must be factored in, and others that are not relevant. As with any of the decisions discussed so far in this chapter, it is only the relevant costs that should be considered in making pricing decisions. In many short-run decisions, unit-level variable costs are the only relevant costs. In other cases, fixed costs or costs at a higher level than unit-level may be relevant.

   b. When used in pricing decisions, relevant costs required to sell and/or produce a good or service should be viewed as the floor—that is, the minimum selling price. Over the long run, this pricing strategy will not work. For instance, the relevant cost of one more passenger on a bus may be close to zero. This may motivate managers to offer free rides to small children if their parents pay for their tickets. If the bus company has excess capacity, this strategy may generate additional profits because it will attract customers with small children who might not otherwise purchase the bus tickets. As capacity is used up though, the free ticket strategy becomes less useful. Paying customers may not be able to buy seats if too many passengers with small children buy tickets.

5. Pricing special orders is another consideration that requires determining which costs are relevant. The most important considerations in deciding whether to accept special orders are the net benefits derived from taking the order, and the amount of productive capacity that must be available to complete the order. If an organization has excess capacity, and is paying for it even though it is not being used, it is to the organization's advantage to take special orders that generate some contribution margin, even if it is lower than the margin generated from regular sales.

REVIEW AND SELF TEST QUESTIONS AND EXERCISES

Matching key terms

Match the following terms to the correct definition by writing the correct letter next to the correct definition.

a. product life cycle costs	b. relevant cost	c. special orders
d. outsourcing	e. target profit	f. make-or-buy decisions
g. decision tree	h. currently feasible costs	i. predatory pricing
j. Robinson-Patman Act		

_____ 1. The amount of cost that is incurred to make product right now.

_____ 2. A cost that differs among alternatives in the future.

_____ 3. A way to depict a problem that helps managers to reach the correct conclusion.

_____ 4. A decision to have some process done by those outside of the organization.

_____ 5. A desired return on revenue, based on selling prices.

_____ 6. An illegal act where prices are initially set artificially low to drive out competition.

_____ 7. This is violated when a company charges one group of customers one price for a product, and charges another group a different price.

_____ 8. Costs associated with a product, from its inception until it is no longer sold.

_____ 9. The decision to obtain components internally or from outside

_____10. A business that has excess capacity might accept these to generate lower-than-normal contribution margin.

Chapter 13

True or False

For each of the following statements enter a T or an F in the blank to indicate whether the statement is true or false.

_____11. A cost is relevant only if it exceeds $1 million.

_____12. Outsourcing may be appropriate if a company lacks expertise.

_____13. Target cost determines what target price should be.

_____14. Sometimes equipment should be replaced even though it is still working.

_____15. If a company uses a secret recipe for making a product, it might not be a good idea to outsource production.

_____16. If a business has a shortage of capacity, that is the best time to accept special orders.

_____17. Dumping is a legal pricing activity in the US.

_____18. A qualitative factor to consider in making a decision to add a business unit may be the political climate.

_____19. If a company charges one price to customers in the US, and another price to customers in Canada, it is practicing price discrimination.

_____20. If a company is losing money on a product, the only solution is to drop it.

_____21. Competition often is the basis for choosing a target price.

_____22. The make-or-buy decision is necessary when a company wants to decide whether to acquire goods or services internally or externally.

_____23. The decision to outsource usually results in increasing an organization's workforce.

_____24. Product costs usually decrease toward the end of a product's life cycle.

_____25. The first step to take when faced with a decision is to figure out the costs of each alternative.

Multiple Choice

Choose the best answer by writing the letter corresponding to your choice in the space provided.

_____26. Which of the following is **not** a stage in the decision-making framework?

a) Gathering information.
b) Setting goals and objectives.
c) Determine product prices.
d) Evaluate alternatives.

_____27. Which of the following is an example of a qualitative factor to consider in making a decision?

a) Hiring qualified employees.
b) Determining how to achieve target cost.
c) Eliminating non-value-added processes.
d) Maintaining employees' morale by guaranteeing that layoffs will not occur.

_____28. Which of the following is **least** likely to be a candidate for outsourcing?

a) A business has no advertising department, but wants to promote a new product.
b) A store has just reduced its hours of operation because of declining sales.
c) A building contractor has seen a sudden rise in business because a competitor's employees are on strike.
d) A manufacturer is losing sales because its production capacity can't keep up with demand.

_____29. Which of the following is a relevant cost when making a decision to drop a product?

a) The factory supervisor's salary of $110,000 will remain the same.
b) Unionized workers' contracts specify that they must be relocated to other departments if their department is closed. They are paid an average of $18 per hour.
c) The department manager will be reassigned to another factory. He makes $75,000 per year.
d) $50 for direct materials is spent for each unit of product.

_____30. Which of the following is the best reason to outsource production activity?

a) Capacity is constantly underutilized.
b) Capacity is inadequate during peak production periods.
c) Capacity is constantly over utilized.
d) Production equipment is obsolete, and needs to be replaced immediately.

_____31. The product life cycle includes all of the following **except**

a) Product design and planning
b) Product promotion
c) Product rollout
d) Product termination

_____32. Which of the following is correct regarding predatory pricing?

a) It is illegal in the US
b) It is illegal in every country
c) It is the primary basis for setting product prices.
d) It is a pricing strategy that attracts competitors.

_____33. When should accepting special orders be considered?

a) When demand for a product is low.
b) When there is a lot of competition.
c) When a company has excess capacity.
d) When prices are regulated by law.

_____34. Which of the following is the correct sequence when using target costing?

a) Determine target price; determine target cost; determine target profit.
b) Determine target profit; determine target cost; determine target price.
c) Determine target cost; determine target price; determine target profit.
d) Determine target profit; determine target price; determine target cost.

_____35. The use of in-house resources is **not** the right choice when

a) You have excess capacity.
b) You want to focus on your core business and marketing activity is a potential for outsourcing.
c) You have a competitive advantage with some production process.
d) You can perform some activity for less if you do it in-house.

_____36. Which of the following is **not** a relevant cost in deciding whether to get rid of old machinery?

a) Costs to overhaul old machinery.
b) Costs of the new machinery that will replace the old machinery.
c) Costs recorded for the purchase of old machinery.
d) Costs of disposing of the old machinery.

_____37. Which of the following is **not** a characteristic of a relevant cost?

a) A relevant cost is the same as a sunk cost.
b) A relevant cost is one that differs among alternatives.
c) A relevant cost is one that differs in the future.
d) A relevant cost is one that has not already occurred.

_____38. Outsourcing occurs when an organization decides to have outsiders perform some activity that could be completed internally. Which of the following is **not** a reason that companies might choose to outsource an activity?

a) The size of their workforce can be increased.
b) The company wants to focus on its core activities.
c) The company has no expertise in performing the outsourced activity.
d) Outsourcing is less expensive than performing the activity internally.

_____39. The make-or-buy decision is one where managers must choose between performing some activity internally, or paying others outside of the organization to perform the activity. Which of the following is a valid reason for choosing to make some production component internally, even if it costs less to buy it?

a) The organization has capacity shortages in the department performing the activity.
b) The organization wants to continue to be able to allocate support department costs to the department performing the activity.
c) The manager of the department performing the activity cannot be reassigned to other work.
d) The activity involves a patented process that would be valuable in the hands of competitors.

_____40. Which of the following is relevant when deciding whether to replace equipment earlier than expected?

a) The new equipment will cost less to operate than the new machinery.
b) The new equipment will require fewer workers, but the workers will be reassigned.
c) The new equipment will cost more than the old equipment did when it was purchased
d) The old equipment has a remaining book value of $40,000.

_____41. The manager of tax services in an accounting firm has determined that the market price for completing an income tax return for an individual with 3 schedules and itemized deductions is $160. If the target return is 20% of revenue, what must target cost be?

a) $192
b) $32
c) $128
d) At least $200

_____42. There are times when it is to the advantage of an organization for it to accept special orders. Which of the following situations should motivate a manager to take a special order?

a) A company is currently doing so well that it is paying all of its production workers overtime, just to keep up with demand.
b) One product's sales are doing so poorly that a recent special order offered to sell it will just barely cover fixed product costs after covering all relevant variable costs for the special order itself.
c) A new company is trying to establish itself in a new geographic market, where its name and reputation are well known. Consumers in that location have been waiting eagerly for the company to begin producing and selling in that geographic area.
d) A company is first to introduce a product that is highly anticipated. One of its major customers wants a special order, and because the order is large, expects a preferential price. Accepting this special order would mean foregoing sales at the regular, higher price.

_____43. There are laws that prohibit certain pricing strategies. One pricing practice that is illegal in the US is predatory pricing. Which of the following correctly describes what predatory pricing is?

a) Predatory pricing is the practice of charging different prices to different customers for the same products.
b) Predatory pricing is the practice of selling products in other countries at lower prices because of inadequate demand in the domestic market.
c) Predatory pricing is the practice of setting prices just below a competitor's price, to attract new customers.
d) Predatory pricing is the practice of selling product at prices that are lower than cost, in order to damage competitors' sales of competing products.

_____44. Organizations in competitive markets that use a cost-plus pricing strategy will suffer lower profits if which of the following is true?

a) Non-value added costs have not been eliminated.
b) Prices are raised to maintain a predetermined profit margin.
c) Prices are lowered, but costs are not lowered.
d) All of the above will lead to lower profits.

_____45. Which of the following is true about a price that is set in an organization that uses target costing?

a) The price can be based on a cost-plus pricing strategy.
b) The price is determined after the target cost is determined.
c) The price will be a market-based, competitive price.
d) The price is set in order to determine the amount of profit to be earned per unit of product.

Exercises

Please use the following to answer the next five questions.

Marian Industries is considering changes in its production activities. One of the products manufactured by Marian Industries is engines for snowmobiles. Because of recent innovations in production technologies, the engines that the company produces can be made differently. Currently, the company uses a combination of machinery and manual labor to make its product. Two alternatives are being considered. One would require that the company lease robotic equipment. This equipment would allow the company to reduce its workforce by a substantial amount. The second alternative would be to outsource a substantial portion of its production activities to a company that specializes in assembling small engines. Regardless of the alternative chosen, the engines will be sold for $400 and the estimated demand is 50,000 engines (**Total revenue of $20,000,000**). The assistant controller in charge of production has compiled the following information so far.

Cost/Quantitative Information	**Alternative 1 Make no Changes**	**Alternative 2 Lease Robotic Equipment**	**Alternative 3 Outsource Motor Assembly**
Units to be produced	50,000	50,000	50,000
Revenue (Price = $400)	$20,000,000	$20,000,000	$20,000,000
Unit level cost per unit	$60	$60	$50
Product level costs:			
Assembly Labor	$4,500,000	$1,400,000	$300,000
Supervision	$2,100,000	$800,000	$100,000
Maintenance	$3,200,000	$500,000	$0
Leasing	$0	$6,000,000	
Training	$60,000	$300,000	$20,000
Outsourcing Contract Payments	$0	$0	$9,000,000
Facility level costs	$5,000,000	$5,000,000	$5,000,000

46. Based on the information accumulated so far, which of the alternatives is the best one for Marian Industries, and why? Give your reasons as dollar amounts and as a return on sales

47. For the alternative that is the best quantitatively, list at least three qualitative reasons for rejecting it.

48. Here is some additional information to consider. An attorney from the company's Legal Department called the assistant controller, and pointed out that the employees who would be terminated based on projections for alternatives 2 and 3 are unionized employees. Although the company has the right to terminate these employees, their union contract has a clause for severance pay, which was not taken into consideration. For alternative 2, severance pay would be an estimated $775,000. For alternative 3, the severance pay would be an estimated $1,050,000. The production manager also provided additional information. She presented projections of maintenance costs based on the rising costs for the past 4 years for the production equipment. Since it is getting old, maintenance costs have been increasing by an alarming 40% each year. Thus, the estimate of $3,200,000 for maintenance, which was last year's actual maintenance cost, should actually be estimated at $1,280,000 more.

Based on this additional information, which alternative now is the best one from a quantitative perspective?

Through some industry contacts, Marian has learned that a bigger company is looking for some temporary production capacity because it can't meet production demand at its own plants. This larger company, Samson's Machines, is willing to pay $375 per engine, and wants the outsourcing company to produce 20,000 machines. If Marian Industries opts to provide the engines it can do so only if it chooses alternative 3. This would free up its existing production capacity, and make it possible for Marian to produce the 20,000 engines for Samson's Machines. The revenues and costs are re-estimated and shown in the table below.

Cost/Quantitative Information	Provide Engines to Samson's Machines	Alternative 3 Outsource Motor Assembly	TOTALS
Units to be produced	20,000	50,000	70,000
Revenue (Price = $400)		$20,000,000	$20,000,000
Revenue (Price = $375)	$7,500,000		$7,500,000
Unit level cost per unit	$60	$50	
Product level costs:			
Assembly Labor*	$2,475,000	$300,000	$2,775,000
Supervision	$1,100,000	$100,000	$1,200,000
Maintenance**	$2,240,000	$0	$2,240,000
Training***	$30,000	$20,000	$50,000
Outsourcing Contract Payments	$0	$9,000,000	$9,000,000
Facility level costs		$5,000,000	$5,000,000

* Assembly labor is less because fewer production workers are needed for production of 20,000 units. However, the amount given includes severance pay for those employees who would be terminated.

** Maintenance costs would be less than the amount given under alternative 1. However, the 40% increase is incorporated into the estimate.

*** Training would be half the original estimate for alternative 1.

Should Marian Industries accept the special order from Samson's machines? Treat this as a fourth alternative. Provide the quantitative reasons for your answer.

50. What is the minimum price Marian Industries should charge Samson's Machines to justify accepting the special order?

Chapter 13

Answers to Questions and Exercises

Matching key terms

1. h   2. b   3. g   4. d   5. e   6. i   7. j   8. a   9. f   10. c

True or False

11. F. A cost is relevant if it differs in the future across different alternatives.
12. T. Companies often choose outsourcing if someone else can perform an activity better (and often for less).
13. F. The opposite is true. Target profit and target price are determined before target cost can be determined.
14. T. Managers should consider whether relevant costs/benefits favor replacing equipment, even if it still works and can produce revenue, if there is a better alternative.
15. T. Even if resources are strained, it may be risky to outsource an activity that gives a company a competitive edge.
16. F. If a business has excess capacity, that is the time to accept special orders, and the lower prices that come with those orders.
17. F. Dumping is illegal in the US.
18. T. No matter how lucrative a business venture may appear, the political climate should be considered, particularly in countries where a business has not operated before.
19. F. Price discrimination refers to prices charged to the same type of customer in the same country or market.
20. F. Before any product is dropped, the company needs to make sure that all costs are necessary, that all costs attributed to the product would stop if production ceased, and that the profits generated from that product are really less than the costs caused by that product.
21. T. In a competitive market, theoretically at least, market price equals target price.
22. T. The make-or-buy decision is related to the decision about which parts of the value chain should be completed internally or externally.
23. F. Outsourcing usually results in downsizing, or reducing an organization's workforce.
24. T. As products reach the end of their "lives", there is less need for marketing and advertising, changes in production facilities, and other product costs.
25. F. Before deciding on alternatives, it is important to decide what goals and objectives are to be met.

Multiple Choice

26. c. Answers a, b, and d are the first three stages of the decision-making framework.
27. d. Employee morale is a qualitative issue. The other three answers are all quantitative.
28. b. For answer a, the business has no expertise in advertising, so might benefit more by hiring outsiders. For answer c, the temporary need for more employees is a good reason to outsource rather than to hire employees. Answer d relates to a need to temporarily outsource until capacity can be increased to meet ongoing demand. For answer b, reduced hours suggests excess capacity rather than not enough capacity, so outsourcing is not needed.
29. d. This is the only cost that will actually go away if the product is dropped.
30. b. This is a temporary lack of capacity. Unless uses for additional capacity can be justified on a more regular basis, it should not be acquired.
31. b. Promotion occurs at various points in the life of a product, but is not a specific stage of the product life cycle.

32. a. This practice is illegal in the US, but is not universally illegal (b). Predatory pricing requires setting prices lower than market price, so should not be the basis for setting prices. The objective of using this practice is to drive away competition.
33. c. When there is excess capacity, special orders should be taken if there is potential for some profit, even if it is less than the normal target profit.
34. d. When target costing is used, target profit and then target price are determined first and second, respectively.
35. b. If a company's core business is the main focus, then it makes sense to outsource other parts of the company's value chain.
36. c. The costs to purchase the old machinery are a past, or sunk cost. The decision to keep or replace the old machinery will not have any impact on this past cost. The other three answers are all relevant because they differ among alternatives in the future.
37. a. A sunk cost is not a relevant cost, because no action taken in the future will change a sunk cost. The other three answers correctly describe characteristics of a relevant cost.
38. a. Usually, if an activity is outsourced, it results in a reduction of the workforce, as employees currently doing the job are no longer needed. The other three answers are all legitimate reasons for outsourcing.
39. d. If the activity must be performed internally to protect trade or patented secrets, the organization will be willing to forego any cost savings that might result from outsourcing. Answer a is incorrect because capacity shortages should motivate an organization to outsource—not motivate it to avoid outsourcing. Answer b is incorrect because allocated costs are irrelevant to the decision to outsource. If outsourcing occurs, support department costs will not change. Answer c is incorrect because the status of the manager's usefulness should not be the basis for making this decision.
40. a. Only answer a relates to future costs that differ between the two alternatives. Answers b is an existing cost that will not change. Answer c includes an irrelevant cost—the purchase price of the old equipment. Answer d is a sunk cost, and is irrelevant.
41. c If 20% of the target price of $160 is target revenue, then 80% of target price is target cost. 80% of $160 is $128.
42. b. Even if the special order does not generate a lot of profit, if it is able to go beyond covering its own costs it will contribute to the company's overall profitability.
43. d. Predatory pricing is illegal because setting prices below cost drives competition away. It is also misleading to consumers, who expect the temporarily low price to remain low. Answer a describes another illegal pricing practice, called price discrimination. Answer b is dumping. Answer c is not illegal.
44. d. All of the answers given, if they occur, will lower profits. Answer a, presence of non-value-added costs will eat directly into profits (unless prices are raised, which can't happen in a competitive market). Answer b would result in losing customers. Lower sales means lower profits. Answer c might result in increased sales volume, but smaller profit margin.
45. c. Companies using target costing determine price based on competitive, market-based demand. Target cost is based on target price minus target profit (the company sets targets for the profit margin they would like to achieve).

Exercises

46. Alternative 3 is the winner. Total costs are summarized below for each alternative.

Cost/Quantitative Information	Alternative 1 Make no Changes	Alternative 2 Lease Robotic Equipment	Alternative 3 Outsource Motor Assembly
Units to be produced	50,000	50,000	50,000
1. Revenue (Price = $400)	$20,000,000	$20,000,000	$20,000,000
2. Unit level cost	$3,000,000	$3,000,000	$2,500,000
Product level costs:			
3. Assembly Labor	$4,500,000	$1,400,000	$300,000
4. Supervision	$2,100,000	$800,000	$100,000
5. Maintenance	$3,200,000	$500,000	$0
6. Leasing	$0	$6,000,000	
7. Training	$60,000	$300,000	$20,000
8. Outsourcing Contract Payments	$0	$0	$9,000,000
9. Facility level costs	$5,000,000	$5,000,000	$5,000,000
10. TOTAL COSTS	$17,860,000	$17,000,000	$16,920,000
11. Total Profit	$2,140,000	$3,000,000	$3,080,000
12. Return on Sales	10.7%	15%	15.4%

Return on sales is Profit/Revenue

47. For the outsourcing alternative, there are several reasons to think twice about accepting it. They include

- Lack of control over quality
- Lack of control over production schedules
- Creates unused capacity
- May have to give processes, patented information to outsiders
- Could cause bottlenecks
- Downsizing could create morale problems among remaining employees

48. For alternative 1, the real costs are higher by $1,280,000. This makes alternative 1 even more unappealing. It would actually generate only **$860,000** in profit. Alternative 2 would generate $3,000,000 – $775,000, or **$2,225,000** in profit. Alternative 3 is no longer the winner. It would generate profit of $3,080,000 – $1,050,000, for profit of **$2,030,000**. This makes alternative 2 the best.

49. This fourth alternative is actually the best. It would generate an incremental profit of $455,000. This result is detailed in the table below.

Cost/Quantitative Information	**Alternative 3 Outsource Motor Assembly**	**Alternative 4 Provide Engines to Samson's Machines (Combine with Alt. 3)**	**Difference between Alternatives 3 and 4**
Units to be produced	50,000	70,000	20,000
Revenue (Price = $400)	$20,000,000	$20,000,000	$0
Revenue (Price = $375)		$7,500,000	$7,500,000
Unit level cost-total	$2,500,000	$3,700,000	$1,200,000
Product level costs:			
Assembly Labor	$300,000	$2,775,000	$2,475,000
Supervision	$100,000	$1,200,000	$1,100,000
Maintenance	$0	$2,240,000	
Training	$20,000	$50,000	$2,240,000
Outsourcing Contract Payments	$9,000,000	$9,000,000	$0
Facility level costs	$5,000,000	$5,000,000	$0
TOTAL COSTS	$16,920,000	$23,965,000	$7,045,000
TOTAL PROFIT	$3,080,000	$3,535,000	$455,000

50. This question is addressing the need to at least break even on the special pricing option. In order to do so, the additional cost of $7,045,000 must be recovered. Take $7,045,000 and divide by 20,000 units, to get **$352.25**

Chapter 14
Strategic Issues in Making Investment Decisions

Chapter Study Suggestions

Chapter 14 presents the topic of long-term investment decisions. These decisions have long-term consequences. The chapter considers two important effects that investment decisions have on time. One is that investments require a long-term commitment of resources that could be used for other purposes. The second is that, since investments are a long-term commitment, managers must be flexible, to allow changes in investment decisions as time passes. Such flexibility allows managers to incorporate events and new information into the management and strategic planning process. This chapter describes how to model strategic investment decisions. It combines earlier chapters' theoretical concepts related to building financial models using relevant information with net present value (NPV) analysis used to make long-term investment decisions. Discounted cash flow analysis is reviewed in the appendix to Chapter 14.

A strategic investment, which is a choice among alternative courses of action is presented while taking into consideration competitors' actions and likely changes in natural, social and economic conditions. The focus of the chapter is to show how to model strategic investment decisions. Two modeling tools are discussed. One is expected value analysis (EVA). The other is real option value analysis (ROV). Expected value analysis attempts to derive an expected value of various decisions based on estimated probabilities of different outcomes resulting from a given decision. Real option value analysis combines NPV and EVA analyses, and allows analysts to consider responses from competitors. The most difficult type of capital investment decision is one that proposes a strategic move. These types of investment decisions require the approval of top management or the board of directors. Strategic moves require detailed analysis of the financial and non-financial implications of making the strategic move.

Chapter Highlights

A. Cost Management Challenges. Chapter 14 presents three cost management challenges.

1. What information is needed in order to make different investment decisions, and what type of analysis should be performed?
2. How can net present value and real option value analyses be used to aid in the long-term decision-making process?
3. How might ethical considerations factor into investment opportunities and choices?

B. Learning Objectives—This chapter has 6 learning objectives.

1. Chapter 14 describes the nature of strategic investment decisions.
2. The chapter discusses external and internal information needed for strategic investment decisions.
3. It shows how to use forecasts of quantitative and qualitative effects of strategic investments in NPV analysis.
4. Chapter 14 models the impact of competitors' actions.
5. The chapter presents real option value analysis, a model useful for assessing investment alternatives.
6. It explains how ethical considerations must be factored into the strategic decision-making process.

C. Investment decisions are major organizational decisions that have long-term consequences. They require commitment of resources for long periods of time, precluding organizations from using those resources for alternative investments. By using models to assess investment options, managers can explore different outcomes given changes in assumptions. This improves the decision-making process.

Financial models are representations of reality in the business world. A model allows one to see how something is supposed to work. A financial model allows an organization to test the interaction of economic variables in a variety of settings.

D. A strategic investment requires choosing among investment alternatives. Since resources are limited, managers want to choose the best investment alternative possible. Once a strategic move is chosen, decision-makers try to anticipate changes in natural, social and economic conditions. They must also consider the possible actions of competitors.

1. There are many factors that are uncontrollable, primarily because they are external to an organization. Uncontrollable external factors can be as obvious as possible changes in climate or environmental change, or as subtle as changes in consumer tastes and preferences. Although managers cannot control these factors, they can try to anticipate and plan for them to occur.

    a. Managers need to identify as many potential uncontrollable events as possible.
    These can include events like the following.

        i. Natural events like climate or environmental change.

        ii. Economic events like recession, increased consumer spending and inflation.

        iii. Social, political or legal events like war, change in political structure or laws affecting specific industries.

    b. Managers should try to gather information about uncontrollable external factors prior to making a strategic move.

    c. Decision-makers must also consider the likelihood of the occurrence of future uncontrollable events. Three commonly used approaches that help managers to assess the impact of uncontrollable future events are sensitivity and scenario analysis, expected value analysis, and real option value analysis. Sensitivity and scenario analysis were discussed in Chapter 12. Expected value analysis and real option value analysis are discussed below.

E. Expected value analysis (EVA) is a mathematical model that measures the likelihood of different outcomes weighted by the probability that each will occur. For instance, suppose an organization estimates a 30% likelihood of a return on an investment project of 8%, and estimates a 70% likelihood of a 12% return. The expected value of undertaking the project is $(.30 \times .08) + (.70 \times .12) = .024 + .084 =$ an expected value of 10.8%. Expected value calculations can be used to evaluate the likelihood of success or failure of different strategic moves. It should be noted that the usefulness of EVA is very closely related to the confidence decision-makers have on the estimates they use.

1. Information used for EVA can be based on internally generated data. It can be based on historical data, or by interviewing knowledgeable people about similar decisions. Experiences of other organizations can also be studied to help decision-makers improve their plans.

2. Information gathered internally or externally can be used to develop forecasts of the outcomes of potential investments. Recall, this information gathering contains many estimates, so sensitivity and scenario analysis should be a part of this process. The information gathered can be used to perform a discounted cash flow (DCF) analysis.

3. If some of the estimates used in the DCF analysis include expected values, managers should try to consider the impact of competition on those expected values. A good way to model the different scenarios is to use an expected value analysis decision tree. This extension of EVA allows the decision-maker to easily compare different results that might occur under different circumstances like entry of competition.

F. A review of or brief introduction to discounted cash flow (DCF) analysis may be useful. The two key performance measurement tools in DCF analysis are net present value (NPV) and internal rate of return (IRR). NPV calculates the cost or benefit of a given project or plan, when cash in- and outflows extend into the future , discounted to today's values. A related DCF measure, IRR calculates what the rate of return on a future project is when the NPV is zero. A simpler performance measure in use is the payback period, which simply shows how many years it would take for a project to recoup the costs associated with the project.

1. NPV calculations include three types of investment cash flows: Asset acquisition dollar impact of taxes resulting from gain or loss of assets to be replaced and tax credits. The calculations include ongoing (periodic) cash flows. These consist of revenues and costs generated from operations. NPV calculations also consider costs of terminating an investment.

   In addition to cash flows, an important component of NPV calculations is the assumed discount rate. This is the estimated opportunity cost of investing in the project. If the NPV is a positive dollar amount, it means the project will generate a higher return than the discount rate.

2. The internal rate of return (IRR) is difficult to calculate, especially if the cash flows for an investment are not uniform. If not using a calculator or Excel or some other electronic method, trial and error is the only way to calculate the IRR.

G. An analytical model that incorporates EVA, DCF and competition is real option value (ROV) analysis. This model allows calculation of the expected values of an outcome given different competitive responses. ROV allows analyses to include assessment of mid-course correction, or of deferring the implementation of a strategic move.

H. Legal and ethical issues must be considered in making strategic decisions. This is especially true when strategic moves are global in nature. In addition to the financial implications of moving operations abroad, organizations must learn about political, social and cultural differences that could affect the outcome of a strategic move. What is normal and acceptable in one country may be unusual and even illegal in another country.

1. Before moving forward with a strategic investment, organizations must conduct an investigation with due diligence. This means that reasonable care is taken to identify potential problems and opportunities of a potential investment.

2. In the United States, recent scandals involving major corporations have led to new laws that require stricter control over unethical or illegal behavior by corporations or top executives or managers.

a. Managers or top executives may behave unethically because of bias for or against particular investment projects, or due to fear of loss of prestige, power, compensation, or simply due to greed.

b. To increase the likelihood that investment practices are ethically correct, organizations can take several steps.

   i. Organizations should hire ethical people.

   ii. A code of ethics should be written and enforced by organizations.

   iii. For investment projects, a system of reporting, review and evaluation should be in place.

   iv. Internal audit of projects should be conducted.

   v. A system of internal controls should be fully developed, implemented and adhered to.

REVIEW AND SELF TEST QUESTIONS AND EXERCISES

Matching key terms

Match the following terms to the correct definition by writing the correct letter next to the correct definition.

a. expected value analysis	b. due diligence	c. strategic investment
d. net present value analysis	e. internal audits	f. code of ethics
g. expected value events	h. DCF analysis	
i. uncontrollable external events	j. decision tree	

_____ 1. A chart that compares two or more possible outcomes.

_____ 2. An evaluation of operations or investment projects in an organization.

_____ 3. A method for comparing different projects by reducing future dollar amounts of cash flows to their current values.

_____ 4. A measure of each possible outcome, weighted by the probability that it will occur.

_____ 5. A complete and thorough investigation of legal, environmental and employee considerations related to a strategic decision.

_____ 6. A way to estimate the benefit of a strategic investment based on the probabilities of various results of that undertaking

_____ 7. A method used to analyze alternative investments.

_____ 8. A type of investment that usually takes organizations into new, untested territory.

_____ 9. Things that might happen, and which should be anticipated in analyzing possible strategic moves.

_____10. A documented set of rules and policies that describe appropriate behavior by employees

True or False

For each of the following statements enter a T or an F in the blank to indicate whether the statement is true or false.

_____11. A strategic investment is one that affects an organization for many years into the future.

_____12. Entry to a market in the emerging countries of Eastern Europe is **not** an example of a strategic investment decision.

_____13. Buying materials for inventory costing $15 million is **not** a strategic decision.

_____14. Strategic moves made by an organization should **not** be in response to strategic moves of their competitors.

_____15. An example of an unexpected external factor is the emergence of religious groups who overthrow the government.

_____16. When expected value analysis is used, the estimates are always somewhat uncertain.

_____17. When gathering information to use for strategic planning, it is not a good idea to research competitors' experiences.

_____18. A good strategic move is best identified by management intuition.

_____19. Due diligence in investigating the prospects for success of an investment includes assessment of the environmental implications of the investment.

_____20. If due diligence is **not** properly carried out, an organization's reputation could be permanently damaged.

_____21. Strategic decisions should be based primarily on internal, historical information.

_____22. A strategic plan to expand operations into a foreign country adds uncertainty to financial information provided for use in deciding whether to proceed with the plans.

_____23. A company entering foreign markets should understand that it will have to violate its own ethical standards in order to succeed in that market.

_____24. Real option value analysis incorporates DCF, EVA and competition into its analysis.

_____25. An audit of a strategic investment project cannot be performed until the project is completely implemented.

Multiple Choice

Choose the best answer by writing the letter corresponding to your choice in the space provided.

______26. Which of the following is **not** a strategic investment decision?

a) $10 million is being spent to roll out a new product line.
b) $10 million is being spent to expand operations beyond the U.S., to Mexico.
c) $10 million is being spent to buy patio sets to sell over the summer season at a lawn and garden chain's 300 stores.
d) $10 million is being spent to upgrade the computerized information system of a major corporation, to make its systems compliant with international accounting standards.

______27. Which of the following is an example of an uncontrollable external factor?

a) A company's oil fields in the Middle East are at risk of attack by terrorists.
b) The CFO of a corporation paid a $5 million bribe to a government official.
c) Production workers are being replaced with robotics production equipment, saving $5 million per year in operating costs.
d) A company has adopted a policy of replacing its fleet of vehicles every 10 years.

______28. A company is considering a move to Eastern Europe. Part of their due diligence investigation should include all **except**

a) study of the legal limits on profits that can be exported.
b) study of the total profits to be generated from the project.
c) study of the environmental laws that the company must comply with.
d) study of cultural norms and expectations with respect to payment of bribes to government officials.

______29. Which of the following is true regarding expected value analysis if used to assess growth?

a) The result of EVA is the likely growth rate.
b) The probabilities used in the EVA are likely to be fairly certain.
c) The estimated growth rates must be obtained from a government entity.
d) The result of EVA is, at best, an estimate and, at worst a guess.

______30. One of the problems of expanding into new countries is that

a) managers lose control of revenues generated there.
b) existing employees cannot be employed there.
c) existing employees may be unfamiliar with cultural norms there.
d) Profits are likely to be very small there.

_____31. Which of the following is the best source of financial information for an organization considering a strategic move to another country?

a) Financial records
b) Interviews with operating and marketing personnel
c) Interviews with managers of competing firms
d) Industry data and competitor analysis

_____32. Which of the following strategic investment decisions are existing employees likely to be most affected by?

a) Replacement of the central air conditioning system in production facilities.
b) Moving some operations overseas.
c) Major overhaul of production equipment, to restore its productive efficiency.
d) Addition of Internet, Web-based product offerings to overseas customers.

_____33. An advantage of real option value analysis is

a) it provides estimates that preclude competition from entering a market.
b) it provides estimates that consider competitors' actions.
c) it shows how to avoid losses, given competition.
d) it shows how to avoid competition in new markets.

_____34. Sensitivity analysis is critical in strategic planning because

a) there are so many variables in the analysis that are estimates, many outcomes are possible.
b) it is an important part of due diligence.
c) it prevents managers from proposing unrealistic capital investments.
d) it assures that the outcomes will meet expectations.

_____35. Strategic investment decisions must normally be approved by

a) top management, regardless of the magnitude or expense of the project.
b) managers directly affected by the project.
c) the board of directors, if the project is a strategic move.
d) the managers directly above those affected by a project, regardless of the magnitude or expense.

_____36. Which of the following should occur with respect to audit activities for capital investment projects that are strategic moves?

a) The project should be periodically audited during implementation and after implementation is complete.
b) The project should be periodically audited only during implementation.
c) The project should be audited only upon completion of its implementation.
d) The project should be audited only if there seems to be a problem.

_____37. Which of the following is true regarding strategic investment estimates and actual outcomes?

a) If the analysis was well done, the actual outcomes will equal the estimates.
b) If actual results of a strategic investment generate losses instead of profits, it is because analysis of the project was poorly done.
c) It is rare that actual outcomes are equal to estimated outcomes for an investment project.
d) If actual results of a strategic investment generate higher than expected profits, it is because estimates used were too conservative.

_____38. All of the following are ethical issues that might occur in investment decisions **except**

a) intentional misstatement of results may occur after the project is implemented.
b) intentional misstatement of information may be submitted for use in making the investment decision.
c) unethical projects may be invested in.
d) the board of directors may approve a project even if it is risky.

_____39. Which of the following is true of non-profit organizations and investment decisions?

a) It is not necessary for non-profit organizations to perform investment analyses.
b) Non-profit organizations perform investment analyses to ensure that limited resources are allocated efficiently.
c) Non-profit organizations can only accept investment projects that allow costs to be recovered.
d) Investment projects for non-profit organizations might be of a duration of one year or less.

_____40. Investment projects in foreign markets may experience cost overruns for all of the following reasons **except**

a) inexperience in working with foreign employees.
b) delays in obtaining approval and licenses to complete work.
c) actual inflation rates are lower than estimated.
d) political intervention has slowed progress.

_____41. Which of the following is **not** a barrier to entering a new geographical market?

a) There is some uncertainty about the government that is about to be elected.
b) There is likely to be competition.
c) Environmental laws in the new market might make the project unprofitable
d) The length of time that benefits can be obtained from the investment is estimated to be too short to generate profit.

_____42. Which of the following non-quantifiable benefits may prompt an organization to **reject** a project that is the best financial choice?

a) The impact on the community is viewed as more important than profits to be gained by the proposed capital investment project.
b) Accepting the capital investment project would violate the company's ethics policies.
c) The potential for damage to the environment outweighs the potential for success of the project, even though the project does not violate any environmental laws.
d) All of the above may prompt an organization to reject a capital project that appears to be the best financial choice.

_____43. Which of the following is a **<u>not</u>** a good way to ensure that unethical behavior is less likely to occur in an organization?

a) Develop and enforce a system of internal controls.
b) Do a background check on all prospects for top management positions.
c) Hire ethical employees.
d) Develop and enforce a code of ethics.

_____44. Which of the following is true of NPV and IRR?

a) If the IRR is lower than the discount rate used to calculate NPV, then the NPV will be a positive dollar amount.
b) If the IRR is greater than the discount rate used to calculate NPV, then the NPV will be a positive dollar amount.
c) If the IRR is lower than the discount rate used to calculate NPV, then the NPV will be $0
d) If the IRR is greater than the discount rate used to calculate NPV, then the NPV will be $0.

_____45. Which of the following is true about a strategic investment?

a) Once a capital investment project is begun, an organization must complete it.
b) A project is not considered to be a strategic investment project unless at least $1 million is spent on it.
c) If, after spending $25 million on a project, management realizes it will not succeed, the management should view the $25 million as a sunk cost and abandon the project.
d) Discounted cash flow (DCF) analysis is the only tool managers should use to decide whether an investment project is viable.

Exercises

Please use the following information to answer the next five questions.

The Elkins Mfg. Company is a large producer of typewriters. The company has been located in Millsville, New Jersey since it began operating in 1922. The firm has one production facility. This facility is used to produce typewriters. The company employs 1,500 people in Millsville. The town has 6,000 people, of whom 4,000 are adults, 2,100 work full-time, and 1,500 work for Elkins Mfg. Most of the town's economy is centered around this one major employer. Aside from Elkins Mfg., most of the people living in Millsville work on farms, or are schoolteachers, shopkeepers or government employees for the town. Elkins Mfg. is publicly traded on NASDAQ.

Gerald Elkins, the grandson of the original owner, and its CEO, has been bothered by the steadily declining profits of the firm. Despite making strategically successful moves into the manufacture of fax machines, shredders and other office equipment, typewriters have remained a major component of their business. He knows that the livelihoods of all of the townspeople depend on the continued existence of his firm. Mr. Elkins has expressed his concerns to his chief financial officer, Deborah (Elkins) McPike, CPA, and to his chief operating officer, Everett Elkins III, about the earnings problems. The top management of Elkins Manufacturing has summarized their concerns below.

- The firm is producing typewriters, which are no longer in demand. The company is losing sales to computer companies, which produce and sell equipment that allows typewriting (word processing) plus a whole lot more.
- The company's owners want to make a strategic change by converting its typewriter business to a keyboard production business. Their company's good name and reputation would help them to enter the computer keyboard industry, and Deborah knows that most computer companies do not have enough production capacity to make the keyboards demanded by consumers.
- Conversion of the typewriter production activities could be accomplished in one of two ways.
    - The typewriter facility in Millsville could be rebuilt and automated, resulting in the loss of 400 production jobs.
    - The entire typewriter production facility in Millsville could be shut down, and the company could purchase a production facility in Mexico, hiring workers at a much lower wage. Moving to Mexico would result in a loss of 1,000 jobs in Millsville, 25 of which would be relocated to Mexico.
- The workers in New Jersey are unionized. Even though they are willing to make concessions to keep the plant in New Jersey, they cannot afford to accept wages comparable to those the Mexican workers would willingly accept.
- If the firm moves to Mexico, the remaining 500 jobs in Millsville would be for administrative, sales and marketing people. All production personnel would lose their jobs.
- The company plans to begin by producing three different keyboard models.
- DCF analysis has revealed that the option to move to Mexico would provide almost twice as much cash flow as the Millsville option would over a 10-year period. NPV of the Millsville option is $4,500,000, and the Mexican option has a NPV of $8,400,000.

46. Discuss at least three quantitative reasons why Elkins Mfg. might choose to stay in Millsville despite the higher expected return from the Mexican option.

47. Discuss at least three qualitative reasons why Elkins Mfg. might choose to stay in Millsville despite the higher expected return from the Mexican option. Then give at least three qualitative reasons why the Mexican option should be chosen.

48. What kinds of ethical predicaments might be encountered if the company decides to relocate to Mexico? How should Elkins Mfg. respond if it moves to Mexico?

49. The company's executives in performing due diligence have learned that there will likely be unexpected competition if they opt for the Mexican investment project. How might this fact influence the company's choice between New Jersey and Mexico?

50. Name some internal control concerns that must be addressed if the company chooses to move to Mexico.

Answers to Questions and Exercises

Matching key terms

1. j 2. e 3. d 4. g 5. b 6. a 7. h 8. c 9. i 10. f

True or False

11. T. Strategic investments are long-term investments that affect assets, revenues and costs.
12. F. Entry to an untested market is a strategic investment.
13. T. Even though millions of dollars may be invested in inventory, the expectation is that it will be sold within a year—thus, it is a short-term investment.
14. F. Sometimes the very survival of an organization rests on its willingness to change its strategy, to remain competitive. Failure to be responsive to competition can lead to organizational failure.
15. T. A change in the political structure of a country creates instability that can have a direct impact on organizations operating in that country.
16. T. Expected value analysis uses estimates of outcomes based on estimated returns for each outcome and estimated probabilities of the outcomes.
17. F. If competitors have had similar experiences, it is informative to learn what mistakes can be avoided and what successes can be repeated.
18. F. Management intuition should be supported by as much analysis and planning as is reasonably possible.
19. T. Due diligence is investigation that is intended to eliminate or minimize any unpleasant surprises. This includes environmental surprises.
20. T. A company's reputation and credibility can be damaged by making a poor investment decision.
21. F. Strategic decisions should be based on historical information, interviews from people in the organization, past experiences of competitors, and uncontrollable external information.
22. T. A company usually has incomplete information, no matter how thorough the preliminary investigation of an overseas project is.
23. F. A company never has to violate its own ethical policies. If the company cannot tolerate the kinds of violations that would occur in the prospective market, it should choose not to operate there.
24. T. Real option value analysis extends DCF and EVA by combining them. It also allows competition to be factored into the analysis explicitly.
25. F. Audits of investment projects should take place periodically, during implementation. That way, problems and successes can be detected early rather than later.

Multiple Choice

26. c. Inventory purchases are not likely to benefit the organization over a period of more than one year. The other three answers all provide benefit to the company for several years, and also should facilitate expansion and growth, and so are strategic investments.
27. a. Organizations should try to anticipate unexpected events like terrorist attacks. The other three answers are all internal events.
28. b. Although financial analysis of the profitability of the move is needed, it is not a part of the due diligence portion of the investigation. The other three answers are examples of due diligence investigating activities.
29. d. Since virtually all of the input to expected value analysis is estimated, it is highly unlikely that the actual growth rate will be the one derived from the analysis (answer a), or that the probabilities used are likely to be fairly certain (answer b). There is no requirement that estimated management information be obtained by the government (answer c). An EVA analysis, if proven to be fairly close to actual results can at best be deemed a good estimate.
30. c. Cultural differences may affect productivity levels, it may influence the way managers and workers interact, and it might even be difficult to communicate. Managers should not lose control of revenues, some employees are normally transferred to new countries to oversee, if not run operations, and profits may be small or large, depending on the success of the project.
31. d. Financial records may not give any clues as to what to expect if an investment project is completely new to the company. Operating and marketing personnel will probably not be well informed either, since they will have had no experience either. Industry data and competitor analysis are the best sources of information. Answer c is wrong because, first of all management at competing businesses will not advise you on how to succeed, and second, if they did, they might be tempted to mislead you.
32. b. If operations are moved overseas, it is very likely due to cost savings that can be obtained by paying workers less in different countries. Existing employees would likely be replaced by workers overseas. Answer c might result in some loss of jobs if the efficiency of the machinery had become so bad that workers were hired to substitute for the inefficiency of the machines, but that is not typically how inefficiencies with equipment are addressed. The other two answers (a and d) should have no effect on production workers.
33. b. Real option analysis explicitly incorporates estimates of expected NPV given competition. It cannot and does not preclude competition, show how to avoid competition, or show how to avoid losses given competition.
34. a. Virtually every financial piece of information in a capital project proposal is an estimate when it is a strategic move. Sensitivity analysis allows managers to consider best and worst-case scenarios.
35. c. Strategic moves affect the whole mission of an organization, or the way in which the mission will be achieved. The board of directors must approve these projects. Top management seldom must approve replacements, and sometimes middle managers can approve expansions.

36. a. A strategic move has many variables that are changeable and unpredictable. Such an undertaking should be audited periodically so that adjustments can be made during the implementation phase. Once a project is completed, it should be audited to evaluate how close to expectations the actual outcomes were. This is useful for future projects, as well as for the continuing operation of the project itself.
37. c. Even for simple investment projects, since estimates of future cash flows are used, it is rare that the actual outcomes equal the original projections.
38. d. The decision by the board of directors to approve a risky project is not unethical. The other three are legitimate ethical problems that might be encountered. Managers may submit intentional misstatement of results or information due to personal biases or personal needs.
39. b. Since non-profit organizations do not exist to make profit, they perform capital investment analyses to determine how best to utilize limited capital resources. They frequently must choose among different projects. Answer a is incorrect because non-profit organizations do perform investment analyses. Answer c is incorrect because all organizations have capital projects that do not generate revenues (for instance, replacing an entire heating system will not make money for anyone—yet such a project is a capital investment). Answer d is wrong because it describes a short-term investment.
40. c. If inflation is **higher** than expected, this will cause cost overruns. The other three answers are all causes of cost overruns in foreign markets.
41. b. Although competition may be a deterrent to entry, it is not, strictly speaking, a barrier.
42. d. All of the answers given are reasons a company may decide against pursuing a capital investment project.
43. b. Doing a background check might be a good idea, but it is not necessarily going to prevent unethical people from joining a company.
44. b. The discount rate, also called the hurdle rate or cost of capital is the opportunity cost of an investment. Since the internal rate of return is the rate at which a project generates a NPV of zero, it must be higher than the hurdle rate or the cost of capital in order for NPV to be positive.
45. c. As difficult as it may be, managers need to realize that failed projects should be discontinued once it becomes clear that a project will generate losses instead of the profits that were expected. It is tempting to try to complete the project, to justify the sunk costs already invested in the project. This is a mistake. Answer a is wrong for exactly this reason. Answer b is wrong because the dollar amount is not the only criteria to use in determining whether an expenditure is a capital investment. Answer d is wrong because managers have come to realize the importance of non-financial factors in analyzing projects.

Exercises

46. (1) The analysis might have ignored the higher expected rate of return needed for operations in Mexico. While the risks of continuing operations in New Jersey could probably be estimated with some degree of confidence, there would be higher risks associated with moving to a foreign country. Assuming moving to Mexico is riskier than staying in New Jersey, the discount rate used in discounted cash flow analysis could be set much higher for the Mexican option. (2) There could be more uncontrollable external factors in Mexico than there are in New Jersey. These include political instability, educational level of workers, cultural differences, and different social norms. (3) Mexican productivity might be slower than the New Jersey workers since NJ workers would have already been familiar with some of the operations of Elkins Mfg. (4) A qualitative factor that may have a quantitative impact is that the quality of work by Mexican workers is unknown. If quality is low, cost of re-work and defects might increase costs. (5) Finally, depending on where the customers are located, there might be additional transportation costs to consider. Elkins Mfg. might have to spend more if its market is located in the northeastern United States.

47. Staying in New Jersey could be justified for a number of qualitative reasons, including (1) the workers there are a known commodity. (2) Managers would know the people, their language, and their culture. (3) Elkins Manufacturing would not have to deal with the uncertainties of political turmoil in Mexico if they stayed in New Jersey. (4) The company could promote itself as an American company that did not abandon American workers. This would place them among other companies who have benefited from being "buy American" companies. (5) Community pride would motivate employees to work harder. (6) History of the company might lead executives to forego some profits. (7) Having control over quality of work might save costs and lessen risk of damaging the company's reputation for producing quality product, and (8) having less of a transition might all be given as reasons for staying in New Jersey.

    On the other hand, moving to Mexico could be beneficial for a number of reasons as well, including (1) getting a fresh start would mean the (Mexican) employees would not have to be re-programmed away from a typewriter mindset to a keyboard mindset. (2) The move might allow expansion into new markets, making the company a global one. The company's reputation could grow as a result. (3) The company, armed with this strategic move and a new location might find that some synergies exist with computer companies, especially since a move to Mexico would place them closer, geographically, to the Silicon Valley in California. This might motivate the company's managers to seek growth in other areas. (4) The move to a new production facility, with new and modern equipment, might make the operation more efficient, and might result in higher quality of product.

48. In Mexico, bribery may be acceptable. Managers might also be tempted to misreport results to make them seem more optimistic than they really are. Given the high rate of unemployment in Mexico, the company may also face attempts by underaged citizens there to seek employment at Elkins Manufacturing. Elkins Mfg. might need to develop more stringent internal controls and create a new code of ethics to address ethical issues that might not have arisen in New Jersey.

49. Entry of competition in Mexico would have an impact on estimated benefits of moving there. Elkins Mfg. should extend their analysis, to incorporate the probable entry of competition. Knowing that there might be competition, estimates of market share should be adjusted using expected value calculations. Going even further, the executives at Elkins Mfg. could also use real option value analysis, considering whether it would be better to defer the move to Mexico, abandon it after competitors move in, or abandon the Mexican option completely.

50. Elkins Mfg. currently operates in a small town, and probably has centralized operations. Since it is publicly traded, it must already have a documented system of internal controls. Expanding to Mexico, where the rules and social norms might be different would warrant development of a code of ethics, as well as requiring changes to the system of internal controls. Internal controls are the policies and practices that are followed to ensure that assets are safeguarded, that operations are performed effectively and efficiently, and that company policies and laws are obeyed. Elkins Mfg. would also need to assess its hiring practices in Mexico, to assure that the company complies with its own hiring practices as well as employment laws in Mexico.

Chapter 15
Budgeting and Financial Planning

Chapter Study Suggestions

Chapter 15 presents the topic of budgeting and financial planning. Budgeting is a planning tool that allows managers to quantify their goals for the coming months, quarters, and for the coming year. Although organizations have strategic plans, and long range goals, they implement activities in shorter blocks of time. Budgets, in particular the master budget, are the financial plans that guide organizational activities. Budgets serve many purposes. In addition to being a planning tool, budgets facilitate communication and coordination among managers; they help managers see how best to allocate resources; Budgets serve as benchmarks against which actual results can be compared, and are often the basis of performance evaluation.

Completion of the master budget is a multi-step process. Beginning with the sales forecast, every phase of activity is planned and quantified in a set of interrelated schedules. The final product of these budget schedules is a set of budgeted financial statements.

The chapter also describes some of the behavioral aspects of budgeting. The appendix explains and illustrates the link between planning for inventory and the economic order quantity model, as well as under JIT inventory management.

Chapter Highlights

A. Cost Management Challenges. Chapter 15 offers five cost management challenges.

1. Why do organizations need an annual budget, and what purposes are served by the budgeting process?

2. How does budgeting facilitate communication and coordination among managers, particularly top management, sales and production personnel?

3. What is a master budget, and what are the five parts of a master budget for a manufacturing firm?

4. How can top management or the board of directors use the budget to influence the future direction of a company?

5. How can participative budgeting be used as an effective management tool?

B. Learning Objectives—This chapter has 7 learning objectives.

1. It describes the key role that budgeting plays in the strategic planning process.

2. Chapter 15 presents and explains five purposes of budgeting systems.

3. The chapter describes and demonstrates how to prepare a master budget, including its components.

4. Chapter 15 illustrates and evaluates a typical organization's process of budget administration.

5. The chapter discusses the behavioral implications of budgetary slack, and explains the workings of a participatory budget.

6. It describes contemporary trends in the budgeting process as an element of a cost management system.

7. The appendix explains and illustrates the use of the economic-order-quantity model, and discusses the implications of JIT on inventory management.

C. Every organization exists for the purpose of accomplishing some set of goals, such as profitability or public service. In order to achieve those goals, an organization's top management engages in strategic planning. One step toward achieving the goals of an organization is identification of critical success factors. These are key strengths felt to be most responsible for making the organization successful. Chapter 14 presented strategic planning concerns as they relate to long-term goals. The focus in the last chapter was on long-term capital investments and planning for strategic moves. Chapter 15 presents budgeting, and budgets represent managers' strategic plan in one-year increments.

1. A strategic long-range plan consists of the steps needed to achieve intermediate and long-range goals. It is a tool used to aid in decisions as they relate to major capital investments in existing facilities, expansion projects, and strategic moves. Strategic plans may include specific objectives such as cost control, increased market share, or introduction of new products.

2. A strategic plan is detailed into year-by-year plans. These yearly guides are referred to as master budgets. A budget is basically a road map, or plan for accomplishing immediate goals. The purposes of budgeting and various types of budgets are presented next. Then the details that go into the master budget will be illustrated.

D. A budget, which is a detailed plan, has five primary purposes.

1. It is a planning tool. It allows managers to quantify their plan of action.

2. A budget facilitates communication and coordination among managers and departments of an organization.

3. They help managers to see how resources should be allocated.

4. Budgets aid in managing financial and operational performance. It is used as a benchmark against which actual results can be compared.

5. Budgets can be used for performance evaluation, both for segments of an organization, managers, and the organization as a whole.

E. Organizations use many types of budgets. The master budget (or profit plan) is a comprehensive set of budgets covering all phases of an organization's operations for a specified time period. Budgeted financial statements (or pro forma financial statements) show how an organization's financial statements will appear if operations proceed according to plan. A capital budget is a plan for acquiring capital assets. A financial budget is a plan that shows how an organization will acquire financial resources, through issuing stock or incurring debt.

Budgets differ also along time dimensions. Budgets may cover a month, quarter, or year (short-range budgets). They may cover periods longer than a year (long-range budgets). Rolling budgets, or revolving or continuous budgets are continuously updated, covering the same amount of time, but dropping older periods which are replaced by newer time periods.

F. The master budget is the main output of a budget system. It is comprised of many separate budgets that are interdependent. The various components of the master budget are outlined below.

1. The sales budget is the first budget to be completed in the master budget. Before the sales budget is even completed though, a sales forecast is completed.

a. The sales forecast is a prediction of sales of goods or services. Sales forecasts are based on past sales, industry trends, general economic trends, political, legal events, pricing policies, planned advertising, planned introduction of products, market research studies, strategic moves planned for the coming year, and other known changes.

b. Sources of sales forecast data are sales staff, market researchers and econometric models (a sophisticated multiple regression time-series model that shows sales trends, given the impact of many variables). A method called the Delphi technique requires that members of a forecasting group submit individual forecasts anonymously. The group then discusses all of the results submitted as a group. This is an attempt to remove biases from the sales forecast.

2. A set of operational budgets is developed next, based on the sales budget. The components of this set of budgets vary, depending on whether the company is a manufacturer, a merchandiser, or a service provider.

   a. A manufacturing firm develops a production budget, which is the basis for a direct materials budget, a direct labor budget, and an overhead budget. These budgets are then used to prepare a schedule of cost of goods manufactured and cost of goods sold. A second set of budgets and schedules is for selling, general and administrative expenses.

   b. A merchandising company does not need a production budget or the budgets prepared from the production budget. Instead, a merchandise purchases budget is prepared. Then, a budget for personnel, overhead, and selling and administrative expenses is prepared.

   c. A service provider, after preparing a sales budget, must prepare a set of budgets showing how those services will be provided. The schedules prepared by service firms vary, depending on the types of service being provided.

   d. A cash budget shows the amount and timing of expected cash receipts and cash disbursements.

   e. A capital budget details plans for major acquisitions and disposals of assets. That portion of the capital which is planned for the coming budget period is included as part of the master budget.

   f. Budgeted financial statements are the final piece of the master budget to be completed. The financial statements include budgeted (pro forma) balance sheet, income statement, and statement of cash flows.

   g. Non-profit organizations also use master budgets, with the notable omission of the sales budget since they do not obtain their financial resources from selling products or services. They usually begin with information showing planned services that will be provided, and the expected funding.

G. Organizations with international operations face a number of challenges in preparing their budgets. For foreign activities, the budget process must incorporate translation of foreign currency into the currency of the home country; adjusting financial information for the inflation rate of the countries where the company operates; and other factors that might affect budget estimates, like consumer demand, costs and availability of skilled labor, legal and political change.

H. Organizations using activity-based costing (ABC) can greatly enhance the quality of their budget process. Such an approach results in activity-based budgeting, which is the process of developing a master budget using information obtained from an ABC analysis.

I. The best way to understand the process of completing a master budget is to walk through each component, describing what goes into it and how the information is obtained. This is shown for a manufacturing company. A manufacturing firm's budget has eight major parts to it:

(1) the sales budget
(2) the production budget
(3) the direct materials budget
(4) the direct labor budget
(5) the manufacturing OH budget
(6) the selling, general and administrative budget
(7) the cash budgets, including budgeted cash receipts and disbursements, and
(8) budgeted financial statements.

Each of these is described in more detail below.

1. The sales budget shows projected sales in units, and multiplies the number of units by price to determine sales revenue. These budgets may be shown by month instead of quarter.

2. The production budget shows the number of units of product that are to be produced during a budget period. In order to determine what production needs are, desired inventory levels must also be budgeted. The production budget is based on the following formulas:

   a. Sales in units + desired ending inventory of finished goods = total units required.

   b. Total units required—expected beginning inventory of finished goods = units to be produced.

3. The direct materials budget is the next to be prepared. This budget shows what materials are needed to produce the units budgeted. The formulas showing how many units need to be produced can also be used to show the raw materials needed:

a. Raw material required for production + desired ending inventory of raw materials = total raw materials required.

b. Total raw materials required—expected beginning inventory of raw materials = raw material to be purchased.

c. The materials to be purchased must be computed for each type of material used in production. Then, estimated cost per unit of material is multiplied by the number of units needed. The direct materials budget shows total units of materials needed, and the cost of those materials.

i. Production and purchasing are linked because the production budget is the basis for determining materials needs. In addition, inventory must be properly managed. Although ideally inventory levels should be minimized to save money, managers do not want to face materials shortages that might delay production.

4. The direct labor budget shows the number of hours of direct labor to be used during the budget period. This budget is based on estimated units to be produced. Then the amount of labor time needed to complete production of these units is determined. Depending on the complexity of production processes, the skill levels of direct labor workers may vary. In this case, the direct labor budget must be more detailed. It must show how much labor of each skill and pay type is needed to complete production.

   The direct labor budget is not a separate budget if labor is included as part of conversion activity. In addition, direct labor may be treated as a facility-level cost instead of unit-level cost if labor costs are not adjusted according to production level changes. The direct labor budget shows the total time and the total cost of direct labor.

5. The manufacturing overhead budget shows the cost of overhead expenses to be incurred in the budget process. The manufacturing overhead budget details each type of overhead cost, and each cost is categorized as unit, batch, product, customer, or facility-level. Overhead costs are also split between cash outlays and non-cash outlays (like depreciation).

6. The selling, general and administrative budget shows the planned amounts of expenditures for these non-production costs. These costs are, like the manufacturing overhead costs, split into unit, batch, product, customer and facility level.

7. The cash budget shows the timing and amounts of cash receipts and cash disbursements. Supplementary budgets are the cash receipts and the cash disbursements budgets.

a. The cash receipts budget shows cash flows generated from sales revenues and other sources of cash.

   i. Especially important is the expected flow of cash from credit sales. Businesses that extend credit to customers must estimate when cash from those sales will be received.

   ii. Uncollectible credit sales must be estimated for those customers who fail to pay what they owe.

   iii. In the case where there are substantial credit sales, a sizable part of the cash receipts from one month may actually be for sales from prior periods. In a given month, the schedule of cash receipts will consist of receipts from cash sales in the current period plus cash receipts for credit sales from past periods.

   iv. Cash receipts may occur when a company borrows funds, sells stock, sells assets, or earns interest or dividends from investments. These receipts are shown on the cash budget, not on the cash receipts budget, which only shows receipts from operating activities.

b. The cash disbursements budget details the expected cash payments for the budget period. Payments may be for materials purchases, payroll, or payment for other goods and services needed to run the business.

   i. Materials purchases are usually paid for over several months, so the timing of cash disbursements must also be estimated.

   ii. The cash disbursements budget is very detailed because it shows all of the items that disbursements are made for. Expenditures from the direct labor, direct materials, manufacturing overhead, and selling, general and administrative budgets appear on the cash disbursements budget.

c. The cash budget combines cash receipts and disbursements. Combining the cash receipts and cash disbursements helps managers to see whether there is adequate cash on hand to pay for all expenditures on a timely basis. The cash budget is organized to show the cash receipts and disbursements from operations first.

   The change in the cash balance due to operations is an important piece of budget information. The expectation is that most of the increase to cash will be the result of profits from operations. Below the change in cash figures, other cash activity is shown. Companies may borrow money for various reasons. If there are loans outstanding, interest must be paid on the loan, and the principal must be repaid.

There may be some months during which cash disbursements exceed the cash balance. In that case, the company should have an established line of credit with banks that they do business with, to cover any shortages until cash flows increase in later months. This is a common practice in companies that have seasonal sales activity.

8. The budgeted schedule of cost of goods manufactured and cost of goods sold combines information from the direct materials, direct labor, and manufacturing overhead budgets. The cost per unit of product is based on absorption costing. This means that unit-level costs are assigned based on budgeted unit-level costs, and higher level costs are allocated based on budgeted activity. The schedule of cost of goods manufactured has the following parts.

   a. Direct materials: Beginning raw materials plus purchases minus raw materials = direct materials used. Direct materials information is obtained from the direct materials budget.

   b. Direct labor. Obtained from the direct labor budget.

   c. Manufacturing overhead. Obtained for the manufacturing overhead budget.

   d. Total manufacturing costs. The sum of direct materials used, direct labor, and manufacturing overhead.

   e. Add the budgeted beginning work in process (if there is any). Deduct the budgeted ending work in process (if there is any), to get cost of goods manufactured. If there are budgeted beginning or ending work in process balances, then a separate schedule showing budgeted equivalent units and their associated costs must be completed.

   f. Add beginning finished goods inventory to cost of goods manufactured, to get cost of goods available for sale. Budgeted beginning finished goods inventory is obtained by multiplying the desired number of units in the production budget by the absorption cost per unit calculated for the schedule of cost of goods manufactured.

   g. Deduct budgeted finished goods inventory from cost of goods available for sale, to get budgeted cost of goods sold. Budgeted ending finished goods inventory is obtained by multiplying the desired number of units in the production budget by the absorption cost per unit calculated for the schedule of cost of goods manufactured.

9. The budgeted financial statements, also referred to as pro forma financial statements consist of the budgeted income statement, the budgeted balance sheet, and the budgeted statement of cash flows.

   a. The budgeted income statement pulls together information from other budgets, to derive the budgeted amount of net income. It shows sales revenue from the sales budget. Cost of goods sold, selling, general and administrative expenses, uncollectible accounts expense, interest expense are all taken from other budgets.

   b. The budgeted balance sheet shows the expected end-of-period balances for the company's assets, liabilities, and owner's equity, assuming that planned operations are carried out. The balance sheet budgeted at the beginning of the year is adjusted to reflect all changes in the balance sheet accounts. All of the changes to the accounts are obtained from other budgets that have already been completed.

      i. The cash balance can be taken directly from the cash budget.

      ii. Accounts receivable can be determined by looking at the cash receipts budget and using the estimated percentage of credit sales still outstanding.
      iii. Inventory balances are obtained from the budgeted cost of goods manufactured.

      iv. If any capital budget items are for capital assets, the capital budget will show changes that should be made to long-lived assets. Accumulated depreciation is updated based on the amount of depreciation appearing on the manufacturing overhead budget (there might also be some depreciation for non-production equipment, on the selling, general and administration budgets).

      v. The balance in accounts payable is obtained from the direct materials budget, and determining what percentage of payments for purchases is still outstanding.

      vi. Owner's equity is updated by adding budgeted net income from the budgeted income statement to the beginning equity balance.

10. The master budget is based on many assumptions. Like any other estimated planning tool, it is a good idea to perform sensitivity analysis by modifying the assumptions. Financial planning models allow computerized analyses of different outcomes, based on various outcomes rather than just one set of budget outcomes.

J. Responsibility for the overall budget process is usually assigned to a budget director, or the controller. The budget director determines how budget data will be gathered, collects the information, and prepares the master budget. Managers responsible for preparing components of the master budget are often guided by a budget manual. Organizations may also have a budget committee to advise the budget director. Final approval of the master budget is usually the responsibility of either the board of directors or board of trustees in non-profit organizations.

K. Since budgeting has an impact on virtually everyone in an organization, there are behavioral implications to budgeting that should be considered. Three behavioral issues are budgetary slack, participative budgeting, and ethical issues in budgeting.

1. Budgetary slack occurs when sales are estimated too low, or costs are estimated to be too high. This provides managers with "budgetary slack". There are three reasons for the presence of budgetary slack.

   a. There is the perception that performance that is better than the budget will look good. If managers are evaluated by comparing actual performance to expected (budgeted) outcomes, then this is a correct perception. If sales are set artificially low, then exceeding targeted sales goals will make it appear that salespeople have done an exceptional job, exceeding expectations. If cost managers estimate costs high, and then costs fall below those estimates, then it appears that cost managers have done an exceptional job of controlling costs.

   b. Budgetary slack is used to deal with uncertainty. Unanticipated events beyond the control of managers may cause the budget to be unattainable. Managers prefer to pad the budget "just in case" something goes wrong.

   c. Managers experienced in the budget process realize that budgets are usually cut before they are finalized. Knowing this, they pad their part of the budget, hoping that the cuts will not chip away at their true resource needs.

2. Participative budgeting involves employees in the budget process. The advantage of participative budgeting is that it gives employees a sense of ownership and a sense of control over the constraints a budget imposes on them. The disadvantage of participative budgeting is that it may result in padding, and can slow down the process since it is more likely that different managers will disagree on uses of the company's resources.

3. Ethical issues related to budgeting arise when employees' actual performance is evaluated based on budgeted or expected performance. For instance, if bonuses are based on exceeding sales figures, then budgeted sales will be lowered to allow salespeople to exceed budget goals, thereby ensuring that bonuses will be paid. Sales employees may even be pressured by their managers to manipulate budget figures, or to shift the timing of reported actual activities, if the manager stands to earn bonuses as well.

L. Zero-based budgeting is a management approach to budgeting that some organizations have tried. Under zero-based budgeting, the budget for every activity starts at zero for each new budget period. Each expenditure proposed for inclusion in the budget must be justified. This forces management to rethink every phase of operations before allocating resources to them. A modification of the zero-based budgeting approach is called "base budgeting", where each department starts with a minimal level. Any expenditures above this amount must be justified.

M. Although budgeting has been and continues to be a widely used management planning tool, the budget process is transitioning from simple budgeting to more sophisticated financial planning activities that incorporate cost management concepts and value-added philosophies to the traditional budgeting process.

REVIEW AND SELF TEST QUESTIONS AND EXERCISES

Matching key terms

Match the following terms to the correct definition by writing the correct letter next to the correct definition.

a. rolling budget
b. budget
c. pro forma financial statement
d. Delphi technique
e. activity-based budgeting
f. master budget
g. econometric models
h. participative budgeting
i. sales forecast
j. budgetary slack

_____ 1. A budgeting approach that includes input from employees at levels other than top management.

_____ 2. A comprehensive set of budgets covering all phases of an organization's operations.

_____ 3. A sales forecasting method where members of the forecasting group each submit forecasts separately. Differences are then reconciled by the forecasting team.

_____ 4. The extra amount of expense added to a budget figure, above the amount a manager thinks the actual expense will be.

_____ 5. A detailed plan expressed in quantitative terms, covering a specific time period.

_____ 6. A statistical method used in sales forecasting where factors that might affect sales are used in a regression model to predict future sales.

_____ 7. Financial statements prepared based on budget information.

_____ 8. Budgets that are updated on a continuous basis.

_____ 9. A prediction of sales of goods or services.

_____10. A budget process used when activity-based costing is being used in an organization.

True or False

For each of the following statements enter a T or an F in the blank to indicate whether the statement is true or false.

______11. One of the purposes of budgeting is to help managers to see how resources should be allocated.

______12. A budgeted income statement is the basis for the sales forecast.

______13. The master budget contains only the sales forecast and the sales budget.

______14. Budgets, when used as an evaluation tool, should be used to punish managers who don't make budget goals.

______15. The sales forecast is a prediction of future sales.

______16. The Delphi technique is used to develop sales forecasts.

______17. A cash budget shows how much money should be made each month.

______18. Budgeted financial statements are the final piece of the master budget.

______19. The production budget for a manufacturing company shows the quantity and cost of units needed for the year.

______20. Manufacturing companies do **not** need to have a selling, general and administrative budget.

______21. One of the challenges in completing the cash receipts budget is that all cash receipts from credit customers may not be collected, so uncollectible accounts must be estimated.

______22. The budgeted schedule of cost of goods manufactured is needed to calculate the budgeted cost of goods sold.

______23. Budgetary slack is built into the master budget by the budget director in case of unforeseen events.

______24. Zero-based budgeting is used by companies that plan to have virtually no increases in budgeted costs.

______25. If bonuses are based on exceeding budget goals, then sales managers might be tempted to set low sales goals.

Multiple Choice

Choose the best answer by writing the letter corresponding to your choice in the space provided.

_____26. The master budget normally covers a period of

a) one week.
b) one month.
c) one quarter.
d) one year.

_____27. Which of the following best describes a rolling budget?

a) A rolling budget always shows two years' budget data.
b) A rolling budget always drops the oldest data, which is replaced by the most recent data available.
c) A rolling budget allows actual results to be incorporated into the budget.
d) A rolling budget can not be used for planning purposes.

_____28. Which types of companies would be likely to include a production budget in their master budget?

a) Merchandisers and service companies
b) Merchandisers and manufacturers
c) Manufacturers
d) Service companies

_____29. Which of the following is **not** a reason for preparing a budget?

a) Budget preparation allows one to evaluate last year's actual financial results.
b) Budget preparation helps managers to properly allocate resources.
c) Budget preparation facilitates communication between departments and their managers.
d) Budget preparation helps managers to plan for the coming year.

_____30. Which of the following comes first in the budget process?

a) Budgeted financial statements
b) The cash budget
c) A production budget
d) A sales forecast

_____31. Which of the following does **not** describe a quality of a sales forecast?

a) A sales forecast is a prediction of sales of goods or services.
b) A sales forecast is the same as the sales budget.
c) A sales forecast is based on past sales and a variety of other factors.
d) A sales forecast might be developed using econometric models as one source of data.

_____32. The production budget is prepared to show which of the following?

a) The total cost of production for the coming year.
b) The number of units to be sold for the coming year.
c) The number of units to be produced for the coming year.
d) The cost per unit of product for the coming year.

_____33. Budgeted financial statements appear at what point in the master budgeting process?

a) They are completed first in the process of preparing the master budget.
b) They are completed during preparation of the other parts of the master budget.
c) They are the final piece of the master budget.
d) They are not a part of the master budgeting process.

_____34. Which of the following correctly describes the formula used to determine the number of units to be produced?

a) Budgeted unit sales minus budgeted beginning inventory plus budgeted ending inventory = budgeted units to be produced.
b) Budgeted unit sales plus budgeted beginning inventory minus budgeted ending inventory = budgeted units to be produced.
c) Budgeted unit sales minus budgeted beginning inventory minus budgeted ending inventory = budgeted units to be produced.
d) Budgeted unit sales plus budgeted beginning inventory plus budgeted ending inventory = budgeted units to be produced.

_____35. The direct materials budget shows all **except** the following?

a) The amounts of each type of direct materials to be used in production.
b) The unit cost of each type of direct material to be used in production.
c) The total budgeted direct materials cost for the coming year.
d) The total actual direct materials cost for the coming year.

_____36. Which of the following items would **not** appear on the manufacturing overhead budget?

a) Budgeted costs of electricity
b) Budgeted depreciation on production equipment
c) Budgeted costs of direct labor
d) Budgeted costs of indirect materials

_____37. Which of the following is true regarding the complexities of completing the budgeted cash receipts budget?

a) Completion of the cash receipts budget is complicated by the need to estimate the timing of cash receipts from credit sales.
b) Completion of the cash receipts budget is complicated by the fact that sales revenues might fluctuate.
c) Completion of the cash receipts budget is complicated by the fact that cash must be used for materials purchases.
d) Completion of the cash receipts budget is complicated by the fact that cash sales are uneven.

_____38. The cash disbursements budget shows all of the following **except**

a) the cash disbursement needs for direct labor workers' salaries.
b) the cash disbursement needs for materials purchases.
c) the cash disbursement needs for payment of interest on loans.
d) the cash disbursement needs for advertising.

_____39. A company has budgeted a loan for $100,000 in the coming budget, to replace equipment used in its business. The repayment will be made over two years (half in the coming budget year, and the rest in the following year). Where will these cash amounts appear?

a) The $100,000 in loan proceeds will appear on the cash receipts budget and the cash budget; the $50,000 repayment will appear on the cash disbursements budget and the cash budget.
b) The $100,000 in loan proceeds will appear on the cash budget, and the $50,000 repayment will also appear on the cash budget.
c) The $100,000 in loan proceeds will appear on the cash receipts budget and the $50,000 repayment will appear on the cash disbursements budget.
d) Neither amount will appear in any of the cash budgets because they are related to capital expenditures.

_____40. Which of the following is true regarding the budgeted cost of goods manufactured?

a) Budgeted cost of goods manufactured should equal budgeted cost of goods sold.
b) Budgeted cost of goods manufactured is needed to determine ending inventory balances for finished goods.
c) Budgeted cost of goods manufactured is needed to compute budgeted cost of goods sold.
d) Budgeted cost of goods manufactured is needed to complete the production budget.

_____41. Which of the following statements is correct regarding completion of the budgeted balance sheet?

a) Information used to complete the budgeted balance sheet comes from last year's actual balance sheet.
b) The budgeted balance sheet must be prepared before the budgeted income statement can be prepared.
c) The cash balance in the budgeted balance sheet seldom agrees with the balance shown on the cash budget.
d) The budgeted balance sheet contains information from many other schedules in the master budget.

_____42. Responsibility for the entire budget process is usually assigned to

a) a budget committee.
b) a budget director.
c) the board of directors.
d) the chief executive officer (CEO).

_____43. Budgetary slack is best described as

a) something that managers do to deal with unforeseen events.
b) an effective way to ensure that managers do not exceed budgeted costs.
c) an activity that top management encourages lower level managers to do.
d) a good way to provide realistic estimates of costs or revenues.

_____44. Which of the following is **not** a reason for padding a budget?

a) People perceive that their performance will look better.
b) Padding is used to provide a cushion against uncertainty.
c) Budget requests are often cut, so padding is used to offset expected budget cuts.
d) Cost managers expect that prices will be artificially inflated by suppliers.

_____45. Zero-based budgeting is used by organizations that

a) want every single cost request in the budget to be justified.
b) start with last year's budget, and build the coming year's budget from that foundation.
c) allocate a minimal amount of resources to each department, and then require that any incremental budget requests be justified.
d) are government agencies or non-profit organizations.

Exercises

Please use the following information to answer the next five questions.

Big Fun Resorts, International sells timeshares to vacationers. It owns properties in the Pocono Mountains in Pennsylvania, in Bermuda, and in the wine country of California. Timeshares are sold by the week for an average $7,500. Thus, one unit, if completely sold out for all 52 weeks of the year, would generate sales of $390,000. The assistant to the budget director has just completed the cash receipts, disbursements, and the cash budgets. The quarter for peak sales is the second quarter, April, May and June. The cash receipts budget for this quarter is shown below, along with the assumptions used for sales revenue, uncollectible accounts, cash sales and cash receipts for credit sales.

- Credit sales are 90% of all sales (Big Fun Resorts provides financing).
- Timeshare purchases on credit are paid for over a 60-month period.
- Timeshare credit purchases require that the first month's payment be received upon closing the sale. It is used as a down-payment, so cash received each month from current credit sales is 1/60 of current credit sales.
- 1/60 of outstanding accounts receivable is received in cash payments each month, except that uncollectibles are estimated at 1% of the balance of Accounts Receivable. Thus, the estimated amount of cash receipts from prior months' credit sales is 99% of 1/60 of the Accounts Receivable balance.

Cash Receipts Budget for the Quarter Ending June 30

	APRIL	**MAY**	**JUNE**	**TOTAL**
Sales Revenue	$1,125,000	$1,500,000	$1,800,000	$4,425,000
Collections from current (cash) sales (10% of revenue)	$112,500			
Collections from prior months' credit sales	$792,000	$811,800	$742,500	$2,346,300
Collections from Current Month's Credit Sales (Down Payments, 1/60 of credit sales)	$16,875**			
TOTALS	$921,375			

**$1,125,000 × 90% × 1/60 = $16,875

46. Complete the Cash Receipts budget shown above.

The budget director wants a more conservative estimate of cash receipts. Re-do the cash receipts budget using the following revised estimates.

- Credit sales are 95% of all sales instead of 90%.
- Timeshare purchases on credit are paid for over a 60-month period (same assumption as before).
- Timeshare credit purchases require that the first month's payment be received upon closing the sale. It is used as a down-payment, so cash received each month from current credit sales is 1/60 of current credit sales (same assumption as before).
- 1/60 of outstanding accounts receivable is received in cash payments each month, except that uncollectibles are estimated at 1.2% of the balance of Accounts Receivable. Thus, the estimated amount of cash receipts from prior months' credit sales is 99% of 1/60 of the Accounts Receivable balance.
- Sales revenue is 2% less than originally estimated.

47. Based on the revised assumptions, what would sales revenue be for each month and for the quarter?

48. Based on the revised assumptions, how much would cash receipts be for cash sales, for each month and for the total? (**HINT: Remember, now cash sales are 5% of the revised sales figures**)

49. Assume the Accounts Receivable balances are revised based on the information given, and they are now the monthly cash receipts for prior months' credit sales are $824,000, $844,600, and $772,500 for April, May, and June, before uncollectible amounts are subtracted. What will the net amount of collections from prior months' credit sales be?

50. Prepare a revised Cash Receipts Budget for the Quarter Ended June 30, using the revised estimates.

Revised Cash Receipts Budget for the Quarter Ending June 30

	APRIL	MAY	JUNE	TOTAL
Sales Revenue (Q. 37)				
Collections from current (cash) sales (5% of revenue) (Q. 38)				
Collections from prior months' credit sales (see Q. 39)				
Collections from Current Month's Credit Sales (Down Payments, 1/60 of credit sales)				
TOTALS				

Chapter 15

Answers to Questions and Exercises

Matching key terms

1. h 2. f 3. d 4. j 5. b 6. g 7. c 8. a 9. i 10. e

True or False

11. T. Since resources are always limited, budget information is used to decide how best to use limited resources.
12. F. The sales forecast is used to start the budget process—the budgeted income statement is one of the final steps.
13. F. The master budget contains budgets for every aspect of an organization's operation.
14. F. Although budgets are used to evaluate managers' performance, they should not be used to punish managers.
15. T. The sales forecast predicts future sales, and that prediction is the basis for the master budget.
16. T. The Delphi technique is used to reduce biases that might exist in budget participants' estimates.
17. F. The cash budget shows changes in the cash balance from month (quarter) to month (quarter).
18. T. The budgeted financial statements cannot be prepared until the other portions of the master budget are prepared. The source of much information appearing on the financial statements is the other budget schedules in the master budget.
19. F. Only the units are shown. Costs appear on later schedules.
20. F. Every company has selling, administrative, and general expenses, so should budget for them.
21. T. There is uncertainty with regard to credit sales, because of the possibility that some customers will fail to pay for their credit purchases.
22. T. The budgeted cost of goods sold cannot be computed without the budgeted cost of goods manufactured.
23. F. Other managers build slack into their budgets. The budget director is usually the one trying to weed slack out of the budget.
24. F. Zero-based budgeting requires that every cost proposed for a budget be justified, including increases from past periods.
25. T. This is budgetary slack on the revenue side.

Multiple Choice

26. d. The master budget covers one year, and it detailed month by month, or quarter by quarter.
27. b. A rolling budget always contains information for a certain length of time (like one year), but the time period it covers is continuously updated.
28. c. Only manufacturers need a production budget.
29. a. A budget for the coming year is not useful for evaluating last year's actual performance. Last year's budget would be more useful for that.
30. d. The sales forecast is the basis for the sales budget, which then is used to complete the rest of the master budget.
31. b. A sales forecast predicts sales. A sales budget shows revenues generated from forecasted sales.

32. c. The main purpose of the production budget is to determine how many units of product must be made.
33. c. The budgeted financial statements cannot be completed until all of the other parts of the master budget are completed because most of the information in the financial statements comes from those schedules.
34. a. Beginning inventory plus units produced minus ending inventory equals units to be sold. Rearrange, and get units sold minus beginning inventory plus ending inventory equals units to be produced.
35. d. Actual costs do not appear on the direct materials budget.
36. c. Direct materials would not appear on the manufacturing overhead budget. If labor is treated as a part of conversion costs, instead of being treated as a separate cost category, it would be included as part of the overhead budget—but this implies there is no direct labor.
37. a. Since customers purchasing goods or services on credit are often given up to 90 days to pay for their purchases, it is hard to predict how much of the balances outstanding will be paid each month. Answers b and d contain true events (fluctuation in sales revenues and uneven cash sales, but these are estimated. It is harder to predict the amount of uncollectibles. Answer c is incorrect because it describes a cash disbursement instead of a cash receipt.
38. c. The payment of interest is not a disbursement that results from operating activities. The cash disbursements budget only shows disbursements related to operating activities. Payment of interest only appears on the cash budget.
39. b. The loan and its repayment do not appear on the cash receipts or cash disbursements budgets because they are not part of operating activities, and the cash receipts and cash disbursements budgets only show receipts and disbursements related to operating activities.
40. c. The main purpose of computing cost of goods manufactured is to determine cost of goods sold. Answer a is wrong because cost of goods manufactured includes ending inventory, but cost of goods sold does not. Answer b is wrong because ending inventory is estimated, and is not based on cost of goods manufactured. Answer d is wrong because the production budget is prepared before the budgeted cost of goods manufactured is.
41. d. Almost all of the information on the budgeted balance sheet either comes from other parts of the master budget, or is updated using information from other parts of the master budget. Answer a is simply not true. Answer b is wrong because the reverse is true. Answer c is incorrect because the cash balance on the balance sheet must agree with the balance on the cash budget.
42. b. The budget director is responsible for coordinating all budget activities, and for putting together the master budget.
43. a. Managers build slack into their budget estimates just in case some unforeseen costs arise.
44. d. The first three answers are the real reasons for padding. Managers do not expect suppliers to artificially inflate prices.
45. a. Zero-based budgeting starts with no budgeted costs being approved. Only costs that can be justified are approved for inclusion in the budget. Answer b describes the traditional budget approach. Answer c describes base budgeting. Answer d is incorrect because any organization can choose to use zero-based budgeting.

Exercises

46. Answers are in bold.

Cash Receipts Budget for the Quarter Ending June 30

	APRIL	MAY	JUNE	TOTAL
Sales Revenue	$1,125,000	$1,500,000	$1,800,000	$4,425,000
Collections from current (cash) sales (10% of revenue)	$112,500	**$150,000**	**$180,000**	**$442,500**
Collections from prior months' credit sales	$792,000	$811,800	$742,500	$2,346,300
Collections from Current Month's Credit Sales (Down Payments, 1/60 of credit sales)	$16,875	**$22,500**	**$27,000**	**$66,375**
TOTALS	$921,375	**$984,300**	**$949,500**	**$2,855,175**

47. through 50. are answered on the table below.

Revised Cash Receipts Budget for the Quarter Ending June 30

	APRIL	MAY	JUNE	TOTAL
Sales Revenue	**$1,102,500**	**$1,470,000**	**$1,764,000**	**$4,336,500**
Collections from current (cash) sales (5% of revenue)	**$55,125**	**$73,500**	**$88,200**	**$216,825**
Collections from prior months' credit sales	**$811,640**	**$831,931**	**$768,300**	**$2,411,871**
Collections from Current Month's Credit Sales (Down Payments, 1/60 of credit sales)	**$17,456**	**$23,275**	**$27,930**	**$68,661**
TOTALS	**$884,221**	**$928,706**	**$884,430**	**$2,697,357**

Chapter 16
Standard Costing, Variance Analysis, and Kaizen Costing

Chapter Study Suggestions

Chapter 16 extends the presentation of budgeting from Chapter 15, to discuss how budget information is used to evaluate actual outcomes. Variance analysis is the comparison between expected outcomes (the budget) and actual outcomes. Chapter 16 focuses on direct materials and direct labor. The use of standard costs to assign materials, labor, and overhead costs to units of product is introduced. A standard costing system is described as an effective way to manage costs. Standard costs are also used as a benchmark against which actual costs are compared.

Variances, which are the difference between expected and actual outcomes, are described for materials and labor based on the underlying cause of the variance. There are two types of variance for both direct materials and direct labor. Direct materials variances are the price variance and the quantity variance. The price variance occurs when the price per unit of materials acquired is more or less than the standard price of materials purchased. The quantity variance for direct materials occurs when the amount of direct materials used in production is more or less than standard quantity allowed for the number of units actually produced.

There are two similar direct labor variances. The direct labor rate variance arises when the hourly labor rate actually paid is different from the standard hourly rate, for actual hours worked. The direct labor efficiency variance occurs because the amount of time taken to complete production of the actual number of units is different than the standard amount of time allowed to complete that much production.

After describing these four variances, the chapter discusses ways to determine when a variance warrants investigation, based on its size or a pattern of recurrence. The issue of controllability of variances and which managers can investigate and explain different variances is presented. Kaizen costing, which relies on continuous improvement of production processes is presented. Finally, the appendix describes variances that are calculated when an organization has two or more types of material inputs, or multiple labor inputs. These result in mix and yield variances.

Chapter Highlights

A. Cost Management Challenges. Chapter 16 offers four cost management challenges.

1. How are standards set for production activities when a company uses standard costing?

2. What are variances, and how can different variances be interpreted?

3. Who is in the best position to control and manage different variances?

4. What are some valid criticisms made about standard-costing systems as they are used in today's business environment?

B. Learning Objectives—This chapter has 10 learning objectives.

1. Chapter 16 discusses how companies use standard-costing systems to manage costs, and describes two ways to set standards.

2. The chapter defines and distinguishes between perfection and practical standards.

3. It shows how to compute and interpret direct-material price and quantity variances, and direct-labor rate and efficiency variances.

4. Chapter 16 describes several methods for determining the significance of cost variances.

5. The chapter discusses the behavioral effects of standard costing, and discusses the controllability of variances.

6. It explains how companies use standard costs in product costing.

7. It summarizes some advantages attributed to standard costing.

8. Chapter 16 describes the changing role of standard-costing systems in today's manufacturing environment.

9. It explains the concept of kaizen costing, and its potential benefits.

10. The appendix shows how to compute and interpret production mix and yield variances.

C. Every control system has three parts: a standard performance level, a measure of actual performance, and a comparison between the two. A cost manager may use a standard costing system in that way. Standards are set, and actual performance is measured and then compared to the standard.

1. A standard cost is established for completion of one unit of product. The difference between a standard cost and the actual cost of one unit is called a cost variance.

2. Managers do not investigate every single variance that occurs. The process of investigating only significant variances is called management by exception.

3. Standards are set using one of two approaches—analysis of historical data or task analysis.

   a. One simple way to set standards is to simply look at the costs that occurred in the past. Using this approach, while simple, has some drawbacks. First, if there are inefficiencies in production activities they are included in the standard. Second, if any changes in production processes occur, the standard may become obsolete. Third, historical data does not exist for new products, so this approach will not work.

   b. Task analysis can be used to establish standards. This approach requires that the process of manufacturing a product to determine what it **should** cost.

   c. Cost managers might use both historical data and task analysis to set standards. This is especially useful when parts of the production process are changed.

   d. Standard-setting may be accomplished with input from accountants (historical cost data), production supervisors and production engineers (task analysis and actual quantities).

4. There are two views of how standards should be set. One view is that standards should be based on the assumption that perfection can be achieved. The other is that standards should be practical.

   a. Perfection standards can be attained only when no mistakes are made. Everything must operate perfectly. Many people believe that perfection standards discourage employees, since they don't believe they can reach these standards.

   b. Practical standards are expected to be attainable. They are set, based on normal (not perfect) operating conditions.

5. Non-manufacturing organizations also use standards. Standards are set for length of time a service call takes; actual time taken to process a federal tax return is benchmarked against a standard; some McDonald's Restaurants guarantee that a breakfast order will be ready in 90 seconds or less.

6. Standard costing systems help managers to control costs. Developing, implementing and maintaining a standard cost system requires a commitment on the part of management, because the standards must be evaluated regularly, and the information it generates is only of value if it is used. The system is used to perform variance analysis.

D. Variance analysis is a comparison of expected outcomes, based on standards, to actual outcomes. This comparison is what variance analysis is. Variances arise for each different type of resource used in an organization. In a manufacturing environment, variances are identified for resources used in production. Two resources for which variance analysis has traditionally been completed are direct materials and direct labor.

1. There are two standards related to direct materials. The first is standard quantity. This standard quantity is the amount that is expected to be used to make one unit of product. The second standard is the standard price. Standard price is the estimated cost per unit of input. Any shipping or delivery costs are added, and any purchase discounts are subtracted to derive the standard cost.

2. There are two direct labor standards. One is the direct labor quantity standard, and it is the estimated direct labor time needed to manufacture one unit of product. The standard direct labor rate is the total hourly cost of labor, including fringe benefits.

3. The standard costs for materials and labor are both based on considering quantity and unit cost of inputs. When actual production occurs, the amount of cost assigned to the units is assigned based on standards. Suppose 500 units were made, and the standard quantity allowed is 10 pounds of material at a standard price of $4 per pound. Then, a total of 500 times 10 pounds times $4 per pound, or $20,000 would be assigned to the inventory account for materials.

4. After actual production activity is complete, and direct materials and labor costs have been determined, the next step is to see how actual cost outcomes varied from the standards. The differences are broken into different types of variances because there are different underlying causes for the variances.

5. There are two variances related to direct materials. They are the direct material price variance and the direct material quantity variance.

   a. The direct material price variance compares the actual cost of materials purchased to the standard price of materials purchased. A formula to express this variance is:

      Direct material price variance = (PQ × AP) – (PQ × SP),

      or

      PQ × (AP – SP)

      where PQ = quantity purchased
      AP = actual price per unit
      SP = standard price per unit

b. The direct material quantity variance compares the standard cost of the actual quantity of materials used to the standard cost of the standard quantity that **should have** been used. The formula to express this variance is:

Direct material quantity variance = (AQ × SP) – (SQ × SP),
or
SP × (AQ–SQ)

where AQ = actual quantity used
SP = standard price per unit
SQ = standard quantity allowed

c. A cost variance is unfavorable if actual costs are higher than the standard allows, and they are favorable if actual costs are lower than the standard allows. If the actual price is higher than the standard price, then the price variance will be unfavorable. If the actual quantity used is higher than the standard quantity allowed, then the variance will be unfavorable.

d. The direct material price variance is based on the actual quantity purchased. The direct material quantity variance is based on the actual quantity of materials used to make the actual number of units produced. The price variance is related to the purchasing function of an organization. The quantity variance is related to production activities.

e. In the case where direct materials are purchased in a country that uses different currency than the home country's currency, there may be a variance that is due entirely to the foreign currency exchange rate. If there are foreign currency exchange rate differences, this piece of the direct material price variance should be separated from the price variance that is normally calculated.

6. There are two variances related to direct labor. They are the direct labor rate variance and the direct labor efficiency variance.

a. The direct labor rate variance is related to differences between the standard hourly labor rate and the actual hourly labor rate. The formula for the direct labor rate is:

Direct labor rate variance = (AH × AR) – (AH × SR) or
AH × (AR – SR)

where AH = actual hours used
AR = actual rate per hour
SR = standard rate per hour

b. The direct labor efficiency variance is related to the differences between the standard labor time allowed for the actual units produced and the actual time taken to make the units produced. The direct labor efficiency variance is:

Direct labor efficiency variance = $(AH \times SR) - (SH \times SR)$ or $(SR \times AH - SH)$

where AH = actual hours used
SH = Standard hours allowed for actual output
SR = standard rate per hour

c. The total direct labor variance is the sum of the rate variance and the efficiency variance. The total direct labor variance can be calculated directly by using the following formula:

Direct labor variance = $(AH \times AR) - (SH \times SR)$

7. When there are multiple types of direct materials, or different classes of direct labor, variances must be computed for each one. Additional variances may be caused by using combinations of inputs that are different from the standard combinations of inputs. These are referred to as mix and yield variances, and are explained in the appendix to Chapter 16.

8. Most production processes have some defects or spoilage. If this is a normal part of the production process, then these amounts and costs must be factored into the standard quantities of materials

E. Cost variances of many types and dollar amounts are possible. Managers cannot investigate every single variance that occurs. Since standards are not perfect, it is not expected that actual outcomes will perfectly match standards. Management by exception requires that managers look only at variances that are significant. The question then becomes what is a "significant" variance? There are a number of guidelines that help managers determine when a variance might need to be investigated.

1. The size of a variance is one determinant of significance. The relative size should be considered. This means a variance should be considered in comparison to the total cost. A \$50,000 direct material quantity variance for the entire Coca-Cola Company's production of Sprite would probably be considered insignificant. A \$50,000 direct material quantity variance for a small independent soft drink bottler whose total direct materials cost is \$500,000 would be quite significant.

   Some companies use a combination of absolute and relative amounts by instituting a policy that says something like, "investigate any variance over \$100,000 or any variance that exceeds 5% of standard cost".

2. The frequency of a variance should also be a basis for deciding whether a variance needs to be investigated. If a variance occurs on a regular basis, it could either mean that a process is out of control, or it could mean that the standard ahs been misestimated. A recurring variance should be investigated even if its size does not warrant investigation.

3. A trend in the variance is often a warning sign of a process that is going out of control. A variance that is moving in an upward or downward direction consistently is usually a sign that it will become significant anyway in the future. An astute manager will recognize the trend, investigate it early, and correct the problem.

4. A variance is more likely to be investigated if a cost manager believes it is controllable. If a variance is occurring because of events that cannot be controlled, there is little point in investigating it since it cannot be corrected.

5. A favorable variance is often viewed as a good thing, because it means that costs are less than expected. However, favorable variances that are outside an acceptable range should be investigated just as unfavorable ones should be.

   a. A favorable variance may be occurring because of true efficiencies or improvements in production activities. managers need to understand them so that future standards can be modified, and so that any improved efficiencies can be adapted to other production activities.

   b. A favorable variance might also mean that some important input is being used too sparingly. Suppose, for instance, that there was a favorable direct labor efficiency variance for the construction of roller coasters. If the variance was favorable because workers were skipping steps needed to ensure that the ride would be safe, the variance would be very unfavorable in the long run.

6. One final consideration in deciding whether to investigate a variance is the benefit that might be derived from the investigation (compared to the cost of investigation).

7. Once a variance is identified as significant, it is then important to try to identify the causes of the variance. A statistical control chart can help managers to separate random variation in productive levels from actual problems. A statistical control chart is used to identify variances that exceed some critical value. Often this critical value is one standard deviation, or a multiple of the standard deviation.

F. Standard costing has some effects on the behavior of managers and other employees. Many organizations reward employees for achieving standards, or to perform at a level that is lower than the cost standard. In some cases this may motivate the correct behavior. Employees may actively seek ways to operate in an efficient, economical way.

Unfortunately, using standards to evaluate and reward employees may also motivate employees to cut corners that should not be cut. Buying lower quality materials to save money on materials costs, or using less than standard amounts to generate favorable materials quantity or labor efficiency variances could affect product quality. That type of behavior, in the long run affects customer loyalty and might even affect company reputation.

G. Different variances are controllable by different managers. The person who is most able to influence a particular variance can often be identified, and be given the responsibility for managing and controlling the amount of variance.

1. The direct materials price variance is the responsibility of the purchasing manager. This individual can avoid unfavorable direct material price variances by ordering materials in bulk, when practical, to take advantage of purchase discounts. At the same time, buying too much leads to higher inventory costs, so the value of purchase discounts should exceed the cost of having extra inventory on hand. Timely ordering of raw materials should also minimize shortages, costly expedited delivery, and production bottlenecks, which can all be costly events.

   If the production manager informs the purchasing manager of materials needs too late, the purchasing manager might not be able to control the related costs of expedited shipping and bottlenecks. These two managers must work together to coordinate materials purchase activities.

2. The direct material quantity variance, and both direct labor variances (rate and efficiency) are the responsibility of the production manager. The production manager should see that there is minimal waste. Material quantity variances may also occur if technical specifications call for inferior materials. This could lead to more waste or higher numbers of defects or reworked units. The production manager may be responsible for reporting on the variances that result, but the production engineers who develop the specifications may be the people who have caused the variance.

   The direct labor rate variance may be caused by the mix of experienced or inexperienced workers. The production supervisor must schedule employees' work in accordance with the labor standards, to avoid labor rate variances. In an environment where employees are a constrained resource, the supervisor may not always have the luxury of scheduling to avoid variances.

   Direct labor efficiency variances can be managed by having the correct mix of skill levels of employees, and by motivating employees to achieve production goals.

3. In many cases there are interactions among variances. Buying inferior materials may cause a favorable direct material price variance. However, the inferior quality may lead to an increase in materials needed for each unit, causing a direct material quantity variance. Having more experienced employees work on product may cause a favorable direct labor efficiency variance. Yet, using this more expensive group of workers may cause an unfavorable direct labor rate variance.

4. By looking at variances from a value-chain perspective, managers can see that the effect of one variance is to cause another variance someplace else. Upstream activities and decisions can have positive or negative effects on downstream activities or outcomes. Unfavorable variances in the production area, for instance, may be due to poor decisions made in the design or supply portions of the value chain.

H. A standard costing system is not used only to manage and control costs. It is also used to assign costs to units of product. Accounting for product costs under a standard costing system is accomplished by assigning only standard costs to units of product, and then using separate accounts to record variances. Accounts are created for direct material price and quantity variances, and accounts are created for direct labor rate and efficiency variances.

1. The flow of product costs in a manufacturing firm is reviewed briefly. Direct materials, direct labor and manufacturing overhead costs are charged to the work-in process inventory account. When a standard cost system is in place, only the standard costs are charged to WIP. When production is complete, the standard cost for completed units is transferred from WIP to finished goods inventory. When product is sold, the amounts in finished goods are transferred to cost of goods sold, which is subsequently closed to an income summary account.

   a. The direct material price variance occurs when materials are purchased. Raw materials inventory is debited for the standard cost of materials purchased. If the price variance is unfavorable, it is treated like a cost, and the direct materials price variance is debited. If the variance is favorable, it is treated as a reduction of a cost, and the variance account is credited.

   b. The direct material quantity variance occurs when production activities take place. Work-in process is debited for materials costs at the standard cost for actual production completed. The difference between the cost of the standard quantity of materials **allowed** and the standard cost of materials **used** is the materials quantity variance. This variance is, like the price variance, treated as a cost if it is unfavorable, and is treated like a cost reduction if it is favorable.

   c. The direct labor rate variance is isolated in a fashion similar to the direct material price variance. The direct labor efficiency variance is isolated in a fashion similar to the direct material quantity variance. Since both of these variances occur during production, they are recorded in the costing system at the same time.

   d. Variance accounts are treated like expense accounts, and are closed at the end of each accounting period. Most companies close out variances to cost of goods sold. If the net amount of variance is favorable, cost of goods sold will be reduced. If unfavorable, then cost of goods sold will be increased. An alternative way to dispose of variances is to prorate them among work-in process, finished goods inventory, and cost of goods sold. This alternative approach reflects the effects of inefficiency or efficiency in all the accounts through which the manufacturing costs flow.

I. Standard costing systems can use information technology to link together several business processes. Standard cost information is loaded onto a computerized costing system. When materials are placed into production the computerized information system assigns materials costs, at standard cost, to work in process. The same thing happens with labor costs. That way, units of product are not contaminated by assignment of costs that are not standard. Use of bar codes and computer-aided design has increased the efficiency of the costing system in manufacturing firms.

1. Bar codes are used to monitor, control, and record the costs of product inputs. When raw materials are purchased and received, they are bar coded. That is, a computer generates an identification tag and the materials are labeled. When materials are sent to production, they are scanned as they leave the raw materials inventory warehouse, and are automatically deducted from raw materials inventory. The materials are then assigned to work-in process. Bar-coding can also be used to assign direct labor costs to a job.

2. Standard costing systems may be integrated with computer-aided design (CAD) systems to assist design engineers in the product design process. This enables product designers to obtain standard cost information, which helps them to determine the cost of new products.

J. Standard costing, which has a long history of use in manufacturing has several advantages. Standard costing is credited for (1) enabling managers to employ management by exception, which conserves management time; (2) providing sensible cost comparisons between benchmarks and actual outcomes; (3) providing a basis for evaluating and rewarding employees for performance; (4) motivating employees to adhere to standards; (5) giving product costs stability not possible if actual costs are used; and (5) providing a costing system that is often less expensive than an actual or normal-costing system.

K. While standard costing has been widely accepted and adopted by many organizations, it has been criticized in recent years for several reasons. There are disadvantages to use of the traditional standard costing system. Others argue that standard costing can be adapted to fit modern management philosophies.

1. Standard costing has been criticized for the following reasons.

   a. Variances calculated are too aggregated, and come too late to be useful. Critics argue that variances should be based on the many activities that occur in an organization. Traditional standard costing also ignores modern management issues such as product quality, processing time, elimination of non-value-activities, and delivery performance.

   b. Traditional standard cost variances are not disaggregated along product lines, batches, or flexible-manufacturing-cells. This makes it difficult for managers to determine the cause of variances.

   c. Traditional systems place too much emphasis on direct labor costs and efficiency. Direct labor is becoming a relatively unimportant factor of production.

   d. Standard costing is based on relatively stable production processes. Modern production processes often contain necessary elements of flexible manufacturing systems that allow frequent switching among a variety of products on the same production line.

e. Standards are only relevant for a short time if a product has a short life cycle.

f. Standard costing focuses exclusively on cost minimization, ignoring product quality and customer service.

g. Variances from standards tend to be very small (insignificant) in highly automated manufacturing processes.

h. Traditional standard costing systems tend to be too broadly defined, and may ignore some of the costs of resources like direct materials.

2. Despite the eight criticisms just listed, some critics argue that standard costing systems can be modified to be compatible with modern management needs. The following adaptations might make standard costing a viable costing system, even in a modern manufacturing environment.

a. Variances focused on direct labor standards should be minimized, as they are losing their relevance. Machine hours, product quality, manufacturing cycle times, and support-department costs have become more important cost control issues than direct labor.

b. Instead of focusing on direct labor, standard costing systems should shift the emphasis to material and overhead costs, and quality management must be incorporated into the standards.

c. Cost-driver analysis should be the unit of analysis rather than units of product, or units of input. Use of cost drivers like machine hours, number of parts, and production runs may be more informative than number of direct labor hours.

d. Cost structures are changing so that unit-level costs like direct material and direct labor are becoming less important, and overhead costs are becoming more important.

e. Total quality management (TQM) and JIT approaches place emphasis on high quality and minimization of costs via reduction of waste and rework. Standard costing can be modified to look for variances from quality standards or rework levels.

f. Standard costing systems need to be modified to aid in efforts to eliminate non-value-added costs. Standards should not be set at levels that allow non-value-added activities to be factored in.

g. Standards must be revised more frequently for products that have short life cycles.

h. Standard costing should not be the only tool used to evaluate performance. Nonfinancial measures must also be used to evaluate outcomes.

i. Benchmarking of processes by comparing them to other units in an organization, or comparing them to other organizations should be used in addition to benchmarking against standards.

j. Computer-integrated manufacturing (CIM) often provides the manager with immediate feedback on actual costs and activities. This allows a quick response to unfavorable variances.

L. Kaizen costing is the process of cost reduction during the manufacturing phase of a product. When kaizen costing is used, improvements occur in small steps. Every employee is responsible for looking for ways to improve production processes and reduce unnecessary costs. Kaizen goals are set based on actual results from the prior year. The goal is to reduce actual costs from the current year in the coming year.

REVIEW AND SELF TEST QUESTIONS AND EXERCISES

Matching key terms

Match the following terms to the correct definition by writing the correct letter next to the correct definition.

a. direct-labor efficiency variance
b. statistical control chart
c. cost variance
d. management by exception
e. practical standard
f. standard cost
g. standard quantity allowed
h. task analysis
i. kaizen costing
j. direct-material price variance

_____ 1. The process of investigating only significant variances.

_____ 2. The technique of analyzing a manufacturing process to determine what it should cost.

_____ 3. The expected, normal amount of some input needed to produce one unit of product.

_____ 4. The difference between actual cost and standard cost.

_____ 5. The difference between actual materials purchased at actual price and actual materials purchased at the standard price.

_____ 6. A continuous improvement costing approach, where manufacturing costs are reduced during the manufacturing phase.

_____ 7. The difference between actual direct labor hours and standard direct labor hours multiplied by the standard direct labor rate.

_____ 8. The budgeted dollar amount for production of a single unit of product.

_____ 9. A plot of cost variances over time that helps identify the need to investigate variances.

_____10. Standards that are difficult but realistically achievable.

True or False

For each of the following statements enter a T or an F in the blank to indicate whether the statement is true or false.

_____ 11. A standard costing system can be used as a benchmark against which actual costs can be compared.

_____ 12. Management by exception refers to the need to treat every variance that occurs as an exceptional event.

_____ 13. Standard-setting is sometimes based on task analysis.

_____ 14. Standard-setting should be based only on input from accountants and the historical cost information they possess.

_____ 15. Perfection standards can be attained only when no mistakes are made.

_____ 16. Non-manufacturing organizations can use standards for performance in ways that are similar to what manufacturing firms do.

_____ 17. Once a standard cost system is developed and implemented, the work on the system is done.

_____ 18. A variance represents the difference between an expected outcome and an actual outcome.

_____ 19. Variance analysis cannot be done unless one has standards, or budgeted cost information available to compare to actual cost information.

_____ 20. Direct materials price variances exist because the prices charged for products sold differ from the original budgeted sales price.

_____ 21. A cost variance is unfavorable if actual costs are higher than standard costs are.

_____ 22. If a company unexpectedly has to hire a lot of inexperienced, untrained workers, then it is likely that there will be a favorable direct labor efficiency variance.

_____ 23. If a company uses a standard cost system, then finished goods inventory will contain only the standard costs of finished units of product.

_____ 24. Variances should only be investigated if they are larger than a preset dollar amount.

_____ 25. One of the criticisms of standard costing and the traditional variances generated from a standard cost system is that the variance information is too detailed.

Multiple Choice

Choose the best answer by writing the letter corresponding to your choice in the space provided.

_____ 26. A variance is favorable if it

a) results in lower operating income than was originally expected.
b) results in higher operating income than was originally expected.
c) results in lower total revenue than was originally expected.
d) results in higher costs than were originally expected.

Please use the following 2 events (Event A and Event B) to answer questions 27–28.
Event A: Very Juicy Juicers Company produces and packages fruit juices. In October of last year, the company bought oranges from its Florida supplier, for use in making orange juice. Because of the excellent weather conditions during the growing season in Florida last winter, the oranges tended to be larger than usual, juicier, and less expensive per pound than the procurement manager originally planned. Oranges actually cost $.30 per pound, instead of the **$.40 standard price**. The **standard quantity of oranges allowed** to make one gallon of orange juice is **2 pounds of oranges**. In October, it took only 1.95 pounds to make one gallon. Despite this, the company made 150,000 gallons of orange juice, which was the amount originally budgeted for. Real Juicy Juicers bought 315,000 pounds of oranges for October's production.

Event B: Very Juicy Juicer's production workers, tired of working for what they called "migrant workers' pay", went on strike in September. In response, the company fired all of their production workers and hired new workers, whom they paid even **LESS per hour than they had been paying the fired workers.** The old workers were paid an average of $12.00 per hour. The new workers were paid an average of $10 per hour. **The new workers began working for Juicy Juice in October.** The new workers were untrained. Their lack of training made them work more slowly than the fired workers could.
The standard time needed to complete production of 150,000 gallons is 8,250 labor hours. The new workers took a total of 9,000 labor hours to complete the 150,000 gallons.

_____ 27. Event A is likely to cause

a) a favorable price variance, and an unfavorable quantity variance for direct materials.
b) an unfavorable price variance and an unfavorable quantity variance for direct materials.
c) an unfavorable price variance and a favorable quantity variance for direct materials.
d) a favorable price variance and a favorable quantity variance for direct materials.

_____ 28. Event B is likely to cause

a) a favorable direct labor rate variance and an unfavorable direct labor efficiency variance.
b) a favorable direct labor rate variance and a favorable direct labor efficiency variance.
c) an unfavorable direct labor rate variance and an unfavorable direct labor efficiency variance.
d) an unfavorable direct labor rate variance and a favorable direct labor efficiency variance.

_____ 29. Which of the following correctly describes a variance?

a) A variance occurs when you have no budgeted expectations.
b) A variance occurs only when some unusual event causes actual outcomes to differ from expected outcomes.
c) A variance is the difference between actual outcomes and expected outcomes.
d) Variances occur only for manufacturing firms.

_____ 30. For production of laser discs, a company plans to switch suppliers. The new supplier promises lower prices, but the discs are also lower quality, meaning the firm will use more discs per unit of product than was originally budgeted. If the firm chose to buy from this supplier, what would it observe for the coming month?

a) An unfavorable direct materials quantity variance and a favorable direct materials price variance.
b) A favorable direct materials quantity variance and an unfavorable direct materials price variance.
c) An unfavorable direct materials quantity variance and an unfavorable direct materials price variance.
d) A favorable direct materials quantity variance and a favorable direct materials price variance.

_____ 31. The direct labor workers for the Tappan Zee Company re-negotiated their union contract for the last four months of 2004, and obtained a substantial raise, to $15 per hour. This raise was not anticipated by the management. Because the workers were so happy about the raises, their productivity increased so that they were able to complete each unit of product in 80% of the time originally budgeted for producing each unit. Based on the originally budgeted standard for direct labor, what should the company observe for the last four months of 2004?

a) A favorable direct labor rate variance and an unfavorable direct labor efficiency variance.
b) A favorable direct labor rate variance and no effect on the direct labor efficiency variance.
c) No effect on the direct labor rate variance and no effect on the direct labor efficiency variance.
d) An unfavorable direct labor rate variance and a favorable direct labor efficiency variance.

_____ 32. Variances arise because actual outcomes are different from expected outcomes. For a direct materials quantity variance, the variance could be due to

a) the supplier's price increased due to inflation (materials cost more than expected)
b) the price decreased due to a change in suppliers (same quality of materials being purchased).
c) direct labor workers were inexperienced, and used more materials than expected
d) production capacity was increased due to purchase of additional machines

_____ 33. Which of the following is **not** true about when to investigate a variance?

a) A variance should be investigated if a trend over time is detected.
b) A variance should be investigated regardless of its size, large or small.
c) A variance should be investigated if it exceeds a predetermined dollar amount.
d) A variance should be investigated if it exceeds a predetermined percentage of cost.

_____ 34. The purpose of a standard cost system is to

a) develop variances.
b) identify problems in production.
c) assign inventory costs to units of product.
d) decrease production costs.

_____ 35. Which of the following is **not** true regarding management by exception?

a) Management by exception is used to identify every variance.
b) Management by exception helps managers to investigate only variances that are worth investigating.
c) Most organizations that use variance analysis also use a management by exception approach to investigating variances.
d) All of the above statements are true.

_____ 36. One source of information for developing standards is historical cost data. Which of the following is **not** a valid criticism of historical data?

a) Any inefficiencies that exist in production activities may be included in the standard.
b) Historical data does not exist for new products.
c) If changes in the production process change over time, the standards may become obsolete.
d) Historical data may be subjective.

_____ 37. Which of the following best describes an example of a standard that can be used in a standard cost system?

a) McDonald's Restaurants promises that its restrooms will always be clean.
b) McDonald's Restaurants guarantees that its breakfasts will be cooked not more than 3 minutes prior to being sold.
c) McDonald's Restaurants guarantees that a management trainee will be promoted within 3 months.
d) McDonald's Restaurants estimates that each order of large fries should contain one-sixth of a pound of potatoes.

_____ 38. A variance may arise for all of the following reasons **except**

a) the price charged for materials is less than the standard purchase price.
b) the quantity purchased was different from the purchase quantity originally budgeted.
c) the quantity of materials used to produce 500 units is higher than the standard quantity allowed for production of 500 units.
d) the number of hours it takes employees to complete production of 500 units is less than the standard time allowed.

_____ 39. Raw materials purchased had a lower price than the standard price. The materials were found to be of inferior quality, causing the time taken to complete production of units to be higher than the standard. Each unit also used more materials than the amount that should have been used. Direct labor workers ended up taking longer to complete products because the inferior materials got jammed in the machinery, and slowed down machinery. Which of the following is likely to be the result of buying the inferior materials?

a) Unfavorable direct labor rate variance and unfavorable direct labor efficiency variance.
b) Favorable direct labor rate variance and unfavorable direct labor efficiency variance.
c) No effect on the direct labor rate variance and unfavorable direct labor efficiency variance.
d) No effect on the direct labor rate variance and favorable direct labor efficiency variance.

_____ 40. Use the information from question 39 to answer question 40. Which of the following is likely to be the result of buying the inferior materials?

a) Unfavorable direct materials price variance and unfavorable direct materials quantity variance.
b) Favorable direct materials price variance and unfavorable direct materials quantity variance.
c) No effect on the direct materials price variance and unfavorable direct materials variance.
d) No effect on the direct materials price variance and favorable direct materials quantity variance.

_____ 41. The direct materials price variance occurs because

a) the price of materials purchased is different from the budgeted (standard) purchase price.
b) the quantity of materials purchased is different from the quantity originally budgeted.
c) the quantity of materials used in production is different from the quantity originally budgeted.
d) the number of units produced differs from the number of units originally budgeted.

_____ 42. A standard costing system is used to assign costs to inventory. The Cinderella Dress Company purchased 10,000 yards of fabric for $2.00 per yard. They used 9,500 yards to produce 2,400 gowns. Standards are 3.8 yards of fabric per dress, and $1.75 per yard. What amount will be assigned to work-in process for materials costs for the 2,400 dresses?

a) $20,000
b) $19,000
c) $18,240
d) $15,960

_____ 43. Which of the following is **not** a valid criticism of traditional standard costing systems and variance information they provide?

a) Variances are too aggregated.
b) Variances are reported too late to be helpful.
c) Standard cost systems place too much emphasis on product quality, and not enough on cost.
d) Standards are too rigid to accommodate modern production processes that use flexible manufacturing systems.

_____ 44. Kaizen costing is an alternative to standard costing. Which of the following best describes kaizen costing?

a) Kaizen costing requires that all non-value-added costs be eliminated during the design phase of a product's life cycle.
b) Kaizen costing is the process of cost reduction during the manufacturing phase of a product.
c) Kaizen costing gives production managers total responsibility for improving production processes.
d) Kaizen costing is based on the assumption that the current year's costs cannot be improved (i.e., reduced) next year.

_____ 45. Critics of standard costing systems suggest that traditional standard costing systems should be modified to allow

a) more frequent revision of standards for products with short life cycles.
b) shift the focus from direct material and direct labor to direct materials and conversion costs, where conversion costs are split into specific costs.
c) cost control should be based on controlling quality, manufacturing cycle times, product quality, and machine hours instead of direct labor hours.
d) all of the above are useful modifications of the traditional standard costing system.

Exercises

Please use the following information to answer the next five questions.

Very Juicy Juicers Company produces and packages fruit juices. In October of last year, the company bought oranges from its Florida supplier, for use in making orange juice. Because of the excellent weather conditions during the growing season in Florida last winter, the oranges tended to be larger than usual, juicier, and less expensive per pound than the procurement manager originally planned. Oranges actually cost $.30 per pound, instead of the $.40 standard price. The standard quantity of oranges allowed to make one gallon of orange juice is 2 pounds of oranges. In October, it took only 1.95 pounds to make one gallon. Despite this, the company made 150,000 gallons of orange juice, which was the amount originally budgeted for. Real Juicy Juicers bought 315,000 pounds of oranges for October's production.

Very Juicy Juicer's production workers, tired of working for what they called "migrant workers' pay", went on strike in September. In response, the company fired all of their production workers and hired new workers, whom they paid even LESS per hour than they had been paying the fired workers. The old workers were paid an average of $12.00 per hour. $12 per hour is the standard rate. The new workers were paid an average of $10 per hour. The new workers began working for Juicy Juice in October. The new workers were untrained. Their lack of training made them work more slowly than the fired workers could.

The standard time needed to complete production of 150,000 gallons is 6,750 labor hours. The new workers took a total of 9,000 labor hours to complete the 150,000 gallons.

46. Calculate the direct material price variance for the oranges.

47. Calculate the direct material quantity variance for the oranges.

48. Calculate the direct labor rate variance for Very Juicy Juicers for October.

49. Calculate the direct labor efficiency variance for Very Juicy Juicers for October.

50. Calculate the total amount of cost assigned to work-in process inventory for direct materials and direct labor for the month of October for Very Juicy Juicers, and the total amount of materials and labor variance for the month.

Answers to Questions and Exercises

Matching key terms

1. d 2. h 3. g 4. c 5. j 6. i 7. a 8. f 9. b 10. e

True or False

11. T. The primary purposes of a standard costing system are to provide standard costs for units of product, and to allow comparison of actual costs to expected (standard) costs.
12. F. Management by exception allows managers to investigate only variances that have been deemed significant, and worthy of investigation.
13. T. Task analysis requires that a manufacturing process be studied, to determine exactly how product is made, and to derive a good understanding of what costs go into making a product.
14. F. Although historical cost information possessed by accountants is useful, it should be supplemented with revisions based on known changes, and where practical, data analysis can be used. Also, input should be obtained from production supervisors and engineers.
15. T. Perfection standards are not realistic since they do not allow for any mistakes. They can be used as a starting point for standard-setting, but perfection standards are not practical to use – practical standards are better.
16. T. Every organization can benefit from establishing standards, so that managers and employees can determine what outcomes are normal or abnormal.
17. F. A standard costing system has to be continually updated, to reflect changes in costs, technologies, and methods of performing tasks.
18. T. The definition of a variance is the difference between some standard (expected) outcome and the actual outcome.
19. T. Standards are the benchmarks used to compare actual outcomes to.
20. F. Direct materials price variances occur when the actual purchase price of direct (raw) materials differs from the standard price of those materials.
21. T. A cost variance is unfavorable when it leads to lower income than was originally planned. Thus, if costs are higher than planned, income will be lower than planned.
22. F. The opposite is true. It is likely that inexperienced, untrained workers will work more slowly than the standards allow, creating unfavorable direct labor efficiency variances.
23. T. Besides serving as benchmarks to evaluate actual outcomes, standards are used to assign costs to units of product.
24. F. Besides significant dollar amounts, variances should be investigated when a trend is apparent, when a variance is larger than some percentage, or if the variance is significant **and** can be controlled.
25. F. The traditional standard costing system has been criticized because it generates variances that are too aggregated. That is, the information is too general and needs to be broken down into more detailed pieces of cost information.

Multiple Choice

26. b. The status of a variance as being favorable or unfavorable is based on its impact on income. If a variance results in operating income that is lower than expected, then it is unfavorable.
27. d. The actual price of oranges is lower than the standard, and the quantity used to produce 150,000 gallons of orange juice was less than the standard quantity allowed.
28. a. The new workers were paid less than the standard hourly rate, but they worked more slowly than the standard allowed. This would cause a direct labor rate variance that is favorable, but a direct labor efficiency variance that is unfavorable.
29. c. A variance is the difference between expected outcomes and actual outcomes, and the expected outcomes are standards. Without budgeted expectations, there is no benchmark to use, to calculate variances (answer a). Variances occur all the time, not just when some unusual event occurs (answer b). Variances occur for any organization that uses a standard costing system, not just manufacturing firms (answer d).
30. a. More discs than the standard allows would be used, causing a quantity variance that is unfavorable. The price variance would be favorable because the actual price per disc would be lower than the standard.
31. d. The rate variance would be unfavorable because the hourly rate is higher than expected. The efficiency variance is favorable because the workers are working faster than the standard.
32. c. If workers are inexperienced and use more materials than the standard amount allowed, the materials quantity variance will be unfavorable. The price charged by the supplier has affects the direct materials price variance (answers a and b). Purchase of additional machines would allow production activity to be higher, but would not be the reason for a materials quantity variance.
33. b. A variance should only be investigated if it is significant. It is only significant if it is a large dollar amount, a large percentage of the, or reflects a trend.
34. c. Standard costs are used to control and manage costs and to assign costs to units of product. Although having a standard cost system may result in variances, or help managers to identify problems in production, they do not exist for those purposes.
35. a. Although it is possible to identify variances via a standard cost system, management by exception is a method for identifying only which variances are important enough to investigate.
36. d. Historical cost data is not subjective – it is objective, which is why it is acceptable to use in formulating standard costs.
37. d. The cost and quantity of inputs can be estimated, and a standard cost for this product can be determined. Although the other three answers may be characterized as goals or standards, they cannot be used to establish standard costs for units of product.
38. b. The quantity purchased does not cause a variance. The price paid for purchases causes a price variance, and the quantity used in production causes a quantity variance.
39. c. The inferior materials would not affect the labor rate. Since the materials slowed down the workers though, it would cause an unfavorable direct labor efficiency variance.
40. b. The price paid was lower than the standard price, causing a favorable price variance. However, the quantity actually used in production exceeded the standard quantity allowed, so the quantity variance would be unfavorable.
41. a. The sole reason for the direct materials price variance is the price per unit of the materials purchased, compared to the standard price per unit of materials purchased.

42. d. The standard cost assigned to inventory is based on the standard cost of $1.75 times the standard quantity per dress, 3.8 yards, times the number of dresses actually made, 2,400. $1.75 × 3.8 × 2,400 = $15,960.
43. c. Standard cost systems are criticized because they place **no** emphasis on product quality, and focus almost exclusively on cost.
44. b. Kaizen costing is a management concept that requires that all employees constantly seek ways to improve products and production processes, while reducing costs. Starting with the current year's costs, targets are set for cost reductions for the following year. This occurs during the manufacturing phase of a product.
45. d. Critics of traditional standard costing systems suggest that the systems be modified to allow more flexibility, more detail, and supply variance information related to product quality, cycle time, and other factors.

Exercises

46. The direct material price variance is $31,500 favorable. Actual price is $.30 per pound. Standard price is $.40 per pound. 315,000 pounds of oranges were purchased. The variance is ($.30 – $.40) × 315,000 = $31,500 favorable.
47. The direct material quantity variance is $3,000 favorable. The actual quantity used to make 150,000 gallons of juice was 1.95 pounds per gallon times 150,000 gallons, or 292,500 pounds. The standard quantity allowed for 150,000 gallons is 2 pounds per gallon times 150,000, or 300,000 pounds. The variance is calculated as (292,500 – 300,000) × $.40 = $3,000 favorable.
48. The direct labor rate variance is $18,000 favorable. The direct labor rate variance is based on the actual hourly rate of $10 per hour, which is $2 less than the standard rate of $12.00 per hour. The new workers were paid for 9,000 hours. The direct labor rate variance is ($10 – $12) × 9,000 hours = $18,000 favorable.
49. The direct labor efficiency variance is $27,000 unfavorable. The new workers took 9,000 hours to make 150,000 gallons of juice. It should have taken 6,750 hours to make the juice. The variance is (9,000 – 6,750) × $12 = $27,000 unfavorable.
50. The total amount of cost is based on the following: 2 pounds of oranges at $.40 per pound, or $.80 per gallon is the standard for direct materials. $.54 per gallon is the cost of labor. This can be determined by dividing 6,750 hours by 150,000, which is .45 of one hour allowed to make one gallon of juice. .45 × $12 = $.54 per gallon. The standard cost for materials and labor, for one gallon of juice is $1.34. $1.34 × 150,000 = $201,000. A simpler way to calculate the cost is calculate the direct materials cost as $.40 × 2 pounds × 150,000 gallons = $120,000. Then, calculate direct labor as $12.00 × 6,750 hours = $81,000. $120,000 + $81,000 = $201,000.

    The total variance for the month is just the sum of the four variances calculated. The direct material variances were $31,500 for the price variance, and $3,000 for the quantity variance. Both were favorable. The direct labor variances were $18,000 favorable for the rate variance and $27,000 unfavorable for the efficiency variance. The total variance recorded for the month was $52,500 favorable, less $27,000 unfavorable, or $25,500 favorable.

Chapter 17
Flexible Budgets, Overhead Cost management, and Activity-Based Budgeting

Chapter Study Suggestions

Chapter 17 presents flexible budgeting and the use of standard costing for overhead costs in manufacturing. As was the case with standard cost systems for direct material and labor costs, explained in Chapter 16, this chapter explains how and why variances occur. Since overhead costs are not traceable to units of product , they must be allocated to units of product. Because of this, the variances for overhead costs are different from variances related to direct materials and labor. The interpretation of variances for overhead costs differs in significant ways from variances for traceable costs.

Overhead costs are split into their fixed and variable components. Variable overhead costs change with production activity. Fixed overhead costs do not change with production activity. There are four overhead cost variances. They are variable overhead spending and efficiency variances, and fixed overhead budget and volume variances. They all occur for different reasons, and are interpreted differently.

An overhead performance report is a report used by managers to evaluate actual activities and outcomes. These actual outcomes are compared to budget goals, and managers try to identify which items on the performance warrant investigation, explanation, and corrective action. The flow of manufacturing overhead costs through the accounting system is illustrated. The traditional standard costing and flexible budgeting system is extended to show how an activities-based system could work. The two appendices show how to prorate variances among work-in process, finished goods inventory, and cost of goods sold, and illustrates and explains backflush costing in a JIT environment.

Chapter Highlights

A. Cost Management Challenges. Chapter 17 offers three cost management challenges.

1. How can a management team use a flexible budget to help manage overhead costs?

2. What are overhead variances, and how can they be interpreted?

3. How can management of overhead costs be improved?

B. Learning Objectives – This chapter has 10 learning objectives.

1. Chapter 17 explains how cost managers use flexible budgets to control overhead costs.

2. The chapter shows how to prepare and interpret a flexible overhead budget.

3. It shows how overhead is applied to work-in process inventory when a standard costing system is used.

4. Chapter 17 discusses issues related to choosing activity measures for overhead budgeting and application.

5. The chapter demonstrates how to compute and interpret variable overhead spending and efficiency variances, as well as fixed overhead budget and volume variances.

6. It shows how to prepare and interpret an overhead cost performance report.

7. Chapter 17 illustrates journal entry preparation, to record manufacturing overhead costs under a standard costing system.

8. The chapter explains why an activity-based flexible budget may provide more useful cost management information than a conventional flexible budget.

9. Appendix A shows how to prorate variances among work-in process inventory, finished goods inventory, and cost of goods sold.

10. Appendix B illustrates and explains backflush costing in a JIT environment.

C. A flexible budget is a cost-management tool used by many companies to control overhead costs. A flexible budget is different from budgets presented in Chapter 15 in one important respect. A flexible budget is not based on one level of activity. A flexible budget for overhead costs is a detailed plan for controlling overhead costs that is relevant within the firm's relevant range of activity.

In order to recognize the way a flexible budget works, one must first understand that fixed overhead costs behave differently than variable overhead costs. This makes it necessary for the costs to be managed differently. Fixed overhead costs do not change as an organization's activity changes. Depreciation on buildings or equipment is examples of fixed overhead costs. Variable overhead costs vary with production activity.

1. Since variable overhead costs vary with production activity, and actual activity is not static, it is useful to have a flexible budget approach, which shows what total costs will be, given different amounts of budgeted activity within the relevant range.

2. A flexible budget can be easily adjusted to show what overhead costs should be, given some actual. Traditional flexible budgets use input levels of activity, like machine hours, to set standards. This approach is particularly useful when there are two or more products manufactured. A flexible budget can be based on standard allowed input, given actual output.

3. The flexible overhead budget is split into variable and fixed cost categories. A formula that shows how to derive total budgeted monthly overhead costs is:

   Total budgeted monthly overhead costs = (budgeted variable OH cost per activity unit × total activity units) plus total budgeted fixed OH cost per month.

   The variable overhead rate is obtained by estimating total variable cost and dividing it by estimated activity level. A commonly used activity is machine hours. By using this formula, total overhead costs can be estimated for any activity level.

4. Overhead costs are applied to work-in process inventory as part of product cost. In a standard costing system, overhead costs are applied based on standard hours allowed for actual output.

5. Common measures of activity to use as the allocation base are machine hours, direct-labor hours, direct labor cost, total process time, and direct material cost.

   a. The activity measure should be chosen because it varies in a similar pattern to the way that variable overhead varies.

   b. Traditionally, direct labor hours has been used as an activity driver. As direct labor costs contribute less to production costs, it becomes less useful as an activity base to use for assigning overhead costs. With increased automation, machine hours or process time have become more informative activity bases.

   c. Dollar measures are occasionally used as activity bases, but there are dangers associated with the use of dollars. Dollar measures are subject to price-level changes, while hours or other quantities do not experience similar fluctuations.

   d. Information technology has simplified flexible budgeting. Once variable rates are determined, a flexible budget can be changed to generate a budget for any activity level.

D. Use of a standard costing system for overhead costs results in overhead cost variances. Variance analysis for overhead costs is broken into fixed and variable components. Variance analysis for overhead costs begins with a flexible budget, and estimation of planned activity

1. Estimated fixed overhead costs must be known. The variable overhead rate must be known. The standard amount of activity allowed for each unit of product must be known. The actual total variable and fixed overhead costs must be known, and the actual quantity of the activity base must be known. The actual number of units must be known.

2. Variable overhead variances are split into two pieces. One is the variable overhead spending variance. The other is the variable overhead efficiency variance.

   a. The variable overhead spending variance compares Actual spending for variable overhead is compared to the amount of spending that should have occurred, given the actual activity of the allocation base. The formula for calculating the variable overhead spending variance is :

      Variable OH spending variance = actual variable overhead – (AH × SVR),

      where AH = actual quantity of the activity base
      SVR = standard variable overhead rate

   b. The variable overhead efficiency variance compares the amount of variable overhead cost that should have occurred given the **actual** quantity of the allocation base to the amount of variable overhead cost that should have occurred given that the standard **allowed** quantity of the allocation base had been used. The formula for calculating the variable overhead efficiency base is:

      Variable OH efficiency variance = (AH × SVR) – (SH × SVR), or
      Variable OH efficiency variance = SVR*(AH – SH)

      where AH = actual quantity of the activity base
      SH = standard machine hours
      SVR = standard variable overhead rate

   c. The variable overhead spending variance is unfavorable if actual variable overhead costs are higher than they should be, given the quantity of the activity base. The variable overhead efficiency variance is unfavorable if the quantity of the activity base is more than the standard quantity allowed for the actual output produced.

   d. The amount of variable overhead applied to work-in process is based on actual number of units produced at standard cost per unit.

e. The efficiency variance is simple to interpret. It measures the efficiency with which the activity base was used in production. If the activity used as the allocation base is machine hours, and actual machine hours exceeds the standard quantity of machine hours allowed for the actual output, then the efficiency variance will be unfavorable. Notice, this variance does not inform managers about the efficiency in the use of variable overhead items like electricity or indirect labor or materials.

f. The variable overhead spending variance is less informative than the efficiency variance. It is caused by two things. First, it is caused by paying more, or less for the various variable overhead items. Second, it is caused by using more, or less of variable overhead items than should have been used for actual activity. This second reason is a measure of the efficiency in the use of variable overhead items. Since variable overhead items are pooled, and then allocated based on one activity, it is virtually impossible to isolate specific causes of the spending variance.

3. There are two fixed overhead variances. One is the fixed overhead budget variance. The other is the fixed overhead volume variance.

a. The fixed overhead budget variance is simply a comparison of actual fixed overhead costs and budgeted fixed overhead costs. The formula is:

Fixed overhead budget variance = actual fixed overhead – budgeted fixed overhead.

b. The fixed overhead volume variance is a comparison between budgeted fixed overhead costs and the amount of fixed overhead applied. The formula is:

Fixed overhead volume variance = budgeted fixed overhead – applied fixed overhead.

Applied fixed overhead is computed as the standard quantity allowed for actual output, multiplied by the fixed overhead rate.

c. An unfavorable fixed overhead budget variance can be interpreted simply, as actual fixed overhead costs being higher than originally expected. The fixed overhead volume variance highlights the two different purposes of the cost-accounting system. The cost-management purpose of a cost accounting system recognizes that fixed overhead cost does not change as production activity changes. Budgeted fixed overhead is the basis for controlling fixed overhead because it is the benchmark for comparing actual expenditures.

The second purpose of a cost accounting system is product costing. The predetermined fixed overhead rate is used to apply fixed overhead costs to work-in process inventory.

d. An incorrect interpretation of a positive volume variance is that it measures the cost of under-utilizing productive capacity. What a positive volume variance does imply is that fewer products were produced than were budgeted. The "cost" is lost contribution margin from units of product not produced for sale. This "cost" may be due to a conscious decision on the part of management to produce less because of lowered demand expectations.

4. The four variances described so far – variable overhead spending variance, variable overhead efficiency variance, fixed overhead budget variance, and fixed overhead volume variance can be combined into two or three variances. Some analyses may combine the variable overhead spending variance with the fixed overhead budget variance, calling this a spending variance. In this case, there are three variances – the overhead spending variance, the variable overhead efficiency variance, and the fixed overhead volume variance.

   Some analyses combine the variable overhead spending variance, variable overhead efficiency variance, and the fixed overhead budget variance, calling this variance the budget variance. In this two-way analysis, there is a budget variance and a fixed overhead volume variance.

E. An overhead cost performance report is used to summarize the budgeted and actual costs and activities, and to compare them by showing the variances. To the extent possible, specific overhead items are presented separately, so that managers can identify, investigate and explain significant variances for specific inputs.

F. Standard cost systems allow product costs to be assigned based on standards instead of using actual costs. Just as standard costs are assigned for direct materials and direct labor, they are assigned for fixed and variable overheads, using the standard rates and standard quantities of the activity base. The flow of costs through the accounting system is outlined below.

1. Actual manufacturing overhead costs are assigned (debited) to the manufacturing overhead account. Various accounts are credited. At the end of the month, when production is completed and accounted for, costs for overhead are assigned using the standard cost per unit of product. Work-in process inventory is debited for the standard overhead cost, and the manufacturing overhead account is credited.

   If the amount of overhead applied is greater than the actual amount of overhead cost incurred, then overhead costs were overapplied. If the amount applied is less than actual overhead costs incurred, then overhead costs were underapplied. In either case, the over- or underapplied overhead costs are reflected in the four overhead variances. In other words, the sum of the four overhead variances will equal the over- or underapplied amounts. The variances are usually closed out to cost of goods sold. An alternative way to close the variances is to prorate them among work-in process, finished goods inventory, and cost of goods sold. This approach is explained in the appendix.

G. The traditional standard costing system and flexible budgets can be modified to have multiple cost drivers instead of just one. Activity-based product costing can be used as the basis for flexible budget planning and management purposes. While the traditional standard costing system used one cost driver like machine hours, an ABC system would split costs according to their relation to machine hours, number of setups, number of production runs, or other activities. Overhead costs that might be fixed with respect to machine hours might vary with more appropriate cost drivers.

H. An ABC flexible budget is more accurate in reporting costs, and allows more accurate cost estimation during the budget process. The performance report would yield more informative variances that could be used to identify true reasons for the variances that occur.

REVIEW AND SELF TEST QUESTIONS AND EXERCISES

Matching key terms

Match the following terms to the correct definition by writing the correct letter next to the correct definition.

a. fixed overhead volume variance
b. applied overhead
c. flexible budget
d. activity-based flexible budget
e. relevant range
f. variable OH spending variance
g. fixed overhead budget variance
h. static budget
i. standard OH rate
j. variable OH efficiency variance

_____ 1. The typical range of activity within which an organization operates.

_____ 2. Budgeted overhead cost divided by planned total activity.

_____ 3. The difference between actual total variable cost and what that cost would have been had the actual cost-driver quantity been multiplied by the standard variable OH rate.

_____ 4. A budget based on a fixed level of activity.

_____ 5. The difference between budgeted fixed OH and applied fixed OH.

_____ 6. The amount of overhead cost assigned to units in work-in-process.

_____ 7 The difference between actual fixed OH and budgeted fixed OH.

_____ 8. A flexible budget used when an organization uses activity-based costing.

_____ 9. A budget that shows expected outcomes within a range of activity levels.

_____10. The difference between the actual quantity of the cost-driver and the standard quantity of the cost-driver for variable costs, multiplied by the standard variable OH rate.

Chapter 17

True or False

For each of the following statements enter a T or an F in the blank to indicate whether the statement is true or false.

_____ 11. A flexible provides budgeted information at just one level of activity.

_____ 12. A flexible budget allows one to adjust fixed production costs based on expected changes in production activity.

_____ 13. In a standard costing system, overhead costs are assigned to units of product based on standard amount of activity allowed for actual output.

_____ 14. In a standard cost system, variable overhead costs are assigned using an activity that varies in a similar pattern to the way variable overhead costs vary.

_____ 15. One of the variances for variable overhead costs is the variable overhead efficiency variance. This variance measures the efficiency of use of overheads like indirect labor.

_____ 16. The variable overhead spending variance is favorable if actual variable overhead costs are lower than they should be, given the actual quantity of the overhead activity base.

_____ 17. The amount of fixed and variable overhead cost assigned to inventory accounts is based on actual number of units produced and actual overhead costs.

_____ 18. The variable overhead efficiency variance informs managers about the efficiency in the use of the activity base used to allocate variable overhead costs to units of product.

_____ 19. The fixed overhead budget variance is affected by the actual amount of activity that takes place in a month.

_____ 20. An overhead cost performance report is used to summarize budgeted and actual overhead costs and activities.

_____ 21. Suppose electricity rates charged by the local utility were exactly as budgeted per kilowatt-hour. Because of production problems, workers were inefficient in the use of electricity. If these events occur, there should be no variable overhead spending variance, but there will definitely be a variable overhead efficiency variance.

_____ 22. If there are unfavorable overhead variances, the simplest way to account for them is to add them to the cost of goods sold.

_____ 23. The traditional standard costing system is more informative if is it modified to have multiple cost drivers.

_____ 24. If actual production is greater than originally budgeted, the fixed overhead costs should not be affected.

_____ 25. A commonly used allocation base used to assign overhead costs to units of product is machine hours. If fewer machine hours were used than the standard allowed for actual production, then the variable overhead efficiency variance will be favorable.

Multiple Choice

Choose the best answer by writing the letter corresponding to your choice in the space provided.

_____ 26. Which of the following is a true statement about the variable overhead efficiency variance (VOHEV) when the allocation base is machine hours?

a) The VOHEV tells you whether one was efficient or inefficient in the use of variable OH resources.
b) The VOHEV tells whether one paid more or less than planned for variable OH resources.
c) Information used to calculate the VOHEV can also be used to determine the direct materials quantity variance.
d) The VOHEV tells you whether one was efficient or inefficient in the use of machine hours.

Please use the following to answer questions 27-28. Very Juicy Juicers Company produces and packages fruit juices. The company had the following budget and standards for each month.

- Budgeted fixed overhead costs were $43,200.
- The variable overhead rate was $7.50 per machine hour.
- The fixed overhead rate was $9.60 per machine hour.
- Budgeted production time for the machines was 4,500 hours.
- The standard quantity of machine time allowed is .03 hour per gallon (1.8 minutes), so the standard cost for a gallon of juice is $.225 for variable overhead costs.
- The standard rate is $.288 per gallon of juice for fixed overheads.

Very Juicy Juicer's production workers, tired of working for what they called "migrant workers' pay", went on strike in September. In response, the company fired all of their production workers and hired new workers, whom they paid even LESS per hour than they had been paying the fired workers. The new workers began working for Juicy Juice in October. After a month of being out of work, some of the old workers came in and sabotaged the machinery, in retaliation for having been fired. Machinery repair costs are treated as part of fixed overhead costs. This slowed the production and machines took 10% longer than the standard to complete production. The slower production rate resulted in much lower production output.

Actual costs for October were as follows:

- Fixed overhead costs were $46,500.
- Variable overhead costs totaled $42,300.
- Actual machine hours totaled 4,800.
- Actual production totaled 135,000 gallons of orange juice, despite original plans to produce 150,000 gallons.

_____ 27. Based on events described, what is the effect on the variable overhead efficiency variances?

a) The result is a favorable variable overhead efficiency variance.
b) The result is an unfavorable variable overhead efficiency variance.
c) The events should have no effect on the variable overhead efficiency variance.
d) The effect cannot be determined based on the information given.

_____ 28. The sabotage of the machinery is likely to cause

a) a favorable fixed overhead budget variance and a favorable fixed overhead volume variance.
b) an unfavorable fixed overhead budget variance and a favorable fixed overhead volume variance.
c) a favorable fixed overhead budget variance and an unfavorable fixed overhead volume variance.
d) an unfavorable fixed overhead budget variance and an unfavorable fixed overhead volume variance.

_____ 29. Which of the following is a correct description of a flexible budget?

a) A flexible budget allows managers to change the variable overhead rates every month.
b) A flexible budget allows managers to see what overhead costs will be at different levels of production.
c) A flexible budget is based on the assumption that fixed overhead costs will fluctuate from month to month.
d) A flexible budget cannot use the same estimated production levels for fixed and variable production activities.

_____ 30. Duke Power Company provides electricity for the factory where Cool Looks Company operates. Cool Looks uses machine hours to allocate variable overhead costs. The state agency that regulates Duke Power has ruled that Duke must reduce its charges to industrial customers like Cool Looks, by 15%. Duke has informed its customers that it will reduce prices by 15%, effective November of the coming year. Because of this unexpected rate **decrease**, the firm's variable OH costs will decrease. A reduction in price won't cause the firm to increase its use of electricity. In November, this unexpected decrease in variable OH costs will cause

a) an unfavorable variable overhead spending variance.
b) a favorable variable overhead spending variance.
c) a favorable variable overhead efficiency variance.
d) an unfavorable variable overhead efficiency variance.

_____31. After replacing old equipment with more efficient machines, a company found that the machine time needed to complete products was reduced by 25%. If the allocation base for variable overheads is machine hours, then which of the following will result from this reduction in production time?

a) There will be an unfavorable variable overhead spending variance.
b) There will be an unfavorable variable overhead efficiency variance.
c) There will be a favorable variable overhead spending variance.
d) There will be a favorable variable overhead efficiency variance.

_____32. Smart Labs recently decided to outsource a part of its production process. All packaging of products will be done by a company that offered a very attractive price, that is less than the cost of packaging internally. Packaging is considered to be part of indirect materials, which is a variable overhead cost. This decision will affect

a) the direct materials price variance.
b) the direct labor rate variance.
c) the variable overhead efficiency variance.
d) the variable overhead spending variance.

_____33. Smart Labs, inc. set a budget for fixed overhead costs at $50,000 for last month. The amount of fixed overhead assigned to inventory was $60,000. Fixed overhead costs are assigned to work-in process inventory based on standard machine hours for actual units of production. Allocation of $60,000 means that

a) the actual number of units produced was higher than the number originally budgeted.
b) the actual number of units produced was lower than the number originally budgeted.
c) the actual number of machine hours must have exceeded the number of machine hours allowed for the number of units produced.
d) actual fixed overhead costs must have been greater than the amount originally budgeted.

_____34. Which of the following is a correct interpretation of the fixed overhead budget variance?

a) A favorable fixed overhead budget variance could be due to efficient use of indirect materials.
b) A favorable fixed overhead budget may be due to overestimation of fixed overhead costs.
c) A favorable fixed overhead budget may be the result of replacing old machinery with new machinery.
d) A favorable fixed overhead budget may be due to outsourcing of support department activities like information systems, to reduce those costs.

_____35. Given that the allocation base is machine hours, the fixed overhead volume variance compares the budgeted fixed overhead costs to

a) the amount that fixed overhead costs should be, given actual units produced and standard rates and standard machine hours allowed for actual production.
b) the amount that fixed overhead should be, given originally budgeted number of units to be produced, standard rates, and actual machine hours used.
c) the amount that fixed overhead should be, given actual units produced, the actual fixed overhead rate, and actual machine hours used.
d) the actual fixed overhead costs.

Please use the following information to answer questions 36–40.

Lumpkins Motors Company manufactures the engines for equipment like riding lawn mowers. The company budgeted production of 2,500 engines in September. Fixed overhead costs were $28,600. Variable overhead costs were budgeted at $32,500. The cost allocation base for both fixed and variable overhead costs is machine hours. 5,000 machine hours were budgeted for the month. Actual fixed overhead costs were $23,600, actual variable overhead costs were $34,400, actual machine hours were 5,200, and 2,700 engines were produced.

_____36. What are the standard fixed and variable overhead rates?

a) The variable overhead rate is $6.50 per engine, and the fixed overhead rate is $5.72 per engine.
b) The variable overhead rate is $6.50 per machine hour, and the fixed overhead rate is $5.72 per machine hour.
c) The variable overhead rate is $6.88 per machine hour, and the fixed overhead rate is $4.72 per machine hour.
d) The variable overhead rate is $6.25 per machine hour, and the fixed overhead rate is $5.50 per machine hour.

_____37. What was the variable overhead spending variance?

a) $1,900 unfavorable
b) $1,300 favorable
c) $700 favorable
d) $600 unfavorable

_____38. What was the variable overhead efficiency variance?

a) $1,900 unfavorable
b) $1,300 favorable
c) $700 favorable
d) $600 unfavorable

_____39. What was the fixed overhead budget variance?

a) $13,156 unfavorable
b) $7,288 favorable
c) $5,000 favorable
d) $2,288 favorable

_____ 40. What was the fixed overhead volume variance?

a) $13,156 unfavorable
b) $7,288 favorable
c) $5,000 favorable
d) $2,288 favorable

_____ 41. After certifying all materials suppliers, the Lumpkin Motors Company found that the quality of materials purchases improved significantly this year. Materials quality affects the amount of time spent assembling engines at Lumpkins Motors, and this year the machine time ended up being less per engine produced than expected. Which effect will the improved materials quality have?

a) It will result in a favorable variable overhead spending variance.
b) It will result in a favorable variable overhead efficiency variance.
c) It will have no effect on variable overhead efficiency variances.
d) There will be an effect on variable overhead variances, but there is not enough information to determine what it is.

_____ 42. Which of the following is true regarding the relationship between the fixed and variable overhead costs and variances?

a) If the variable overhead spending variance is favorable, the fixed overhead budget variance will also be favorable.
b) If the variable overhead efficiency variance is unfavorable, the fixed overhead volume variance will also be unfavorable.
c) If the number of units produced is higher than the number originally budgeted, then the amount of fixed and variable overhead applied to inventory will be higher than originally budgeted.
d) If the variable overhead spending variance is favorable, the fixed overhead budget variance will be unfavorable.

_____ 43. If an overhead cost variance is unfavorable, which of the following will result (assuming the company uses the simple approach to disposing of variances)?

a) Cost of goods sold will be increased.
b) Cost of goods sold will be decreased.
c) Manufacturing overhead costs will be increased.
d) Non-production costs will be increased.

_____ 44. A modification to the traditional standard costing system would allow the use of more than one cost driver, like machine hours. Which of the following would be a **least** likely addition to the cost drivers for variable overhead costs?

a) Number of setups
b) Number of production runs
c) Dollar amount of direct labor costs
d) Kilowatts of electricity used in production

_____45. A performance report, prepared by the production manager reports on overhead variances. Explanation of the variances would be the responsibility of

a) top management.
b) the production manager.
c) production workers.
d) the accountants and other cost managers.

Exercises

Please use the following information to answer the next five questions.

Very Juicy Juicers Company produces and packages fruit juices. The company had the following budget and standards for each month.

- Budgeted fixed overhead costs were $43,200.
- The variable overhead rate was $7.50 per machine hour.
- The fixed overhead rate was $9.60 per machine hour.
- Budgeted production time for the machines was 4,500 hours.
- The standard quantity of machine time allowed is .03 hour per gallon (1.8 minutes), so the standard cost for a gallon of juice is $.225 for variable overhead costs.
- The standard rate is $.288 for fixed overheads.

Very Juicy Juicer's production workers, tired of working for what they called "migrant workers' pay", went on strike in September. In response, the company fired all of their production workers and hired new workers, whom they paid even LESS per hour than they had been paying the fired workers. The new workers began working for Juicy Juice in October. After a month of being out of work, some of the old workers came in and sabotaged the machinery, in retaliation for having been fired. Machinery repair costs are treated as part of fixed overhead costs. This slowed the production and machines took 10% longer than the standard to complete production.

Actual costs for October were as follows:

- Fixed overhead costs were $46,500.
- Variable overhead costs totaled $42,300.
- Actual machine hours totaled 4,800.
- Actual production totaled 135,000 gallons of orange juice.

46. Calculate the variable overhead spending variance.

47. Calculate the variable overhead efficiency variance.

48. Calculate the fixed overhead budget variance.

49. Calculate the fixed overhead volume variance.

50. Calculate the total amount of cost assigned to work-in process inventory for overhead product costs. Calculate the total variance between actual overhead costs and costs assigned to work-in process.

Answers to Questions and Exercises

Matching key terms

1. e 2. i 3. f 4. h 5. a 6. b 7. g 8. d 9. c 10. j

True or False

11. F. A flexible budget allows managers to see what budgeted amounts would be at various levels of activity.
12. F. Fixed production costs should not change as a result of expected changes in production activity.
13. T. Costs for units of product are based on standard cost.
14. T. The cost driver used to assign variable costs should bear some relationship to that pattern of variable costs.
15. F. The variable overhead efficiency variance measures efficiency in the use of the activity base – not efficiency in the use of overhead resources. Those efficiency measures are included in the variable overhead spending variance.
16. T. Calculation of the variable overhead spending is actual variable overhead costs minus the actual quantity of the activity base times the standard variable OH rate.
17. F. The overhead cost assigned to inventory accounts is based on actual number of units produced and **standard** costs allowed per unit.
18. T. The variable overhead efficiency variance informs managers about the use of the activity base – not efficiency in the use of variable overhead resources.
19. F. Fixed overhead costs do not vary in proportion to production activity. That's why they are viewed as fixed.
20. T. The overhead cost performance report summarizes actual activity and costs, and compares them to budgeted activity and standard costs.
21. F. Even if the rate charged for electricity is as budgeted, the variable overhead spending variance will contain variances due to differences in the quantity of electricity used. There is likely to be a variance in usage because electricity usage was more than expected. However, this variance shows up in the spending variance, not in the efficiency variance.
22. T. Since a standard costing system assigns only standard costs to inventory accounts, any variances are either written off to cost of goods sold (the simplest approach), or can be prorated among work-in process, finished goods inventory, and cost of goods sold.
23. T. One of the criticisms of a standard costing system is that the information is too aggregated. Allowing an activity-based set of cost drivers to set standards and assign product costs will be more informative.
24. T. Fixed overhead costs should not be affected by production activity.
25. T. The variable overhead efficiency variance is due entirely to the difference between expected use of the activity base for actual output and actual use of the activity base for actual output.

Multiple Choice

26. d. The variable overhead efficiency variance is informative about only one thing – that is, the efficiency in the use of the cost driver, which in this question, is machine hours.
27. b The efficiency variance will be unfavorable because the machines took 10% longer than the standard allows.
28. d. Both variances are unfavorable. The budget variance is unfavorable because of the maintenance costs. The volume variance is unfavorable because of the lower output.
29. b. The budget is flexible because it allows managers to estimate costs at different activity levels. Variable costs change at different production levels.
30. b. The variable overhead spending variance contains differences because of how variable overhead inputs are used, and because the cost of those inputs is different from the budgeted cost. This situation describes the latter occurrence.
31. d. The machine time will be shorter for every unit produced, which will affect the variable overhead efficiency variance in a favorable way.
32. d. The cost of this variable overhead will decrease, affecting the variable overhead spending variance.
33. a. The standard rate per unit of product is assigned to actual units produced, so if more units than originally budgeted are produced, then more fixed overhead cost will be assigned to units of product in inventory. Answer c is wrong because the actual number of machine hours is not used to calculate either of the fixed overhead variances. Answer d is incorrect because it describes the fixed overhead budget variance.
34. b. If budget estimates are inaccurate, then variances are caused by poor estimation rather than unexpected actual costs. Use of indirect materials affects the variable overhead spending variance (answer a). Replacing old machinery with new would likely cause an unfavorable fixed overhead budget variance (answer c). Support department costs are not fixed overhead costs (answer d).
35. a. The volume variance for fixed overheads compares the fixed overhead budget amount to the amount of fixed overhead applied to work-in process, which is based on actual units times the standard rate times the standard quantity of the allocation base (machine hours).
36. b. The variable overhead rate is $32,50/5,000 machine hours = $6.50 per machine hour. The fixed overhead rate is $28,600/5,000 machine hours = $5.72 per machine hour.
37. d. $600 unfavorable. The actual variable overhead cost was $34,400. Compare this to 5,200 actual machine hours times the standard rate of $6.50, or $33,800. The variance is $600 unfavorable (it cost more than it should have cost, given actual quantity of machine hours).
38. b. $1,300 favorable. Compare the actual machine hours times the standard rate, $6.50, or $3,800 to the standard machine time allowed times number of units produced times the standard rate per machine hour, or 2 hours per engine × 2,700 engines times $6.50 = $35,100. $35,100 was applied, and is compared to $33,800, the flexible budget amount. The variance is $1,300 favorable. Work completed took 5,200 hours, when it should have taken 5,400 hours.
39. c. $5,000 favorable. The fixed overhead budget variance compares actual fixed overhead costs to budgeted fixed overhead costs. Actual costs of $23,600, compared to budgeted fixed overhead costs of $28,600 caused a favorable variance of $5,000.
40. d. $2,288 favorable. The amount budgeted, $28,600 is compared to the amount applied, $5.72 × 2,700 engines × 2 hours = $30,888. The difference is $2,288. $2,288 more was applied than was originally budgeted.

41. b. Even if variable overhead costs do not change as a result, the variable overhead efficience variance will be favorable because the machine time will decrease. To the extent that machine time is a true cost driver for variable overhead costs, the costs should actually decline as a result of the improved quality of materials.
42. c. There is really no relationship between fixed and variable overhead variances. They occur for two different reasons. The only way in which events are the same for both costs is the way in which costs are assigned to units of product.
43. a. If a cost variance is unfavorable, it means that costs were higher than expected. Thus, an unfavorable cost variance can be viewed as an additional cost. The simplest way to dispose of variances is to write them off to cost of goods sold. If a cost variance is unfavorable, it is closed by increasing cost of goods sold, and crediting (decreasing) the variance.
44. c. Direct labor costs are becoming increasingly less important. Therefore, it would not be helpful, in most cases to use direct labor cost as a cost driver for overhead costs.
45. b. The production manager is responsible for explaining the variances related to overhead costs. Top management would not know the reasons for the variances (answer a). Production workers may have something to do with why there are variances, but it is not their responsibility to explain them (answer c). Accountants and other cost managers would not know the reasons for the variances either (answer d).

Exercises

The following notation is used in calculating the variances in questions 46-50:

- AC = Actual total cost
- AQ = Actual quantity of machine hours
- AQP = Actual number of units produced
- FOH = Fixed overhead
- FOHBC = Fixed overhead budgeted cost
- FOHSR = Fixed overhead standard rate per machine hour
- SQ = Standard quantity of machine hours allowed per unit
- VOH = Variable overhead
- VOHSR = Variable overhead standard rate per machine hour

46. The variable overhead spending variance is:
AC for VOH – AQ × VOHSR = $42,300 – 4,800 × $7.50
= $42,300 – $36,000 = **$6,300 unfavorable.**
47. The variable overhead efficiency variance is:
(AQ × VOHSR) – [(SQ × AQP) × VOHSR] = (4,800 × $7.50) – [(.03 × 135,000) × 7.50]
= (4,800 × $7.50) – (4,050 × $7.50)
= $36,000 – $30,375 = **$5,625 unfavorable.**
48. The fixed overhead budget variance is:
(AC for FOH) – FOHBC = $46,500 – $43,200 = **$3,300 unfavorable.**

49. The fixed overhead volume variance is:
FOHBC – (SQ × AQP) × FOHSR)) = \$43,200 – (.03 × 135,000) × \$9.60 = \$43,200 – 4,050 × \$9.60 = \$43,200 - \$38,880 = **\$4,320 unfavorable.**

50. Actual costs were \$46,500 for fixed overhead costs and \$42,300 for variable overhead costs. Total actual overhead costs were \$88,800. Total costs applied to work-in process is \$.288 per gallon for fixed overhead costs, and \$.225 per gallon for variable overhead costs, or \$.513 times 135,000 gallons = **\$69,255** assigned to work-in process. Total variance for overhead costs is **\$19,545 unfavorable**, which is more than 28% of the overhead cost allowed under the standards originally set.

Chapter 18
Organizational Design, Responsibility Accounting, and Evaluation of Divisional Performance

Chapter Study Suggestions

Chapter 18 introduces the organizational structure of large organizations, and discusses the need for decentralization in these organizations. Decentralization, which is the dividing up of large organizations into smaller units, results in the delegation of management decision-making authority to employees other than top management. Because top management relinquishes control of many decision-making activities, there must be mechanisms in place to ensure that managers will seek goals that are congruent with the goals of the organization. A responsibility accounting system is that mechanism.

A responsibility center is a subunit of an organization, which is assigned particular responsibilities. People placed in charge of these subunits, managers, are accountable for the subunit achieving the goals of the subunit. There are five types of responsibility centers. They are cost centers, discretionary cost centers, revenue centers, profit centers, and investment centers. The manager of an investment center is responsible for a division of an organization and its costs, revenues and profits. The manager is also given the authority to make capital investment decisions as they relate to his or her division.

The measurement of performance of investment centers and their managers is accomplished using three financial measures of performance. They are return on investment (ROI), residual income (RI), and economic value added (EVA). All of these performance measures have advantages and disadvantages. In addition, the ways to measure a division's income and invested capital (assets) varies, and the advantages and disadvantages of each measurement approach are described.

Chapter Highlights

A. Cost Management Challenges. Chapter 18 offers five cost management challenges.

1. As companies grow, what is the best way to manage them? What are some benefits and costs of decentralization?

2. How can a responsibility accounting system foster goal or behavioral congruence for an organization?

3. What are the major types of responsibility accounting centers?

4. What is the key feature of activity-based responsibility accounting?

5. How is investment center performance typically measured?

B. Learning Objectives – This chapter has 8 learning objectives.

1. Chapter 18 explains the role of responsibility accounting in fostering goal or behavioral congruence.

2. The chapter lists several benefits and costs of decentralization.

3. It describes the distinguishing characteristics of responsibility centers and the various types: a cost center, a discretionary cost center, a revenue center, a profit center and an investment center.

4. Chapter 18 shows how to prepare a performance report for various responsibility centers.

5. The chapter demonstrates how to compute an investment center's return on investment (ROI), residual income (RI), and economic value added (EVA).

6. It explains how a manager can improve ROI by increasing either the sales margin or capital turnover.

7. The chapter describes the pros and cons of using ROI and RI as divisional performance measures.

8. Chapter 18 explains various approaches for measuring a division's income and invested capital.

C. Most large organizations are divided into smaller units, each of which is assigned particular responsibilities. The people placed in charge of these units should be motivated to strive toward the goals that the organization wants to achieve. Goal congruence results when managers of subunits throughout an organization have incentives to perform in the common interest.

Ideally, members of an organization have such a strong team spirit that goal congruence is a natural outcome of that spirit. In most cases, however, employees must be motivated to behave as if their personal goals were congruent with organizational goals through a set of performance evaluation and incentive systems. This results in behavioral congruence.

Responsibility accounting, which is comprised of the tools and concepts used to measure performance of people and departments, is used to foster behavioral congruence. The fundamental purpose of a responsibility accounting system is to reap the benefits of decentralization, while minimizing the costs of decentralization.

1. Decentralization of large organizations became necessary as organizations became too large and complex to be under the authority of just a few people. A centralized organization has a small group of decision makers at the top. Subordinates carry out the decisions as they are handed down, but the subordinates do not participate in any decision making. A decentralized organization, on the other hand, allows people at lower levels of management to make key decisions in the subunits that they are responsible for. Top management makes the major, strategic decisions. Decentralization has some benefits, but also has some costs.

2. Large organizations benefit from decentralization the most if there is a system in place to ensure that lower-level managers will do a good job without day-to-day oversight of their activities. Six benefits of decentralization are as follows. (1) Decentralization allows managers with particular skills to manage those parts of the organization where those skills are needed. This eliminates the need for top managers to be skilled in all areas of operation. (2) Giving managers autonomy and responsibility prepares them for higher-level management positions. (3) Managers with decision-making authority usually exhibit greater motivation than those who merely follow directions of others. (4) Delegating decisions to lower-level managers frees up time of higher-level managers to make strategic decisions instead of being bogged down in daily decision-making. (5) Empowering employees to make decisions makes use of their knowledge and expertise of day-to-day operations. (6) Delegating decision-making authority to lower levels allows an organization to respond on a timely basis to opportunities and problems that arise.

3. In addition to the benefits of decentralization, there are also some costs. They are as follows. (1) Managers may have a narrow focus on their own unit's performance instead of the overall goals of the organization. (2) If managers have a narrow focus on their subunit, they may ignore the consequences of their actions on other subunits. (3) Decentralized organizations run the risk of having duplication of tasks or services. For instance, a decentralized organization that authorizes departments to purchase their own office equipment may find that two departments, right next to each other purchase copiers, when the two departments probably could have shared one.

D. Responsibility accounting is a systematic way to ensure that workers in an organization will work toward achieving the organization's goals. The basis of a responsibility accounting system is the designation of each subunit as a particular type of responsibility center. A responsibility center is a subunit in an organization whose manager is held accountable for specified financial and nonfinancial results of the subunit's activities. There are five types of responsibility centers.

1. A cost center is a subunit whose manager is responsible for the cost of an activity for which a well-defined relationship exists between inputs and outputs. In manufacturing, production departments are usually designated as cost centers.

2. A discretionary cost center is a subunit whose manager is held accountable for costs where the input-output relationship is not well defined. Support departments in organizations are discretionary cost centers.

3. A revenue center is a subunit whose manager is held accountable for the revenue attributed to the subunit. The manager of Ladies Dresswear in a department store is a revenue center manager

4. A profit center is a responsibility center where the manager is responsible for profits. Since profits are obtained by subtracting costs from revenues, the manager of a profit center is accountable for both costs and revenues.

5. An investment center has a manager who is accountable for the subunit's profits as well as invested capital used to generate its profits. A division of a large corporation is typically designed as an investment center. Managers of investment centers usually have the authority to make some capital investment decisions. Some organizations use the terms profit center and investment center interchangeably.

E. Performance reports are prepared by the manager of each responsibility center. A performance report shows budgeted and actual amounts of key financial results appropriate for the type of responsibility center involved. The performance report for a cost center of a manufacturing facility would contain budgeted and actual activity, and then would report cost variances, as described in Chapters 16 and 17. A manager of a revenue center would complete a performance report showing budget and actual information, and would include variances like those presented in the appendix to Chapter 17. This performance report might also summarize customer profitability.

A performance report is completed and submitted to the next higher-level manager. The lower-level manager's subunit is a part of the higher-level manager's larger subunit.

1. Responsibility accounting, budgeting, and variance analysis are closely related. The flexible budget provides the benchmark against which actual revenues, expenses and profits are compared.

2. Contemporary cost management systems extend the basic measures of financial performance of cost, revenue and profit by incorporating activity-based analysis of costs, revenues and profits. Activity-based responsibility accounting directs management attention to costs and revenues, and also places emphasis on activities.

F. The purpose of having a responsibility accounting system is to elicit certain types of behavior. Unless the system is developed and used properly, an organization runs the risk of eliciting inappropriate behavior.

1. The proper focus of a responsibility accounting system is information. One danger in having a responsibility accounting system where managers must explain unfavorable outcomes is that there may be some sense that unfavorable outcomes should be **blamed** on managers. If this is how managers feel about the responsibility accounting system, they may take steps to manipulate data, or undermine it in other ways.

2. A performance report is even more informative if the costs and revenues are split between those that are controllable by the reporting manager, and those that are not controllable. Segregating costs or revenues is not an easy task, but to the extent it can be done, it aids higher-level managers to more accurately evaluate the performance of lower-level managers.

3. The best result of a responsibility accounting system is one that motivates the desired behavior of managers. For instance, the sales manager, whose main focus is on making sales, may be motivated to accept rush orders without regard to the additional production costs that might result. A responsibility accounting system that charges the sales manager for the production costs of an expedited order might be more careful about making promises of fast delivery to customers.

G. Although managers of cost, revenue and profit centers are evaluated based on controlling costs or achieving revenue or profit goals, the highest-level responsibility center, an investment center is probably given the closest scrutiny by top management. In addition to the fact that these managers' performance reports include the results of lower-level units, they are held accountable for the effective use of investment resources. There are three common measures of performance for managers of investment centers. They are return on investment, residual income, and economic value added.

1. Return on investment (ROI) is the most commonly used measure of investment center performance. It is calculated as:

   ROI = Income/Invested capital

   ROI makes different investment centers in an organization comparable to each other. Absolute dollar amounts of profit can be misleading. Suppose two investment centers generated $10 million and $20 million in profits. Just looking at the profits, it appears that the second subunit's performance was better than the first. But suppose it took investments of $100 million and $400 million to generate those profits. The ROI for the first investment center is 10%, while the ROI for the second investment center is only 5%.

   a. The ROI can be expressed in a different way. An alternative calculation is:

      ROI = (Income/Sales Revenue) × (Sales Revenue/Invested capital)

By canceling out the sales revenue terms, ROI can be more readily calculated. However, it is useful to determine ROI using the longer expression because it highlights the fact that the return on investment is actually earned for two reasons. The longer expression is sometimes referred to as the DuPont model.

i. Income/Sales revenue is called sales margin. This part of ROI shows how much of the profit was generated as a percentage of sales revenue. Clearly, the higher this percentage is, the higher the return on investment will be.

ii. Sales revenue/Invested capital is called capital turnover. This expression shows how much revenue is generated for every dollar of capital investment. A higher number for this expression implies that invested capital is being used effectively.

2. Improving a division's ROI can be accomplished by increasing sales margin or by increasing capital turnover. It is useful to look at the DuPont model expression of ROI to see what needs to be done to improve profitability. Suppose sales revenues are increased but income and invested capital are held constant? ROI will be exactly the same as before. Thus, increasing sales without increasing profits will not increase overall profitability.

   a. Increasing income is the most obvious way to increase ROI, but it is not an easy way. Income can be increased by either increasing revenues (higher sales) or by decreasing costs. Income can also be increased by raising prices, but selling less product. In this case, total revenue is held constant but income is higher.

   b. The other way to increase ROI is to raise capital turnover. It should be noted that, turnover could be increased by raising sales revenue or lowering invested capital. However, if revenue is raised without raising income as well, or lowering invested capital as well, there will be no effect on ROI. Decreasing invested capital is a challenging goal. Large chunks of invested capital are committed, long-term, fixed assets. These cannot be easily eliminated.

   c. Although ROI is widely used as a performance measure, it has one important drawback. Since managers are evaluated based on their division's ROI, there may be some disincentives for managers to make capital investments that are good for the organization as a whole, but not good as it relates to divisional ROI. For instance, if a manager" division has an ROI of 15%, and a capital investment has a ROI of 11%, the new ROI for the division would become something less than 15%. Thus, even if an ROI of 11% is acceptable for the organization as a whole, because it exceeds organizational cost of capital, the manager might be tempted to reject it because of the effect it would have on his or her division's ROI.

   d. There is an ethical component to the situation just described. Recall, the responsibility accounting system is supposed to motivate behavioral congruence for the good of the organization. In the situation just described, the manager would be tempted to reject a viable investment option because of the effect on his or her own interests. This is especially true if bonuses, promotions, or even one's job could be at risk if divisional ROI declines.

This highlights the dangers of using just one performance measure. Residual income or economic value added are other performance measures that may be used to supplement ROI.

3. An alternative performance measure for investment centers is residual income (RI). ROI is computed without regard to the cost of capital. Residual income looks at the profitability of a prospective capital investment based on how much income remains after accounting for the organization's cost of capital. If residual income with the proposed investment is higher than residual income is without the investment, then the proposed capital project should be accepted.

   Residual income is calculated as:

   RI = Investment center's profit – (investment center's invested capital × Imputed interest rate)

   The imputed interest rate is the firm's cost of acquiring investment capital.

   a. Residual income is a dollar amount, not a percentage like ROI. This is, in fact, one of the drawbacks of using it. Since RI gives an absolute dollar amount, it cannot be used to evaluate different investment centers with differing investment decisions to make. A very large division with RI of $40,000 for a project should not be evaluated the same as a very small division with RI of $20,000 (the first project is probably not twice as beneficial as the second).

   b. RI and ROI should both be used for different purposes, or in conjunction with each other.

4. Economic value added (EVA) is the third measure used to evaluate performance of investment centers. EVA is:

   Investment center's after-tax operating income – [(Investment center's total assets – Investment center's current liabilities) × Weighted-average cost of capital)].

   EVA is similar to residual income, except for three things. First, income tax effects are explicitly incorporated into the calculations by using the after-tax operating income, and by using the after-tax cost of debt capital. Second, an investment center's current liabilities are subtracted from total assets. Third, the weighted average cost of capital is used instead of an imputed interest rate. The weighted average cost of capital WACC) takes into account the two sources of long-term capital – debt and equity.

   WACC is calculated as:

[(After-tax cost of debt capital) × (Market value of debt) + (Cost of equity capital) × (Market value of equity)]

divided by

(Market value of debt + market value of equity)

a. The EVA is expressed as a dollar amount. The advantage of calculating EVA is that it evaluates overall performance of the division like ROI does, but it tells top management fairly readily when a division is in trouble. If the EVA is negative, it means the division is a financial drain on the company's resources. It sounds an alarm that management can respond to immediately.

H. ROI, RI, and EVA all use profit and invested capital in their formulas. This raises the question of how to measure divisional profit and invested capital. There are various ways to do this.

1. There are several ways to measure an investment center's capital. Here are some considerations.

a. Asset balances (or invested capital) may be averages of beginning and ending balances. ROI, RI and EVA are measures of performance over a period of time, while asset balances are measured at one point in time. Average asset balance is used because it, at least, gives a simple measure of the asset base over the time period being evaluated.

b. How much of the asset base should be included for a division? Some companies use total assets. Other companies use total productive assets, excluding nonproductive assets. A third view is that total assets less current liabilities should be used, based on the logic that current liabilities must be paid with current assets, so current assets should be reduced by this much. A fourth consideration is whether gross or net book values should be used. Using gross book value when a considerable portion of the asset base has been depreciated might distort results. This last consideration deserves more discussion.

i. Net book value has two advantages over gross book value. First, it is consistent with balance sheet information prepared for financial reports, and allows for a more meaningful comparison of ROI measures across different companies. Second, net book value is more consistent with net income used in calculating ROI. The income figure deducts the current period's depreciation expense.

ii. Proponents of the use of gross book value argue that depreciation methods are arbitrary, and so they should not be included in performance measures. Perhaps a more compelling argument is that the net book value artificially inflates the ROI, RI and EVA over time. This being the case, managers might be motivated to hang on to old equipment too long, and they might be reluctant to acquire new, more efficient assets.

c. The asset base for a division might also include allocated assets. For instance, divisions may have accounts receivable allocated when customers purchase product from several divisions.

2. Choosing the method for measuring investment center income is another concern for managers. One factor to consider is how controllable is the income attributed to a division? A division's net income figure may be derived from including several allocated expenses, like allocated income taxes, facility-level expenses allocated from corporate headquarters, interest expenses allocated from corporate headquarters, expenses traceable to the division but controlled by others, and general and facility-level expenses controllable by the division manager. An argument could be put forth that no allocated expenses beyond the control of the division manager should be factored into that manager's performance measures.

3. One point to keep in mind when considering what information to use for estimating assets and income is that ROI, RI and EVA are used to evaluate managers' **and** divisions' performance. In evaluating the manager's performance, one should consider only costs and revenues that the manager can control. Evaluation of a division is done for a different purpose. The main purpose of evaluating a division is to see if it is viable in terms of profitability. Traceability of costs is more important than controllability.

4. Even though costs like allocated income taxes, and other costs allocated from corporate headquarters are not controllable by division managers, they are routinely included in performance reports to remind division managers that there are other costs that must be covered by the profits of various divisions in order for the organization as a whole to be profitable.

5. During periods of inflation, or for global companies operating in high-inflation countries, it could be justifiably argued that historical-cost asset valuation should be supplemented with replacement-cost asset values.

I. ROI, RI, and EVA are all short-term performance measures, that evaluate performance one year at a time. An investment center is comprised of the product of strategic decisions intended to benefit the organization over long periods of time. A correct evaluation of multiperiod strategic decisions is to look at a longer window of time.

1. A more appropriate evaluation of a long-term investment is to perform a postaudit of an investment decision. The problem with this approach, however, is that strategic decisions are made on an ongoing basis, and are usually part of a bundle of investments that are used together.

2. Another way to evaluate long-term investment is to use a balanced scorecard approach. The balanced scorecard is presented in Chapter 21.

J. Large, decentralized nonprofit organizations need to evaluate performance of divisions and managers just as much as for-profit organizations do. It is especially challenging to do this because the profit motive is not there to elicit efficient, productive activity. Often, managers of nonprofit and government organizations are working there for reasons that are not purely financial. They may be less receptive to formal control procedures than their business counterparts.

The goals of nonprofit organizations may be less clear-cut than for –profit organizations. Some goals may contradict. For instance, an organization may have the goal of providing medical care to a rural, impoverished community. It may have another goal to stay within its budget. Clearly these goals conflict if the budgeted is fixed.

K. Top management must be conscious of the need to modify its performance evaluation system in accordance with the changes in its organization. Some warning signals that may indicate a need to modify or add performance measures include: (1) a change in organizational strategy; (2) an absence of nonfinancial performance measures; (3) no measures associated with a critical process or success factor; (4) adoption of new technology or organization structure; (5) market share drop; (6) financial crisis; (7) reports that are ignored by managers; (8) managers motivated to do non-value-added tasks; (9) performance measures monitor only costs; (10) measures are all short-term in nature; (11) product has moved into a new phase of its life cycle; (12) measures do not tell how one can do better; (13) functional groups do not work well together; (14) measures are extremely precise; (15) measures are only internally focused; (16) managers and employees cannot articulate critical success factors for organization.

REVIEW AND SELF TEST QUESTIONS AND EXERCISES

Matching key terms

Match the following terms to the correct definition by writing the correct letter next to the correct definition.

a. return on investment
b. responsibility accounting
c. investment center
d. economic value added
e. residual income
f. sales margin
g. cost center
h. behaviorial congruence
i. decentralization
j. weighted-average cost of capital

_____ 1. The case where an individual acts in the best interests of the organization, regardless of his or her own goals.

_____ 2. An investment center's profit less the product of cost of capital times invested capital.

_____ 3. A way to manage an organization where decisions are made by managers at levels below top management.

_____ 4. A subunit of an organization whose manager is authorized to make cost, revenue, profit and investment decisions.

_____ 5. The average of the cost of debt and equity capital.

_____ 6. Net income divided by invested capital.

_____ 7. Net income divided by sales revenue.

_____ 8. An investment center's profit less the product of net invested capital times weighted average cost of capital.

_____ 9. A subunit of an organization whose manager is held accountable only for costs.

_____ 10. An accounting system that holds managers accountable for financial and nonfinancial results under their control.

True or False

For each of the following statements enter a T or an F in the blank to indicate whether the statement is true or false.

_____11. Responsibility accounting is more effective in a decentralized organization than in a centralized organization.

_____12. Goal congruence results when managers are motivated to perform in ways intended to achieve organizational goals.

_____13. Decentralized organizations require approval of most activities from someone in top management.

_____14. One of the problems associated with decentralization in organizations is that managers may focus so much on their own department that they lose sight of the goals of the entire organization.

_____15. A profit center is a kind of responsibility center where the manager is only in charge of revenues and profits.

_____16. An investment center's manager is accountable for costs, revenues, and profits, as well as being authorized to make investment decisions.

_____17. Return on investment (ROI) is best used to evaluate the performance of a revenue center.

_____18. ROI can be split into two parts. One is sales margin, and the other is called invested capital.

_____19. Residual income is a measure of an investment center's profitability without regard to its cost of capital.

_____20. In order to calculate residual income, one piece of information that must be known is the imputed interest rate.

_____21. When comparing economic-value-added (EVA) to ROI and RI, it is the most similar to ROI.

_____22. One of the decisions to be made in calculating ROI is whether to use net book value of assets or gross book value of assets. If net book value is used, it means that accumulated depreciation is subtracted from the depreciable asset base.

_____23. A large, decentralized nonprofit organization needing to evaluate performance can use ROI, just like a for-profit organization can.

_____24. ROI, RI and EVA are all short-term performance measures.

_____25. EVA and ROI can both be used to evaluate divisions' performance.

Chapter 18

Multiple Choice

Choose the best answer by writing the letter corresponding to your choice in the space provided.

_____26. Which of the following best describes a decentralized organization?

a) Small organizations with one manager in charge are usually decentralized.
b) Small organizations with several managers in charge are usually decentralized.
c) Large organizations with one manager in charge are usually decentralized.
d) Large organizations with many managers in charge are usually decentralized.

_____27. Responsibility accounting is used to foster behavioral congruence. Which of the following is correct regarding responsibility accounting?

a) Responsibility accounting allows large, decentralized organizations to trace costs and revenues to particular divisions.
b) Responsibility accounting is useful primarily as a tool to evaluate which managers to discipline for not working hard.
c) Responsibility accounting does not work very well in a decentralized organization.
d) Responsibility accounting can only be used by organizations that use an ABC system of accounting for costs.

_____28. One of the **disadvantages** of decentralization is

a) it assigns most of the responsibility for making decisions to top management.
b) it does not allow lower level managers to gain any decision-making experience
c) it may cause some duplication of activities to occur.
d) it may lead to managers getting promoted into higher positions.

_____29. Which of the following is a **disadvantage** of decentralization?

a) Decentralization allows large, complex organizations to delegate responsibilities to lower-level managers.
b) Decentralization could result in poor decisions being made by lower-level managers without approval by top managers.
c) Decentralization provides lower-level managers with management experience that prepares them for higher-level positions.
d) Decentralization allows top managers to focus on the strategic plans of an organization instead of the day-to-decision making.

_____30. The manager of a profit center is responsible for

a) only the profits of a division (not costs or revenues).
b) only the profits and revenues of a division (but not costs).
c) only the profits and costs of a division (but not revenues).
d) only costs, revenues, and profits of a division (but not investments).

_____31. Which of the following correctly describes the roles of cost center managers and investment center managers?

a) A cost center manager is evaluated using ROI, and an investment center manager is evaluated using EVA.
b) A cost center manager is evaluated based on division budgeted and actual costs, and variances, while an investment center manager may be evaluated based on ROI, RI, or EVA.
c) The manager of a cost center is never evaluated, but an investment center manager may be evaluated based on ROI, RI or EVA.
d) The managers of cost and investment centers are both evaluated based on company-wide profits.

_____32. Which of the following is a short-term controllable cost, from the perspective of the cost manager of a production department?

a) The per unit cost of raw materials purchased for use in production
b) Depreciation expenses for production equipment
c) Costs of defective product.
d) The hourly pay of unionized production workers.

_____33. Investment centers and their managers are evaluated based on ROI, RI, and EVA. In comparing these three performance measures, which of the following is true?

a) ROI is a percentage, while RI and EVA are absolute dollar amounts.
b) ROI and RI are absolute dollar amounts, while EVA is a percentage.
c) ROI and RI are percentages, while EVA is an absolute dollar amount.
d) ROI is an absolute dollar amount, while RI and EVA are percentages.

_____34. ROI can be calculated as follows: ROI = (Income/Sales Revenue) × (Sales Revenue/Invested capital). Which of the following is another way to calculate ROI?

a) Income times sales revenue
b) Invested capital divided by income
c) Sales revenue divided by income
d) Income divided by invested capital

_____35. Which of the following correctly describes sales margin and capital turnover?

a) Sales margin shows income as a percentage of revenue, while capital turnover shows how much revenue is generated for each dollar of capital investment.
b) Sales margin shows income as a percentage of revenue, while capital turnover shows how much capital investment is required to generate a dollar of revenue.
c) Sales margin shows how much income it takes to generate a dollar of revenue, while capital turnover shows how much revenue is generated for each dollar of capital investment.
d) Sales margin shows how much profit is earned on an investment, and capital turnover shows the same thing.

_____36. Capital turnover is the part of ROI that tells

a) whether production capacity is being over- or underutilized.
b) whether an organization needs to acquire more capital assets.
c) whether the money invested in capital assets is generating a large amount of revenue.
d) whether production workers have been efficient or inefficient in production activities.

_____37. Residual income is calculated as:

a) Investment center's profit minus investment center's ROI
b) Investment center's ROI divided by the investment center's income
c) Investment center's revenues minus the investment center's costs
d) Investment center's profit minus the investment center's cost of capital

_____38. The imputed interest rate, used in the calculation of residual income is

a) the estimated cost of a firm's acquiring investment capital.
b) the estimated interest rate that a bank would charge to loan money to the company.
c) the estimated rate of return on an investment in capital assets.
d) the minimum rate of interest available to a company for its investment needs.

_____39. Economic value-added is defined as

a) the weighted cost of investment capital.
b) the net financial benefit, in absolute dollars, of a capital investment.
c) the market value of the capital investment.
d) the estimated rate of return on a capital investment.

_____40. Which of the following is one of the biggest advantages of the use of EVA to evaluate performance?

a) It helps managers to increase profits immediately.
b) It identifies ways to reduce the cost of investment capital.
c) It exposes financially troubled divisions.
d) It provides an evaluation measure that allows comparability to ROI.

_____41. EVA, RI, and ROI all use investment capital in their calculations. Which of the following is **not** a correct way to estimate asset balances?

a) Use the average gross asset balance for the investment center being evaluated.
b) Use the average net asset balance for the investment center being evaluated.
c) Use the average total asset base less nonproductive assets for the investment center being evaluated.
d) Use only the assets acquired in the current year for the investment center being evaluated.

_____42. One of the problems with the use of gross book value as the invested capital base is

a) it cannot be determined easily.
b) it distorts the true value of assets by subtracting depreciation from the original acquisition costs of the assets.
c) it ignores the age of assets in the investment base.
d) it includes too many assets that are not productive assets.

_____43. ROI can be improved several ways. Which of the following is **not** a way to make ROI higher?

a) Increase income
b) Increase investment in capital assets (invested capital)
c) Reduce costs
d) Decrease the invested capital

_____44. RI calculations can be manipulated by changing the assumptions about the imputed interest rate. Raising the imputed interest rate will

a) cause the residual income to be lower than before.
b) cause the residual income to be higher than before.
c) have no effect on residual income.
d) cause an investment center's profit to decrease.

_____45. EVA calculations use a weighted average cost of capital. This is an improvement over the residual income calculation because

a) it gives a result that is more acceptable to financial accounting standard setters, like FASB.
b) it leads to a more concise estimate of the cost of investment capital than RI.
c) it leaves out the more uncertain component of cost of capital, which is equity capital.
d) it uses only equity capital, so cost of borrowed investment funds can be left out of the calculations.

Exercises

Please use the following information to answer the next five questions.

McAllistair Systems has three divisions, which operate independently of each other. Their results for the third quarter of 2001 were as follows:

	McMillan	McBride	McAdams
Sales revenue	$49,500,000	$7,000,000	$10,000,000
Operating Income	$19,800,000	$3,500,000	$5,040,000
Current Liabilities	$7,920,000	$1,400,000	$2,800,000
Invested Capital	$178,200,000	$20,000,000	$28,000,000

- Assume the imputed interest rate is 10%
- Assume the weighted average cost of capital is 13.5%
- Assume the company's tax rate (on operating income) is 16% for McMillan and McBride. The tax rate is 25% for McAdams, because it is located in a less favorable tax climate in another country.

Use the table below to show your answers to questions 46-50.

46. Compute the sales margin and the capital turnover for all three divisions.

47. Compute the ROI for all three divisions.

48. Compute the residual income for the three divisions.

49. Compute the economic value added for the three divisions.

50. Based on ROI, rank the divisions from most to least profitable. Based on EVA, rank the three divisions. Do the same thing based on RI. Comment on the rankings you obtain, and discuss how you would use the information to evaluate the performance of the three divisions.

	McMillan	McBride	McAdams
Capital Turnover			
Sales margin			
ROI			
Residual Income			
Economic Value-Added			
Rank, based on ROI (1 is the highest)			
Rank, based on RI (1 is the highest)			
Rank, based on EVA (1 is the highest)			

Answers to Questions and Exercises

Matching key terms

1. h 2. e 3. i 4. c 5. j 6. a 7. f 8. d 9. g 10. b

True or False

11. T. Responsibility accounting provides a link between top management and lower level managers. Since the size of large organizations precludes their management of a handful of people at the top, authority to perform many management duties is delegated to lower level managers. A responsibility accounting system gives information to top managers about how well the lower level managers are performing these duties.
12. T. Goal congruence refers to the need for managers to feel that their personal goals are compatible with the goals of the organization that they work for.
13. F. The purpose of decentralization is to break up large organizations into smaller units, with managers who are responsible for the smaller units.
14. T. One of the dangers of giving managers authority over one area of operations is that they care only about the successful operations of their own division, even if it is to the detriment of the organization as a whole.
15. F. The manager of a profit center is responsible for revenues and costs, which is how profits are derived.
16. T. An investment center's manager is authorized to make investment decisions as they relate to their division. They are also accountable for earning a return on the investments made, by earning revenues, managing costs, and generating profits.
17. F. ROI is used to evaluate the performance of an investment center.
18. F. ROI can be split into sales margin and capital turnover.
19. F. Residual income is calculated as the investment center's profit minus invested capital times imputed interest rate. Invested capital times the imputed interest rate is the cost of capital.
20. T. The imputed interest rate must be known in order to compute estimated cost of capital.
21. F. EVA is essentially the same as residual income, with a few modifications to invested capital and the way that cost of capital is determined.
22. T. The asset base is reduced by the amount of depreciation that has been expensed so far on the plant assets when net assets are used in the ROI calculation.
23. F. ROI, or return on investment cannot be earned in a nonprofit organization since profits are not earned. A nonprofit organization is expected to, at best, break even.
24. T. One of the criticisms of all three of these performance measures is that they motivate managers to focus only on short-term profits.
25. T. EVA and ROI provide absolute dollar amounts and a percentage, respectively. There are times when EVA may be a more useful measure of performance. There are other times when ROI may be more informative.

Multiple Choice

26. d. Small organizations do not usually require decentralization, since decentralization is normally required only when an organization becomes too large for top management or the owners to make all of the decisions.
27. a. Responsibility accounting extends an accounting system to allow coding of transactions and activities in such a way that they can be traced to a particular responsibility center. It is not a disciplinary tool (answer b); it works best in a decentralized organization (answer c); and any accounting system can be extended to include codes for responsibility centers (answer d).
28. c. Since managers are authorized to make decisions for their own divisions, there may be instances where two (or more) managers will make similar decisions about resources that would be shared in a centralized organization. Answers a and b are simply untrue (the opposite is true in both cases); answer d is true, but it is an advantage instead of a disadvantage.
29. b. Since decision-making authority is delegated to lower level managers, top management accepts the risk of having managers making poor decisions.
30. d. The manager of a profit center is responsible for the revenues and costs of his or her division. Since revenues minus costs equal profits, the profit center manager is also responsible for profits. However, these managers are not authorized to make decisions for capital investments.
31. b. A manager of a cost center is evaluated based on their ability to meet targeted goals for managing costs. The manager of an investment is expected to meet targets related to earning a pre-determined profit on capital investments. ROI, RI, and EVA are three commonly used evaluation measures.
32. c. Even though all four of the costs listed may be included in a performance report for a cost center, the cost manager can probably only control the costs of defects, at least in the short run. The investment manager who makes decisions about acquiring capital assets will affect depreciation expenses. The purchasing manager is responsible for the cost of raw materials. The hourly pay of unionized workers can probably be managed to some extent by the production manager when the labor contract is negotiated, but short-run effects would be negligible at best.
33. a. ROI is a percentage, while RI and EVA are absolute dollar amounts.
34. d. Since sales revenue cancels out in the expression given, ROI can be calculated by dividing income by invested capital.
35. a. Sales margin shows how much profit was generated as a result of sales activity. Capital turnover shows how effectively the capital investment was used to generate sales.
36. c. Capital turnover explains one part of the earnings result. It shows whether the investment in capital assets is resulting in a lot of sales revenue. Sales revenue alone though is not enough to evaluate profitability. Revenue results in income, which is measured in the other piece of ROI's calculation.
37. d. The investment center's profit or income is reduced by the return required on the invested capital. Residual income shows how much income is left **after** taking into account the cost of acquiring investment capital – interest paid to lenders and returns paid to investors.
38. a. The cost of acquiring investment capital is a combination of debt and equity. Answer b is incorrect because borrowed capital is not always obtained from a bank. Answer c is incorrect because all investment capital is not equity capital. Answer d is incorrect because the imputed rate is not necessarily the minimum and it is not necessarily all debt.

39. b. EVA is similar to residual income, with two notable exceptions. It reduces the capital investment by current liabilities, so **net** assets are used instead of gross assets. Second, EVA takes into consideration the fact that funds for capital investment come from borrowings and from equity. The cost of debt capital is the after-tax cost. Answers a and c are pieces of the EVA calculation, while answer d is wrong because EVA is a dollar amount rather than a rate.
40. c. EVA for a financially troubled division will be negative. This implies that the division is actually a drain on the financial resources of the company.
41. d. Use of only those assets acquired in the current year would ignore the fact that revenues and profits are earned as a result of all productive assets – not just the ones acquired recently. The other three answers are all acceptable ways to value the asset base.
42. c. Use of the gross value of assets ignores any depreciation on assets that are not new. Answer a is wrong because the gross book value is just the acquisition cost, which is easy to determine. Answer b is incorrect because it describes the net book value. Answer d is incorrect because the gross book value can always be adjusted to exclude nonproductive assets.
43. b. Unless the increase in invested capital also increases income, this change, by itself, will decrease ROI rather than increasing it. The other three changes would, by themselves, increase ROI. This can be seen most easily by considering that ROI is income/invested capital. Suppose income is $12 million and invested capital is $100 million, giving an ROI of 12%. Increasing income without changing invested capital will result in higher ROI (answer a). Increasing invested capital (e.g., to $110 million) without increasing income will decrease ROI. Reducing costs (answer c) will increase income, so this change will have the same effect as increasing income. Decreasing invested capital without changing income (say, to $90 million) would increase ROI.
44. a. The imputed interest rate is used to calculate the cost of capital. If the imputed interest rate is higher, this means that more of the division's profits must go toward covering the cost of capital, leaving less residual income.
45. b. EVA takes into account the fact that debt capital's cost is interest. Interest expense is deductible for income tax purposes. Thus, the true cost of capital for debt is the after-tax interest rate. This is a more accurate measure of the cost of borrowed money used for capital investments. Also, the use of a weighted average cost of capital factors in the relative proportions of investment capital financed by debt and equity. The imputed rate may be derived using much simpler assumptions.

Exercises

Answers to questions 46-50 are shown in the table below.

	McMillan	McBride	McAdams
Capital Turnover	.27777	.35	.3571428
Sales margin	.40	.50	.504
ROI	11.11%	17.5%	18%
Residual Income	$1,980,000	$1,500,000	$2,240,000
Economic Value-Added	($6,355,800)	$429,000	$378,000
Rank, based on ROI	3	2	1
Rank, based on RI	2	3	1
Rank, based on EVA	3	1	2

Capital turnover is $49,500,000/$178,200,000 =**.27777** for McMillan; $7,000,000/$20,000,000 = **.35** for McBride; and $10,000,000/$28,00,000 = **.3571428** for McAdams.
Sales Margin is $19,800,000/$49,500,000 = **.40** for McMillan; $3,500,000/$7,000,000 = **.50** for McBride, and $5,040,000/$10,000,000 = **.504** for McAdams.
ROI is just Capital Turnover × Sales Margin, or 11.11% for McMillan, 17.5% for McBride, and 18% for McAdams.
Residual Income is $19,800,000 – (178,200,000 × 10%) = **$1,980,000** for McMillan; $3,500,000 – ($20,000,000 × 10%) = **$1,500,000** for McBride, and $5,040,000 – ($28,000,000 × 10%) = **2,240,000** for McAdams.
EVA is ($19,800,000 × (1–.16)) – (($178,200,000–$7,920,000) ×.135) = $16,632,000 – $22,987,800 = **($6,355,800)** for McMillan; ($3,500,000 * (1–.16)) – (($20,000,000 – $1,400,000) ×.135) = $2,940,000 – $18,600,000 = **$429,000** for McBride; ($5,040,000 × (1 – .25) – (($28,000,000 – $2,800,000) ×.135) = $3,780,000 – $3,402,000 = **$378,000** for McMillan

50. The rankings for the divisions differ from one evaluation method to another. The largest division, McMillan, is clearly not doing well based on ROI and EVA. However, if one considered RI alone, it would appear that McMillan was performing better than McBride. This result highlights the dangers of using absolute dollar amounts to compare dissimilar divisions. It took an additional $158 million to generate less than half a million additional income. When comparing divisions, inside or outside of an organization, it is best to use ROI. RI or EVA are more useful for comparisons of the same investment center over time, or compared to budget objectives.

    Use of ROI to compare McBride and McAdams shows the two divisions are very similar as far as the returns generated. When RI and EVA are used to evaluate McBride and McAdams, another problem emerges. Ignoring tax effects on income in the RI calculation makes the McAdams division's financial results appear to be more profitable than McBride's. Factoring in the taxes taken from operating income gives a more accurate picture of the performance of all of the divisions. The McMillan division is clearly in trouble, based on EVA. Given the choice between RI and EVA, EVA is the better, more accurate measure of performance.

Chapter 19
Transfer Pricing

Chapter Study Suggestions

Chapter 19 presents the topic of transfer pricing. A transfer price is the amount charged when one division sells goods or services to another division. Since managers of investment centers are evaluated based on the profitability of their division, transfer pricing presents a challenge to the selling division manager who wants to maximize profits and the buying division manager, who wants to minimize costs.

A general model for setting the transfer price is explained. Transfer prices can be set based on the used capacity levels of the selling division. If the selling division has excess capacity, the transfer price should be lower than it would be if there is no excess capacity. Theoretically, the general rule for setting transfer price should work. In reality, there are some instances where this rule must be modified. The transfer price can be set based on market price, based on product cost, or based on negotiations between the buying and selling divisions' managers.

The last part of Chapter 19 discusses the implications of transfer pricing in a multinational company, particularly as they relate to international tax and tariff laws.

Chapter Highlights

A. Cost Management Challenges. Chapter 19 provides four cost management challenges.

1. What is the primary purpose of establishing a transfer price policy?
2. What are four methods for setting transfer prices?
3. What is the significance of excess capacity in the transferring division, and what impact does that have on the transfer price?
4. Why might income-tax laws affect the transfer-pricing policies of multinational companies?

B. Learning Objectives – This chapter has 5 learning objectives.

1. Chapter 19 explains the purpose and role of transfer pricing.
2. The chapter explains how to use a general economic rule to set an optimal transfer price.
3. It explains how to base a transfer price on market prices, costs, or negotiations.
4. Chapter 19 discusses the implications of transfer pricing in a multinational company.
5. The chapter discusses the effects of transfer pricing on segment reporting.

C. A transfer price represents the amount charged when one division sells goods or services to another division within an organization. Transfer pricing is a challenge for cost managers because it represents an economic event that must be recorded in the accounting system. Deciding what the transfer price should be is the challenge. Transfers of goods and services within an organization do not impact the organization's profits as a whole organization. However, the buying and selling divisions' profits are affected by transfer prices charged. A high transfer price increases profits for the selling division and increases costs for the buying division.

If divisions are evaluated using ROI, residual income, or economic value added, then the transfer price can affect the performance of each division. This fact may motivate managers to pursue strategies for transfer pricing that are not congruent with organizational goals.

1. In a highly decentralized organization, managers are given the autonomy to decide whether to accept or reject orders and whether to buy from inside the organization of from outside.. The goal in setting transfer prices is not to motivate managers to buy internally. It is to motivate managers to make decisions that support the overall goals of the organization. Thus, the transfer price chosen should allow each division manager to maximize his or her own profits while also maximizing the company's profit.

2. There is a general transfer-pricing rule that ensures goal congruence. It is:

   Transfer price = Additional outlay cost per unit incurred because goods are transferred + Opportunity cost per unit to the organization because of the transfer.

   a. This general rule separates the transfer price into two pieces. The first piece is just the additional costs incurred to manufacture the product (or provide the service), plus any applicable costs that are directly related to the transaction to transfer goods internally.

   b. The second piece of the transfer price, the opportunity represents the amount of contribution margin given up to make the sale internally. In other words, if a sale could be made to an outside buyer, the difference between the outside buyer's price and the additional outlay costs per unit equals the opportunity cost. The opportunity cost of selling internally depends on whether the selling division has excess capacity or not.

3. Assume the selling division has no excess capacity. This means that all production capacity is currently being used to sell product at the market price. The transfer price is the outlay cost plus foregone contribution margin. This is just the existing market price. That is the case because for every unit sold internally, one less unit can be sold to external customers.

   a. Given the case that the selling division has no excess capacity, how can the general transfer-pricing rule be used to promote goal or behavioral congruence? One should next look at the buying division's situation. Suppose the transfer price for a part is $40. Suppose the buying division can obtain the same item from another supplier for $35? The buying division should buy from the other supplier. Why? Because the selling division can sell the product to external customers instead of selling internally. The buying division can buy externally at $5 less than it could if the item was purchased internally. This will increase profits for the company as a whole.

   b. Suppose the selling division has no excess capacity, its transfer price is $40, and other suppliers' charge $45. In this case, it is better for the buying division to buy internally. The selling division should be indifferent since the transfer price is the same amount that would have been charged to external buyers.

4. Now, consider the case where the selling division has excess capacity. In this case, the general rule for a transfer price would assume that opportunity costs are zero. All demand for external sales can be met, and excess capacity can be used to satisfy internal demand. Now, suppose again that the price charged to external customers is $40. Suppose further that this $40 price included contribution margin of $14. The opportunity cost of $14 becomes $0 when there is excess capacity. In this case, the transfer price is $26.

   a. Suppose, as described earlier, that the buying division could buy an item for $35 from another supplier? In the case where the selling division could sell the item for $40, it would be better not to transfer the item internally. In the case of excess capacity, where the transfer price is now $26, it makes sense for the selling division to accept the internal order, and it makes sense for the buying division to buy internally. In this case, it is unlikely that the buying division could find the item externally for less than the transfer price.

5. Theoretically, the general rule for transfer pricing should work well, and should promote goal or behavioral congruence. In reality, there are some challenges associated with setting the transfer price, outlined below.

   a. The external market may not be perfectly competitive, so the opportunity cost is
   not always easy to determine. In a perfect competitive market, the market price does not depend on the quantity sold by any one producer. Under imperfect competition, a single producer can effect the market price by varying the amount of product available in the market. This makes the opportunity cost variable because it depends on decisions about the amount available to external buyers.

   b. Another complication arises when there is no outside market for the item to be
   sold internally. In the most extreme of these cases, the company may even combine the buying and selling divisions, so the transfers occur without a need to set transfer prices.

   c. A third complication arises when the goods being transferred are unique, or when special equipment must be acquired to produce the items being transferred. These special situations could be viewed as opportunity costs since the producing division could have used those resources for more profitable activities.

   d. A fourth complication arises when the selling manager has excess capacity, and has no opportunity cost. It is to the advantage of the organization for the selling division to manufacture and sell product to the buying division using excess capacity. Yet, the selling manager is evaluated based on the profitability of his or her division. If items are produced and sold (transferred) without any contribution margin, the selling manager's profitability will not increase as a result.

   e. Because of the complexities encountered in real transfer pricing situations, the general rule for transfer pricing is sometimes modified, as described below.

6. In the simplest case, the transfer price equals the external market price. This occurs when the market is perfectly competitive, and the selling division has no excess capacity.

7. There may be occasions where an industry experiences a period of significant excess capacity and extremely low prices. Under such extreme conditions, transfer price cannot equal market price. In this unusual case, the transfer price should be based on the long-run external market price instead of the current, artificially low market price.

8. Many companies use negotiated transfer prices. Division managers may start at the external market price, and seek reductions based on savings that may occur because the internal transfer may involve less cost than external sales. For instance, sales commissions are not necessary, and transportation and shipping costs may be less if the two divisions share facilities. Negotiated transfer prices may also be used when there is no external market.

   a. Negotiated transfer prices have two drawbacks. Negotiations can cause divisiveness and competition between division managers. This can undermine cooperation and unity.

   b. A second drawback is that negotiating skill can erroneously become an evaluating mechanism for managers. If, for instance, the selling division manager is very effective at negotiating the transfer price, the selling division may look better simply because of the selling manager's negotiating ability.

9. An alternative to a market-based or negotiated transfer price is a cost-based transfer price.

10. In general, when making a transfer pricing decision, the transfer price should be based on standard costs instead of actual costs. If actual costs were used, the costs of any inefficiencies would be passed on to the buying division.

11. Cost-based transfer pricing can be improved by adopting activity-based costing. This would improve the accuracy of costs used to determine transfer price.

12. When the producing division is not provided with financial motivation for selling product internally, motivational problems can arise. There are several remedies to this problem.

   a. A supplying division whose transfers are almost all internal could be organized as a cost center. Then the manager is not responsible for generating profit, and the manager's performance is not based on profit measures.

   b. A supplying division who sells externally could be structured so that external sales activity is treated as profit center activity, and internal sales activity could be treated as part of cost center activity.

13. A tempting solution to disputes between managers regarding transfer price disagreements is to have upper management intervene. Once a company establishes a transfer pricing policy, and gives managers autonomy to accept or reject orders or transfer prices, it is best not to intervene directly.

14. In the case where the transfer price could cause the buying and selling managers to reject internal transfers when they should not, a dual transfer pricing system could be set up. Using this approach, the buying division is charged with only the cost of the transferred product, while the selling division is given credit for some profit.

D. The transfer pricing issue becomes much more complex and controversial in a global environment. This is true because of tax laws, royalties, and other laws related to definition of cost and transfer of profits outside of a country. Since tax rates vary among countries, companies are motivated to set transfer prices that will increase revenues in low-tax countries, and increase costs in high-tax countries.

1. International tax authorities look closely at transfer prices when examining tax returns of companies engaged in related-party transactions that cross national boundaries. Companies often are required to provide support for the transfer prices they use.

2. In addition to the tax effects on transfer pricing decisions, import duties may influence the transfer prices chosen by companies. Import duties, or tariffs, are fees charged to importers that are based on the value of the goods being imported. If there are import tariffs, a company will be motivated to set the transfer price low, to minimize the amount of import tariffs assessed.

E. The Financial Accounting Standards Board (FASB) requires companies engaged in different lines of business to report certain information about segments. This includes segmented reporting of revenue, profit or loss, assets, depreciation and amortization, capital expenditures, and certain specialized items. International organizations must also report segmented information by geographic region. The FASB promotes the use of market-based transfer prices for financial (external) reporting purposes. The determination of market price is not always feasible, as has been discussed earlier in this chapter. Companies usually are forced to estimate market price of items for which a market price is not readily available.

F. Although most of the discussion in Chapter 19 revolves around the transfer pricing issue for a manufacturing firm, it is also used in service sector firms and in nonprofit organizations.

REVIEW AND SELF TEST QUESTIONS AND EXERCISES

Matching key terms

Match the following terms to the correct definition by writing the correct letter next to the correct definition.

a. transfer price
b. imperfect competition
c. segment revenue
d. cost-based transfer price
e. segmented income statement
f. distress market price
g. divisional autonomy
h. dual transfer prices
i. import duties
j. general transfer pricing rule

_____ 1. A transfer pricing system where the buying division pays at cost, and the selling division gets credit for a profit.

_____ 2. The amount charged when one division of an organization sells goods or services to another division.

_____ 3. Fees charged by countries when goods are transferred between divisions across borders. An incentive to lower transfer prices.

_____ 4. The case where a single producer has the ability to affect the market by controlling the amount of product available.

_____ 5. A financial report structured so that each division's profit can be determined.

_____ 6. The authority given to managers of division that allows them to set their own transfer prices.

_____ 7. An unusually low market price caused by excess capacity.

_____ 8. Transfer price equals outlay cost plus opportunity cost.

_____ 9. Revenues that can be traced to a single division of a company.

_____ 10. A transfer price that does not include profit.

True or False

For each of the following statements enter a T or an F in the blank to indicate whether the statement is true or false.

_____ 11. A transfer price is the cost of transferring a company's goods from one warehouse to another.

_____ 12. The general rule for setting a transfer price says that the transfer price should be the cost of additional outlay per unit plus the opportunity cost per unit because of the transfer.

_____ 13. A transfer pricing problem does **not** exist in a centralized organization.

_____ 14. If a division is selling goods to another division in the same organization, and the selling division has excess capacity, then the opportunity cost of selling additional units is greater than zero.

_____ 15. If a selling division is producing and selling all production, and is operating at full capacity, it should always be willing to forego outside sales in order to sell to other divisions within its own company.

_____ 16. If a division has an opportunity to buy product it needs from another division in its own company, and the internal (transfer) price is higher than the price it can obtain from an outside supplier, then it is better for the organization as a whole for the buying division to buy from the external supplier.

_____ 17. In a decentralized organization, where investment center managers are evaluated based on their unit's' profitability, the transfer price is usually **not** set based on the general transfer pricing rule when the selling division has excess capacity.

_____ 18. A cost-based transfer price normally allows the selling manager to set the transfer price at cost plus whatever profit could be obtained by selling the product to outside customers.

_____ 19. When there are disagreements about what the transfer price should be, the best solution is for top management to intervene and set the transfer price.

_____ 20. In a transfer pricing situation, the transfer price represents a cost to one division, and revenue to another division.

_____ 21. The transfer price determines total profits earned by the organization as a whole.

_____ 22. A multinational company is likely to set transfer prices in a way that minimizes the total amount of taxes and tariffs paid for international transfers.

_____ 23. Transfer pricing issues are a concern for all types of businesses who transfer goods or services, not just for manufacturers.

_____ 24. The Financial Accounting Standards Board, which issues standards for US firms' financial reporting, promotes the use of market-based transfer prices for segmented financial reports.

_____ 25. Market-based transfer prices are always possible to determine.

Multiple Choice

Choose the best answer by writing the letter corresponding to your choice in the space provided.

_____ 26. Transfer prices are best described as

a) prices charged to customers when a company sells only to other businesses.
b) prices paid for materials and supplies needed to complete production.
c) prices charged when one division sells goods or services to another division within an organization.
d) prices charged when there is a shortage of capacity.

_____ 27. The general transfer-pricing rule states, basically, that

a) the transfer price is the opportunity cost per unit to the organization because of the transfer.
b) the transfer price is the additional outlay cost per unit incurred because goods are transferred.
c) the transfer price should never be greater than the cost to make additional product.
d) the transfer price is the additional outlay cost per unit incurred because goods are transferred plus opportunity cost per unit to the organization because of the transfer.

_____ 28. The opportunity cost of selling goods internally is

a) zero when the selling division has excess capacity.
b) zero when the buying division has excess capacity.
c) zero when the selling division has no excess capacity.
d) zero when the buying division has no excess capacity.

_____ 29. If the selling division has no excess capacity, then

a) the transfer price should be higher than cost.
b) the transfer price should be lower than cost.
c) the transfer price should be equal to cost.
d) the transfer price should be zero.

_____ 30. If the selling division is a cost center, then what is true about the manager and the transfer price?

a) The manager will not be evaluated based on profits, so should set the transfer price at cost regardless of capacity constraints.
b) The manager will be evaluated based on profits, so should set the transfer price at market value regardless of capacity constraints.
c) The manager will not be evaluated based on profits, so should set the transfer price at cost if there is excess capacity.
d) The manager will not be evaluated based on profits, but should set the transfer price at market value if there is excess capacity.

_____ 31. When the selling division has excess capacity, the opportunity cost of internal sales is

a) market price.
b) the difference between market price and the cost of making additional product.
c) cost of making additional units of product needed for internal sales.
d) zero.

_____ 32. Which of the following is a reason for the general transfer-pricing **not** being workable in practice?

a) The product does not have an external market.
b) There is no excess capacity.
c) The external market is perfectly competitive.
d) The product in question can be sold internally or externally.

_____ 33. Even if a selling division has excess capacity, the manager may be reluctant to make and sell product at cost, because

a) it may cause unnecessary additional costs that cannot be recovered based on the transfer price.
b) it will lower the profit margin earned by the division.
c) it will make it necessary for the manager to temporarily hire production workers.
d) it will mean the division has to give up sales to external customers.

_____ 34. A negotiated transfer price might be the best approach in all of the cases **except** which one?

a) There is excess capacity, but the selling division is an investment center.
b) There is no excess capacity, but there would be some cost savings if units were sold internally.
c) There is no excess capacity, and there would be additional costs if units were sold internally.
d) There is excess capacity, but the selling manager is not evaluated based on profit.

_____ 35. When does it make the most sense to use a cost-based transfer price?

a) When the organization is highly decentralized, and top management makes most of the decisions related to operations.
b) When the organization is highly decentralized, and managers of investment centers make most of the decisions related to operations.
c) When the organization is highly decentralized, and production departments are all cost centers.
d) When the organization is highly decentralized, and all production departments are profit centers.

_____ 36. What is the best strategy for top management to use when buying and selling divisions disagree on the correct transfer price?

a) Allow an independent arbitration process to be used to resolve the price.
b) Intervene, and set the price based on what is best for the company.
c) Use the transfer price of the most convincing manager.
d) Always choose the transfer price that is the lowest.

_____ 37. In a global environment, where income may be affected by the taxes or import tariffs of other countries, a transfer price should be

a) set high when the selling division is in a high-tax country.
b) set low when the selling division is in a high tax country.
c) set low when the selling division is in a low tax country.
d) the tax situation of the country where the selling division operates should not have any impact on the transfer price.

_____ 38. The Financial Accounting Standards Board's (FASB) position on transfer prices is that, to the extent possible,

a) the transfer price should only be based on cost.
b) the transfer price should only be based on market value.
c) the transfer price should always be negotiated.
d) the FASB does not have a position regarding how transfer prices should be set.

_____ 39. Which of the following is an example of a transfer pricing problem in a nonprofit organization?

a) The university charges every school and department of the university $10,000 plus $.10 per call for the use of the long-distance 800 phone services.
b) The university has an agreement with the local community college that allows community college students to register for certain classes at the university. The School of Business wants to charge students who are not enrolled at the university to pay an extra $350 per class.
c) The Finance department in the School of Business wants the university to charge finance majors an extra $200 per course if they want to take a finance course. They currently have no excess capacity, and want to restrict enrollment.
d) The School of Business is holding a retreat for faculty and student leaders of student organizations on campus. The School of Business thinks the catering charges from the university's Food Services Division are too high. The Food Services Division caters affairs to private parties on campus, and charges the same fee per person as it is charging the School of Business.

_____ 40. A division has products that other divisions want to buy. The selling division is an investment center with no excess capacity. The product is sold by the selling division for $100. Competitors offer the same type of product for $95. Which of the following is true based on this information?

a) The buying division should buy internally at a transfer price of $95.
b) The selling manager should reduce the transfer price from $100 to $95, to allow product to be sold internally.
c) The buying manager should buy from the external source at $95, and the selling manager should sell all product externally.
d) The buying manager should buy internally at a transfer price of $100.

_____ 41. A division with excess capacity sells its product for $50 per unit to external customers. It costs $35 to make each unit of product. The selling division is an investment center. Which of the following is **not** true regarding what the transfer price should be?

a) The transfer price should not be below $35.
b) The transfer price should not be above $35.
c) The transfer price should not be above $50.
d) The transfer price should be between $35 and $50.

_____ 42. Wilson, Wilson and Quinn, CPAs is a public accounting firm with a Tax, Audit and Management Consulting Divisions. All three divisions offer services to clients. Which of the following cases would **not** be a good example of a transfer pricing problem in a service firm like this one?

a) The Tax Division wants to charge the Management Consulting Division for doing that segment's tax reports.
b) The Management Consulting Division wants to charge the Tax Division for reengineering the activities in the Tax Division.
c) Wilson, Wilson and Quinn has recently acquired a bookkeeping practice (a new profit center). The Audit Division wants to charge the recently acquired bookkeeping practice, for the assurance services it will provide.
d) The Human Resources Department (a support department) wants to charge the Tax Division a fee each time a new employee is hired in the Tax Division.

_____ 43. Suppose the selling division has excess capacity, and is selling its product for $75. A division within the company has recently started making a product that requires the product made by the selling division. The buying division has an external supplier who is willing to sell the product for $65. The cost to make the product is $50. What should be done under these circumstances?

a) The selling division should change the price on its external sales to $65, and sell internally and externally at $65.
b) The buying division should buy internally, at $75 per unit.
c) The buying division should buy externally, paying $65 per unit.
d) The selling division should leave its external price alone, but should sell internally at no more then $65 per unit.

_____ 44. Which of the following is **not** a reason for using market-based transfer pricing?

a) Decentralized organizations evaluate managers of profit and investment centers based on profits, whether those profits are generated internally or externally.
b) Market-based transfer pricing is a good way to increase overall profits.
c) Use of market-based transfer pricing highlights the opportunity costs of selling internally to the buying managers.
d) A market-based transfer price can be compared to the prices charged by competitors for the same product.

_____ 45. Given that the selling division has excess capacity, the buying division has cheaper external alternatives, the transfer of goods is all in one country, and the transfer price is the market price, how will total operating income for the entire company be affected?

a) Setting the transfer price at market will reduce profits because the buying division will buy externally rather than pay the market price.
b) Setting the transfer price at market will increase overall profits for the company.
c) Setting the transfer price at market will have absolutely no effect on overall operating income for the company.
d) Setting the transfer price at market will cause operating income to decline because of income taxes.

Exercises

Please use the following information to answer the next five questions.

Lindsey's Linens Company manufactures bedding products. One division (Sheets and Window Treatments Division) produces and sells sheets and pillowcases, and color-coordinated window treatments. A second division (Bedding Division) sells comforters, bedspreads, pillows and shams. Both divisions sell their products individually, to department stores, linen stores and other retailers. They also sell to a third division (the Sets Division). This division sells the bedding, sheets and window treatments as packages through a catalog and mail-ordering systems. The Sets Division also sells the packaged items to retailers. For instance, "bed in a bag" consists of a sheet set with a comforter, one pillow sham, and a curtain set for one window (including the balloon valance). The Sets Division does not manufacture any of the products it sells. It buys everything it sells from the two production divisions and from outside suppliers. The Sheets and Window Treatments Division and the Bedding Division are investment centers. The Sets Division is a profit center. Lindsey's Linens has the following policies for transfer pricing:

- The two selling divisions can sell product at market when they are operating at full capacity.
- The two selling divisions are entitled to a minimum markup of 12% of cost when operating at less than full capacity. The transfer price can be higher than cost plus 12%, but cannot be lower than that.
- The buying division (Sets Division) can buy internally or externally, without regard to surplus inventory or excess capacity of the selling divisions.
- The selling divisions can sell internally or externally, without regard to the purchasing needs of the buying division.

The following information has been accumulated for each division, for last month.

- The Sheets and Window Treatment Division:
  - Operating at full capacity (even if the Sets Division does not buy from them)
  - A twin sheet set is sold for $5.00, and includes a flat sheet, a fitted sheet and one pillowcase
  - The cost to make the sheet set is $3.00
  - A small window set, consisting of curtains and a balloon valance sells for $7.50
  - The small window set costs $4.50 to make
- The Bedding Division:
  - Operating at less than full capacity
  - A comforter for a twin bed is sold for $15
  - The cost to make the comforter is $8.00
  - The matching sham for the comforter sells for $4.75
  - The cost to make the sham is $2.50

46. What is the transfer price that should be charged to the Sets Division for the sheet set and window treatment for a twin bed?

47. What is the transfer price that should be charged to the Sets Division for the comforter and sham?

48. An external supplier offers a sheet set and window treatment that is almost identical to the sheets and curtains produced by the Sheets Division. The price for this set is $12.00, and the manager of the Sets Division has decided to order through this supplier. Explain the effect of this decision on the Sheets and Window Treatments Divisions' profits, and on the company's profits.

49. After finding the supplier who can beat the price offered for the sheets and curtains by the Sheets Division, the manager of the Sets Division (Ellen Michaels) finds out, to her dismay, that the supplier cannot match the design of the comforter and shams that she was planning to buy internally, from the Bedding Division. The outside supplier offers to make the entire set, with a design that is very similar to the one being made by the divisions within Lindsey's Linens. The Sheets Division's manager has already informed Ms. Michaels that he cannot reduce the price from $12.50, but has agreed to re-arrange production activity to accommodate the sale to her division if she wants to buy from his division. What is the maximum price Ms. Michaels should be willing to pay to the external supplier for the complete sets?

50. Some of the sales made to the Sets Division are made to its offices in a European country. The income tax rate in this country is approximately 18%. The tax rate in the home country, the United States, is 11%. The Sets Division is interested in placing an order for 10,000 complete sets for its European offices. Ignoring any transfer pricing issues related to capacity, what would be the most beneficial transfer price for a complete set? Use the cost plus the 12% markup as the minimum, and market price as the maximum. Answer this question from the perspective of the company as a whole – not from the perspective of the buying or selling divisions. Assume the Sets Division will sell the sets for $100 each.

Chapter 19

Answers to Questions and Exercises

Matching key terms

1. h 2. a 3. i 4. b 5. e 6. g 7. f 8. j 9. c 10. d

True or False

11. F. A transfer price is the price charged by one division when it sells product to another division in the same organization.
12. T. Theoretically, the transfer price should always be based on this general rule. Practically speaking, there are several reasons why this general rule does not work.
13. T. Employees in a centralized organization do not have the authority to set transfer prices, and in fact there is no such thing as a transfer price in a centralized organization.
14. F. The opportunity cost is the amount given up when product is sold internally instead of it being sold externally. If there is excess capacity, then demand for external sales has already been filled. In that case, there is no opportunity cost because the "alternative" is to have idle capacity.
15. F. A decentralized organization gives each manager the authority to decide how to prioritize sales, meaning the selling division does not have to forego external sales in order to satisfy internal demand.
16. T. If the selling division can demand a higher price, and is selling all it can make, then the organization as a whole will be better off if the buying division goes to the external supplier. The selling division will have higher profits than it would if it sold at lower prices internally. The buying division would have lower costs if it bought from the outside supplier.
17. T. If the selling manager is in charge of an investment, then his or her performance will be based on profits. If the transfer price is based only on additional cash outlay, then there is no profit included in the transfer price. There is no financial incentive for the selling manager to produce and sell the additional units of product if there is no profit.
18. F. Cost-based transfer prices do not allow the selling manager to sell at market price. The transfer price is usually well below the market price when cost-based pricing is used.
19. F. In a truly decentralized organization, where division managers are authorized to make their own decisions, it is wrong for top managers to intervene. When there are disagreements regarding what the transfer price should be, the best thing for top managers to do is to stay out of it in the short run. In the long run though, the transfer pricing policies probably need to be evaluated if they result in dysfunctional managers' decisions about transfer pricing.
20. T. This fact is what can sometimes make the transfer price controversial. The buying manager is trying to minimize costs, while the selling manager is trying to maximize profits.
21. F. Transfer prices do not affect the profits of the organization as a whole. They only affect the profits of the buying and selling divisions. If the selling division makes $100,000 more from selling product internally, then the buying division will make $100,000 less because of that transaction.

22. T. To the extent legally possible, companies set transfer prices in a way that minimizes the amount of taxes and tariffs imposed on goods being sold between divisions from one country to another.
23. T. Any company that sells goods or services internally is subject to a transfer pricing problem. Even nonprofit organizations may have transfer pricing problems.
24. T. The FASB promotes the use of market-based transfer pricing. It argues that products sold between divisions should be treated as any other arms' length transaction would be handled.
25. F. Two instances where market prices can't be determined will illustrate why a market price can't always be determined are (1) there may not be an external market for the product, and (2) if the product is offered under imperfect markets, where prices are influenced by one or a few producers, the market price can be manipulated by the decisions of the producers who control the market.

Multiple Choice

26. c. Transfer prices are called that because goods and services are transferred between divisions within one organization.
27. d. Answers a and b are each one-half of the correct answer. Answer c would be a cost-based transfer price, but is not the only way to set the transfer price.
28. a. The opportunity cost represents contribution margin given up when external sales must be foregone to satisfy internal demand. If there is excess capacity, internal demand can be met without sacrificing any external sales. The capacity levels of the buying division are not relevant to the transfer price (answers b and d). If there is no excess capacity in the selling division, the opportunity cost is non-zero (answer c).
29. a. Since the opportunity cost is the contribution margin given up to make the sale internally, opportunity cost is greater than zero. In that case, the transfer price should be greater than the additional costs incurred to manufacture additional units of product.
30. c. If the manager will not be evaluated based on profits generated from selling product internally, then it is to the advantage of the buying division to be offered the product at cost. It is also better for the company as a whole, because the buying division will not have to buy externally at a higher cost. In addition, underutilized production capacity in the selling division will be better utilized.
31. d. When the division has additional capacity, the opportunity cost is zero because no contribution margin is given up.
32. a. If there is no external market, then lost contribution margin cannot be determined. If there are several divisions demanding the products of the selling division, there may be an artificially determined transfer price.
33. b. If the selling manager is in charge of a profit or investment center, then transfer prices that are equal to cost would result in lower overall profits for the division, because there is no profit for these units. Then, even though it would be better for the company as a whole for the selling division to make and sell the product at cost, the selling division's manager would be reluctant to do so.

34. d. To decide if a negotiated transfer price is needed, consider the positions of the two managers involved. If there is excess capacity, and the selling manager is going to be unfavorably evaluated for lowered profits, that manager will be unwilling to sell at cost, and the buying manager will be unwilling to buy at market (answer a). If there is no excess capacity, the selling manager will be unwilling to sell below market, and might even be unwilling to forego external sales to existing customers, even if there is an internal demand. The buying manager, however, would argue against market price if some cost savings exist (answer b). In answer c, the selling manager would want to sell above market, but the buying manager probably would argue that the selling manager wants to charge too much. If the selling manager is not evaluated based on profits, there is really no reason to set transfer price above cost.

35. c. If all transfers made are between cost centers, none of the managers are evaluated based on profit. This would make the use of a simple, cost-based transfer pricing approach a reasonable solution. Answer a is incorrect because transfer pricing is not needed if the organization is centralized. Answers b and d are incorrect because managers of profit or investment centers are usually reluctant to offer cost-based transfer prices unless they are modified to include a profit element.

36. a. If an organization is truly decentralized, and managers are given the authority to set prices for their divisions, then top management should avoid intervention when disagreements arise about the appropriate transfer price. Choosing the lowest price or the one of the most convincing manager is sure to alienate the other manager. Although the transfer price should ideally be the best one for the company (as alluded to in answer b), if it is not, top management's response should be to make modifications to the managers evaluation structure to motivate them to choose goal congruent transfer prices.

37. b. Setting the transfer price low will make revenues lower for the selling division. This would result in lower income taxes. Answer d is wrong because global transfer prices are very much impacted by the tax structure of different companies where a company operates.

38. b. The FASB's position is that transfers between autonomous divisions within an organization should be treated as arms-length transactions just like transactions between unrelated businesses are treated.

39. d. Both the School of Business and the Food Services Divisions are separate units, responsible for costs and revenues. Food Services has internal customers and external customers, like the School of Business and private parties. Answer a is an example of a support department allocation problem. Answers b and c are not transfer pricing problems because they are not between two units – they are between the university and external customers (students).

40. c. The best solution for the company as a whole is for the buying division to buy at the lower price offered by an external supplier. The selling division should continue to sell all product externally. The opportunity cost of selling internally for $95 is $5 per unit.

41. b. It is not true that the transfer price should not be above $35. Since the selling division is an investment center, it should be allowed to set the transfer price above $35, to earn a profit. The transfer price **should** be above $35, but should be below $50.

42. d. The Human Resources Department is a cost center, and does not offer its services outside of the organization.

43. d. The selling division could not justify selling its product internally for $75 if it has excess capacity. There is no reason to reduce the price of outside sales to $65. However, there is a reason to reduce the price to $65 internally, since the manager of the buying division would be motivated to buy externally at $65 unless that price could be matched internally.
44. b. The transfer price does not have any effect on overall profits for the company.
45. a. The buying division will buy externally. The price paid externally will be higher than the cost to make the product internally, so the costs for the buying division will be higher than they would be if the buying division bought internally.

Exercises

46. **$12.50.** Since the Sheets and Window Treatments Division is operating at full capacity, the transfer price should be market price, or $5.00 + $7.50 = $12.50.
47. **$11.76.** Since the Bedding Division is operating at less than full capacity, the transfer price should be cost plus the 12% markup. This is ($8.00 + $2.50) * 1.12 = $11.76.
48. If the Sets Division orders from the external supplier, the Sheets and Window Treatments Division should not be affected at all if they can sell all of their product to outside customers. The company as a whole will be paying $4.50 above the internal cost for each sheet set purchased from the outside supplier. However, the Sheets and Window Treatments Division will make $5.00 above cost for every set they sell. Thus, the company is better off with the Sets Division buying from the outside supplier.
49. **$24.26**. The maximum price should be based on the maximum price that would be charged for the internal sale. The Sheets and Window Treatments Division will not sell for less than its market price of $12.50. The Bedding Division, however, will sell for $11.76 since it is operating at less than full capacity. $12.50 + $11.76 = $24.26. This is probably far below the price that would be offered by the external supplier since the markup on the Bedding Division's products is much lower than its market price markup.
50. To arrive at the correct conclusion, you must determine the taxes on the sale to the buying division, which will be taxed at the US rate, and you must determine the taxes on the sale of the sets in Europe. Cost of goods sold must be considered as well. The cost of making the complete set is $3 + $4.50 + $8.00 + $2.50 = $18. This is the total cost of goods sold per set for the two selling divisions. If sold at the minimum transfer price, revenues for the selling divisions will be $18 * 1.12 = $20.16 per set. If sold at the maximum transfer price, the revenue will be $5 + $7.50 + $15 + $4.75 = $32.25.

First, look at the taxes from the selling divisions' perspectives. If sold at $20.16, 10,000 sets would generate revenues of $201,600. Cost of goods sold totals $18 * 10,000 = $180,000. Gross margin is $21,600. Taxed at the US rate of 11%, income taxes are $2,376. If sold at market, the revenues would be $32.25 * 10,000 = $322,500. Subtract cost of goods sold of $180,000, to get gross margin of $142,500. Tax on $142,500 is $15,675.

Next, look at the taxes from the perspective of the buying division. If the Sets Division pays $201,600, and sells for $1,000,000, gross margin is $798,400. Income taxes will be at the European rate, 18%, and would be $143,712. If the Sets Division pays $322,500, gross margin is $677,500, and European taxes are $121,950.

Total taxes paid if the floor ($20.16) is used will be $2,376 + $143,712 = $146,088. If the market price, $32.25 is used, the total taxes paid will be $15,675 + $121,950 = $137,625. The company will be better off as a whole to use the market-based transfer price. Note, however, that if the tax rates had been reversed the cost-based transfer prices would have been more favorable.

Chapter 20
Strategy, Balanced Scorecards, and Incentive Systems

Chapter Study Suggestions

This chapter describes the use of leading and lagging measures, and illustrates their use in balanced scorecards. Leading and lagging measures are used by managers to motivate employees to excel in the performance of their duties. Identification of indicators, especially leading indicators is an important part of modern cost management. Lagging indicators, used primarily for reporting results are measures of the final outcomes of management plans and their execution. Leading and lagging indicators are used with the balanced scorecard. This management tool combines some of the dimensions of leading indicators of performance with some lagging indicators of performance. The objective of having a balanced scorecard is to show managers and others in an organization how each person contributes to the success of the organization. The balanced scorecard contains financial measures of performance, but also evaluates performance from the perspectives of learning and growth, the customer, and the internal business and production process. This method can be effective in motivating managers to achieve financial goals as well as non-financial goals.

The chapter also discusses the importance of developing incentive systems to motivate employees to perform in a manner that ensures that an organization's goals will be achieved. Discussion includes the use of non-financial and financial performance measures to evaluate performance. The chapter presents discussion of incentive compensation plans, including discussion of six different incentive system choices that should be considered during the plan design phase. The chapter discusses the pros and cons of giving cash, stock or stock options, or non-monetary prizes to reward managers for good performance. The chapter concludes by relating the use of balanced scorecards to the use of incentive systems to maximize employee performance.

Chapter Highlights

A. Cost Management Challenges. Three questions are answered in this chapter.

1. How does the balanced scorecard differ from other measures of organizational cost and performance? What does it do that other measures have not been able to do?

2. How can an employee incentive system be designed to increase customer satisfaction?

3. How can organizations weigh the tradeoffs of various incentives for improving financial performance?

B. Learning Objectives – This chapter has 7 learning objectives.

1. The chapter demonstrates the importance of using of leading and lagging indicators to build a balanced scorecard for communication, motivation, and evaluation.

2. It explains how organizations select related measures for a balanced scorecard.

3. Chapter 20 evaluates the benefits and costs of a balanced scorecard.

4. The chapter explains how a balanced scorecard is implemented.

5. It introduces the key principles of performance-based incentive systems.

6. It evaluates the advantages and disadvantages of alternative incentive features.

7. The chapter discusses ethical issues related to incentive systems.

C. Leading indicators are measures that identify future financial and non-financial outcomes used to help managers make the right decisions. Lagging indicators are measures of performance based on actual outcomes. These actual results are compared to expected outcomes. Lagging indicators, while useful to report results are derived too late to be useful for decision-making. Although they should not (and cannot) be ignored, lagging indicators are not very helpful for making decisions about future operations or future activities. Indicators can be used to help employees understand the impact of their activities on customers and profitability. This can be achieved by using a balanced scorecard.

The main inputs to a balanced scorecard are leading indicators. A balanced scorecard consists of four areas of strategic performance. They are learning and growth performance, business and production process performance, customer performance, and financial performance. Each of these parts of the balanced scorecard is discussed below.

Incentive compensation is another way to motivate employees. It goes beyond the balanced scorecard which measures performance. Incentive systems offer financial rewards to employees who achieve or exceed goals and expectations of the organization.

D. Leading indicators are measures of organizational performance. Leading indicators should motivate employees by communicating plans and results to employees.

1. Leading indicators, if used to communicate strategy to employees can help employees to see why their activities contribute to the success of an organization. Giving employees information about why they are there should provide motivation to them. Feedback as simple as employee of the week, to incentive structures that pay bonuses based on achieving some pre-announced goals can be motivating forces.

2. Leading indicators of current successes can be used as predictors of future successes.

3. Leading indicators are used to identify future financial and non-financial outcomes to guide management decision-making.

E. A balanced scorecard is a performance measure that relies heavily on leading indicators, and to a lessor extent on lagging indicators. Using leading and lagging indicators in the framework of a balanced scorecard is an appropriate model when the goal is to attain improvement in areas of organizational learning and growth, improved business and production process efficiency, customer service and satisfaction, and improved financial results. Each of these strategic areas is discussed further below.

1. Organizational learning and growth is the direct result of improved performance of employees. Employees cannot possibly know how to improve their performance unless they understand what it is that the organization wants them to do. Enhancement of employee knowledge can be achieved in several ways.

    a. Provide employee training and education. Training can be developed in-house, or can be brought to an organization. Employees may also be reimbursed for training and education obtained from external sources.

    b. Improve employee satisfaction and morale. Determine what it takes to maximize employee morale. High morale among employees can increase retention, productivity, quality of customer service and product, and improved response to problem-solving.

    c. Minimize employee turnover. Employees become more valuable to an organization as they develop knowledge about the organization's operations. Employees are an important non-financial asset to the company. Moreover, it is costly to replace key employees because of training costs and lost productivity.

    d. Seek and reward innovation. In a competitive market, innovation in product design and offerings can contribute to achieving financial goals.

    e. Organizations should seek and embrace opportunities for improvement. Encouraging employees to suggest improvements and innovations can leading to higher financial rewards for the organization.

f. Evaluate measures of organizational growth. Although use of the balanced scorecard presumably results in making choices about costs and benefits of implementing things like training to improve employee performance, the financial benefits are not always the deciding factor. Quantification of the benefits from initiatives like improving employee morale or implementing employee suggestions is soft quantitative information at best.

2. Business and process performance is a second area of strategic performance that is factored into the balanced scorecard. Business and process efficiency should improve if there is organizational learning and growth. Some common areas of business and process improvements to consider for any organization include new product or service development, employee productivity and error rates, costs of service, process improvements, and supplier relations.

a. New product or service development is an important strategy to stay ahead of the competition. New product offerings or entry to new locations is most beneficial if a business is the first one to offer it. This requires that new product development time be as short as possible.

b. Employee productivity and error rates are often measurable and quantifiable. Measuring actual productivity (lagging measure) against a benchmark (leading measure) provides managers with useful feedback to give to employees, so those employees can improve if they don't achieve, or more important, be rewarded if they exceed the benchmark.

c. Service costs must be managed in service companies. Since higher costs eat directly into profits, cost management is a critical factor.

d. Incentives for improving processes are also necessary. Improving processes may result in the shortening of cycle time.

e. Supplier relations are an important component of the internal business perspective. The rise of outsourcing has made the need for reliable suppliers even more critical. Companies have begun to certify suppliers, based on whether product can be received without inspection. Managers should be given incentives to get suppliers certified, working with them to reduce costs and increase quality.

3. Customer value is the third of the four types of leading indicators. There are four important leading indicators related to customer value. They are customer satisfaction, customer retention and loyalty, market share, and customer risk.

a. Measuring customer satisfaction is a leading indicator of future sales. Customer satisfaction measures whether a product or service meets customer needs. Satisfaction is related to characteristics of the product itself - performance of the product, style, adaptability, durability, reliability, safety, and technical specifications. Customer satisfaction is also related to the quality of customer service (before and after the sale). Finally, customer satisfaction is based on customers' willingness to pay the price based on product quality and competitors' product offerings.

b. Measuring customer retention and loyalty refers to the likelihood that there will be repeat sales. This metric is a lagging indicator since it measures how customers have behaved in the past. However, it is also a leading indicator because it gives managers information about retention of customers for new product offerings. Customer retention or loyalty measures indicate how well a company is doing in keeping its customers. A rule of thumb in business is that it costs five times as much to get a new customer as it costs to keep an existing customer. Managers should be motivated through the incentive structure to keep existing customers happy, and loyal.

c. Market share is another measure of how a company is doing from the perspective of customers. Market share measures a company's proportion of the total business in a particular market. If managers are rewarded for bringing in new customers, market share will grow.

d. Depending on the type of product offerings, or whether customers are generally extended credit, customer risk is another measure of performance. Being able to predict the patterns for customer default or late payments are useful pieces of information for evaluating the potential quality of actual revenues.

4. Financial performance is the more traditionally thought of measure of performance, and relies heavily on lagging indicators. The leading indicators in the areas of organizational learning and growth, business and production processes, and customer value are the inputs to the process that result in financial performance. Financial performance can be measured in many ways. For instance, Chapter 6 presents customer profitability. Chapter 18 discusses return on investment. Net income, profit margin, and growth of revenue are some other commonly used measures of financial results. The balanced scorecard combines the leading indicators with the lagging indicators of financial performance to help managers and employees to better understand why the financial outcomes attained happened.

F. The main benefit of using the balanced scorecard is that it links the performance measures based on leading indicators with the performance measures based on lagging indicators. It gives employees the opportunity to see and consider the impact that their decisions and actions have on profitability. A balanced scorecard models causes and effects.

A balanced scorecard can be adapted to practically any type of organization. Adopting, developing and implementing a balanced scorecard is not costless. It is difficult to assess the exact cost, and it is often also difficult to assess the financial rewards of having used a balanced scorecard approach to measuring performance. At a minimum, there are costs of measuring leading and lagging indicators, education costs and use costs to consider.

G. Incentive compensation plans have been in existence at least as early as 1918, at General Motors Corporation. Today, virtually all large companies and some nonprofit organizations have incentive compensation plans. Everyone knows that employees must be paid for the work that they do. Incentive compensation plans go beyond this basic idea, because they pay employees for performance. With incentive compensation plans, at least some portion of a manager's income is not guaranteed, but is dependent on a measure of organizational performance. There are two key elements of incentive compensation plans. They are (1) the measure of performance and (2) the method of compensation.

1. An article from 1975, entitled "On the Folly of Rewarding A While Hoping for B", explained the problems with incentive plans that did not motivate employees to do the things the plan was supposed to motivate them to do. A danger to avoid in designing an incentive plan is to motivate undesirable behavior among employees.

2. The starting point in designing an incentive plan is to decide on what the desired behavior of employees is. The organization must have a clear vision of what goals it wants to achieve before developing an incentive structure that will motivate employees to achieve them. In addition, even if an organization wants to reward behavior that benefits the organization in the long run, managers want to be rewarded now and into the future. There are three theories of human behavior that address key motivational aspects of incentive compensation plans. They are expectancy theory, goal-setting theory and agency theory. Incentive systems use components taken from these theories to motivate managers.

H. Agency, goal-setting and expectancy theories all have some useful components. Several guidelines are extracted from these theoretical models. These guidelines can be used when organizations are implementing new incentive systems or modifying existing systems. They are listed below.

1. Most individuals are motivated by self-interest, so performance-based rewards should be
greater than rewards from nonperformance.

2. Companies get the behavior that they reward, so performance measures and rewards must reflect organizational goals.

3. Effort follows rewards, so employees must believe that their efforts influence performance and will be rewarded.

4. Fairness is a basis for sustained motivation, so the reward system should be fair and consistent.

5. Manipulation undermines fairness and effort, so performance measures must be observable and verifiable.

6. Different rewards can motivate effort, so rewards must meet market conditions and different rewards should be incorporated into the incentive structure.

7. Every incentive system involves tradeoffs, so minimizing costs of aligning goals and monitoring behavior must be factored into the incentive plan.

I. Performance-based incentive systems can be structured in many ways. There are six commonly used choices for design of incentive systems. They are (1) whether evaluation should be based on absolute or relative performance; (2) whether valuation measures should be formula-based (quantitative) or subjective; (3) whether incentives should be financial or non-financial; (4); whether performance variables should be broadly defined or narrowly defined; (5) whether rewards should be current or deferred; and (6) whether financial rewards should be paid as salaries or bonuses, and if bonuses, should they be paid as cash, stock or stock options. Each of these is described in more detail below.

1. Absolute performance versus relative performance.

   a. Absolute performance measures employee performance against some standard, norm or benchmark. Employees are then rewarded based on whether they meet or exceed those benchmarks. The disadvantage of doing this is that the benchmark may be unfair for managers of divisions where the outcome is normally lower than the company's average because of the nature of the division. For instance, a division with a new, very highly demanded product may earn a return of 30%, while the division with a mature product may earn a return of only 8%. The 8% return may actually be a high return, based on the maturity and demand for the mature product, and the 30% may be low considering the high level of demand for the new product.

   b. Relative performance evaluation measures one employee's performance to other employees' performance, and rewards based on which employees' performance was the best. Relative performance evaluation may also be based on comparison of a division manager's performance to other division managers in the same industry.

   Both methods have incentive problems to consider. For instance, if the standard or benchmark is too high, employees may feel that the goal is unattainable, and give up. For relative performance evaluation, employees may feel that they are pitted against each other and may take steps to lower the performance of others to increase their own success rate. Relative performance evaluation also does not motivate managers to aspire toward harder, higher positions. If they are already at the top of one department in terms of performance, they may hesitate to transfer to other departments where they would no longer be the top performer.

2. Formula-based compensation versus subjective performance evaluation.

   a. Formula-based performance evaluation is used to reward employees based on achievement of specific objectives. For instance, an employee may have to reach a targeted sales growth percentage in order to get a bonus. If the target is 2% increase, and a sales rep achieves 5%, he or she might receive a bonus of 1% of salary times one point for each percentage point above the target (or 3 points times 1% times annual salary).

   b. Subjective performance evaluation incorporates evaluation of performance based on goals that may not be strictly financial, or even quantitative in nature. For instance, if a goal is to serve an underrepresented part of the community, and a division achieves that, the division's employees may be rewarded based on achieving that goal. Formula-based and subjective performance evaluation can be used separately or jointly.

3. Should evaluation be based on financial performance or non-financial performance?

   a. Financial performance is usually based on either financial results of the company or market price of the company's stock. Some common measures of financial performance are based on the amount, or changes in the amount of revenues, costs, cash flow, operating income, return on investment (ROI), residual income (RI) or economic value added (EVA). Stock-based incentive plans are most commonly based on stock price. ROI, RI, EVA, and stock price are commonly used to evaluate performance for individual business units. These performance measures are explained further in Chapter 18.

      i. ROI is a popular measure because it is an easy to compute, objective measure of results. EVA, a more recently introduced performance measure, is viewed as a more accurate measure of performance, but it is harder to compute and harder to understand.

      ii. EVA's main benefit is also the major criticism of it. EVA can be modified to adjust for "accounting distortions" in a way that ROI cannot. Some companies adjust EVA for things like capitalization of certain expenditures like R&D, customer development, advertising and promotion, and employee training that benefits future years, instead of expensing such expenditures. Organizations may also adjust EVA to reflect replacement cost of inventory; to reflect expensing goodwill instead of amortizing it; to show impact of using current values instead of historical costs for certain assets, revenues and expenses; and by using gross or restated values of assets. The criticism of these adjustments is that it allows the opportunity to subjectively select the adjustments to make it appear that desired performance outcomes were attained.

      iii. Evaluating performance based on stock price is an often-used performance measure. Stock awards align the interests of managers with those of the stockholders. In many companies, there are restrictions on the sale of stock by participants in the stock compensation plans until they leave the company or retire.

   b. Non-financial performance measures are typically included in incentive plans with financial performance measures. Companies using a balanced scorecard approach include both financial and non-financial measures in this way.

4. Should rewards be based on narrow or broad responsibility of performance? There are mixed views of the best approach, and the answer is company-specific. There are advantages and disadvantages of each approach.

   a. If incentives are provided to improve division performance, the manager's focus may be too narrow. Narrow incentives alone might motivate managers to lose focus of overall company objectives, lessening cooperation among managers.

   b. Evaluation based on the broader performance measures should increase the likelihood that managers will cooperate for the greater good of the organization. Moreover, performance measures of financial performance are easier to develop than individual, divisional measures. A compromise is to use both performance measures as part of the incentive structure.

5. Should performance rewards be current or deferred?

   a. If the rewards are based on current performance, the compensation is usually given in the form of cash or stock that can be cashed immediately or soon after the award.

   b. If the reward is based on future performance, the compensation may be deferred. For instance, a manager may be promised stock options if earnings increase by 10% over the next three years. Two advantages of rewarding future performance are that managers will establish long-term profit goals instead of only short-term goals, and they will have incentives to stay with the company. A disadvantage of deferred compensation is that if it is too far in the future, managers might not be motivated to try to achieve it.

   c. Most companies use combinations of current and deferred rewards for top managers, but use current rewards for lower managers and their subordinates.

6. Should rewards be given in the form of salary or bonus? Most incentive plans include some combination of salary, bonus, stock and stock options.

   a. Paying a manager a straight salary protects managers when they make risky decisions. However, it may deter taking risk since there is no reward for doing so. If risk-taking can improve performance and profits, then managers should be compensated for that behavior by receiving bonuses.

   b. Cash bonuses are relatively easy to develop and implement. Usually, they are based on achieving specific financial or non-financial goals. The obvious advantage of cash bonuses is that they are immediate and liquid.

   c. Giving stock awards links performance by managers to market perceptions of company performance. Tying performance to stock performance should align managers' incentives with those of shareholders. Although this should give the manager proper motivation, it may be difficult for the manager to see the link between divisional performance and stock performance. Also, the stock's value may fluctuate for reasons that are out of the control of managers. Stock bonuses can be awarded either as stock appreciation rights or as stock options.

i. Stock appreciation rights (SARs) give bonuses to employees based on increases in stock prices for a predetermined number of shares.

ii. Stock options give people the right to purchase a certain number of shares of stock at a specified price. Managers rewarded with options have an incentive to increase the value of stock.

J. Incentive systems have come under scrutiny in recent years, and have been criticized because of the negative impact such reward structures have had on top managers in large corporations. Top executives should not be financially rewarded by the incentive system when the company is losing money, stockholders are losing value, and employees are making financial sacrifices. One result of poor design of incentive systems and/or poor oversight of the system of rewards in the U.S. was the passage of the Sarbanes-Oxley Act. One intended result of this new federal law is that it will force companies to align incentive structures in a reasonable fashion, and ensure that there is adequate oversight of performance.

K. Large nonprofit organizations need to have incentive systems to motivate employees just as much as for-profit organizations do. Managers must be motivated to perform well based on non-financial dimensions since there are no profit goals to achieve. Financial performance is likely to be related to accountability in the handling of funds.

If a nonprofit organization is organized as a bureaucracy, then managers may be evaluated based on adherence to the rules of the bureaucracy (as in the military). In charitable organizations, the rewards received by employees may be intrinsic. Helping others less fortunate may be the reward gained instead of receiving a cash bonus. Some nonprofit organizations are adopting evaluation methods and incentive structures that mirror their for-profit counterparts. The balanced scorecard has been successfully implemented in universities.

Chapter 20

REVIEW AND SELF TEST QUESTIONS AND EXERCISES

Matching key terms

Match the following terms to the correct definition by writing the correct letter next to the correct description. Some of the indicators may be used more than once.

a. benchmark
b. relative performance evaluation
c. leading indicator
d. absolute performance evaluation
e. balanced scorecard
f. stock options
g. lagging indicator
h. incentive compensation plan
i. bonus
j. subjective performance evaluation

_____ 1. Financial compensation beyond employee salary.

_____ 2. Rights to purchase shares of stock at a specified price over a specified time; a stock-based piece of incentive plans.

_____ 3. A measure of future financial and non-financial outcomes.

_____ 4. A way to evaluate employee performance based on comparison of one employee's performance to other employees.

_____ 5. A measure of performance based on actual outcomes.

_____ 6. A way to evaluate employee performance based on some fixed benchmark or standard.

_____ 7. A standard used to compare actual employee performance to expected employee performance.

_____ 8. A way to evaluate employee performance based on the employee reaching non-quantifiable goals.

_____ 9. An evaluation tool that uses leading and lagging indicators to help organizations to see past and future performance.

_____10. A way to compensate employees that motivates them to act in the best interest of the company and shareholders.

True or False

For each of the following statements enter a T or an F in the blank to indicate whether the statement is true or false.

_____11. Leading indicators are the same thing as lagging indicators.

_____12. Lagging indicators are more commonly used for measuring final financial outcomes than leading indicators are.

_____13. A balanced scorecard uses both leading and lagging indicators.

_____14. The balanced scorecard is a way to evaluate performance that excludes any financial measures.

_____15. The balanced scorecard evaluates activity based on the customer's perspective, among others.

_____16. The main benefit of using the balanced scorecard is that it is completely based on events that have already happened.

_____17. A balanced scorecard does not help employees to see how their actions affect organizational profits.

_____18. An incentive compensation plan may result in payment to employees in part based on organizational performance.

_____19. The key to developing an effective incentive plan is knowing what the goals of an organization are.

_____20. Paying employees a straight salary is a good incentive to encourage them to take risks.

_____21. Cash bonuses paid at the end of the year are an example of current rewards for good performance.

_____22. Incentive compensation is best when it only bases rewards on quantifiable goals.

_____23. An important consideration when designing a proper incentive structure is whether managers should be rewarded for current performance or future performance.

_____24. Nonprofit organizations do not need incentive compensation since there is no profit motive.

_____25. If a manager is given stock options as an incentive to improve future earnings, the options have value only on the day the options are awarded.

Multiple Choice

Choose the best answer by writing the letter corresponding to your choice in the space provided.

_____26. Leading indicators are useful for all of the following **except**

a) assessment of progress toward meeting performance goals.
b) assessment of the likelihood of success in launching new products.
c) management decision-making about portions of value chain activities.
d) measurement of final financial outcomes of management plans.

_____27. A valid criticism of lagging indicators is

a) they measure results too late to affect processes.
b) they cannot be linked in any way to leading indicators.
c) they are not useful in a competitive environment.
d) they do not provide information on profitability.

_____28. Which of the following is an example of a leading indicator?

a) An income statement showing net income (profit) for 2003.
b) The wage expenses for all of the service technicians at an appliance sales company for 2003.
c) Total revenue in Europe for an international corporation in 2003.
d) The number of hours of continuing professional education (CPE) each CPA will be provided with at a public accounting firm this year.

_____29. The balanced scorecard has four perspectives. Which of the following is **not** a balanced scorecard perspective?

a) The learning and growth perspective.
b) The internal business perspective.
c) The external business perspective.
d) The customer perspective.

_____30. Which of the following correctly describes the balanced scorecard?

a) It is compatible with most current management styles.
b) It is a causal model of performance.
c) It only shows managers (not lower level employees) how their jobs contribute to the ultimate goal of the organization.
d) It is primarily a model useful for evaluating financial performance.

_____31. The internal business perspective of the balanced scorecard refers to

a) how goods and serviced are transferred from one division to another.
b) how smoothly things run internally in an organization.
c) ways to measure managers' performance when they do not interact with external customers.
d) measurement of employee satisfaction.

______32. A primary benefit of using the balanced scorecard is that

a) it helps management to see which employees to dismiss.
b) it helps management to cut costs.
c) it links leading indicators with lagging indicators to help managers make decisions about the future
d) it helps managers to supervise employees better.

______33. Which of the following is **not** correct regarding the use of information from a balanced scorecard?

a) Financial results from last year should be used to predict sales growth for the coming year.
b) Sales growth from next year should be used to predict sales returns for next year.
c) Repeat sales from last year should be used to predict sales growth for this year.
d) Employee turnover rates should be used to predict hiring needs for the coming year.

______34. Which of the following is **not** a critical element of incentive compensation plans?

a) They must allow measurement of employee performance.
b) They must be structured to cause behavioral congruence.
c) They must include methods of compensation.
d) They must include methods for punishing poor performance.

______35. One obstacle to achieving desired goals through use of an incentive compensation plan is that the plan might

a) motivate employees to do the wrong thing.
b) set goals so they are too easy to achieve.
c) compensate different employees differently.
d) offer compensation based on measurable outcomes.

______36. Which of the following correctly describes absolute performance evaluation?

a) Absolute performance evaluation makes managers compete against each other.
b) Absolute performance evaluation is based on exceeding last year's goals.
c) Absolute performance evaluation is based on standards or benchmarks being met or exceeded.
d) Absolute performance evaluation cannot be used when division managers' jobs are all equally challenging.

______37. If a formula-based incentive structure is in place, which of the following would be the **least** likely item to be included in the incentive plan?

a) Employee retention must be at least 95%.
b) Revenue growth must be 5% or more.
c) Bonus equals 3% of base salary if revenue exceeds budgeted growth.
d) A bonus is given based on division income performance exceeding target division income performance.

_____38. What is the difference between a formula-based reward structure and one based on subjective performance?

a) A formula-based reward structure gives managers financial incentives to exceed financial goals; rewards based on subjective performance are based on how much the manager likes an employee.
b) A formula-based reward structure gives managers financial and non-financial incentives; rewards based on subjective performance are based only on non-financial incentives.
c) A formula-based reward structure gives managers financial incentives to exceed financial goals; rewards based on subjective performance are often based on non-financial criteria.
d) A formula-based reward structure only pays cash bonuses; rewards based on subjective performance are based only on stock options as rewards.

_____39. Which of the following incentives is most likely to motivate a division manager to perform well?

a) Exceeding targeted return on investment (ROI) will result in a bonus.
b) Market price of stock exceeding option price will result in increased value of options.
c) Division managers who meet targets will be given a raise at year-end comparable to last year's raise.
d) Exceeding division sales targets will result in a bonus.

_____40. A good example of an appropriate reward for a manager in a nonprofit organization is

a) Bonus paid for increasing dollars directly benefiting recipients of services offered by a nonprofit agency
b) Bonuses for creating a surplus (i.e., profit for the nonprofit)
c) Bonuses for managers who cut costs by eliminating services.
d) Bonuses for managers who maintain the status quo

_____41. Which of the following is a legitimate way to structure rewards in incentive plans?

a) Managers should be rewarded on a salary basis alone.
b) Managers should be evaluated and rewarded based strictly on expected future performance.
c) Managers can be evaluated based on how comparable managers' performance is.
d) Managers can be evaluated and rewarded based strictly on current performance.

_____42. The incentive structure may contain incentives that motivate actions that affect current performance. Which of the following would be the **least** useful reward to motivate improved current performance?

a) Cash bonuses given at year-end.
b) Stock options given at year-end, to be exercised within 3 years.
c) Stock awards given at year-end.
d) Gifts, awards, and prizes given at year-end.

_____43. Which of the following is correct regarding stock options?

a) Stock options have value whether the market price of the stock goes above or below the price offered in the options.
b) Stock options are the best way to motivate managers to improve short-term profits.
c) Stock options can only be offered to top managers.
d) Stock options give managers incentives to increase the value of the company's stock.

_____44. What is the purpose of rewarding employees with company stock?

a) It is intended to make managers' goals consistent with shareholders' goals
b) It keeps the company from having to pay salaries.
c) It is a necessary component of an incentive plan.
d) It makes employees feel valued

_____45. One of the criticisms of incentive-based compensation is that

a) it is unfair to hard-working managers.
b) it sometimes causes managers to behave unethically.
c) it is illegal in most countries.
d) it is usually unfair to employees.

Exercises

Please use the following information to answer the next five questions.

Traveltime.com is a new company that sells airline, train, and other transportation tickets over the Internet. The company also sells travel packages and hotel room accommodations. The company, in its third year, has finally made a profit. Stock for the company is publicly traded, and it is now considering implementing an incentive compensation plan for its employees. There are four different bonus plans being considered to compensate the employees.

1. Cash bonuses paid at year-end, based on profits. Because profit margins are low right now, the bonuses would be fixed at 2% of each employee's annual salary if operating income exceeds 5% of the target set for operating income. The average salary of top managers is $75,000. The average salary of all other employees is $25,000.
2. Cash bonuses paid at year-end, plus stock, based on profits. Because cash available to pay cash bonuses is minimal, the bonuses would be fixed at ½ of 1% of each employee's annual salary if operating income exceeds 5% of the target set for operating income. In addition, top management would receive 500 shares each. Other employees would also receive 50 shares each of stock if the profit goal is met.
3. Shares of stock would be given to employees. Top management would each receive 1,000 shares of stock, and all other employees would receive 100 shares of stock. No cash would be paid.
4. Stock options would be given to employees. The option price is $7.25 per share, and top management can buy up to 10,000 shares over the next three years. Other employees can buy up to 1,000 shares for $7.25 over the next three years.

Some other information to consider:

- The stock traded for $7.50 at the end of last year.
- Traveltime.com has been widely viewed by market analysts as a company with a bright future. Its initial public offering sold at $2.25 per share. It's stock is currently trading for about $7.50 per share.
- Stock analysts project growth in its market price at 5% per year for the next three to five years.

46. For a top manager, what is the value of each of the four options?

47. For an employee who is **not** a top manager, what is the value of each of the four options?

48. If the company has 10 top managers, and 90 other employees, what would be the value of the bonuses given to all employees under options 1, 2 and 3?

49. If the company has 10 top managers and 90 other employees, what would be the value of the bonuses given to all employees under option 4 based on (a) assuming the stock market analysts' predictions are correct and the options are exercised after three years, (b) assuming the options are exercised immediately, and (c) assuming the price drops below \$7.25?

50. Which of the four options would you recommend for the company? Explain your choice.

Answers to Questions and Exercises

Matching key terms

1. i 2. f 3. c 4. b 5. g 6. d 7. a 8. j 9. e 10. h

True or False

11. F. Leading indicators are used to predict future performance, while lagging indicators measure final outcomes of management plans
12. T. Lagging indicators report on financial results and other measures of performance, without necessarily providing information about how future activities should be modified.
13. T. The fact that the balanced scorecard uses both leading and lagging measures of performance is what distinguishes it from other performance measures.
14. F. The balanced scorecard uses both financial and non-financial performance measures.
15. T. Customer value is an important component of the balanced scorecard.
16. F. The main benefit of the balanced scorecard is that it uses leading indicators, which are useful estimators of future performance.
17. F. One benefit of using a balanced scorecard is that it gives employees useful information on how they can do a better job.
18. T. In addition to fixed salaries, employees may be compensated based on the degree of success in achieving goals of the organization.
19. T. Companies are sometimes disappointed when employees do not achieve the desired goals of the company, but it could be because goals are not clearly spelled out, or because employees are not given clear guidelines on how to achieve the goals.
20. F. Employees who are paid only salaries and no other form of compensation gain nothing by taking risks for the company, so are not motivated to do so.
21. T. A year-end bonus is an almost immediate reward for good performance.
22. F. There are many non-financial, non-quantitative incentives that can be used to motivate employees.
23. T. Ideally, there should be a balance between the need to give managers immediate positive feedback for good performance and the need to motivate them to work toward achieving ongoing and long-term success on behalf of the organization.
24. F. Even though profit is not a motivator, achieving the goals of a nonprofit organization are just as important as achieving the goals of a for-profit organization.
25. F. Stock options are valid for a specified period of time.

Multiple Choice

26. d. Lagging indicators are used to measure final financial outcomes, not leading indicators.
27. a. Lagging indicators report **results**, which are not useful for changing a current process.
28. d. All of the other answers are examples of lagging indicators. The number of hours of CPE could be used to assess the effect of education on performance.
29. c. Answers a, b, and d are components of the balanced scorecard. The fourth component is financial performance.

30. b. Answer a is incorrect because the balanced scorecard is not consistent with most current management styles. Answer c is not correct because it should help employees at any level within the organization. Answer d describes the more traditional measures of performance, based primarily on lagging indicators.
31. b. Answers a and c have nothing to do with the balanced scorecard. Answer d relates to the learning and growth perspectives.
32. c. It is the ability to link leading and lagging indicators that makes the balanced scorecard a unique model for evaluating performance.
33. b. You cannot use sales growth projections to predict sales returns.
34. d. An incentive compensation plan must include methods for rewarding good behavior rather than punishing bad behavior.
35. a. If, for instance a plan is structured to motivate higher short-term profits, but the goal is to generate higher long-term profits, the long-term profits may not occur because employees are not motivated to work toward that goal.
36. c. Absolute performance measures typically set some fixed benchmark or standard which managers must exceed in order to be rewarded. Answer a is more closely associated with relative performance evaluation. Answer b is incorrect because there are many benchmarks – not just last year's goals. Answer d is incorrect because absolute performance evaluation can be used without regard to managers' jobs being comparable.
37. a. Employee retention is not a formula-based incentive.
38. c. While a formula-based incentive structure is based on fairly rigid, financial goals being met, subjective performance measures are geared toward achieving non-financial goals.
39. d. To motivate division managers, the incentive should be directly linked to the manager's efforts. Answers a and b are incentives linked to overall company performance and/or outside factors. They are beyond the manager's direct control. Answer c is not a strong incentive to go beyond the minimum amount of effort needed to get a raise.
40. a. Ideally, money contributed to a nonprofit organization should use as much money as possible for the recipients of its services. Generating profit is not a goal for nonprofits (answer b), and cutting costs that result in provision of less service is also not an appropriate goal (answer c). Maintaining the status quo is also not useful since incentive programs should motivate employees to achieve higher results than those obtained in the past.
41. c. This describes relative performance evaluation. The other three answers are all too restrictive.
42. b. Stock options, to be exercised in future years will motivate managers to improve long-term performance. The other rewards in answers a, c, and d motivate actions to improve short-term performance.
43. d. Stock options give employees the right to purchase stock in a corporation in the future. If high performance improves profitability of the corporation, the market value of its stock will rise, making the options more valuable. Answer a is incorrect because a market price below the price in the options makes the options worthless. Answer b is incorrect because stock options motivate managers to improve long-term performance instead of short-term performance. Stock options can be offered to anyone in the corporation, so answer c is incorrect.
44. a. If overall company performance improves, stock price will increase. This is a result resired by shareholders, so employees will aspire to achieve these results.

45. b. Recent corporate scandals in the U.S. and Europe have caused stockholders, regulators and others to criticize incentive plans for top executives because they led to fraudulent financial reporting. These types of fraud benefit executives when their compensation is partly based on the value of the corporation's stock. If properly designed, incentive plans reward hard-working managers (answer a), and are fair to workers (d). Incentive plans are not illegal (c).

Exercises

46. The first three options, if chosen at the end of the year, would be worth **$1,500, $4,125**, and **$7,500**, respectively, for top managers. This is based on a stock price of $7.50. The fourth option can viewed many ways. The most optimistic view is that stock market analysts are correct. If they are, and stock appreciates in value for the next three years, then the options would be worth **$14,320** (rounded) if exercised at the end of three years. If the market value of the stock increased by 5% each year, then after three years, the stock would be worth $8.682 per share, or $1.432 per share more than the exercise price. This difference, multiplied by 10,000 shares is $14,320. Even if one takes into consideration the need to discount the value of the stock options based on a 20% return, it still has a present value of $8,288 ($14,320 × .579 - see the present value tables in the Appendix to Chapter 14). If exercised immediately, the options would be worth **$2,500**. The market price is $7.50, and the option price is $7.25, so each share can be bought for $.25 less than market price. $.25 × 10,000 shares = $2,500.

The most pessimistic view of the value of the options is based on the assumption that the market price of the stock drops below the exercise price of $7.25. In that case, the value of the options is **zero**. A manager with great confidence in the company's future would prefer the fourth option, because its value exceeds the values of the other three options. A manager with little confidence in the company's future would probably prefer the third option, assuming he or she could immediately sell the shares for $7,500.

47. The value of the first three options would be **$500, $500**, and **$750** for the employee who is not top management. The fourth option would be **$1,432.19** at best, **$250** if exercised immediately, and **zero** if stock prices fell below $7.25. Just as is the case with top management, lower-level employees should prefer the stock options if they have confidence in the future of the company, and should prefer the third option if they don't. Notice that the first and second options are both $500 bonuses. The lower-level employee should (theoretically) be indifferent between these two options. However, if you consider risk preferences of investors, the values of these two bonuses may differ.

48. Assuming 10 top executives and 90 lower-level employees, the value of option 1 is $1,500 × 10 plus $500 × 90 = **$60,000**. The value of option 2 is $4,125 × 10 plus $500 × 90 = **$86,250**. The value of the third option is $7,500 × 10 plus $750 × 90 = **$142,500**.

49. Assuming the market analysts are correct, the stock options for the executives would be worth **$143,219**, and the value of the options for lower-level employees would be **$128,897**, for a total of **$272,116**. If exercised immediately, they would be worth **$25,000** for top executives and **$22,500**, for a total of **$47,500**. If the stock price drops below $7.25, the value of the options would be **zero**.

50. Making the choice among the four bonus options should not be based purely on the dollar amount of the bonus. If the value of the option is the only choice, then Option 1 is preferable to options 2 and 3, and is preferable to option 4 if it is assumed that the stock will appreciate in value. One of the problems with choosing option 1 is that it puts pressure on the company to use cash, which may be in short supply for a start-up company. Rewarding employees with stock instead of cash conserves cash, and also motivates employees to behave in ways that are congruent with shareholders.

    Offering stock options has several benefits. First, it requires no cash outlay unless or until the options are exercised, conserving cash. Second, because the greatest benefit is derived several years in the future, and then only if the employees ensure that profits are achieved over the next several years, it will motivate employees to make decisions that benefit the organization over the long-term. Third, it will engender loyalty and commitment on the part of employees, who must stick around and work toward generating profits, for at least three years.

    For a new company, the best option is probably the fourth one because it ensures that the successes obtained under the current leadership can continue to occur.